Norwegian
A Comprehensive Grammar

Norwegian: A Comprehensive Grammar is a complete reference guide to modern Norwegian (the Bokmål standard). The *Grammar* is an essential source for the serious student of Norwegian, and for students of comparative linguistics. It is ideal for use in colleges, universities and adult classes of all types.

The volume is organised to promote a thorough understanding of Norwegian grammar. It presents the complexities of Norwegian in a concise and readable form. Explanations are full, clear and free of jargon. Throughout, the emphasis is on Norwegian as used by present-day native speakers.

An extensive index, numbered paragraphs, cross-references and summary charts provide readers with easy access to the information they require.

Philip Holmes is Reader Emeritus in Scandinavian Studies at the University of Hull, UK, and co-author of four grammars of Swedish and Danish for Routledge, as well as *Colloquial Swedish* (2016).

Hans-Olav Enger is Professor of Scandinavian Linguistics at Institutt for lingvistiske og nordiske studier at Oslo University, Norway. He has edited *Norsk Lingvistisk Tidsskrift*, is currently editor of *Maal og Minne* and is the author of many articles and book chapters on the Norwegian language, as well as co-author of *Innføring i norsk grammatikk – Morfologi og syntaks*.

Routledge Comprehensive Grammars

Comprehensive Grammars are available for the following languages:

Bengali
Burmese
Cantonese
Chinese
Catalan
Cantonese
Danish
Dutch
Finnish
French Creoles
Greek
Indonesian
Japanese
Kazakh
Korean
Modern Welsh
Modern Written Arabic
Norwegian
Panjabi
Persian
Polish
Slovene
Swedish
Turkish
Ukrainian

Other titles in this series can be found at www.routledge.com/languages/
series/SE0550

Norwegian

A Comprehensive Grammar

 **Philip Holmes and
Hans-Olav Enger**

Routledge
Taylor & Francis Group

LONDON AND NEW YORK

First published 2018
by Routledge
2 Park Square, Milton Park, Abingdon, Oxon OX14 4RN

and by Routledge
711 Third Avenue, New York, NY 10017

Routledge is an imprint of the Taylor & Francis Group, an informa business

© 2018 Philip Holmes and Hans-Olav Enger

British Library Cataloguing-in-Publication Data
A catalogue record for this book is available from the British Library

Library of Congress Cataloging-in-Publication Data
Names: Holmes, Philip, 1944– author. | Enger, Hans–Olav, 1965– author.
Title: Norwegian : a comprehensive grammar / Philip Holmes and
    Hans–Olav Enger.
Description: Milton Park, Abingdon, Oxon ; New York, NY : Routledge,
    [2018] | Series: Routledge comprehensive grammars | Includes
    bibliographical references and index.
Identifiers: LCCN 2017053103 | ISBN 9780415831352 (hardback : alk.
    paper) | ISBN 9780415831369 (pbk. : alk. paper) | ISBN 9781351059831
    (ebook)
Subjects: LCSH: Norwegian language—Grammar—Study and teaching. |
    Norwegian language—Study and teaching.
Classification: LCC PD2623 .H575 2018 | DDC 439.8/25—dc23
LC record available at https://lccn.loc.gov/2017053103

ISBN: 978-0-415-83135-2 (hbk)
ISBN: 978-0-415-83136-9 (pbk)
ISBN: 978-1-351-05983-1 (ebk)

Typeset in Sabon and Gill Sans
by Apex CoVantage, LLC

Contents

Preface

Our aims in writing this book are both to describe the structure and usage of contemporary written and spoken Norwegian Bokmål and to provide a source of reference in English for the more advanced student or even teacher so as to help non-native learners develop fluency when using Bokmål.

As far as we are aware, this is the first attempt to write a truly comprehensive English-language grammar of Bokmål. Because of restrictions on time and the length of this book, we have sadly not simultaneously been able to cover Norwegian Nynorsk.

A substantial index is provided to both Norwegian and English key words as well as grammatical concepts.

We have attempted to employ a terminology that is comprehensible to the learner whose mother tongue is not Norwegian and one not too far removed from the established terminology used in Norwegian language grammars which such a learner may also encounter. Where we have differed in our usage from these standard works of reference in Norwegian, such as the incomparable *Norsk referansegrammatikk (NRG)*, we have pointed this out.

Bokmål is not uniform. Unlike Swedish and Danish, Norwegian has no standard written language, and we have tried to steer a middle course in guiding the learner through the minefields of on the one hand ultra-conservative and on the other ultra-radical views respectively on Bokmål.

A book of this kind requires hundreds of examples. Many have been taken from the Oslo Corpus in order to ensure high frequency. In some cases, these have been adapted to help in the learning/teaching process. The English translations are our own.

The book is intended to be comparative, and our own translations have been provided for the vast majority of examples as an additional aid in the task of learning how to render Norwegian accurately into English.

Preface

Norwegian: A Comprehensive Grammar is not of course primarily intended for Norwegians, but for intermediate and advanced foreign learners of Norwegian, and therefore concentrates on the questions these learners frequently raise, in some cases with their teachers, and it is our hope that it may provide some answers to these.

We are indebted to scholars who have written on Scandinavian grammars before us (not only those listed in the bibliography), to our teachers, colleagues and students.

Philip Holmes and Hans-Olav Enger
Kineton, England, and Oslo, Norway, 2017

Symbols and abbreviations

(at), teat(e)ret	word or part of a word is or can be omitted or added; alternative form
fnyste/fnøs	alternatives
*mellom klokka åtte til ti	incorrect usage
–C	ends in a consonant
–V	ends in a vowel
–ske, –inne, etc.	word ending in –ske, –inne, etc.
/er, –t, –ne	inflexional endings
skriv/er	verb stem + inflexional ending
x → y	x changes into y
I, II, III	numbers of verb conjugations
hund /hun/	approximate pronunciation using standard Norwegian spelling
<kj>	grapheme
/øi/	phoneme
mil [approx. 6 miles]	clarification
'forsvar	stress on syllable following mark
for|be|red|ende, bil|tak	division into word formation elements or morphemes
NRG	Norsk referansegrammatikk
Språkrådet	The Norwegian Language Council
adj.	adjective
adv.	adverb
art.	article
aux.	auxiliary
C	complement
CA	clausal adverbial
cf.	compare
coll.	colloquial
conj.	conjugation

conj.	conjunction
conjunct.	conjunctional
cons.	consonant
def.	definite
DO	direct object
end art.	end (definite) article
Eng.	English
fem.	feminine
FS	formal subject
FV	finite verb
gen.	genitive
H	head word
indef.	indefinite
inf.	infinitive
intr.	intransitive
IO	indirect object
lit.	literally
masc.	masculine
MC	main clause
n.	neuter
neg.	negation
NFV	non-finite verb
NP	noun phrase
O	object
OA	other adverbial
obj.	object(ive)
OC	Object complement
part.	participle
pl.	plural
prep.	preposition
– prep.	no preposition
+ prep.	with preposition
PS	Potential subject
S	subject
SC	1. subordinate clause, 2. subject complement
sing.	singular
subj.	subject
T	topic
tr.	transitive

Introduction
What is Norwegian?

This is a grammar of Norwegian. Norwegian is spoken and written by roughly 5 million Norwegians, who mostly live in Norway; it is also spoken by expatriate Norwegians elsewhere in the world. There are additionally some few residents of the American Midwest who still have Norwegian as a hereditary language.

All languages vary. American spelling differs slightly from English spelling, and the language spoken in Grand Rapids, USA, differs considerably from that spoken in Greymouth, New Zealand, to say nothing of Glasgow, Scotland.

This makes the life of any grammar writer more difficult (and more interesting). The difficulties in the case of Norwegian are compounded by several interesting facts. Firstly, Norwegian comes in two different written standards; secondly, each of these standards contains a great deal of variation.

Let us first look at the fact that there are two written standards. One is referred to as Bokmål (literally 'book language'), the other as Nynorsk (literally 'New Norwegian'). These labels are perhaps not particularly apt; from an historical point of view, some might argue, Nynorsk is 'older than' Bokmål; Nynorsk reflects Old Norse (the language used in Iceland, Norway and the Faroe Islands, say, around 1200 CE) more closely than does Bokmål. Conversely, at least some speakers of Norwegian might perceive Nynorsk as being more bookish than Bokmål; they could argue that they hardly ever encounter Nynorsk in 'popular culture', only in 'serious novels', for example. Anyway, the two written standards are very similar; many words are written in exactly the same way, and a sentence such as **Han kasta ballen over til kona** 'He threw the ball over to [his/the] wife' might be either. But, then, also American and English spelling are very similar, yet they are perceived by some as two different standards.

Learning a foreign language is not necessarily plain sailing, and meeting a lot of variation from the very outset can be confusing. Therefore, this grammar is restricted to one of the two written standards of Norwegian, namely Bokmål. We do not write much about Nynorsk. The volume you are holding in your hands is, to the best of our knowledge, the first comprehensive grammar this size of Norwegian Bokmål written in English. (There is, to be sure, a comprehensive grammar of Nynorsk [in 250 pages] from 1983, by Peter Hallaråker.) Today, a reasonable guess is that 7 out of 8 Norwegians write Bokmål – if they have to write one of the two official standards. In restricting ourselves to Bokmål, we are not saying that Bokmål is any 'better' than Nynorsk, or denying that Nynorsk conforms better to a large number of dialects than does Bokmål, for that matter; we are merely making a practical choice. This choice may be regretted by a number of our fellow linguists in Norway; but this book is not primarily targeted at Norwegian linguists, but at the Anglophone student who needs to see Norwegian contrasted with English, if anything, and not to see one kind of Norwegian contrasted with another, a third, a fourth, and Old Norse.

Our second problem noted above has to do with the fact that both Nynorsk and Bokmål allow for considerable variation, more than the reader may be used to. For example, in Bokmål, an alternative to **kasta** is **kastet** – both mean 'threw'. All verbs that can take –a in the past tense can alternatively take –et. An alternative to **kona** is **konen**; all nouns that can take –a in the definite singular can alternatively take –en. Thus, an alternative to 1 **Han kasta ballen over til kona** is 2 **Han kastet ballen over til konen**; alternative 3 is **Han kasta ballen over til konen**; alternative 4 **Han kastet ballen over til kona**.

Again, we shall make a choice that may cause some dissatisfaction among our fellow linguists but which to us seems reasonable: We do not constantly present and emphasise all the variations that can be found within Bokmål. Some lesser used options may be left out or downplayed in this book. The reason for this is, again, our belief that meeting a lot of variation almost from the outset can hamper learning. Furthermore, all animals (and written variants) may be created equal; yet it is a (perhaps sad) fact that some are created more equal than others. Returning to the ball and wife example, it would make little sense to present all four options above as equal, given that the third one practically never occurs, the first is definitely possible, but infrequent, and the last is the one probably chosen by the majority. Rather than presenting so many options at each stage, we try to focus on what we take to be most common. Those who wish to find out, for example, exactly what the twelve accepted written versions of the adjective **lavtlønnet** 'low-paid' are can easily do that by turning to an excellent dictionary found free of charge on the web, viz. *Bokmålsordboka* on http://ordbok.uib.no/.

 ## What is in a grammar?

By its origin, the word 'grammar' is related to the word for 'writing'. The minimum included in a reference grammar for a particular language is a description of the morphology – in particular, the inflectional morphology – and syntax of said language. Some grammars, however, also include chapters on phonology, discourse and other things.

We have chosen not to include a chapter on phonology. There are several reasons for this choice. We walk in the footprints of our predecessors. For example, *Norsk referansegrammatikk* of 1997 does not include a chapter on phonology. An important reason for this is that Norwegian is spoken in so many ways; the written standard is comparatively clear-cut, compared to the spoken one. More positively phrased, Norwegian society is characterised by a relatively large tolerance of dialectal variation. To promote one particular 'standard' of spoken Norwegian would, therefore, seem a futile exercise and raise many eyebrows. Any grammar worth its name must include morphology and syntax; it can also include other subjects, including phonology, text and other things. In order for this book to materialise at all, we have chosen a restrictive definition.

 ## Why can Norwegian grammar vary so much?

To outsiders, the Norwegian situation may seem exotic. Why should a country which is so small (in population) and so relatively homogeneous have two written standards, especially when those two standards are so similar and represent basically one and the same spoken language? And why does each of these two standards display so much 'internal' variation?

A large part of the answer is historical. Norwegian (Old Norse) is amply attested from runic inscriptions and written documents from the Middle Ages (and earlier). However, the power of the Norwegian kingdom waned in the late 14th century; Norway came to be ruled from Denmark and to be seen as part of that kingdom. Once Norway was administered largely from Copenhagen and the written language was associated with church and crown, it is understandable that the language of written texts came to be Danish. Perhaps paradoxically, the Lutheran Reformation, which meant a huge leap forward for national languages in many European countries, and which was adopted by the Danish king in 1536, meant, in Norway, the final ousting of Norwegian – by Danish – as a written language.

That is how things may look from the 21st century. Yet Danish and Norwegian were more similar around 1500 CE than they are now – and even today, they are more similar than, say, the German spoken in Bremen and that in Basel; this has not prevented the Swiss from writing 'High German'. Moreover, national identities can hardly have been relevant then in the same way as they arc now, and the concept of a 'written standard national language' is anachronistic when applied to the 14th or 16th century. It is not clear that 16th century Norwegians felt Danish to be a different language any more than, say, present-day Londoners perceive Glaswegian to be a different language. (In fact, those Norwegians would probably have been less likely to make that judgment, had they given the issue any thought.)

In the aftermath of the Napoleonic wars, Norway was given from the Kingdom of Denmark to the Kingdom of Sweden in 1814. Thus, the prime political reason for Danish being the written language of Norway was removed. As we have noted, the written Danish language was fairly close to the spoken Norwegian language, so the discontinuation of Danish in Norway was by no means logically necessary. However, given the powerful influence of nationalism and romanticism, widespread across Europe in the 19th century, the use of the Danish standard came to be seen as problematic. Furthermore, this standard was perceived as more problematic when all Norwegians – not just members of the elite, partly Danicized, anyway – were expected to be able to read and write, as a result of the introduction of obligatory schooling for all. The difference between the dialects of rural Norway and written Danish was then perceived as a problem.

One response, suggested by the great grammarian Ivar Aasen, was to devise a new written standard – basically, the one known today as Nynorsk. This standard, which was launched in the 1850s and of limited practical importance until the 1880s, was built on the dialects, but Aasen also took Old Norse into consideration and, as a result, not all dialects were given equal weight, and Nynorsk did not always reflect the dialects. Aasen's motivation was twofold; both nationalist and social/pedagogical. Another response to the situation, suggested by Knud Knudsen, was to reform the

Danish standard on the basis of the Dano-Norwegian spoken by the urban elite. If Aasen can be called the father of Nynorsk, Knudsen is at least the godfather of Bokmål (up to 1929 known as Riksmål). Knudsen argued that Aasen's aim was unrealistic; the elite would not accept a written standard based on the speech of the peasants. A third response, quite popular in some circles, was to 'stay the course' and change nothing. It was argued that the Danish language had served as a bridge to European culture for 400 years. (It is telling that, even though many of Knudsen's suggestions for reform were actually implemented, they were not implemented until after his death.) At the other end of the spectrum from the 'Danophiles', Aasen's language, from 1929 known as Nynorsk, was seen as a powerful expression of a truly Norwegian mind – an important argument in a period of nationalism.

In the late 19th century, the language issue came to be intertwined with the great political divide in Norway at that time, between 'conservative' civil servants and 'liberal' farmers. (This is a gross simplification, but it must suffice here.) Aasen's language, more suitable to the political agenda of the farmers, was given equal rights with the 'ordinary book language' in 1885, one year after the overturn of a conservative ministry. In the 1890s, Aasen's written standard gradually came to be chosen for the schools in many districts/municipalities, especially in western Norway. If Aasen's standard had not been so successful and made such advances, Knudsen's preferred option for the reform of Danish would perhaps not have carried the day against the 'no change' wing, but the spelling reform of 1907 may be said to mark 'the birth of Bokmål'.

It is a remarkable testimony not only to Aasen's genius, but also to the political force of the language issue in Norway, that Nynorsk today is used by roughly one eighth of the population. However, Knudsen has been proved right in a sense; the urban elite has not accepted Nynorsk as an equal contender. This gradually became very clear in the 20th century. In 1917 and especially in 1938, the government introduced major spelling reforms in both Nynorsk and Bokmål (as that language came to be called). The aim was ultimately to unify the two standards in one common Norwegian, referred to as Samnorsk. Part of the strategy was to introduce several options into the written standard on each side. For example, while the tradition on each side had **solen** (in what later is called Bokmål) and **soli** (in later Nynorsk) for 'the sun', the idea was to introduce **sola** as a 'common denominator'. In 1917, **sola** was introduced as an alternative in both standards, and in 1938, **solen** was taken out of Bokmål, while **soli** was given a second-class status in Nynorsk. During the 1950s, popular opposition to this course became fierce on the Bokmål side – even the word 'Skamnorsk', i.e. 'shameful Norwegian', was used. In the 1960s, the Samnorsk policy was in practice abandoned. (And today, both **solen** and **sola** are accepted within the Bokmål norm; after 2012, however, only **sola** is accepted in Nynorsk.) While the opposition against Samnorsk in the 1950s is often (and partly justifiably) associated with an urban elite, it actually had support from many quarters of Norwegian society.

One may speculate that Nynorsk lost some of its attraction during the German occupation (1940–45), when there were more potent ways of showing loyalty to the country than e.g. the choice of inflectional suffix or a particular word (such as Nynorsk **eg** vs. Bokmål **jeg**, both meaning 'I'). Alternatively, perhaps the force of nationalism simply could not go on forever after 1905 (when the union with Sweden was dissolved). Anyway, it is clear that centralisation, in Norway as elsewhere in the Western world, has been a boon to Bokmål and not to Nynorsk. No city in Norway has Nynorsk as the language taught in its schools. Also, Western Norway, the 'heartland' of Nynorsk, and to some extent of associated counter-cultures, had a larger proportion of the population in Aasen's day. While approximately one third of the pupils in primary schools used Nynorsk before the second world war, today, one out of eight does.

Be that as it may; any language displays variation, and Norwegian is far from unique in that respect (see above). Nor is there anything unique in language variation being linked to geographical, cultural and social factors. The question 'Why have more than one different standard for what seems to us outsiders to be clearly one and the same language?' could well be applied to British vs. American English or, more dramatically, to the four languages Bosnian/Serbian/Croatian/Macedonian, three decades ago referred to by laymen as one language, 'Serbo-Croat'.

In short, then, the brief answer to 'Why have two different standards?' is that the Norwegians could not settle on one. The answer to 'Why have so much variation within each standard?' is that much variation came in with the Samnorsk strategy, and that some have thought it was a good thing to allow for so much variation; it was thought to be pedagogical, not to foreigners, but to Norwegians. However, many other written standards also display variation. Within British English, one may choose whether to write '-ize' or '-ise', in Swedish, you may choose whether to write **simmade** or **sam** 'swam', in German, both **gebacken** and **gebackt** are available as participles of **backen** 'bake'.

It may seem ridiculous to take out societal conflicts in language planning, but a more positive version is that societal conflicts, just like murder, will out, and that language planning can be a harmless way of bringing such conflicts out in the open. The discussions on written language in Norway have always been intertwined with the discussion on what it takes to be Norwegian, and hence with a fight for cultural supremacy; it may be a good thing if such fights are not definitely won.

Chapter 1

Nouns

1.1 Introduction

1.1.1 *Different types of noun*

Nouns comprise two main groups: proper nouns (or names) and common or generic nouns (those denoting non-specific people, places, things or ideas).

1.1.1.1 *Proper nouns*

Bergen; **Synnøve** [woman's name]; **Per** [man's name]; **Aftenposten** [newspaper]; **Statoil**; **Tyskland**, Germany

As in English, proper nouns are written with an initial capital letter (12.3.1), unlike common nouns. They also differ from common nouns in that they do not generally have a definite form or a plural form, though this does occasionally occur, e.g. **Volvoen**, 'the Volvo'; **Dolomittene**, 'the Dolomites'. They do, however, in many instances have an –s genitive form: **Pers mor**, 'Per's mother'; **Norges Bank**, 'the Bank of Norway'.

1.1.1.2 *Common nouns*

datamaskin, computer; **hus**, house; **jente**, girl; **katt**, cat; **natt**, night

Types of common noun:

(a) Count nouns are nouns denoting an individual countable entity and, therefore, usually possess a plural form. In the examples, the indefinite plural is used for illustration:

kake – kaker, cake – cakes; **lærer – lærere**, teacher – teachers;
hus – hus, tree – trees

Some abstract nouns are count nouns:

farge – farger, colour; **glede – gleder**, joy; **sykdom – sykdommer**,
illness

(b) Non-count nouns often denote an abstract concept or substance and are
therefore usually without a plural form:

frykt, fear; **kjærlighet**, love; **håp**, hope; **søvn**, sleep

Many non-count nouns denote substances:

bensin, petrol; **luft**, air; **vann**, water

Most abstract nouns are non-count (cf. (a) above):

hvithet, whiteness; **lykke**, happiness; **musikk**, music

1.1.2 *Three genders or two?*

See also 1.2.1f.

1.1.2.1

Grammatical gender, which is not found in English, is a system of noun classification in which most common nouns belong to one category or another
(but see 1.2.1). Some nouns, such as those only existing in the plural (1.2.1,
1.5.2), have no gender. Gender is revealed when words related to the noun,
such as articles, pronouns, determiners or adjectives, change their form
according to the gender of the noun (see below). This is called 'agreement'.

Nouns in Norwegian Bokmål officially have one of three genders: *masculine, feminine* and *neuter.*

Masculine
en blomst, a flower; **blomsten**, the flower; **blomsten min**, my flower
(see also 4.4.1.1); **denne blomsten er liten**, this flower is small;
(cf. **den er liten**, it is small)

en gutt, a boy; **gutten**, the boy; **gutten min**, my boy (see also 4.4.1.1); **denne gutten er liten**, this boy is small (cf. **han er liten** he is small)

Feminine

en/ei hytte, a cottage; **hytten/hytta**, the cottage; **hytten min/hytta mi**, my cottage; **denne hytten/hytta er gammel**, this cottage is old (cf. **den er gammel** it is old)

en/ei jente, a girl; **jenten/jenta**, the girl; **jenta mi**, my girl; **denne jenta er klok**, this girl is sensible (cf. **hun er klok**, she is sensible)

Neuter

et brev, a letter; **brevet**, the letter; **brevet mitt**, my letter; **dette brevet er langt**, this letter is long (cf. **det er langt**, it is long)

| 1.1.2.2 |

But the feminine–masculine division is not applied consistently. Since 2005, it is no longer obligatory in Bokmål to use the specifically feminine forms, and instead the masculine form is often used for feminine nouns. For this reason, it is possible to think of Norwegian Bokmål as possessing just two grammatical genders for nouns (in the same way as Danish and Swedish); these genders are then called *common gender* and *neuter*. (There are more than two genders for pronouns. See Chapter 4.)

In referring to nouns denoting inanimates (i.e. lifeless things), there are two pronouns: **den** (for nouns that are masculine or feminine) and **det** (for neuter nouns), cf. 4.2.4.6, 1.

Masculine (common) gender nouns take the determiner (indefinite article) **en**, feminine nouns take **ei** and neuter nouns **et**. In the definite form, the masculine (common gender) noun ends in –(e)n, the feminine in –en/–a, and the neuter in –(e)t. In the Oslo Corpus of Bokmål, only 1% of nouns in actual use are feminine, i.e. may have **ei**. See 1.2.3.

| 1.1.3 | *Indefinite plural forms*

For definite plural forms, see 1.10.3.

Norwegian nouns form their indefinite plural in three main ways, by adding either the endings –(e)r, –e or zero (no ending). These are the main rules:

Masculine
en by – by/er, town – towns
en time – time/r, hour – hours
en lærer – lærer/e, teacher – teachers

Feminine
en bygd/ei bygd – bygd/er, district – districts
en krone/ei krone – krone/r, crown – crowns

Neuter
et eple – eple/r, apple – apples
et språk – språk, language – languages

See 1.4. For plurals of loanwords see 1.4.7.

1
Nouns

1.1.4 | *The genitive in –s*

Norwegian nouns have a basic (unmarked) form and a genitive form in –s.
See 1.8.

Basic form	*Genitive form*
en gutt, a boy	**en gutts hånd**, a boy's hand
gutten, the boy	**guttens hånd**, the boy's hand
gutter, boys	**gutters hender**, boys' hands
guttene, the boys	**guttenes hender**, the boys' hands

1.2 An outline of gender

1.2.1 | *General points on gender*

1.2.1.1

Normally, a noun will have only one gender. Thus, the neuter noun **hus**, 'house' will take the determiners **et** or **det** and can take the adjective form **stort**, 'big'. Compare **et stort hus – det huset er stort** 'a big house' – 'that house is big'. Similarly, the common gender noun **mus**, 'mouse' will take the determiner **en** or **den** and the adjective form **stor**, and cannot take **et** or **stort**.

11

1.2.1.2

There are some exceptions, however:

(a) Some common gender nouns can be used as feminines (1.1.2). This goes for **mus**, for example; some people can and do write **ei mus, den musa**, 'a mouse, that mouse', others **en mus, den musen** (or even **en mus, den musa**). In principle, this applies to a sizeable proportion of common gender nouns.

(b) Some nouns have a 'mixed' agreement pattern. That is, they may select, for example, a masculine determiner but a feminine pronoun. For example, **en skiløper**, 'a skier' has the masculine determiner **en**. But, if we are talking about a woman skier, we will still refer to her using the feminine pronoun **hun**, 'she'. These cases are not infrequent. Unlike **mus**, there is no way of avoiding the feminine pronoun here. Similarly, **et postbud**, 'a postie' will not normally be referred to as **det**, 'it' but as **han** or **hun**.

(c) A very few nouns that have different genders in different types of Norwegian such as **ekorn**, 'squirrel', **lås**, 'lock' and **strekk**, 'stretch' may be either masculine or neuter gender, and a few nouns may take any of three genders, for example **gardin**, 'curtain'; **greip**, 'pitchfork' and **nyre**, 'kidney'.

(d) Some noun homonyms (nouns with the same spelling but different meanings, see 1.7) have different genders. For example, **lem** can either mean 1 'limb', in which case it is neuter, or 2 'shutter', in which case it is a common gender noun. Notice that this example is very different from **mus** and **gardin**, as they will always have the same meaning whatever gender they have. They remain the same word. By contrast, **lem** 1 and **lem** 2 are two different words. These cases are rare, however.

(e) Nouns that are only used in the plural, such as **opptøyer**, 'riots', do not have a gender for the simple reason that gender only shows in the singular.

(f) Similarly, nouns that are only used in fixed expressions, such as **kapp** in the phrase **om kapp**, 'in competition', cannot be said to have any gender (as there is no agreement evidence).

1.2.2 Introduction

1.2.2.1

(a) About 75 percent of all nouns are masculine or feminine gender, and about 25 percent are neuter gender. Loan nouns are predominantly masculine (but see 1.3.2.2). Whilst it is clearly advisable to learn each noun with its gender, the guidelines in 1.2.4ff should provide some help in predicting gender. In many cases, either the meaning of the noun or its suffix provides a clue as to its gender.

1.2.2.2

Gender also determines the form of the adjective in the indefinite singular and the form of some determiners and pronouns, as these usually agree in gender and number with nouns (see 2.1.1 and 2.1.4):

	Indefinite	Definite
Masculine	**en stor by** a large town	**den store byen** the large town
Feminine	**en stor seng/** **ei stor seng** a large bed	**den store sengen/** **den store senga** the large bed
Neuter	**et stort skap** a large cupboard	**det store skapet** the large cupboard

Similar examples:

Byen er stor.	The town is large.
Sengen/Senga er stor.	The bed is large.
Skapet er stort.	The cupboard is large.
Den store byen er pen.	The large town is pretty.
Det store skapet er pent.	The large cupboard is pretty.

Han har kjøpt en stor ring til henne. Den er vakker.
He has bought a large ring for her. It is beautiful.

Han har kjøpt et stort hus. Det er vakkert.
He has bought a large house. It is beautiful.

1.2.3.1

Feminine nouns with the definite form −a sometimes appear with the indefinite article ei:

bygda, the district   **ei bygd**, a district

The indefinite article **ei** is not much used in Bokmål, cf. 1.1.2.2 (but is frequent in the spoken language). When it is used, it is often found with nouns which have a form that is specifically Norwegian (i.e. one that differs from the written Danish that for a long period was used in Norway), nouns such as **ei ku**, 'a cow'; **ei øy**, 'an island' (cf. Danish 'en ko', 'en ø'). Some authors use the feminine determiner **ei** more frequently. Ei can also be used as a stylistic device, for example in fiction in order to render speech. The common gender indefinite form **en** is, therefore, commonly found with the feminine noun: **en ku**, 'a cow'; **en øy**, 'an island'.

1.2.3.2

As regards article use and the use of the possessive with the feminine noun, there is considerable variation, though the following pattern is frequent in the written language.

en bygd is more frequent than **ei bygd**   a district
min bygd is much more frequent than **mi bygd**   my district
bygden/bygda are both frequent   the district
bygden min/bygda mi   my district
(Not *__bygda min__ or *__bygden mi__) are both frequent

1.2.3.3 *a-forms*

In written Bokmål, the a-form, where −a is the definite marker (see also 1.10.2.3), has become the preferred form in a number of cases such as the following, in all of which it is also possible to use the alternative form −en:

boka, the book; **gata**, the street; **katta**, the cat; **lomma**, the pocket; **uka**, the week

Note 1 – Before 2005 some feminine nouns had an obligatory –a ending in the definite singular, but the –a ending is now optional:

en/ei hytte – hytta/hytten   cabin

Note 2 – Before 2005 nouns ending in **–ning** were masculine; they are now either masculine or feminine:

en/ei setning – setninga/setningen   sentence

Note 3 – The definite plural form of neuter nouns can have **–a** as an alternative to **–ene**, but this is less common (see 1.10.3.1 Note 6):

barna, the children; **beina**, the legs

1.2.4 | *Common gender by meaning*

For the sake of simplicity, in this book we will often only use the indefinite article **en** with feminine nouns and refer to both masculines and feminines as 'common nouns'.

1.2.4.1 | *Words for human beings*

Natural gender usually coincides with grammatical gender:

Masculine (**en**)	*Feminine* (**en/ei**)
en mann, a man	**en/ei kvinne**, a woman
en gutt, a boy	**en/ei jente**, a girl
en bror, a brother	**en/ei søster**, a sister
en far, a father	**en/ei mor**, a mother
en vert, a host	**en/ei vertinne**, a host

Note 1 – Exceptions. Some nouns denoting people are neuter, including:

et barn, a child; **et bud**, a messenger; **et geni**, a genius; **et individ**, an individual; **et medlem**, a member; **et menneske**, a human being; **et vitne**, a witness

When referring to **barn** and **menneske**, the pronoun **det** is often used:

Barnet hadde lagt seg, så vi fikk ikke se *det*.
The child was in bed so we couldn't see it.

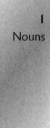

But in many other cases of neuter nouns referring to human beings, such as **vitne**, 'witness', and **postbud**, 'postie', **han/hun** 'he/she' are usually found:

> **Da det verdenskjente geniet reiste seg, kunne alle se hvor høy hun er.**
> When the world-famous genius stood up, everybody could see how tall she is.

Note 2 – With nouns of common gender describing people, **han** or **hun** is used rather than the common gender pronoun **den** when referring to an individual:

> **en gjest**, a guest; **en lege**, a doctor; **en person**, a person

> **Legen var på vei hjem fra sykehuset da hun ble arrestert.**
> The doctor was on the way home from the hospital when she was arrested.

Note 3 – Words denoting human beings of unspecified sex normally take the common gender determiner:

> **en agent**, an agent; **en baptist**, a Baptist; **en kunde**, a customer; **en lærer**, a teacher; **en sjåfør**, a driver; **en skotte**, a Scot

Note 4 – Nouns of neuter gender do not alter their gender when used to depict a human being:

> **Han er et svin.**   He is a swine.

| 1.2.4.2 | *Words for animals*

It is more difficult to generalise as to the gender of words for animals:

(a) If there is one word for the male and another for the female, natural gender coincides with grammatical gender:

Masculine – Male	*Feminine – Female*
en hane, a cockerel	**en/ei høne**, a hen
en galt(e), hog	**en/ei sugge**, a sow
en okse, an ox	**en/ei ku**, a cow
en vær, a ram	**en/ei søye**, a ewe

(b) However, in some cases one gender possesses a specific denotation, while the other also denotes the entire species:

Species name

en bukk, a (male) goat; **en/ei geit**, a goat/(female) goat; **en/ei binne**, a (female) bear; **en bjørn**, a bear

(c) Species names are usually but not always common gender:

en elg, an elk; **en hare**, a hare; **en hest**, a horse; **en hund**, a dog; **en katt**, a cat; **en spurv**, a sparrow; **en tiger**, a tiger; **en løve** (m/f), a lion; **en mus** (m/f), a mouse; **en svane** (m/f), a swan; **et ekorn**, a squirrel; **et lam**, a lamb; **et lemen**, a lemming

1.2.4.3 *Words for domestic plants and trees*

These are often feminine:

en/ei bjørk, a birch; **en/ei blomst**, a flower; **en/ei eik**, an oak; **en/ei nøtt**, a nut; **en/ei plante**, a plant

Exceptions include:

et bær, a berry, compounds in **–bær**; **et stikkelsbær**, a gooseberry; **et jordbær**, a strawberry; **et eple**, an apple; **et frø**, a seed; **et tre**, a tree

compounds in **–frø**: **et valmuefrø**, a poppy seed
compounds in **–tre**: **et grantre**, a spruce,

1.2.4.4 *Rivers and bodies of water*

These often have common gender:

en/ei elv, a river; **en fjord**, a fiord; **en innsjø**, a lake; **en strøm**, a stream; **Storsjøen**; **Tanaelva**

Note – Exceptions: Names ending in –vann/–vatn: Røssvatnet

1.2.4.5 *Cardinal numbers and fractions ending in –del*

en toer, en treer	a two, a three
en tre(dje)del	a third
en fem(te)del	a fifth

1.2.5 Common gender by form

Nouns with the following suffixes are usually common gender:

–ans	**en instans**, an instance; **en stimulans**, a stimulus; **en substans**, a substance
–ant	**en representant**, a representative; **en restaurant**, a restaurant; **en variant**, a variant
–dom	**en barndom**, a childhood; **en sykdom**, an illness; **en ungdom**, a youth
–else	**en foreteelse**, a phenomenon; **en skuffelse**, a disappointment; **en øvelse**, an exercise
–ens	**en intelligens**, an intelligence; **en konsekvens**, a consequence
–er	Occupations, nationalities, people; **en dommer**, a judge; **en politiker**, a politician; **en trener**, a coach; (cf. 1.2.4.1, Note 3 above); **en tysker**, a German; **en røyker**, a smoker; **en sjusover**, someone who sleeps a lot (includes many *nomina agentis*); **en samboer**, a life partner. Others: **en alder**, an age; **en hammer**, a hammer

Note – Exception: **et lager**, a storeroom; **et nummer**, a number

In the examples below the bracketed articles indicate that the noun is usually non-count. See 1.1.1.2(b).

–graf	**en biograf**, a biographer; **en koreograf**, a choreographer
–het	**(en) arbeidsløshet**, unemployment; **en hemmelighet**, a secret; **(en) trygghet**, security
–ing	**en forening**, a society; **en handling**, an action; **en regjering**, a government
–isme	**(en) lokalpatriotisme**, local patriotism; **(en) realisme**, realism; **(en) turisme**, tourism
–ist	**en journalist**, a journalist; **en komponist**, a composer; **en pensjonist**, a pensioner (cf. 1.2.4.1, Note 3 above)
–log	**en biolog**, a biologist; **en gynekolog**, a gynecologist
–sjon	**en aksjon**, an action; **en leksjon**, a lesson; **en situasjon**, a situation
–tet	**en aktivitet**, an activity; **en realitet**, a reality; **en stabilitet**, a stability

Note – Exceptions: **et fakultet**, a faculty; **et universitet**, a university

–(i)ør	**en direktør**, a director; **en entreprenør**, an entrepreneur; **en leverandør**, a supplier; **en ingeniør**, an engineer

Note – Some feminines with the suffixes: –esse, –inne, –erske, –ske (see also 1.3.4.2): **en/ei prinsesse**, a princess; **en/ei sangerinne**, a female singer; **en/ei sykepleierske**, a nurse

1.2.6 Neuter by meaning

The following types of noun are often neuter.

1.2.6.1 Words for substances

(et) brød, bread; **(et) kjøtt**, meat; **et papir**, a piece of paper; **(et) regn**, rain; **(et) sølv**, silver; **(et) støv**, dust

Note – There are a number of exceptions, including:

en jord, earth; **(en) luft**, air; **en vin**, wine; **en ull**, wool

1.2.6.2 Areas and localities

et fylke, a county; **et kontinent**, a continent; **et land**, a country; **et sogn/sokn**, a parish; **et torg**, a square

Note – Exceptions:

en by, a town; **en elv**, a river; **en gard/gård**, a farm; **en verden**, a world

Names that refer to Norwegian rivers and islands are often feminine or common gender in the agreement of adjective complements (2.1.1):

Glomma er bred.   The River Glomma is wide.

Norwegian towns are often regarded as having common gender in the agreement of adjective complements (2.1.1):

Bergen er gammel.   Bergen is old.

The names of towns used with a preposed adjective attribute tend, however, to be treated as neuter:

det gamle Roma   ancient Rome
det nye Oslo   the new Oslo
et vakkert Tromsø   a beautiful Tromsø

When adjectives or pronouns qualify the names of countries, they have neuter form:

Norge er rikt på olje.   Norway is rich in oil.
Russland er stort.   Russia is big.

Neuter by form

Nouns with the following suffixes are usually neuter:

-em   **et problem**, a problem; **et system**, a system
-gram   **et diagram**, a diagram; **et program**, a programme
-iv   **et alternativ**, an alternative; **et fjellmassiv**, a mountain massif;
    et kollektiv, a collective

Note – Exceptions:

Grammatical terms vary: **en akkusativ**, an accusative; **en genitiv**, a genitive;
but: **et adjektiv**, an adjective; **et substantiv**, a noun

-ment   **et departement**, a department; **et instrument**, an instrument
-(e)ri   **et bakeri**, a bakery; **et bedrageri**, a fraud; **et fyrverkeri**, a
    firework

Note – Exceptions: **en geometri**, a geometry; **en industri**, an industry

-um   **et faktum**, a fact; **et maksimum**, a maximum; **et publikum**, an
    audience; **et sentrum**, a centre
-tek   **et apotek**, a pharmacy; **et bibliotek**, a library; **et diskotek**, a
    discotheque

1.3   Miscellaneous points of gender

| 1.3.1 | **Difficult suffixes**

It is always a good idea to check nouns of uncertain gender in a reliable
dictionary. Here are a few cases where the suffix does *not* give a reliable
clue as to gender:

-al   **et areal**, a surface area; **et kvartal**, a quarter of a year; **et
    potensial**, a potential
    BUT: **en festival**, a festival; **en filial**, a branch office; **en kapital**,
    a capital
-ar   People: **en antikvar**, a second-hand bookseller; **en bibliotekar**,
    a librarian; **en notar**, a notary public (cf. 1.2.4.1 Note 3)
    BUT: **et ansvar**, a responsibility; **et forsvar**, a defence; **et rep-
    ertoar**, a repertoir
-at   **et apparat**, an apparatus; **et format**, a format; **et internat**, a hall
    of residence; **et mandat**, an authorisation; **et sitat**, a quotation

BUT: **en advokat**, a lawyer; **en kamerat**, a friend (cf 1.2.4.1); **en undulat**, a budgerigar (cf 1.2.4.2(c)); **en automat**, a vending machine; **en tomat**, a tomato

–e   **en mage**, a stomach; **en pinne**, a stick are masculine; **en/ei jente**, a girl; **en/ei dame**, a lady; **en/ei kåpe**, a coat are feminine
BUT: **et jorde**, a field; **et stykke**, a piece, item are neuter

–el   **et exempel**, an example; **et fengsel**, a prison; **et kapittel**, a chapter; **et middel**, a means
BUT: **en himmel**, a sky; **en lengsel**, a longing; **en mangel**, a shortage; **en terskel**, a threshold; **en trussel**, a threat

–ent   **et dokument**, a document; **et engasjement**, a commitment; **et moment**, a factor; **et talent**, a talent
BUT: Words for people are common gender (cf. 1.2.4.1); **en betjent**, a police officer; **en dirigent**, a conductor; **en konsulent**, a consultant

–i   **en kopi**, a copy; **en ideologi**, an ideology; **en melodi**, a melody; **en regi**, a production; **en økonomi**, an economy.
BUT: **et byråkrati**, a bureaucracy; **et havari**, a shipwreck; **et parti**, a political party; **politiet**, the police

–skap   **et landskap**, a landscape; **et mesterskap**, a championship; **et selskap**, a society; **et vennskap**, a friendship; **et forfatterskap**, an authorship
BUT: (largely abstracts); **en egenskap**, a property; **en kunnskap**, a knowledge; **en vitenskap**, a science

1.3.2 | *Gender of abbreviations and nouns of foreign origin*

1.3.2.1 | *Abbreviations*

In most cases the gender follows that of the unabbreviated noun:

en bh (cf. **brystholder –en**)	brassiere
en tv (cf. **televisjon –en**)	a tv
et wc (cf. **vannklosett –et**)	a wc

1.3.2.2 | *Gender of loan words*

The gender in many cases conforms to the word's original gender, as in the following cases.

(a) Many early loans were from Latin and Greek and have the same gender in Norwegian:

–um   **et album**, an album; **et laboratorium**, a laboratory; **et museum**, a museum

–ment   **et arrangement**, an arrangement; **et engasjement**, a commitment

–rie   **en arterie**, an artery; **en bakterie**, a germ

–tek   **et kartotek**, a card file

(b) Most modern loans are from English, which has no grammatical gender, and the vast majority of such loans are of common gender:

–er   **en computer**, a computer

–ing   **(en) dumping**, dumping

–or   **en koordinator**, a coordinator

–sjon   **en integrasjon**, an integration

These include many nouns ending in –ing, –er:

en ranking, en container

Exceptions are nouns ending in –**ment** (cf. 1.2.7): **et understatement**

Monosyllabic loans are also frequently neuter, particularly when the noun has a related verb in Norwegian:

et krash   cf. **krashe**
et push   cf. **pushe**

(c) Where there is formal similarity to a Norwegian noun, the loan may adopt the same gender:

Loan	*By analogy with:*	
et college	**et kollegium**	a college
et cover	**et omslag**	a cover
et senter	**et sentrum**	a centre
et card	**et kort**	a card

In some cases, the gender of the closest translation may influence the choice of gender:

en weekend	cf.	**en helg**	a weekend	**I** Nouns
et band	cf.	**et orkester**	a band	
et game	cf.	**et spill**	a game	
et team	cf.	**et lag**	a team	

1.3.3 Compound nouns

See also 11.2.

Compound nouns almost always take the gender of their second element, to which the inflectional endings are added:

en skifer a slate	+	**et tak** a roof	→	**skifer|taket** the slate roof
et tak a roof	+	**en/ei panne** a tile	→	**tak|pannen/tak|panna** the roofing tile

1.3.4 Masculines and feminines

1.3.4.1 Lexical differences

Lexical distinctions are often used to indicate the gender of humans (compare also 1.2.4.2 (a)):

Male	*Female*
gutt, boy	**jente**, girl
enkemann, widower	**enke**, widow
fetter, male cousin	**kusine**, female cousin
konge, king	**dronning**, queen

1.3.4.2 Matrimonial feminines

Honorary titles ending in –**inne** and –**esse** were previously given to the wives of office holders or members of the nobility or royalty. They were common until the 20th century, but have now almost died out:

bisp, bishop	**bispinne**, bishop's wife
prost, dean	**prostinne**, dean's wife

A few such titles are, however, still used:

hertug, duke	**hertuginne**, duchess
prins, prince	**prinsesse**, princess

Some titles indicating gender have no matrimonial connotation:

diakon, deacon	**diakonisse**, deaconess
helt, hero	**heltinne**, heroine

Note the still frequent: **elskerinne**, mistress; **svigerinne**, sister-in-law; **venninne**, (female) friend; **vertinne**, hostess. Cf. also 11.1.3.2.

1.3.4.3 Functional feminines and gender-neutral terms

(a) *Språkrådet* gives some basic guidelines for gender-balanced language, which include:

1. Using gender-neutral terms as far as possible for functional titles. Use, for example, **arbeidsleder**, 'supervisor' instead of **formann**, 'foreman'.
2. Avoiding the use of **kvinnelig**, 'female' and **mannlig**, 'male' with occupations when there is no reason for them, e.g. avoiding **kvinnelig tannlege**, 'female dentist' or **mannlig sykepleier**, 'male nurse', etc.

(b) In the past half century, there has been a move away from the use of feminine suffixes to indicate the female gender of a professional person. A female teacher, **en lærerinne**, is often now **en lærer** like her male counterpart. A female writer, **en forfatterinne**, is often **en forfatter**. An actress, **en skuepillerinne**, is now often described as **en skuespiller**, though all of the feminine forms above are still in use.

(c) The suffix **–mann**, which had already to a great extent lost its original sense in job titles, has nevertheless in many cases also been replaced (as has ' –man' in English):

brannmann, fireman → **brannkonstabel**, firefighter
postmann, postman → **postbud**, postal worker, postie
stortingsmann, member of parliament → **stortingsrepresentant**
talsmann, spokesman → **talsperson**, spokesperson

Surviving nouns in – **mann** include: **embetsmann**, senior civil servant
fylkesmann, county governor; **lagmann**, Appeals Court judge
tjenestemann, civil servant

Note that, similarly, **en nordmann**, 'a Norwegian', is not really gender-neutral and is best avoided in contexts such as, for example *nordmannen Emma Hansen. *Hun er nordmann might be replaced by Hun er norsk, 'She is (a) Norwegian'.

(d) The suffix –folk is useful to replace –menn/ –kvinner: idrettsfolk, 'sportsmen and women'; politifolk, 'police officers'; sjøfolk, 'seafarers'.

1.4 Plural noun forms – the declensions

1.4.1 Indefinite plural of indigenous nouns

1.4.1.1 Basic forms

Norwegian has three indigenous ways of forming the indefinite plurals of nouns (declensions):

Ending in **–(e)r**		Ending in **–e**		Ending in zero (No separate plural form)	
en blomst a flower	**to blomster** two flowers	**en lærer** a teacher	**to lærere** two teachers	**et land** a country	**to land** two countries
en skole a school	**to skoler** two schools	**et teater** a theatre	**to teatre** two theatres	**en troende** a believer	**to troende** two believers
				(en sko (a shoe	**to sko)** * two shoes)
et ansikt a face	**to ansikter** two faces				
et eple an apple	**to epler** two apples				
*There are very few nouns of this type.					

These declensions are outlined in 1.4.3–1.4.5, where some irregular plural forms are also detailed. The inflection of loanwords is shown in 1.4.7. For some hints as to how to predict plural forms, see 1.4.2.

1.4.2 Nouns: indefinite plural forms – predictability

The indefinite plural of Norwegian nouns is to some extent predictable. The determining factors are listed below. Note that these provide only general rules and there are some exceptions.

Gender

Gender is not a perfectly reliable predictor of the plural form, but some general guidelines can be given. See also 1.4.3ff and 1.4.8. Most common gender nouns take –er or –r, with one easily identifiable group (nouns whose stem ends in –er) ending in the plural in –e. Many neuter nouns, especially the monosyllabic ones, have a zero plural, but there are also substantial groups of bi- or polysyllabic neuter nouns in –er or –r.

1.4.2.2 Complexity

(a) Monosyllabic common gender nouns generally take –er:

en bygd	**to bygder**	district

(b) Monosyllabic neuter nouns generally take a zero ending:

et folk	**to folk**	people

(c) Polysyllabic nouns ending in –e generally take –r:

en brygge	**to brygger**	jetty
et stykke	**to stykker**	piece

(d) Polysyllabic nouns ending in a consonant (but not compounds) generally take –er:

en virkning	**to virkninger**	effect
et ansikt	**to ansikter**	face

(e) Polysyllabic common gender nouns ending in –er generally take –e:

en trener	**to trenere**	coach

1.4.2.3 Stress

(a) Polysyllabic nouns (often originally loanwords) with end stress (stress is indicated by ' before the stressed syllable) generally take –er:

en trafi'kant	**to trafi'kanter**	road user
en servi'tør	**to servi'tører**	waiter

(b) Common gender nouns ending in a stressed vowel take –er:

en 'by	**to 'byer**	town

(c) Polysyllabic common gender nouns take –er:

en lektor   **to lektorer**   upper secondary
school teacher

(d) Common gender nouns ending in unstressed –er take –e:

en dommer   **to dommere**   referee

| 1.4.2.4 | *Derivatives with certain endings* |

Nouns ending in the following suffixes all take –er:

–dom	en eiendom	to eiendommer	property
–het	en dumhet	to dumheter	blunder
–i	en verdi	to verdier	value
–ing	en endring	to endringer	change
–nad	en kostnad	to kostnader	cost
–sjon	en situasjon	to situasjoner	situation
–skap	en egenskap	to egenskaper	property

| 1.4.3 | **Nouns with a plural in –(e)r** |

| 1.4.3.1 | *This declension includes the following types of noun* |

(a) Monosyllabic common gender nouns ending in a consonant.
In the plural these take –er.

en bil	**biler**	car
en dag	**dager**	day
en gutt	**gutter**	boy

(b) Many polysyllabic common gender nouns ending in a consonant.
In the plural these take –er.

en assistent	**assistenter**	assistant
en billett	**billetter**	ticket
en datamaskin	**datamaskiner**	computer
en fotball	**fotballer**	football

(c) Many polysyllabic nouns of either gender ending in a vowel.

   (i) In the plural, both common and neuter nouns ending in –e take –r:

en forbindelse	**to forbindelser**	link
et bilde	**to bilder**	picture

Others include:

en foreteelse, a phenomenon; **en hage**, a garden; **en kirke**, a church; **en måne**, a moon; **en tanke**, a thought; **en uke**, a week; **et anliggende**, a concern; **et eple**, an apple; **et møte**, a meeting; **et område**, an area; **et skifte**, a shift; **et utseende**, an appearance; **et værelse**, a room

   (ii) In the plural, common gender nouns ending in a vowel other than –e add –er:

en mamma	**mammaer**	mum
en baby	**babyer**	baby

en pappa, a dad; **en valuta**, a currrency; **en industri**, an industry; **en melodi**, a tune; **en bru**, a bridge; **en hustru**, a wife; **en ku**, a cow; **en hobby**, a hobby; **en paraply**, an umbrella

---

<u>1.4.3.2</u> *Basic rule 1*

Most common gender nouns add the plural ending –er to the stem. Neuter nouns in –eum, –ium also take –er, but drop the syllable –um before adding the plural ending:

en stol	**to stoler**	chair
et museum	**to museer**	museum

<u>1.4.3.3</u> *Basic rule 2*

Nouns of both genders ending in unstressed –e add –r to the stem:

et stykke	**to stykker**	piece
en time	**to timer**	hour

| 1.4.3.4 | *Exceptions to the basic rules*

See also 1.4.3.5f.

(a) Common gender nouns denoting non-humans (cf. 1.4.4) with stems ending in –el usually drop an –e in the stem before adding –er:

en ankel – ankler, ankle; **en bibel – bibler**, bible; **en regel – regler**, rule; **en singel – singler**, single

Note 1 – If the first syllable ends in a double consonant, one of the consonants is dropped before adding the plural ending (See 12.2.1.1):

en artikkel – artikler, article; **en sykkel – sykler**, bike; **en tittel – titler**, title

Note 2 – Neuter nouns whoses stems end in –el have –er as an alternative to a zero plural, and then always drop the stem –e:

et eksempel – to eksempel/eksempler, example; **et møbel – to møbel/møbler**, piece of furniture

(b) Common gender nouns ending in –mmer drop the stem –e and an –m in the plural:

en hammer – to hamrer (hammere/hamre), hammer; **en sommer – to somrer (sommere/somre)**, summer

Note 1 – Neuter nouns whose stems end in –er have a plural in –e, but then usually drop the stem –e. See 1.4.4.3(a) Note:

et mønster – to mønster/mønstre, pattern

(c) Many polysyllabic neuter nouns (often loanwords) possess two alternative plural forms, with either an –er plural or a zero plural:

et prosjekt, to prosjekter/prosjekt, a project; **et vindu, to vinduer/vindu**, window

Others:

et dokument, a document; **et hotell**, a hotel; **et kontor**, an office; **et problem**, a problem; **et universitet**, a university; **et drama**, a drama;

et firma, a firm; **et kamera**, a camera; **et parti**, a party; **et intervju**, an interview; **et nivå**, a level

---

$\boxed{1.4.3.5}$ *Doubling the* **m**

Norwegian words never end in **–mm**. The **–m** that follows a short vowel is doubled before the plural ending is added:

en ungdom   **ungdommer**   young person

Also:

en dam, a dam; **en drøm**, a dream; **en klem**, a hug; **en sykdom**, an illness; **et lem**, a limb; **et medlem**, a member

---

$\boxed{1.4.3.6}$ *Modification of the stem vowel*

Some nouns ending in a consonant modify the stem vowel as well as adding **–er**.

(a) The following vowel changes occur:

A → E

and – ender, duck; **hovedstad – hovedsteder**, capital city; **kraft – krefter**, power; **natt – netter**, night; **rand – render**, stripe; **strand – strender**, beach; **stang – stenger**, pole; **tang – tenger**, pair of tongs; **tann – tenner**, tooth

But note also that modification in some cases occurs together with plurals that do not end in **–er**:

far – fedre, father; **mann – menn**, man

O → Ø

bok – bøker, book; **bot – bøter**, fine; **not – nøter**, seine net; and doubling the final consonant; **fot – føtter**, foot; **rot – røtter**, root

Note also modification occurring together with an **–e** plural in:

bror – brødre, brother; **mor – mødre**, mother

hånd – hender, hand

(b) Note also modification occurring together with a zero plural in:

gås – gjess, goose

Note also the following nouns ending in a vowel with vowel modification that take –r:

bonde – bønder, farmer; **glo – glør**, ember; **klo – klør**, claw; **kne – knær** (alt. **kne**), knee; **ku – kyr**, cow; **rå – rær**, yard (on a ship); **tre – trær** (alt. **tre**), tree; **tå – tær**, toe

(d) Note also modification occurring with an –e plural in:

datter – døtre, daughter

| 1.4.3.7 | *Recent loanwords with* **–er** *plurals*

layout – layouter, layout; **policy – policyer**, policy; **weekend – weekender**, weekend; **franchise – franchiser**, franchise

This group includes some loans ending in –is, –us:

kjendis – kjendiser, celebrity; **bonus – bonuser**, bonus; **minus – minuser**, minus

But a few loans in –a, –is or –us may drop these final syllables before adding the plural ending –er:

kollega – kolleger (or **kollegaer**), colleague; **amanuensis – amanuenser**, amanuensis; **radius – radier**, radius

See also 1.4.7.2.

| 1.4.4 | *Nouns with a plural in* –e

| 1.4.4.1 | *This declension includes*

(a) Most common gender nouns ending in –er denoting people, occupations, relationships, frequently *nomina agentis*, etc.

en arbeidsgiver, an employer; **en eier**, an owner; **en lærer**, a teacher; **en løper**, a runner; **en medarbeider**, a co-worker; **en motstander**, an opponent; **en norgesmester**, a Norwegian champion; **en partner**, a partner; **en politiker**, a politican; **en spiller**, a player; **en utenriksminister**, a foreign minister

(b) This group also includes many nationality words and some loanwords denoting occupations:

en amerikaner, an American; **en italiener**, an Italian; **en tysker**, a German; **en manager, en scorer**

(c) Some nouns, often describing instruments or agents used for an activity:

en container, a container; **en grøsser**, a thriller; **en server**, a [computer] server; **en trailer**, an articulated lorry

(d) A few neuter nouns that end in –er. These usually drop the final stem –e:

et monster – monstre, a monster; **et teater – teatre**, a theatre

(d) A number of names for fauna, several of which are *nomina agentis*:

en gnager, a rodent; **en støver**, a hound; **en gråfluesnapper**, a spotted flycatcher; **en kjernebiter**, a hawfinch; **en toppdykker**, a great crested grebe

(e) Some nouns in –er taking either –e or –er:

en seier, to seiere/seire/seirer, victory

Also: **en alder**, an age; **en tiger**, a tiger

1.4.4.2 Basic rule

Most common gender nouns ending in –er add the plural ending –e to the stem:

en begynner   **to begynnere**   beginner

| 1.4.4.3 | *Exceptions to the basic rule*

Cf. 1.4.3.4.

(a) Some nouns of either gender with stems ending in –er can drop the –e of the stem before adding the plural ending:

en finger – to fingre, finger; **en skulder – to skuldre**, shoulder; **en tiger – to tigre**, tiger; **en vinter – to vintre**, winter

Note – Neuter nouns with stems ending in –er either have a zero plural or a plural in –e, in this latter case dropping the stem –e and reducing any double consonant in the stem:

et offer – to offer/ofre, victim; **et kammer – to kammer/kamre**, room; **et lager – to lager/lagre**, storeroom; **et senter – senter/sentre**, centre

(b) The following words for family relationships modify the root vowel (see 1.4.3.6) and drop the stem –e (if there is one) before adding the plural ending –e:

en bror – to brødre, brother; **en datter – to døtre**, daughter; **en far – to fedre**, father; **en mor – to mødre**, mother

| 1.4.5 | **Nouns with a zero plural**

| 1.4.5.1 | *This declension includes*

(a) Most monosyllabic neuter nouns ending in a consonant:

et barn, a child; **et bær**, a berry; **et dyr**, an animal; **et egg**, an egg; **et fjell**, a mountain; **et glass**, a glass; **et hjem**, a home; **et hus**, a house; **et land**, a country; **et liv**, a life; **et navn**, a name; **et ord**, a word; **et rom**, a room; **et skip**, a ship; **et språk**, a language; **et tall**, a number; **et år**, a year

(b) Many polysyllabic neuter nouns ending in a consonant:

et besøk, a visit; **et fjernsyn**, a television; **et forhold**, a relationship; **et forslag**, a suggestion; **et samfunn**, a society; **et spørsmål**, a question; **et øyeblikk**, a moment

(c) A few common gender nouns, including those that are formed from present participles:

> **en feil**, a fault; **en lus**, a louse; **en mus**, a mouse; **en sko**, a shoe; **en ting**, a thing; **en pårørende**, a next of kin; **en reisende**, a traveller; **en troende**, a believer

(d) Some common gender nouns for units of measurement:

> **en dollar**, a dollar; **en/et kilo**, a kilo; **en liter**, a litre; **en meter**, a metre; **en mil**, a (Norwegian) mile, 10 km; **en øre**, an øre

1.4.5.2 Basic rule

Many neuter and a few common gender nouns add no plural ending:

et bad	**to bad**	bath, swim
et forsøk	**to forsøk**	attempt
en besøkende	**to besøkende**	visitor
en sko	**to sko**	shoe

1.4.5.3 Exceptions to the basic rule

(a) Some monosyllabic neuter nouns possess two alternative plural forms, with either a zero plural or an –er plural:

et bord	**to bord/border**	table
et verk	**to verk/verker**	work composition

Others include:

> **et blad**, a leaf; **et brev**, a letter; **et fat**, a dish; **et kurs**, a course; **et punkt**, a point; **et skjørt**, a shirt; **et stoff**, a material

For most of these neuters, the zero plural is much more frequent.

Note also one common gender noun with this alternative:

> **en ski – to ski/skier**, a ski

(b) Note the change of stem vowel in the following nouns (1.4.3.6 (b)):

en gås – gjess, goose; **en mann – menn**, man

1.4.6 | Plurals and compound nouns

For the gender of compound nouns, see 1.3.3. The second element in a noun compound takes the plural ending:

et skole|barn – skole|barn   **en barne|skole – barne|skoler**
a schoolchild – schoolchildren   a junior school – junior schools

1.4.7 | Plurals of loanwords

Some foreign loans have not adapted completely to the Norwegian system of plural endings.

1.4.7.1 | English loans

(a) Most foreign loans, especially those borrowed from English previously with a plural in ' –s', now have Norwegian plural forms (see also 11.4.8.3). They vary as to their new plural ending:

- Common gender nouns tend to favour –er like native nouns:

  baby – babyer, baby; **buss – busser**, bus; **film – filmer**, film;
  jeep – jeeper, jeep; **jobb – jobber**, job; **lift – lifter**, lift; **playboy –
  playboyer**, playboy; **tripp – tripper**, trip

- Common gender loans ending in –er take –e like native nouns:

  entertainer – entertainere, entertainer; **gangster – gangstere**,
  gangster; **reporter – reportere**, reporter; **sweater – sweatere**,
  sweater; **trailer – trailere**, trailer

- Loans ending in a silent –e take –r:

  franchise – franchiser, franchise; **guide – guider**, guide; **jingle –
  jingler**, jingle

- The very few neuter loans have a zero plural like native nouns:

  et heat – heat, heat (in a race); **et show – show**, show; **et
  team – team**, team

l Nouns

(b) The English plural in '-s' is retained in Norwegian in loan nouns occurring mostly or only in the plural or collective (non-count) forms:

cornflakes; chips; jeans; koks, coke; nikkers, knickers; odds, pikkels, pickles; pyjamas, shorts, snacks (cf. also 11.4.8.3)

(c) Some loanwords, especially those that still feel alien and have not been integrated into Norwegian, may retain their '-s' plural:

callgirl - callgirls; audition - auditions; joystick - joysticks

(d) In a few cases, Norwegian has borrowed an English '-s' plural as a singular form in so-called 'kaps-words':

en fans/fan (pl. fans), a fan; en kaps (pl. kaps or kapser), a cap; en kjeks (pl. kjeks), a biscuit; en pyjamas (pl. pyjamaser), a pair of pyjamas; shorts (pl. shorts), a pair of shorts

Note – Neuter nouns of this type usually have a zero plural:

et tips (or et tipp) - flere tips (or tipp), a tip - several tips

(e) Words retaining the '-s' are often characterised by foreign pronunciation or spelling; in some cases, these are a loan phrase or quotation:

et keyboard – keyboards; en negro spiritual – negro spirituals; en royalty – royalties

1.4.7.2 Latin loans ending in -a, -um, -ium, -us

(a) Neuter nouns in -a have two alternative plural endings:

et drama drama/dramaer drama

Also:

dilemma, dilemma; skjema, scheme; tema, theme

But note the common gender noun en kollega – kollegaer, colleague

(b) Some neuter nouns ending in −um have an obligatory Latin plural in −a added to the stem:

et faktum fakta fact

Others include:

kvantum, quantum, and, usually in the plural; **antibiotika**, antibiotics; **narkotika**, narcotics

(c) Some neuter nouns in –**um** have alternative Norwegian plurals in –**er** or –**a** added to the Latin stem:

et forum   **fora/forumer**   forum

Others are:

maksimum, maximum; **serum, ultimatum**; **visum**, visa

(d) Most nouns ending in –**ium** have alternative plural endings in –**ier** or –**ia**:

et kriterium   **kriterier/kriteria**   criterion

Also:

akvarium, aquarium; **auditorium**, auditorium; **kjemikalium**, chemical; **kollegium**, college; **laboratorium**, laboratory; **medium**, medium; **stadium**, stage; **studium**, study; **territorium**, territory

Note 1 – With the exception of the word **media**, the –**ia** plural is little used.

Note 2 – Alternative short singular forms have been created from a number of loans of this type:

et akvarie (et akvarium), an aquarium; **et laboratorie**, a laboratory

(f) Common gender nouns ending in –**us** take –**er**:

en bonus   **bonuser**   bonus

Also:

status, status; **rebus**, rebus

(g) Neuter nouns ending in –**us** take either a zero plural or –**er**:

et fokus   **fokus/fokuser**   focus

Also:

manus, manuscript; **opus**, opus; **sirkus**, cirkus

Notice also:

et/en genus	**genus/genera**	gender

1.4.7.3 *Nouns ending in –o*

(a) Most such nouns are common gender with a plural in –er:

en video	**videoer**	video

Also:

avokado, avocado; **cello**, cello; **dato**, date; **fiasko**, failure; **getto**, ghetto; **konto**, account; **lasso**, lasso; **radio**, radio; **risiko**, risk; **saldo**, credit balance

(b) A few are neuter:

et foto	**foto/fotoer**	photo

Cf. also **piano**, piano; **veto**, veto; **tempo** (with a further alternative plural **tempi**)

1.4.8 **Nouns – plural indefinite forms: summary chart**

	Singular	Plural	Meaning	Para
Nouns with a plural in –er				
Common gender				
	en sak	**saker**	thing	1.4.3.1
	en match	**matcher**	match	1.4.3.1
	en villa	**villaer**	detached house	1.4.3.1
	en gutt	**gutter**	boy	1.4.3.1

en sannhet	sannheter	truth	1.4.2.4
en løsning	løsninger	solution	1.4.2.4
en eiendom	eiendommer	property	1.4.3.5
en natt	netter	night	1.4.3.6

Neuter

| et medium | medier | medium | 1.4.7.2 |

Nouns with a plural in –r
Common gender

| en klasse | klasser | class | 1.4.3.1 |
| en jente | jenter | girl | 1.4.3.1 |

Neuter

| et teppe | tepper | carpet | 1.4.3.3 |
| et gjerde | gjerder | fence | 1.4.3.3 |

Nouns with a plural in –e
Common gender

en spiller	spillere	player	1.4.4.1
en container	containere	container	1.4.4.1
en finger	fingre/fingrer	finger	1.4.4.3
en datter	døtre	daughter	1.4.4.3

Neuter

| et teater | teatre | theatre | 1.4.4.1 |

Nouns with a zero plural
Common gender

| en feil | feil | fault | 1.4.5.1 |
| en mann | menn | man | 1.4.5.1 |

Neuter

et dyr	dyr	animal	1.4.5.1
et besøk	besøk	visit	1.4.5.1
et brev	brev/brever	letter	1.4.5.3
et kjøkken	kjøkken/ kjøkkener	kitchen	1.4.5.3
et faktum	fakta	fact	1.4.7.2

For the definite plurals, cf. 1.10.3.

1.5 Nouns with no plural form or no singular form, collective nouns and nouns expressing quantity

1.5.1 Nouns with no plural form

The following types of noun generally speaking have no plural form.

1.5.1.1 Abstract nouns

ansvar, responsibility; **fred**, peace; **frihet**, freedom; **hat**, hatred; **håp**, hope; **kjærlighet**, love; **kynisme**, cynicism; **kulde**, cold; **mot**, courage; **sannhet**, truth; **søthet**, sweetness; **søvn**, sleep; **vennskap**, friendship

Plurals of abstract nouns (if found) denote a countable quality. Compare usage in the following pairs of sentences:

Susanne minnes sin ungdom.
Susanne recalls her youth.

Ungdommene hjalp Susanne.
The youngsters helped Susanne.

Friheten blir satt høyt i Vesten.
Freedom is highly valued in the West.

Tony tok seg friheter.
Tony took liberties.

1.5.1.2 Substances and materials

gress, grass; **gull**, gold; **kjøtt**, meat; **luft**, air; **melk**, milk; **olje**, oil; **sand**, sand; **snø**, snow; **støv**, dust; **vann**, water; **øl**, beer

(a) Plurals of nouns denoting substances usually indicate a type:

hvite viner, white wines; **vegetabilske oljer**, vegetable oils

(b) Some nouns with a zero plural can form a compound or derivative to which an explicit plural ending may more easily be added:

dåp, baptism	–	**dåp|s|handlinger**, baptisms
gjeld, debt	–	**gjeld|s|poster**, debts
håp, hope	–	**forhåp|ninger**, hopes

| 1.5.1.3 | *Nouns denoting measurement or currency*

See also 1.5.4.

en liter, one litre — **femti liter**, fifty litres

Like this go:

fot, foot; **meter**, metre; **dollar**, dollar; **euro**, euro

See also the collective noun **mann** (1.5.3.1).

| 1.5.2 | *Nouns with no singular form*

Normally, nouns have both a singular and a plural form. There are nouns that have no singular – that occur only in the plural – but these are much less numerous than nouns that have no plural – that occur in the singular only.

| 1.5.2.1 |

The following nouns are usually only found in the plural:

aner, ancestry; **briller**, spectacles; **finanser**, finances; **godterier**, goodies; **grønnsaker**, vegetables; **hengsler**, braces; **innvoller**, bowels; **klær**, clothes; **kontanter**, cash; **matvarer**, foodstuffs; **opptøyer**, riots; **penger**, money

Some of these nouns are occasionally used in the singular form:

internasjonal finans, international finance; **verdens sunneste grønnsak**, the world's healthiest vegetable; **en billig penge**, an affordable price

This group includes some words for articles of clothing in two pieces:

jeans, shorts

| 1.5.2.2 | *Collectives denoting people* |

These nouns, though most often used in the plural, can also have singular forms:

foreldre, parents; **småbarn**, infants; **søsken**, siblings

| 1.5.2.3 | *Some illnesses* |

meslinger, measles; **røde hunder**, German measles; **vannkopper**, chickenpox

| 1.5.2.4 | *Some place names* |

Alpene, the Alps; **Færøyene**, the Faeroes; **Maldivene**, the Maldives; **Pyreneene**, the Pyrenees

| 1.5.3 | **Collective use** |

| 1.5.3.1 | **Mann** |

The noun **mann** usually has the plural form **menn**, but when an organised unit or band of men is involved, the plural form used is **mann**:

To menn fikk alvorlige brannskader.
Two men received serious burns.

cf. **en besetning på 23 mann**   a crew of 23 men

| 1.5.3.2 | *Groups of animals* |

In describing groups of animals or fish, the singular of the species name is sometimes used:

tre spurver	three sparrows
cf. **en flokk spurv(er)**	a flock of sparrows
tre sild og to laks	three herring and two salmon

1.5.4 | *Nouns expressing quantity*

In expressions such as those given below, the noun indicating the measure of quantity usually has a zero plural. Notice that, in cases where English uses 'of', Norwegian has no direct equivalent. See also 7.7.3.7.

en fot	one foot
Den er 5 fot lang.	It is five foot long.
en liter	one litre
Vi har to liter melk.	We have two litres of milk.
en meter	a metre
Tunnelen er 600 meter lang.	The tunnel is 600 metres long.
en kilo	a kilo
Peter veier 100 kilo.	Peter weighs a hundred kilos.
en kilometer	a kilometre
De kjørte 1750 kilometer.	They drove 1,750 kilometres.
en mil	a (Norwegian) mile [=10 km]
åtte mil øst for Røros	eight miles [80 km] east of Røros

Note – The noun **krone** is, however, used in the plural form:

en krone	one crown [unit of currency]
ti kroner	ten crowns

1.6 Differences in number between English and Norwegian

1.6.1 | *Nouns which are usually singular in English but plural in Norwegian*

A number of singular nouns in English correspond to plural nouns in Norwegian:

forretninger, business; **inntekter**, income; **kontanter**, cash; **møbler**, furniture; **nyheter**, news; **opplysninger**, information; **penger**, money; **utgifter**, expenditure

Nouns which are usually singular in Norwegian but plural in English

1.6.2.1

A number of singular nouns in Norwegian correspond to plural nouns in English:

> **aske**, ashes; **havre**, oats; **innhold**, contents; **lønn**, wages; **middelalderen**, the Middle Ages; **moral**, morals; **protokoll**, minutes; **rikdom**, riches; **sprit**, spirits; **takk**, thanks; **tollvesen**, the Customs; **utseende**, looks

1.6.2.2

This group includes words for tools and instruments where English has 'a pair of':

> **en pinsett**, (a pair of) tweezers; **en saks**, (a pair of) scissors; **en tang**, (a pair of) pliers; **en vektskål**, (a pair of) scales

1.6.2.3

In reciprocating constructions, the Norwegian singular corresponds to the English plural:

De byttet plass.	They changed places.
Mennene tok hverandre i hånden	The men shook hands.

1.7   Noun homonyms

1.7.1   *List of Norwegian noun homonyms*

Some Norwegian nouns with the same spelling have two very different meanings shown either in different genders or different plural forms or both. They are usually regarded as being different words. Below is a brief list of some frequent homonyms.

en ark –er	1 dormer window 2 ark	et klapp –	pat
et ark –	sheet of paper	en legg –er	folio
		et legg –	calf (of leg)
en bank –er	1 bank 2 knocking sound	en lem –mer	shutter
et bank –	knocking sound	et lem –	limb
		et lokk –	lid
en bar –er	1 bar 2 sandbank	en lokk –er	lock of hair; song
et bar –er	conifer sprig	en plan –er	plan
		et plan –	plane
en bruk –	1 use 2 custom	en rev –er	fox
et bruk –	1 farm 2 factory	et rev –	reef
en dam –mer	1 pool 2 dam 3 puddle	en rom –	rum
en dam –	draughts, checkers	et rom –	room
et egg –	egg	en rot – røtter	root
en egg –er	1 cutting edge 2 ridge	et rot –	mess
en fyr –er	1 light 2 chap	en slått –	haymaking
et fyr –	beacon	en slått –er	folk tune
en kar –er	fellow	en tall –er	pine tree
et kar –	container	et tall –	number
en klapp –er	valve		

1.8 The genitive

Modern written Norwegian has an unmarked form of the noun and one adding an –s indicating possession. See also 1.8.1.7 for the **sin** genitive, and for the periphrastic genitive using a preposition, predominantly in spoken language, see 1.8.1.6, 7.7.3. For remnants of the dative case, see 1.8.1.4(c).

1.8.1 The form of the genitive

1.8.1.1 Basic rule

To form the genitive, −s is added to the form of the indefinite or definite singular or plural.

Indefinite singular	Definite singular
en students fag	**studentens fag**
a student's subject(s)	the student's subject(s)
et folks helse	**folkets helse**
a people's health	the people's health

Indefinite plural	Definite plural
studenters fag	**studentenes fag**
students' subjects	the students' subject(s)
folks helse,	**folkenes helse**,
peoples' health	the peoples' health

See also the group genitive (1.8.1.3), renderings of 'of' (see 7.7) and the prepositional genitive, 1.8.1.6.

(a) After a noun in the genitive form, the noun following *never* takes an end article:

the school's headteacher	**skolens rektor**
the girls' parents	**pikenes foreldre**
the roof of the car	**bilens tak**

This often involves a conscious change when translating from English, as it involves dropping an article on the 'possessed' noun:

The will of *the* people	→	**folkets vilje**
Definite article Definite article		*Definite article No article*
		lit. the people's will

Note – A rare exception is when the noun is a title or proper noun:

Jan Kjærstads 'Forføreren' ble innspilt som TV-serie.
Jan Kjærstad's *The Seducer* was made into a TV series.

(b) The –s genitive may occur with adjectival nouns:

de unges røykevaner	young people's smoking habits
det godes seier	the victory of good
den døendes ansikt	the face of the dying person

(c) Proper nouns (especially names of people) also take the –s ending:

Griegs komposisjoner	Grieg's compositions
Ibsens geni	The genius of Ibsen
Ivar Aasens innsats	Ivar Aasen's achievement

(d) Acronyms (see 11.4.5) that are proper nouns also take an –s ending:

EUs direktiv	the EU directive
USAs president	the president of the USA
NRKs seertall	Norwegian Broadcasting's viewing figures

1.8.1.2 | *After proper names ending in* **–s, –x, –z** *an apostrophe is added instead of* **–s**

Claes' venner	Claes's friends
Sveits' banker	Switzerland's banks
Harrods' fasade	the façade of Harrods
Marx' utsagn	Marx's statement
Berlioz' symfonier	Berlioz's symphonies

1.8.1.3 | *The group genitive*

When a name consists of a group of words, the genitive –s is placed on the last word. This is the 'group genitive':

Kongeriket Norges grunnlov
the Constitution of the Kingdom of Norway

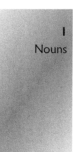

Asbjørnsen og Moes eventyr
Asbjørnsen and Moe's stories
(cf. **Garborgs og Lies romaner,** Garborg's and Lie's novels)

Asbjørnsen and Moe wrote their stories together, while Garborg and Lie were two distinct novelists.

This also occurs with noun phrases comprising common nouns:

mannen i gatas innstilling	the view of the man in the street
for hustru og barns skyld	for the sake of wife and children
en av mine venners hjem	one of my friends' homes

It is not the street that holds the view, but the man in the street. The home does not belong to the friends collectively, but to one of them.

___

1.8.1.4 *Remnants of old case endings in set expressions*

(a) Expressions with a genitive in –s after **til** include:

gå til alters, get married; **til bords**, at table; **til bunns (i noe)**, to the bottom (of something); **til fjells**, into the mountains; **til fots**, on foot; **spørre noen til råds**, ask someone's advice; **til sengs**, abed; **(høyt) til værs**, (high up) in the sky

(b) Expressions with an old genitive in –e after **til**:

komme til orde, get a word in; **gå til spille**, go to waste; **komme til syne**, appear

(c) Notice also the following relict datives in –e after different prepositions:

gå fra borde, go ashore; **i drømme**, in one's dreams; **være i live**, be alive

___

1.8.1.5 *Latin genitives are used in a very few names*

Kristi himmelfart	cf. **Kristus**	the Ascension
Jesu oppstandelse	cf. **Jesus**	Jesus's Resurrection

| 1.8.1.6 | *Periphrastic genitives* |

See also 7.7.3.

(a) Particularly in spoken Norwegian, there are many prepositional expressions that may serve as an alternative to the –s genitive, among others **av, i, på, til**:

utsiden av huset	the outside of the house
Universitetet i Oslo	the University of Oslo
taket på bilen	the car roof
kompisen til Erik	Erik's friend

(b) In the case of the objective genitive (1.8.2.1(f)), the –s genitive may feel too formal, and **av** is normally used instead:

vaksinering av barn	vaccination of children

(c) Another alternative to the genitive in –s is the compound noun:

huseieren	the owner of the house/
cf. **husets eier**	house owner
saksbehandling	legal procedure
cf. **sakens behandling**	

| 1.8.1.7 | *The* **sin** *genitive* |

This originally dialectal western and northern feature, in which the possessive determiner **sin** (**sitt, sine**) is postposed after the noun as an alternative to the –s genitive, has over the last half century spread to the spoken language of Eastern Norway. Although it is used in Nynorsk, it is still considered by some Bokmål writers to be childish or awkward, but it is gaining ground among young people and has become common in written Bokmål. Note that the determiner has to agree with the noun following.

Olav si(n) bok	Olav's book
cf. **Olavs bok**	
mannen sin hatt	the man's hat
cf. **mannens hatt**	
NRK sitt arkiv	NRK's archive

There is a tendency to use the **sin** genitive after an /s/ sound:

SAS sine ruter	SAS's routes
Anders sin leilighet	Anders's flat.

The **sin** genitive is also found in group genitives (cf. 1.8.1.3):

Vesaas og Duun sine romaner	Vesaas's and Duun's novels

1.8.2 The use of the genitive

1.8.2.1 Categories of the genitive

See also periphrastic forms in 1.8.1.6.

In terms of the relationship between the nouns in the genitive phrase, the following distinctions are sometimes made.

(a) Possessive genitive
This is the most easily distinguished category. The referent of the first noun 'owns' or 'possesses' the second:

fars briller	father's glasses
naboens hund	the neighbour's dog
Annas bror	Anna's brother

Frequent prepositional alternatives include **av, på, til**:

boka til/av Knut Faldbakken	Knut Faldbakken's book
slutten av/på boka	the end of the book

(b) Genitive of origin
Similar to the possessive.

Sigrid Undsets berømte formulering
Sigrid Undset's famous phrase

(c) Partitive genitive (only a part is inferred)

fjellets topp (cf. **fjelltoppen**)	the top of the mountain
barnets øyne	the baby's eyes

(d) Descriptive genitive

The –s genitive is a modifier where the first noun (phrase) describes or classifies the second noun.

en seksårs gutt	a six-year-old boy
en fem binds historie	a five-volume history
et drama i tre akter	a three-act play

Note that in many cases where English has a descriptive genitive, Norwegian has a compound noun: 'girl's school' = **jenteskole**; 'farmer's wife' = **bondekone**.

(e) Subjective genitive

In an equivalent sentence, the first noun is subject:

Darwins reise	Darwin's journey.
(cf. **Darwin reiste.**	Darwin travelled.)
menneskers forbruk	people's consumption
(cf. **Mennesker forbruker.**	People consume.)

Compare also the use of **av**:

en tale av helseministeren	a speech by the Health Minister
(cf. **Helseministeren taler.**	The Health Minister speaks.)

(f) Objective genitive.

In an equivalent sentence, the first noun is object:

Australias oppdagelse	the discovery of Australia
(cf. **Man oppdaget Australia.**	They discovered Australia.)
firmaets grunnlegger	the founder of the company
(cf. **Han grunnla firmaet.**	He founded the company.)

This usage is rather literary. Compare the use of **av**:

oppdagelsen av Australia	the discovery of Australia
grunnleggelsen av et firma	the founding of a company

(g) Measurement genitive

en times busstur   one-hour bus trip

See 1.8.2.2(b).

(a) The –s genitive corresponds to both the English genitive in 's or s'
and the 'of' genitive:

guttens far	the boy's father
guttenes far	the boys' father
Norges høyeste fjelltopper	Norway's highest peaks
gårdens eier	the owner of the farm
En handelsreisendes død	*Death of a Salesman* (drama)

(b) The genitive of measurement

en åttetimers arbeidsdag	an eight-hour working day
en tre roms leilighet	a three-room apartment
en 700 kroners drosjetur	a 700-kroner taxi ride

(c) Notice also the use of the –s genitive in Norwegian to indicate a quality:

et herrens vær	terrible weather
den helvetes bilen hans	that bloody awful car of his

Note that (b) and (c) are much more restricted than (a).

1.9   The form of the indefinite article

The indefinite article is **en** for common gender nouns and **et** for neuter
nouns:

en blomst, a flower; **et land**, a country; **en skole**, a school; **et eple**,
an apple

For feminine nouns with the indefinite article **ei** see 1.2.3 and 1.1.2.2.

1.10 The form of the definite article

1.10.1 Introduction

The definite or end article singular has the forms –en, –n, (in the masculine), –a (feminine, 1.10.2.3) and –et, –t (neuter). The definite plural has the forms –ene or –ne or occasionally, with neuter nouns, –a (1.10.2.3). These are not strictly 'articles' in the same way as the front article (determiner); they are suffixes (endings) added to the noun.

When the definite noun is preceded by an adjective, definiteness is expressed by both a front or adjectival article or determiner (den, det or de) and an end article (–en, –n, –et, –t or –a) as well as a definite ending –e on most adjectives. See 2.3.

1.10.2 The form of the definite singular with end article

1.10.2.1 Basic rule

Most Norwegian nouns add the end article –en or –et:

en **hånd**, a hand	**hånden**, the hand
en **melodi**, a tune	**melodien**, the tune
et **barn**, a child	**barnet**, the child
et **galleri**, a gallery	**galleriet**, the gallery

Neuter nouns in –um follow the main rule.

albumet, the album; **vakuumet**, the vacuum; **volumet**, the volume

Note – Neuter nouns in –eum –ium generally drop the –um of the stem before adding any endings:

museet, the museum; **podiet**, the podium; **studiet**, the study

1.10.2.2 Exceptions

Nouns of either gender ending in unstressed –e add –n or –t according to gender:

en **kirke**, a church	**kirken,** the church
et **møte**, a meeting	**møtet,** the meeting

(a) Common gender nouns in –e take –n in the definite form:

en bonde – bonden, farmer; **finne – finnen**, Finn; **hage – hagen**, garden; **en måte – måten**, way; **en serie – serien**, series and many in **–else**; **en avgjørelse – avgjørelsen**, decision; **en mottakelse – mottakelsen**, reception

(b) Neuter nouns in –e take –t in the definite form:

et løfte – løftet, promise; **et menneske – mennesket**, person; **et område – området**, area; **et stykke – stykket**, piece; **et tilfelle – tilfellet**, occurrence, case; **et værelse – værelset**, room

Note – If the feminine is used, the unstressed –e– from the indefinite singular is dropped before the ending –a is added: **ei jente – jenta**, girl.

1.10.2.3 The –a form

For feminines, see 1.2.1ff, 1.1.2.1 and 1.2.3.

(a) The feminine definite ending in –a in written Bokmål is the preferred form in only a restricted number of cases such as the following (in which it is also perfectly possible to use –en):

geita, the goat; **hytta**, the cabin; **jenta**, the girl; **kua**, the cow; **øya**, the island

Note – In the language reform of 1917 –a forms were either obligatory or optional for "names of indigenous fauna and flora, indigenous natural phenomena, rural life and superstition". In the reform of 1938, approximately 1,000 nouns had obligatory –a endings. The ending proved contentious in the debate in the immediate post-war period on bringing Nynorsk and Bokmål closer together. After the 2005 reform, the ending –a is never obligatory. See also 1.1.2.2.

(b) Some neuter nouns often have a plural definite form in –a:

et barn – barna, child; **et bein – beina**, leg

| 1.10.2.4 | *Contraction* |

In some cases, nouns drop the stem vowel in inflected forms.

(a) Neuter nouns that in their uninflected form end in –el usually drop the stem vowel –e before adding the definite article, though they also possess an uncontracted alternative:

et fengsel – fengslet/fengselet, prison

Other examples:

et eksempel – eksemplet, example; **et kapittel – kapitlet**, chapter; **et middel – midlet**, means; **et stempel – stemplet**, stamp

Note – Neuter nouns ending in –en, –er have an uncontracted form in the definite:

kjøkkenet, the kitchen; **våpenet**, the weapon; **nummeret**, the number; **senteret**, the centre

(b) Neuter nouns ending in –eum, –ium often drop the –um of the stem before adding any inflexional endings:

et museum – museet, museum; **et auditorium – auditoriet**, auditorium; **et mysterium – mysteriet**, mystery; **et stadium – stadiet**, stage

Note – Words denoting the chemical elements have uncontracted forms:

kalium – kaliumet, potassium; **kalsium – kalsiumet**, calcium

See also 1.4.7.2.

| 1.10.3 | **Choice of the definite plural ending** |

For indefinite plural forms, see 1.1.3, 1.4.1.

Basic rule I

Nouns with indefinite plurals in –er drop the –r of the indefinite plural ending before adding the definite plural ending –ne:

en blomst	blomsten	blomster	blomstene	flower
en skole	skolen	skoler	skolene	school
et ansikt	ansiktet	ansikter	ansiktene	face
et eple	eplet	epler	eplene	apple

Note 1 – Neuter nouns ending in –eum, –ium drop the –um of the stem before adding any inflexional endings:

et jubileum	jubileet	jubileer	jubileene	jubilee
et medium	mediet	medier	mediene	medium

Note 2 – All common nouns that in the indefinite singular end in –el and most that end in –er show contraction of the final stem vowel in their plural forms:

en regel	regelen	regler	reglene	rule
en finger	fingeren	fingre/fingrer	fingeren	finger

Neuter nouns that end in –el, –er can also show contraction, though they have an alternative zero indefinite plural:

et fengsel	fengslet	fengsler/ fengsel	fengslene	prison
et kapittel	kapitlet	kapitler/ kapittel	kapitlene	chapter
et orkester	orkestret	orkestre/ orkester	orkestrene	orchestra

Note 3 – Nouns whose indefinite singular end in –en have an uncontracted form in the definite plural:

aftenene	the evenings
lakenene	the sheets
tallerkenene	the plates

Note 4 – In the case of **bror, mor** and **far**, the stem vowel is modified and there is also contraction (and addition of –d):

en bror	broren	brødre	brødrene	brother
en mor	moren	mødre	mødrene	mother
en far	faren	fedre	fedrene	father

Note 5 – Modification of the stem vowel and contraction is also found in:

en datter – datteren – døtre – døtrene, daughter

Note 6 – Neuter nouns may alternatively take –**a** (cf. 1.10.2.3(b)), which may involve dropping both the –**e** and the –**r** of the indefinite plural ending:

barna (cf. **barnene**), the children; **eksempla** (cf. **eksemplene**), the examples; **epla** (cf. **eplene**), the apples

---

| 1.10.3.2 | *Basic rule 2*

Plurals of common gender nouns ending in their uninflected form (indefinite singular) in –**er** retain the stem –**r** in the definite plural:

en bruker	brukeren	brukere	brukerne	user
en leder	lederen	ledere	lederne	leader
en spiller	spilleren	spillere	spillerne	player

Note – A small number of nouns ending in a root vowel which change their stem vowel in the plural retain the –**r** of the indefinite plural ending in their definite plural form:

en klo	kloen (kloa)	klør	klørne	claw
en ku	kuen (kua)	kyr (kuer)	kyrne (kuene)	cow
en tå	tåen (tåa)	tær	tærne	toe
et kne	kneet	knær (kne)	knærne	knee
et tre	treet	trær (tre)	trærne	tree

1.10.4	Nouns – forms with end article: summary

Paragraph	Common gender	Neuter
Singular		
1.10.2.1	**avisen** the newspaper	**salget** the sale
1.10.2.1	**sagaen** the tale	**temaet** the theme
1.10.2.1	**ideen** the idea	**treet** the tree
1.10.2.1	–	**albumet** the album
1.10.2.1n	**museet** (from **museum**) the museum	**stadiet** (from **stadium**) the stage
1.10.2.2	**skiven** (from **skive**) the slice	**løftet** (from **løfte**) the promise
1.10.2.3	**hytta** (from **hytte**) the cabin	–
1.10.2.4	–	**eksemplet** (from **eksempel**) the example
Plural		
1.10.3.1	**klubbene** the clubs	**lagene** the teams
1.10.3.1	**reglene** (from **regel**) the rules	**midlene** (from **middel**) the funds
1.10.3.2	**ministrene** (from **minister**) the ministers	**teatrene** (from **teater**) the theatres
		museene (from **museum**) the museums
1.10.3.1	**brødrene** (from **bror**) the brother	–
1.10.3.2	**deltakerne** (from **deltaker**) the participants	–
1.10.3.2	**kyrne** (from **ku**) the cows	–
1.10.3.1	–	**eplene** (from **eple**) the apples

1.11 The use of the indefinite and definite article and the noun without article

1.11.1 Introduction

The same principle usually applies in Norwegian as in English, namely that unfamiliar concepts take an indefinite article while concepts that are already familiar from the context take a definite article.

Vi kjøpte *en* stol. Stol*en* var gammel.
We bought a chair. The chair was old.

Vi kjøpte en ny stol. *Den* nye stol*en* var billig.
We bought a new chair. The new chair was cheap.

Vi kjøpte to roser. Rosen*e* var dyre.
We bought two roses. The roses were expensive.

With assumed common knowledge (1.11.1.2):

Eva har tatt bil*en* til arbeidet.   Eva has taken the car to work.

Article use in Norwegian may be regarded as a series of choices between the three forms of the noun outlined in 1.11.1.1 to 1.11.1.3.

1.11.1.1 Noun without article

The noun without article has restricted fields of use. These include words for substances (**De byr på kaffe**, 'They offer us a coffee'), abstracts (**Han har skaffet seg arbeid**, 'He has found work'), nouns in proverbs and fixed expressions (**Liten tue kan velte stort lass**, 'A small tussock can topple a big load', i.e. small details can destroy large projects) and nouns in rubrics in newspapers (**Fem skadd i trafikkulykke**, 'Five hurt in traffic accident'). It is also general when the noun is a complement (**Hun er musiker**, 'She is a musician') (see 1.11.5.1). In legal and bureaucratic language, the noun without article has generic reference, as it also does in the following cases shown here for comparison with the form with indefinite article:

Generic reference	Specific reference
Kjører du bil?	**Vinn en bil!**

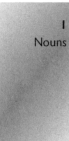

Generic reference	*Specific reference*
Do you drive (a car)?	Win a car!
De sitter og spiser kylling.	**Hvordan dele en kylling?**
They sit eating chicken.	How to joint a chicken?
Nils er ute på reise.	**Han planlegger en reise.**
Nils is away on a trip.	He is a planning a trip.
De jaktet elg.	**Vi så en elg i skogen.**
They hunted elk.	We saw an elk in the forest.
Det er en øde høyslette av stein.	**Han plukket opp en stein.**
It is a desolate plateau of rock.	He picked up a rock.

With a noun indicating a substance such as **stein, vin** the use of the indefinite article stresses type:

	Type or sort
et hus av stein	**Gneis er en hard stein.**
a house (built) of stone	Gneiss is a resistant rock.
Hun drakk vin.	**Hun tok en fransk vin.**
She drank wine.	She took a French wine.

In contrast with the articleless noun, the noun with indefinite article may have a figurative or subjective sense (cf. 1.11.5.1):

Literal	*Figurative*
Han er klovn.	**Sjefen er en klovn.**
He is (employed as) a clown.	The boss is a clown. [i.e. a fool].

1.11.1.2	*Noun in the definite*

The listener/reader is usually aware of what is being referred to. For example, **kongen** 'the king' to a Norwegian might logically refer to King Harald V of Norway. When there is assumed common knowledge of the context, Norwegian often has a definite form, even when English does not:

Skolen begynner i august.	School starts in August.
Han havnet i retten.	He ended up in court.

A whole species or family may be denoted by either the definite singular or indefinite plural:

Delfinen/Delfiner er et pattedyr.
The dolphin is a mammal./Dolphins are mammals.

1.11.2 | *Definite article in Norwegian – no article in English*

1.11.2.1 | *Abstract nouns in a generic sense*

Many abstract nouns in a generic sense are usually found in the definite in Norwegian, including:

(a) Nouns denoting aspects of human life and thought such as:

Døden snakker vi helst ikke om.	We don't mention death.
Livet er ikke en dans på roser.	*Lit.* Life is not a dance on roses.
	Life is not a walk in the park.

Others include:

arbeidet, work; **barndommen**, childhood; **menneskeheten**, humankind; **naturen**, nature; **skjebnen**, fate; **vitenskapen**, science

(b) Nouns denoting human qualities and emotions:

Erfaringen viste at dette ikke var riktig.
Experience showed that this was not the case.

Others include:

helsen, health; **kjærligheten**, love; **lykken**, happiness; **skjønnheten**, beauty

1.11.2.2 | *Proverbs*

Proverbs include many special cases of 1.11.2.1.

Historien gjentar seg.	History repeats itself.

Kunsten er lang, livet kort.	Art is long, life is short.
Slik er livet.	Such is life.
Mennesket spår, Gud rår.	Man proposes, God disposes.
Arbeidet adler mannen.	Works ennobles Man.
Gråten letter sorgen.	Tears ease grief.

1.11.2.3 *Idiomatic prepositional phrases*

In some idiomatic prepositional phrases indicating location the noun is found in the definite form in Norwegian:

Vi er i/drar til byen.	We are in/are going to town.
De går i kirken.	They go to church.
Guttene er på skolen.	The boys are at school.

1.11.2.4 *Days of the week, etc*

Days of the week, seasons and festivals are more often used in the definite in Norwegian than in English.

om natten/fredagen/vinteren	at night/on Friday/in winter
i julen/pinsen/skumringen	at Christmas/Whitsun/dusk

Note – Exceptions: Festivals ending in –**aften**:

på julaften/påskeaften/sankthansaften
on Christmas Eve/Easter Saturday/Midsummer's Eve

1.11.2.5 *Other phrases*

på byen, in (the) town; **i utlandet**, abroad; **gjennom tollen**, through Customs; **i posten**, by post

1.11.2.6 *Public places, etc*

Names of some public places and geographical locations:

Domkirkeplassen, Storgata, Majorstuen, Hardangerbrua, Blåfjellet, Geirangerfjorden, Victoriasjøen, Lake Victoria

Note – When used as the first element in a compound, names drop the end article:

|---|---|
Atlanteren	the Atlantic
cf. **Atlanter|havet**	the Atlantic Ocean
Nordsjøen	the North Sea
cf. **nordsjø|olje**	North Sea oil

1.11.2.7 *With nouns after hele, halve*

hele uken	all week
(cf. **en hel uke**	a whole week)
halve natten	half the night

1.11.3 *Definite article in Norwegian – indefinite article in English*

This is found in expressions indicating frequency of occurrence.

to ganger i uken	twice a week/a month
300 kroner i timen	300 kroner an hour
1 000 kroner i året	1,000 kr per annum

1.11.4 *No article in Norwegian – definite article in English*

1.11.4.1 *With certain adjectives*

This is found with certain adjectives (that in some way restrict the reference) in the definite form. The form without a front article is more common in the spoken language (see 2.3.5ff):

samme tid/måte/periode/størrelse
the same time/way/period/size

første gang/del/runde
the first time/part/round

siste instans/runde/øyeblikk
the last resort/lap/minute

neste utgave/århundre/årtusen
the next edition/century/millenium

But constructions with the front article and end article are also possible and frequent in the written language:

den forrige statsministeren	the previous Prime Minister
den neste utgaven	the next edition
det neste århundret	the next century

1.11.4.2 Instruments

In some phrases involving instruments and hobbies:

Mia spiller piano.	Mia plays the piano.
Far hører på radio.	Dad is listening to the radio.
Sara prater i telefon.	Sara is speaking on the phone.

1.11.4.3 Latin and Greek loans

(a) With many linguistic terms, medical terms and other words from Latin:

i infinitiv/presens/futurum/preteritum
in the infinitive/present tense/future/ past tense

i singularis/pluralis	in the singular/plural
i utrum/nøytrum	in the common/neuter gender

This also applies to their Norwegian equivalents:

i entall/flertall	in the singular/plural
i felleskjønn/intetkjønn	in the common/neuter gender

(b) In titles, mainly but not only from Latin or Greek:

Ved Universitetet i Oslo har rektor/dekanus besluttet å utvide.
At the University of Oslo, the Vice Chancellor/the Dean has decided on expansion.

1.11.4.4 Directions

In phrases involving compass points and directions:

i nord/syd	in the north/south
til venstre/på venstre side	to the left/on the left-hand side

| 1.11.4.5 | Superlatives |

With superlatives, usually in the definite form in English:

av beste kvalitet	of the best quality
i høyeste grad	to the highest degree
av billigste sort	of the cheapest kind

| 1.11.4.6 | Rivers |

In the majority of river names:

Donau, the Danube; **Kongo**, the Congo; **Mississippi**, the Mississippi; **Volga**, the Volga

Note – Exceptions include some well-known Norwegian and other rivers:

Drammenselva; Elben, the Elbe; **Nilen**, the Nile; **Rhinen**, the Rhine; **Themsen**, the Thames

| 1.11.4.7 | Some set phrases |

i håp om at	in the hope that
med unntak av	with the exception of
under innflytelse av noen	under the influence of someone
Han er forfatter av boken.	He is the author of the book.
Bjørn var sønn av Harald Hårfagre.	Bjørn was the son of Harald Fairhair.

1.11.5 No article in Norwegian ('naked noun') – indefinite article in English

See also 1.11.1.1.

| 1.11.5.1 | Nationality, profession, etc |

With nouns denoting nationality, profession, trade, political or religious belief:

Wolfgang er tysker.	Wolfgang is a German.
Ingrid er lærer.	Ingrid is a teacher.
Sofia er sosialist.	Sofia is a socialist.
Kari er muslim.	Kari is a Muslim.

Exceptions:

The article is, however, used:

(a) When the noun is of a more subjective kind:

Mor var et geni/en engel/en kverulant.
Mum was a genius/an angel/a cantankerous person.

(b) When the noun is qualified by an adjective:

Hun er *en god* lærer.   She is a good teacher.

(c) When the noun is qualified by a restrictive relative clause:

Hun var en lærer *som kunne sine ting*.
She was a teacher who knew her stuff.

| 1.11.5.2 | *After* **som** |

When the noun follows **som** (= 'in the capacity of'):

Som professor fikk hun det meget travelt.
As a professor, she became very busy.

Som barn var han smart og kreativ.
As a child, he was clever and creative.

Note – When the noun follows **som** means 'like a', an indefinite article is used, as in English:

"Da jeg var barn, talte jeg som et barn …"
"When I was a child I spoke as a child …" (I Corinthians 13)

| 1.11.5.3 | *Generality* |

See also 1.11.1.1.

With singular count nouns when a general idea is inferred rather than a specific example. The noun is unmodified:

Det er vanskelig å skaffe leilighet i Oslo.
It is difficult to get a flat in Oslo.

Vi går ikke ut på restaurant så ofte.
We don't go out to a restaurant so often.

Anna venter barn.	Anna is expecting a baby.
Håkon skriver brev.	Håkon is writing a letter (or several letters).
Familien har hund.	The family has a dog.

1.11.5.4

After the verb **ha** (and **få**) and with an adjective attribute the naked noun is often found in phrases describing the characteristic external or internal qualities of people and objects. Here there is a great deal of variation in use, however.

Han har dårlig rygg/stor nese/god samvittighet.
He has a bad back/ a big nose/ a good conscience.

Katten har kort pels.   The cat has a short coat.

At times, this construction occurs with other verbs:

Han var kledd i hvit skjorte.   He was wearing a white shirt.
Olav kjøper ikke ny dress.   Olav is not buying a new suit.

1.11.5.5 Idiomatic phrases

The naked noun is also used in other idiomatic phrases when English has an indefinite article:

med stort flertall, with a large majority; **ha hastverk**, be in a hurry; **i godt humør**, in a good mood; **ha feber**, have a high temperature; **ha rett til å**, have a right to; **på avstand**, at a distance; **i nødsfall**, in an emergency

1.11.6 Indefinite article in Norwegian – no article in English

The following expressions using **en** (or its neuter equivalent **et**) denote 'about, approximately':

De forsøkte en fire, fem ganger.   They tried four or five times.
Firmaet har et femtitall biler.   The firm has about 50 cars.

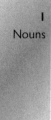

| **1.11.7** | **Use of the definite article to indicate possession** |

| **1.11.7.1** | *Parts of the body and articles of clothing* |

The end article is often used in Norwegian with parts of the body and articles of clothing when it is clear who these belong to. In these cases, English uses a possessive (cf. also 4.4.4):

Han river seg i håret.	He is tearing his hair out.
Vi fryser på føttene.	Our feet are cold.
De tok ikke av seg skoene.	They didn't take off their shoes.
Keeper fikk hendene på ballen.	The goalkeeper got his hands on the ball.

Note – Exception: Where precise ownership needs to be indicated or in order to avoid ambiguity, the possessive adjective is used, as in English:

Jenta la sin hånd i min.	The girl put her hand in mine.

| **1.11.7.2** | *Aches and pains* |

Notice the following construction locating various aches and pains, which requires a different rendering in English:

Hun har vondt i ryggen/hodet/magen/halsen/skulderen.
She has backache/a headache/a stomach-ache/a sore throat/shoulder pain.

| **1.11.8** | **Differences in the position of the article in Norwegian and English** |

en halv time	half an hour
en slik fremgangsmåte	such a procedure
en ganske lang vei	rather a long way

Chapter 2

Adjectives

2.1 Form and order

2.1.1 Introduction to forms and use

Adjectives are inflected in Norwegian (for gender, number, definiteness and degree). Both attributive and predicative adjectives adopt a form according to the gender and number of the noun or pronoun to which they refer. This is called 'agreement'. The indefinite forms of the adjective are used both attributively – before the noun – and predicatively – after the verb –, while the definite forms are only used attributively:

	Indefinite	Definite
Attributive	**en lang film** a long film	**den lange filmen** the long film
	et langt dikt a long poem	**det lange diktet** the long poem
	lange filmer/dikt long films/poems	**de lange filmene/ diktene** the long films/poems
	varm luft hot air	**den varme luften** the hot air
	varme vinder hot winds	**de varme vindene** the hot winds

Indefinite	Definite
en lukket beholder a closed container	**den lukkede** **beholderen** the closed container
et lukket møte a closed meeting	**det lukkede møtet** the closed meeting
lukkede dører closed doors	**de lukkede dørene** the closed doors

Predicative

filmen er lang the film is long	**filmene er lange** the films are long
diktet er langt the poem is long	**diktene er lange** the poems are long
luften er varm the air is hot	**vindene er varme** the winds are hot
døren er lukket the foor is closed	**dørene er lukkede** the doors are closed
møtet er lukket the meeting is closed	**møtene er lukkede** the meetings are closed

2.1.1.1 *Front article/Determiner*

Notice that the definite declension of the adjective usually employs the determiner we have called a front (or adjectival) article **den, det, de**. See 2.3.3.1.

2.1.1.2 *Adjective as predicative complement*

After *copular verbs*, such as **være**, 'be'; **bli**, 'be(come)'; **hete**, 'be called'; **virke**, 'seem', the adjective comprises a *predicative complement* (10.3.5) and is inflected according to the subject or object to which it refers (2.2.1.3f.). See also 2.1.1 above.

2.1.2 | The basic rule

2.1.2.1 | Markers for neuter singular and for plural

There is no distinctive marker for the common gender singular indefinite (basic or dictionary 'look-up') form of the adjective, but the neuter singular form usually adds –t, and both the plural indefinite and the definite (singular and plural) add –e. The basic rule is shown for the adjective **fin**, 'fine', in the diagram below:

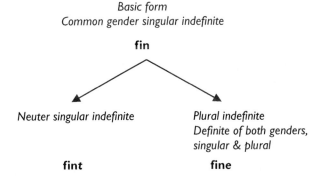

Basic form
Common gender singular indefinite

fin

Neuter singular indefinite

fint

Plural indefinite
Definite of both genders,
singular & plural

fine

Notice that no distinction is made between the common gender and neuter plural form. Examples:

en fin bok
a fine book

et fint stykke
a fine piece

fine bøker, fine stykker
fine books, fine pieces

den fine boken, det fine stykket
the fine book, the fine piece

Adjectives may be grouped into inflection classes on the basis of how they form their paradigms.

2.1.3 | Class 1: Endings in zero, –t, –e

These adjectives follow the basic rule with only minor variations (2.1.3.1ff).

The table is shown in this form for comparison with the paragraphs that follow.

Ending:	Basic form **–**	Neuter **–t**	Plural/Definite **–e**	
	dyr	**dyrt**	**dyre**	expensive
See 2.1.3.1(a)	**grå**	**grått**	**grå(e)**	grey
See 2.1.3.2(a)	**enkel**	**enkelt**	**enkle**	simple
See 2.1.3.1(b)	**tynn**	**tynt**	**tynne**	thin
See 2.1.3.2(b)	**dum**	**dumt**	**dumme**	stupid

Examples:

en dyr fornøyelse	an expensive entertainment
et dyrt helsevesen	an expensive health system
dyre medisiner	expensive medicines

The large group of adjectives which inflect according to this rule includes:

• Many monosyllabic adjectives ending in a consonant or consonant group:

   frisk, healthy; **hvit**, white; **høy**, high; **jevn**, even; **kald**, cold; **pen**, pretty;
   rik, rich; **rød**, red; **sterk**, strong; **stor**, big; **søt**, sweet; **ung**, young

• Polysyllabic adjectives ending in stressed –al, –bar, –ell, –iv, –ær, –(i)øs:

   minimal, minimal; **kostbar**, expensive; **spesiell**, special; **positiv**,
   positive; **populær**, popular; **religiøs**, religious; **nervøs**, nervous

| 2.1.3.1 | *Variations – neuter form*

The basic pattern shown in 2.1.3 displays a number of minor variations for
some adjectives, which are, however, relatively frequent. (In the summary
of form given below: –V = vowel, –$\underline{V}$ = long vowel, –C = consonant.)

(a) A number of adjectives ending in a long vowel shorten the vowel (even if
   this does not show orthographically, cf. 12.2.1.1) and take –**tt** in the
   neuter form:

Ending:	*Basic form* –$\underline{V}$	*Neuter* –V+**tt**	*Plural/Definite* –$\underline{V}$+**e**	
	fri	**fritt**	**frie**	free

This large group includes:

blå, blue; **grå,** grey; **ny,** new; **rå,** coarse; **små** (pl. only), small

The vowel is shortened in the neuter form. In the plural, three of these words possess alternative forms without an ending:

blå/blåe, grå/gråe, rå/råe

Note 1 – **Små** is a suppletive form for the plural of **liten.** See 2.1.3.4.

Note 2 – There are a number of exceptions that are indeclinable, for example **bra,** 'good'; **sta,** 'stubborn'. See also 2.1.5.

(b) Adjectives ending in a double consonant in their basic form drop one consonsonant in the neuter form, cf. Orthography 12.2.1.1(a).

Basic form	Neuter	Plural/Definite	
trygg	**trygt**	**trygge**	secure
sann	**sant**	**sanne**	true
aktuell	**aktuelt**	**aktuelle**	topical

Others include:

hvass, sharp; **kjekk,** decent; **knapp,** scarce; **spesiell,** special; **stinn,** full

---

2.1.3.2 | *Variations – plural/definite form*

(a) Adjectives ending in –**el,** –**en,** –**er** in their basic form drop the final –**e** before adding the plural/definite ending:

Basic form	Neuter	Plural/Definite	
travel	**travelt**	**travle**	busy
voksen	**voksent**	**voksne**	adult
munter	**muntert**	**muntre**	merry

Other adjectives of this kind are:

disponibel, disposable; **enkel,** simple; **risikabel,** risky; **erfaren,** experienced; **naken,** naked; **åpen,** open; **dyster,** gloomy; **mager,** thin

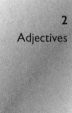

This is a very large group of adjectives, particularly those ending in –en.

(b) Adjectives of this kind also simplify the double consonant in the plural form (cf. 12.2.1.1 a):

Basic form	Neuter	Plural/Definite	
gammel	**gammelt**	**gamle**	old
frossen	**frossent**	**frosne**	frozen
sikker	**sikkert**	**sikre**	certain

(c) Adjectives with a short vowel ending in –m double this consonant in the plural form:

Basic form	Neuter	Plural/Definite	
dum	**dumt**	**dumme**	stupid
lam	**lamt**	**lamme**	lame
morsom	**morsomt**	**morsomme**	amusing

2.1.3.3 | Inflexion of past participles in –en and/or –et

See also 5.3.12.

The past participles of strong verbs inflect in one of two ways:

(a) When the participle no longer corresponds to a verb, it inflects in the same way as other adjectives in –en. See also 2.1.3.2(a). Many of these words are derivatives or compounds and have a static, adjectival sense.

holden	**holdent**	**holdne**	wealthy
slagen	**slagent**	**slagne**	beaten

Others include:

erfaren, experienced; **fullkommen**, complete; **overdreven**, exaggerated; **storslagen**, magnificent; **velkommen**, welcome; **veloppdragen**, well-behaved

(b) When the participle has a clearly verbal sense, it has the ending –et in the indefinite singular both in the common and the neuter gender:

omskrevet	**omskrevet**	**omskrevne**	rewritten

Others:

beskrevet, described; **omkommet**, died by accident; **overstrøket**, deleted

Some adjectives formed from the past participles of strong verbs fall between these two types, and there is considerable variation in individual cases, which may lead to differences in similar words. In the case below, **stjålen** is used literally and more like a verb with **bil** and **kredittkort** and figuratively and more like an adjective with **blikk**:

Verbal sense	Adjectival sense
en stjålen/stjålet bil	**stjålen lykke**
a stolen car	stolen joy
et stjålet kredittkort	**et stjålent blikk**
a stolen credit card	a stolen glance

For past participles of weak verbs, cf. 2.1.4.6(a) below.

2.1.3.4 *Liten*

Liten, 'little', is unique in several respects:

(a) It changes stem in the plural:

	Basic form	Neuter	Plural
Indefinite	**liten**	**lite**	**små**
	en liten skole	**et lite hus**	**små skoler/hus**
	a small school	a small house	little, small
			small schools/
			houses

(b) The neuter form **lite** is unique, and should not be confused with **litt**, 'a little': **Vent litt**, 'Wait a bit'. (See further 4.6.8.2 on **litt**.)

(c) **Liten** possesses a singular definite form, **lille**, which differs from its plural form. Compare 2.3.1ff.

	Basic form	Neuter	Plural
Definite	**lille**	**lille**	**små**
	den lille skolen	**det lille huset**	**de små skolene/husene**
	the small school	the small house	the small schools/houses

Note 1 – The rare feminine form **lita** can be used with the feminine indefinite article **ei**, (1.2.3) **ei lita jente**, 'a small girl', or predicatively: **Jane er lita**, 'Jane is small'.

Note 2 – Notice the adjectival noun **en liten**, 'a little baby'.

Note 3 – It is possible to form a neuter indefinite form from **små**, namely **smått**, but this is usually found only in set phrases, with a collective noun or else nominally or adverbially:

Det er smått med penger.   Money is short.
Smått er godt.   Good things come in small packages.
det smått legendariske bandet   the almost legendary band

Note 4 – There is an alternative to **lille** as the definite singular, viz. **vesle**, which is formed suppletively and not much used in the written language.

2.1.4 | Class 2: No neuter form

These adjectives do not add –t in the neuter form, but they do have an –e added in the plural/definite. Compare 2.1.3.

2.1.4.1 | Adjectives ending in –ig, –lig

	Basic form	Neuter	Plural/Definite	
Ending:	**nyttig**	**nyttig**	**nyttige**	useful
	tidlig	**tidlig**	**tidlige**	early

This group includes:

alvorlig, serious; **enig**, united; **forsiktig**, careful; **forskjellig**, different; **vanlig**, usual; **vanskelig**, difficult; **viktig**, important

Examples:

en kraftig økning, a powerful increase; **et kraftig regnvær**, a powerful downfall; **kraftige advarsler**, powerful warnings

2.1.4.2 | Nationality adjectives ending in –sk

Basic form	Neuter	Plural/Definite
gresk	**gresk**	**greske** Greek

This group includes many others:

> **amerikansk**, American; **engelsk**, English; **indisk**, Indian; **norsk**,
> Norwegian; **tysk**, German

Note – Other monosyllabic adjectives in **–sk** belonging to Class 1 include:

> **falsk – falskt – falske**, false; **fersk – ferskt – ferske**, fresh; **frisk –**
> **friskt – friske**, healthy; **rask – raskt – raske**, quick

---

| 2.1.4.3 | *Polysyllabic adjectives ending in* **–sk, –isk** |

Basic form	*Neuter*	*Plural/Definite*	
himmelsk	**himmelsk**	**himmelske**	heavenly
pittoresk	**pittoresk**	**pittoreske**	picturesque
realistisk	**realistisk**	**realistiske**	realistic

Examples:

> **en sosialistisk filosof**, a Socialist philosopher; **et sosialistisk parti**, a
> Socialist party; **sosialistiske ideer**, Socialist ideas

Others include:

> **trøndersk**, from Trøndelag; **grotesk**, grotesque; **muslimsk**, Muslim;
> **nordisk**, Nordic; **økonomisk**, economic

| 2.1.4.4 | *Some adjectives ending in* **–d, –id** |

Basic form	*Neuter*	*Plural/Definite*	
redd	**redd**	**redde**	afraid
fremmed	**fremmed**	**fremmede**	foreign

This group includes among others: **nitid**, careful; **solid**, solid

---

| 2.1.4.5 | *Adjectives ending in* **–tt** *or a consonant* **+t** |

Basic form	*Neuter*	*Plural/Definite*	
svart	**svart**	**svarte**	black
trett	**trett**	**trette**	tired

Others include:

absolutt, total; eksakt, exact; intelligent, intelligent; interessant, interesting; komplett, complete; kort, short; perfekt, perfect; rett, right; stolt, proud; vanntett, waterproof

2.1.4.6 Adjectives ending in **-et**

See 2.1.3.3.

Basic form	Neuter	Plural/Definite	
lukket	lukket	lukkede/	closed
		lukkete	
ubegrenset	ubegrenset	ubegrensede/	unlimited
		ubegrensete	
blomstret(e)	blomstret(e)	blomstrete	flowery

This is a large and complex collection of adjectives. They all have the same form in the neuter as in the basic form, but also possess a possible variant form in the singular or plural. *Språkrådet* distinguishes several types:

(a) Past participle (see 5.3.12) forms of weak verbs that are not compounds may have optional –a:

dannet	dannet	dannede	educated
(danna)	(danna)	(dannete, danna)	

The forms in parentheses are perfectly acceptable (and such forms as danna are probably more frequent in speech), but they are less used in writing.

Others include:

elsket, loved; kastet, thrown; samlet, collected; tørket, dried; ventet, awaited; ønsket, wished

(b) Compound adjectives in -et with optional -a:

firkantet	firkantet	firkantede	square
(firkanta)	(firkanta)	(firkantete, firkanta)	

The forms in parentheses are perfectly acceptable (and such forms as firkanta are probably more frequent in speech), but they are less used in writing.

Others include:

> **helhjertet**, whole-hearted; **kortermet**, short-sleeved; **rakrygget**, upright; **storsinnet**, magnanimous; **ublandet**, unalloyed

(c) Adjectives in –et(e) derived from nouns and meaning 'full of X':

> **steinet(e)**   **steinet(e)**   **steinete**   rocky

Others include:

> **bakket(e)**, hilly; **flekket(e)**, speckled, stained; **håret(e)**, hairy

In practice, –ete is much more common than –et.

2.1.5 | *Class 3: Indeclinable adjectives*

The following types of adjective are indeclinable, i.e. do not add an inflexional ending in either the indefinite or the definite declension.

Basic form	Neuter	Plural/Definite	
moderne	**moderne**	**moderne**	modern
bra	**bra**	**bra**	good
gratis	**gratis**	**gratis**	free of charge

Examples:

> **en ekte gentleman**, a real gentleman; **et ekte dilemma**, a real dilemma; **ekte menn**, real men

---

2.1.5.1 | *Adjectives ending in* **–e**

> **det tidligere Tsjekkoslovakia**   the former Czechoslovakia

This group includes most adjectives ending in unstressed –e:

(a) All present participles. See 5.3.13.

> **følgende**, following; **flytende**, liquid; **grunnleggende**, fundamental; **omfattende**, comprehensive

(b) Many participial adjectives, i.e. adjectives that were originally participles but which have subsequently become independent of the verb:

> **beklemmende**, depressing, disconcerting; **enestående**, exceptional; **rasende**, furious; **uvedkommende**, irrelevant

(c) Adjectives ending in –e that are not participles:

nøye, careful; **stille**, calm; **ymse**, different, varied; **øde**, desolate; **beige**, beige; **oransje**, orange

(d) Comparative forms in –ere/ –re. See 2.5.1f.

et høyere tak	a higher ceiling
et yngre par	a rather young couple

2.1.5.2 *Adjectives ending in* **–a**

fem bra filmer   five good films

This group includes:

ekstra, extra; **lilla**, mauve; **prima**, first class; **rosa**, pink

Note – Some have an alternative plural in –e: **sta**, 'stubborn'; **gra(e)**, 'uncastrated, eager'.

2.1.5.3 *Adjectives ending in* **–o, –u** *and* **–y**

These include:

tro, loyal; **tabu**, taboo; **ublu**, exorbitant; **kry**, proud, and some English loans: **macho, sexy, sporty**

Note 1 – Some adjectives ending in –u or –y have an alternative plural form in –e:

edru(e), sober; **sjalu(e)**, jealous; **sky(e)**, shy; **slu(e)**, cunning

Note 2 – **ru**, 'rough' and **ublu**, 'exorbitant' have alternative forms for both the neuter and plural:

ru – ru (rutt) – ru (rue); ublu – ublu (ublutt) – ublu (ublue)

Note 3 – The frequent adjective **ny**, 'new' follows the pattern in 2.1.3.

2.1.5.4 *Many adjectives ending in* **–s**

gratis	free
innvortes	internal
landsens	from the country

This group includes:

(a) Adjectives ending in a consonant +s:

alskens, all sorts of; **nymotens**, modern; **sams**, common; **stakkars**, poor, pitiable

(b) Adjectives ending in –es:

annerledes, different; **avsides**, secluded; **felles**, common; **innbyrdes**, mutual, internal

Note – Adjectives ending in stressed –is, –os, –us, –(l)øs inflect according to the basic rule (2.1.2):

en nervøs student	**et nervøst barn**	**nervøse studenter/barn**
a nervous student	a nervous child	nervous students/children

Other examples like **nervøs**:

vis, wise; **grandios**, grandiose; **diffus**, diffuse; **løs**, loose; **rastløs**, restless; **seriøs**, serious; **trådløs**, wireless

2.1.5.5 *Others, including some adjectives formed from nouns and adverbs*

feil, wrong; **kvitt**, quit; **slutt**, finished

Some loans belong to this group:

allround, selfmade, up-to-date

Most loans tend after a while to inflect in the same way as ordinary Norwegian adjectives. Compare **kjip** (English 'cheap') 'sad, bad, mean': **Livet er for kjipt** (pop song) 'Life is too sad'; **Guttene var kjipe** 'The boys were mean/nasty'.

2.1.6 *Order of adjective attributes*

2.1.6.1 *General guidelines*

The order of adjective attributes in Norwegian is not always the same as in English, and the rules are not entirely categorical in either language. It is only possible to provide some general guidelines:

(a) The more permanent the quality indicated (e.g. nationality and colour), the closer it is placed to the noun it qualifies:

langt rødt hår	long red hair
de største norske byene	the largest Norwegian towns
en sint ung mann	an angry young man

Sometimes adjective and noun form a fixed expression and cannot be separated:

en godlynt irsk setter	a good-natured Irish Setter

(b) Generally speaking, the longer or more complex adjective is placed closest to the noun. Participles are often found in this position:

slitte umoderne fabrikker	decrepit old-fashioned factories
en trendy prisbelønnet forfatter	a trendy prize-winning author

2.1.6.2 *Differences between English and Norwegian*

Notice the difference between English and Norwegian word order in:

et slikt system	such a system	cf. 4.9.5, 1.11.8
et halvt kilo	half a kilo	cf. 3.4.2.1, 1.11.8

2.2 The indefinite (strong) declension

2.2.1 The use of the indefinite form

2.2.1.1 *With no word preceding the adjective*

The indefinite form of the adjective may be used attributively with no word preceding the adjective + noun if the noun is non-count (1.1.1) or plural:

Ikke alle har råd til *varm mat* hver dag.
Not everyone can afford a hot meal every day.

Det blir *pent vær* i Oslo i dag.
There will be fine weather in Oslo today.

Det er kjedelig med *lange, rette veistrekninger.*
It is boring to have longstraight stretches of road.

2
Adjectives

2.2.1.2 *After a determiner, etc*

The indefinite form of the adjective may be used attributively after, for example:

1 the indefinite articles **en (ei), et**
2 determiners or adjectives: **noen, ingen, hver, hver annen, en annen** and their inflected forms (4.6.3, 4.6.6f, 4.9.3).
3 **hvilken, slik, sånn** and their inflected forms (4.8.2, 4.9.5)
4 **flere, alle, mange, få** (4.6.8.3, 4.6.1.1, 4.6.2.2, 4.6.8.1)
5 cardinal numbers from two onwards (3.1.1)

Table of examples

Non-neuter	Neuter	Plural
1 **en ny bil**	**et nytt hus**	**to nye biler**
a new car	a new house	two new cars
–	–	**to nye hus**
		two new houses
en ond gjerning	**et ondt varsel**	**mange onde gjerninger**
a bad deed	a bad omen	many bad deeds
2 **noen politisk leder**	**noe annet navn**	**noen få måneder**
some political leader	some other name	some few months
3 **ingen god start**	**intet enkelt valg**	**ingen nye spillere**
no good start	no easy choice	no new players
en annen mulig løsning	**et annet nordisk land**	**andre danske aviser**
another possible solution	another Nordic country	other Danish newspapers
hver nyoppført hytte	**hvert nyoppført hus**	_
every newly built	cabin	every newly built house
4 **hvilken sosial bakgrunn**	**hvilket politisk parti**	**hvilke skjulte talenter**
which social background	which political party	what hidden talents

83

en slik stor dag	et slikt stort hotell	slike små bedrifter
such a big day	such a big hotel	such small businesses
5 –	–	**flere væpnede ran**
		several armed robberies
	–	**få konkrete forslag**
		few concrete proposals
6 –	–	**tjue røde roser**
		twenty red roses

2.2.1.3 *Predicative use*

The indefinite form of the adjective may be used predicatively and agrees with its noun (see 2.2.1.4):

(a) As a subject complement:

Maten var god.	The food was good.
Ølet var godt.	The beer was good.
Kanapéene var gode.	The canapés were good.

(b) As an object complement:

Han malte veggen grønn, taket brunt og veggene gule.
He painted the wall green, the ceiling brown and the walls yellow.

(c) As a predicative attribute:

Ingrid gikk skuffet hjem.	Ingrid went home disappointed.
De døde lykkelige.	They died happy.

2.2.1.4 *Agreement in predicative use*

(a) When used predicatively, the adjective (complement, see 10.3.5) normally agrees with the noun or pronoun (subject or object) (cf. 2.2.1.3):

Non-neuter	**Hagen er vakker.**	The garden is pretty.	**2**
	Subject ↔ Subject		Adjectives
	complement		

Neuter	**Huset er vakkert.**	The house is attractive.
	Subject ↔ Subject	
	complement	

Plural	**Værelsene/Husene er vakre.**	The rooms/houses are attractive.
	Subject ↔ Subject	
	complement	

Plural	**Stress gjorde lærerne syke.**	Stress made the teachers ill.
	Subject Object ↔ Object	
	complement	

(b) However, in 2.2.2–2.2.6 various cases are detailed in which agreement deviates from this norm. An important case is where the adjective as subject complement agrees with a subordinate clause or an infinitive phrase as subject (in other words, agreement is not with a noun phrase). In this case, the adjective takes a neuter ending:

Subordinate clause as subject

At han aldri får Nobelprisen, er åpenbart.
It is obvious that he will never win the Nobel Prize.

Infinitive phrase as subject

Å gå i skogen i skumringen er makeløst.
To wander in the forest at dusk is without equal.

Note – Infinitive phrases and subclauses are also referred to with the neuter pronoun **det**, cf. 4.2.4.6, 2.

2.2.2 | Coordinated subjects

2.2.2.1 | *Two or more subjects*

When there are two or more subjects, the complement is usually in the plural:

Erik og Anders var trette og glade.
Erik and Anders were tired and happy.

Både Jonas og Mia er intelligente.
Both Jonas and Mia are intelligent.

2.2.2.2 *Verken . . . eller*

With verken . . . eller, 'neither . . . nor' Norwegian has a plural complement, whereas English has a singular verb.

Verken Jonas eller Mia er intelligente.
Neither Jonas nor Mia is intelligent.

2.2.2.3 *Ingen + plural*

Notice also the use of the plural adjective in:

Ingen av dem er intelligente.
Neither of them is intelligent.

Note – **Ingen av dem er intelligent** is also possible, but less frequently used. Note the contrast with such general statements as **Ingen er bare snill,** 'Nobody is only good-hearted', usually with a singular adjective.

2.2.2.4 *Agreement with the closest noun*

In cases where the coordinated subjects do not refer to people and the nouns differ in gender or number, the adjective tends to agree with the noun closest to it:

Verken kneet hans eller ryggen var sterk.
Neither his knee nor his back was strong.

Verken ryggen eller kneet var særlig sterkt.
Neither the back nor the knee was particularly strong.

Ikke bare faren, men også barna var intelligente.
Not only the father, but also the children were intelligent.

Ikke bare barna, men også faren var intelligent.
Not only the children were intelligent, but also the father.

2.2.3 *Constructions according to meaning*

In these cases, the inherent meaning of the subject overrides its grammatical number/gender; in other words, sense overrides form. One such case is the neuter noun denoting a person (see 1.2.4.1, Note 1) where the predicative adjective is usually in the common gender form (and the pronoun is not in the neuter), such as:

Vitnet var ikke *sikker* på om det var Olsen *hun* så.
The witness was not certain that it was Olsen she saw.

With subjects denoting a collective, the complement is often found in the plural. See 2.2.3.1f. Cf. also 4.7.1.3.

| 2.2.3.1 | *Collective nouns*

These tend to have a plural complement, especially when the noun has neuter gender:

Familien er lykkelige.   The family is/are happy.
Folk er fornuftige.   People are sensible.

Paret er nervøse for fremtiden.
The couple are nervous about the future.

Italia er ikke lette å slå.
Italy [the team] are not easy to beat.

When referring to **par**, 'couple', the pronoun **de** is used:

Det unge paret er forelsket. *De* er overlykkelige.
The young couple are in love. They are on top of the world.

Cf. also 4.7.1.3.

| 2.2.3.2 | *Man*

The pronoun **man** (4.7.1.1), 'one, they, people' is singular, but is often found with a plural complement:

Man var enige/enig om beslutningen.
They were united on the decision.

Man er avhengige/avhengig av pressens velvilje.
They are dependent on the goodwill of the press.

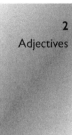

2.2.3.3 *Barn*

Barn, 'child' (in the singular) usually has a neuter complement:

Barnet er sykt. The child is ill.

When referring to **barn** with a pronoun, however, **han/hun** (or **ham/henne** respectively) are often used:

Hvem skal holde barnet når presten døper *ham/henne?*
Who will hold the child when the priest christens him/her?

2.2.3.4 Titles of published works

Titles of published books and newspapers which are plural are regarded as common gender singular for purposes of agreement (cf. the noun **boken**, 'the book'):

Mange vil finne Amtmandens døtre tung.
Many people will find *The District Governor's Daughters* heavy.

2.2.4 Words indicating measurement or degree

2.2.4.1

These cases are rather similar to those in 2.2.3.1. If the whole (group or collective) is intended rather than the part, the singular form of the complement should be used:

Antallet anmeldelser er lavt. The number of reports is low.

2.2.4.2

If the noun denotes quantity, then the plural is normally used:

Halvparten av kundene er unge.
Half the customers are young.

Flertallet av befolkningen er positive til det.
The majority of the population is positive towards it.

Fixed expressions with an uninflected adjective

2.2.5.1

When an adjective forms part of a fixed expression, often comprising verb + adjective + preposition with a single meaning, the adjective may not be inflected:

Politikerne *var klar over* problemet.
The politicians were aware of the problem.

Vi *er glad i* landet vårt.
We love our country.

Hermine og Harry *blir veldig lei av* Ronny iblant.
Sometimes, Hermione and Harry really get tired of Ronny.

Compare with 'normal' inflection:

Bussene er klare.	The buses are ready.
Vi er glade i dag.	We are happy today.
De bakkene var jammen leie.	Those uphills were really nasty.

2.2.5.2

When the adjective is part of a fixed expression, the subject is typically human (or a 'higher' animal). While a bus, for example, can be **klar**, 'ready', it is only people and animals that can be **klar over**, 'aware of'. While an uphill or a task can be **lei**, 'hard, nasty', it is only people that can become **lei av**, 'fed up with'. The difference in the meaning of the adjective within the fixed expression and outside of it can thus sometimes be considerable.

Others include: **være ferdig med**, be finished with; **bli klok på**, figure out; **være redd for**, be afraid of; **være sikker på**, be certain of; **være vant til**, be used to

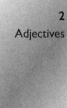

| 2.2.6 | *Bøker er dyrt* |

| 2.2.6.1 |

In cases where the subject is inanimate and has a general, abstract or collective sense, the neuter indefinite form of the adjective is often used as subject complement:

| **Bøker er dyrt.** | (Noun is plural) | Books are expensive. |
| **Sild er godt.** | (Noun is common gender) | Herring is good. |

Here it is not the books/herring *per se* which are expensive/nice, but the idea of (buying) books/(eating) herring. The adjective often expresses a judgement. Expressions of this kind may often be regarded as ellipted forms, reflecting an underlying clause or phrase:

Cf. **Sild er godt.**	Herring is good.
Å spise sild er godt.	Eating herring is good.
Det er godt med sild.	Herring tastes good.
Sild, det er godt, det.	Herring tastes good, it does

The neuter complement is also found with disciplines, sports and pastimes, etc.:

Grammatikk er morsomt.	Grammar is fun.
Skiløping er populært i Norge.	Skiing is popular in Norway.
Røyking er nok usunt.	Smoking is probably unhealthy.

| 2.2.6.2 |

This lack of agreement occurs only when the noun is in the form without article (singular or plural). It is especially frequent with subjects not normally found in the plural (mass nouns) or where the plural form has a collective sense:

| **Politikk er morsomt.** | Politics is fun. |
| **Meslinger er smittsomt.** | Measles is contagious. |

But when the meaning is more restricted, by the end article or an additional complement, the adjective usually agrees:

Silden er god.	The herring is good.
Silden *jeg kjøpte*, er god.	The herring I bought is good.
Bøkene *jeg behøver*, er dyre.	The books I need are expensive.

2.2.7 | Indefinite use of adjectives: summary

(Not including the comparative or superlative)

	Common singular	Neuter singular	Plural
Attributive			
2.2.1.1	**pen musikk**	**pent vær**	**pene øyne**
2.2.1.2	**en**	**et**	**to**
	noen	**noe**	**noen**
	ingen	**intet**	**ingen**
	en annen ny seng	**et annet** nytt bord	**andre** nye senger/bord
	en slik	**et slikt**	**slike**
	hver	**hvert**	–
	hvilken	**hvilket**	**hvilke**
Predicative			
2.2.1.3(a)	**Hagen er stor, men huset er lite.**		
2.2.1.3(b)	**Han farget taket grønt og veggene gule.**		
2.2.2.1	**Både Jonas og Mia er intelligente.**		
2.2.3.1	**Folk er fornuftige.**		
2.2.6	**Bøker er dyrt.**		

Translations: beautiful music; beautiful weather; beautiful eyes; a etc new bed; a etc. new table; two etc. new beds/tables. The garden is big but the house is small. He painted the ceiling green and the walls green. Both Jonas and Mia are intelligent. People are sensible. Books are expensive.

2.3 The definite declension

2.3.1 | The definite form of the adjective

2.3.1.1 | Form

The ending indicating the definite declension of the adjective is the same as for the indefinite plural, with –e being added to the basic form (2.1.2.1). In the definite declension, the front article/determiner **den**, **det** or **de** is added.

See 2.3.3.1. Notice that there is no distinction made in the definite declension between gender in the common and neuter singular or between singular and plural, unlike the indefinite declension. But see 2.1.3.4 for **lille, små**.

Indefinite		*Definite*	
Singular	*Plural*	*Singular*	*Plural*
en stor hage	**store hager**	**den store hagen**	**de store hagene**
a large garden	large gardens	the large garden	the large gardens
et stort hus	**store hus**	**det store huset**	**de store husene**
a large house	large houses	the large house	the large houses

2.3.1.2 Indeclinable adjectives

Indeclinable adjectives (2.1.5) have no special definite form:

> **den gnagende mistanken**, the nagging suspicion; **det øde landskapet**, the desolate landscape; **de bra bilene**, the good cars; **deres felles interesser**, their common interests

Note 1 – **Små** does not take the plural/definite ending:

> **de små guttene**   the small boys

Note 2 – The ending in –e is optional (and rare) for **blå, grå, rå.** See 2.1.3.1(a).

> **det blå(e) havet**   the blue ocean

2.3.2 The use of the definite (weak) declension – introduction

There are four types of definite construction in which adjective and noun may be combined:

2.3.3 Type I – Front article and end article (double definition)

2.3.3.1 Front article/Determiner

When the adjective precedes the noun in the definite form, a determiner is usually added in front of the adjective.

Determiner	Definite adjective	Noun	End article	Section
TYPE 1	Front article, etc. and end article (double definition)			2.3.3
den the	**lange** long	**reise** journey	**–n**	2.3.3.1
dette that	**unge** young	**landslag** national team	**–et**	2.3.3.2
TYPE 2	Front article but no end article (single definition)			2.3.4
Den The Church of Norway	**norske**	**kirke**	–	2.3.4
TYPE 3	No end article after genitive, possessive, etc.			2.3.5
Norges Norway's	**nye** new	**statsminister** prime minister	–	2.3.5.1
hennes her	**fine** fine	**hus** house	–	2.3.5.2
samme the same	**lange** long	**vei** road	–	2.3.5.3
hele all	**siste** last	**uke** week	–	2.3.5.4
TYPE 4	Neither a determiner nor an end article			2.3.6
Kjære Ulf! Dear Ulf				
i høyeste grad to the highest degree				
på indre bane in the inside lane				

This determiner or front (or adjectival) article has the following forms (see also 4.3.2.1f):

(a) **den** for common gender singular nouns:

cf. **reisen**	the journey
den lange reisen	the long journey

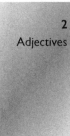
(b) **det** for neuter singular nouns:

| cf. **huset** | the house |
| *det* **store huset** | the big house |

(c) **de** for plural nouns irrespective of gender:

| cf. **reiser – *de* lange reisene** | journeys – the long journeys |
| cf. **hus – *de* store husene** | houses – the big houses |

This is the most frequent use of the definite declension.

Examples:

den nye veien, the new road; **den clektroniske utgaven**, the electronic edition; **det totale arealet**, the total area; **det uoppklarte ranet**, the unsolved robbery; **de nordiske landene**, the Nordic countries

2.3.3.2 *Denne, dette, etc*

The noun also takes an end article after the demonstratives/determiners denne, dette, disse, 'this (common), this (neuter), these'. See 4.3.2.6.

denne sterke reaksjonen, this strong reaction; **denne positive trenden**, this positive trend; **dette lille diktet**, this little poem; **dette fine været**, this fine weather; **disse viktige spørsmålene**, these important questions; **disse fortapte sjelene**, these lost souls

2.3.3.3 Double definition

The presence of both a front article and an end article is termed 'double definition' (also 'double determination, double definiteness') because the noun is marked as definite while the 'front article' in itself marks definiteness. These two markers correspond to a single article in English:

| *the* new car | *den* **nye bilen** |
| *the* old ladies | *de* **gamle damene** |

'Double definition' might be considered a misnomer, since the noun phrase is usually defined at least three times, once by adding the definite ending to the adjective:

den nye bilen

cf. en ny bil

Notice that one kind of construction with a postposed possessive pronoun is realised using this structure (but see also 2.3.5.2):

den nye bilen din

your new car

Note 1 - In certain fixed expressions with rene, skjære the determiner is omitted:

rene galskapen

sheer madness

rene og skjære propagandaen out and out propaganda

Note 2 – The determiner is often omitted where the noun is a name:

kiære Biørn!

dear Biørn

vesle Eva

little Eva

Gamle Bybro

the Old Town Bridge

See also 2.3.6.1

2.3.4 Type 2 - Front article but no end article (single definition)

2.3.4.1

Single definition is a construction without the end article on the noun. It is often a remnant of the Danish formerly used in writing in Norway, and is found in formal or literary style and officialese. Double definition therefore by contrast distinguishes indigenous written Norwegian style.

den vestlige halvkule

the western hemisphere

Single definition tends to be used in the following:

(a) In some proper names:

De britiske øyer, the British Isles; Det hvite hus, the White House; Det røde kors. The Red Cross: Den norske kirke. The Church of Norway; De forente nasjoner, the United Nations

But compare double definition in:

Det Norske Teatret [a theatre in Oslo]; de franske myndighetene, the French authorities

Adjectives

For some abstract concepts:

> **den kristne lære**, Christian teaching; **den totale krig**, total war; **det frie ord**, freedom of speech; **den hellige ånd**, the Holy Spirit; **det evige liv**, eternal life

(b) In some cases, to distinguish between general and specific reference:

General reference	*Specific reference*
den lille mann i kamp mot óvermakten	**den lille mannen reiste seg opp**
the little man struggling against the odds	the little man got up
en offiser av den gamle skole	**den gamle skolen i byen**
an officer of the old school	the old school in town

2.3.4.2

A traditional institution such as the church has tended to use single defini-tion. Notice the change, however, in a recent translation of the Bible into Norwegian:

1985	**Gud kalte *det faste land* for jord ...**	*Single definition*
2011	**Gud kalte *det tørre landet* jord ...**	*Double definition*
	And God called the dry land Earth. (Genesis 1:10)	

Note – There is also a tendency to omit the expected definite suffix with common gender nouns whose stems end in –n: **av den grunn**, 'for that rea-son'. This is also the case with neuter nouns in –e where in speech the –t of any end article is not pronounced: **det første møte**, 'the first meeting'.

See also determinative pronouns, 4.3.2.

2.3.5 | *Type 3 – No end article after certain words*

After the types of word described in 2.3.5.1–4 the adjective is in the definite (and takes the definite ending, if possible) but the noun does not take an end article.

Genitive expressions

See 1.8.1f.

Sofies gamle morfar	Sofie's old grandfather
bilens nye eier	the car's new owner
høstens nye krimromaner	the autumn's new crime novels
årets beste TV-program	the best tv programme of the year
parets første barn	the couple's first child

Note – Exceptions: In the following cases the adjective is inflected according to the indefinite declension (–, –t, –e). See 2.1.2ff.

(a) The genitive of measurement. See 1.8.2.2(b).

en to timers dramatisk jakt	a dramatic two hour-long chase

(b) With **en slags**, 'a kind of', **all slags**, 'all kinds of'.

en slags offentlig hemmelighet	a kind of open secret
et slags uoffisielt resultat	a kind of unofficial result
all slags god musikk	all kinds of good music

(c) After a genitive or possessive **egen**, 'own', is inflected according to the indefinite declension (–, –t, –e).

hans eget grundige arbeid	his own thorough work

2.3.5.2 *Possessives*

See 4.4.

After the possessive as determinative, the noun has no end article:

mitt andre hjemland	my second homeland
hennes beste venn	her best friend
(cf. **den beste vennen hennes**	her best friend)
vårt lille kontor	our small office

2.3.5.3 Samme, etc

After the words **samme**, 'the same'; **neste**, 'the next'; **følgende**, 'the following, the noun need not always have an end article. See 1.11.4. These words to some extent 'determine' the noun following; they do some of the same work as the definite article.

samme høye kvalitet	the same high quality
neste russiske presidentvalg	the next Russian presidential election
følgende generelle råd	the following general advice

Note, however, that **den samme høye kvaliteten, det neste russiske presidentvalget** are also possible.

2.3.5.4 Hele

hele første omgang	the whole of the first half

Note that, when **hele** and **halve** are used with the noun alone, the noun takes an end article:

hele familien, the entire family; **halve boken**, half the book

2.3.6 Neither a determiner nor an end article

There are four main types of this construction.

2.3.6.1 In some forms of address, with expressions denoting relationships

Kjære venn!	Dear friend!
Snille mamma!	Dear Mum

2.3.6.2 With some ordinal numbers

første etasje, the ground floor; **annen verdenskrig**, the second world war

2.3.6.3 *With the words **øvre, nedre, indre, ytre, store** often in proper nouns*

Store Bjørn, Ursa Major; **Øvre Eidfjord**

When not in proper nouns, determiners and end articles are possible:

(den) nedre halvdel(en) av tabellen, the lower half of the table;
(det) indre eksil(et), internal exile

2.3.6.4 *With some superlatives*

See also 2.5.12.

i siste instans	in the last resort
på beste måte	in the best way

2.4 Adjectival nouns

2.4.1 *Introduction*

The adjective is normally subordinated to the noun, but in certain cases it may attain a degree of independence. In the following cases the adjective is used independently of the noun.

2.4.1.1 *The noun may readily be supplied*

Nye biler bruker mindre bensin enn gamle (biler).
New cars use less petrol than old ones.

Det er bedre å være storaksjonær i et lite selskap enn liten aksjonær i et stort (selskap).
It's better to be a major shareholder in a small company than a small shareholder in a large one.

Note – Unlike English, Norwegian does not require the additional word 'one' in cases where the count noun (1.1.1) is omitted.

In cases like those above, the adjectival noun retains its adjectival inflexion in the singular and plural:

en langhåret mann – den langhårete (mannen) – de langhårede
a long-haired man – the long-haired man – the long-haired men

2.4.1.2 *The noun is not usually supplied*

(a) This is the type usually regarded as the 'adjectival noun'.

en ansatt, an employee; **en arbeidsløs**, an unemployed person; **en blind**, a blind person; **en døv**, a deaf person; **en handikappet**, a person with a disability; **en kristen**, a Christian; **en liten**, a baby; **en uskyldig**, an innocent person

A common gender form is generally used to refer to a person or to a common gender noun omitted but understood (normally, only humans can, for example, be Christian, unemployed or disabled).

den ukjente, the stranger; **de blinde**, the blind; **de døve**, the deaf; **de handikappede**, (the) people with disabilities; **Du er den eneste**, You are the only one.

Schuberts beste symfoni er Den ufullendte.
Schubert's best symphony is *The Unfinished.*

Hun er hjemmehjelp for de eldre (menneskene).
She is a home help for the elderly.

(b) A neuter form generally refers to an unlimited, unspecified amount or quantity or to a neuter noun that is omitted but understood:

det eneste som er sikkert	the only thing that is certain
det siste hun gjorde	the last thing she did
det nye i boken	the new element in the book
det verste vi har vært med på	the worst thing we've experienced
det beste jeg vet	the best thing I know

| 2.4.1.3 | *An adjectival noun may take a genitive in* **–s** |

den avdødes enke   the widow of the deceased
det muliges kunst   the art of the possible
de voksnes ansvar   the responsibility of the adults

| 2.4.2 | **The forms and use of the adjectival noun** |

| 2.4.2.1 | *As in English* |

Both English and Norwegian often use adjectival nouns in the plural definite to indicate persons:

de arbeidsløse, the unemployed; **De nakne og de døde**, *The Naked and the Dead* [novel by Norman Mailer]; **de fattige**, the poor; **de gamle**, the old; **de syke**, the sick; **de unge**, the young

| 2.4.2.2 | *Norwegian uses an adjectival noun in the singular* |

As may be seen from the examples in 2.4.1, Norwegian goes much further than English in its use of adjectival nouns, as the article form alone indicates number. In Norwegian, adjectival noun phrases can consist of:

(a) Indefinite article common gender + the indefinite form of the adjective:

en bekjent, an acquaintance; **en blind**, a blind person; **en død**, a dead person

These will typically refer to persons, unless another noun can be inferred from the context.

Hun tok en rød ballong, men jeg ville ha en blå.
She took a red balloon, but I wanted a blue one.

(b) Definite article common gender + the definite singular form of the adjective:

den gamle, the old person; **den enkelte**, the individual

These will typically refer to persons, unless another noun can be inferred from the context.

Hun tok den røde ballongen, men jeg tok den blå.
She took the red balloon, but I took the blue one.

(c) Definite article neuter + the definite singular form of the adjective:

det gode, the good thing, goodness; **det nye**, the new thing; **det positive**, the positive thing

These will typically refer to general abstract concepts and qualities, unless another noun can be inferred from the context:

Ella likte best det nye opptaket, men Duke foretrakk det gamle.
Ella liked the new recording best, but Duke preferred the old one.

(d) The definite superlative form of the adjective:

det minste, the least (thing); **det viktigste**, the most important thing

(e) Present participles:

en forbipasserende, a passer-by; **de sørgende**, the mourners; **de tilstedeværende**, those present

(f) Past participles or words derived from them:

den ukjente, the stranger; **undertegnede**, the undersigned

2.4.2.3 *English equivalents*

Adjectival nouns in Norwegian may correspond to the following in English:

(a) A common noun:

de ansatte, the employees; **de reisende**, the travellers

(b) An adjective + an abstract noun:

det ironiske er ...   the ironic thing is...

(c) A clause:

Dette er det avgjørende.   This is what is decisive.

(d) Adjectives that in English are now treated as nouns with a plural in ' –s':

de grønne, the Greens; **de nygifte**, the newly-weds; **de voksne**, the adults

2.4.3 | Nationality words

2.4.3.1 | Nationality words

Adjectives and nouns of nationality are not written with capital letters unless they begin a sentence. See 12.3.1.2 (b). There are three types.

Country	Inhabitant	Adjective	Language	Translation
I Inhabitant in **–mann**				
Norge	nordmann	norsk	norsk	Norway
Frankrike	franskmann	fransk	fransk	France
England	engelskmann	engelsk	engelsk	England
2 Inhabitant in **–e**				
Danmark	danske	dansk	dansk	Denmark
Sverige	svenske	svensk	svensk	Sweden
Storbritannia	brite	britisk	engelsk	Great Britain
Finland	finne	finsk	finsk	Finland
3 Inhabitant in **–er**				
USA/De forente stater	amerikaner	amerikansk	engelsk	the USA
Tyskland	tysker	tysk	tysk	Germany
Russland	russer	russisk	russisk	Russia
Kina	kineser	kinesisk	kinesisk	China
Nederland	nederlender	nederlandsk	nederlandsk	the Netherlands

2.4.3.2 'The English', etc

English nationality expressions of the type 'the English', 'the French' 'the Dutch' are never translated using the adjectival noun. There are separate common nouns for these in Norwegian:

engelskmennene, franskmennene, nederlenderne, etc.

2.5 Comparison of adjectives (gradation)

2.5.1 Introduction

Norwegian adjectives possess a basic (positive) form which is inflected according to number, gender and definite/indefinite (2.1.1), a comparative form which is uninflected and a superlative form which is inflected only for definiteness. There are four main types of adjective comparison:

1   The endings –ere, –est are added to the positive. See 2.5.2.

   glad, gladere, gladest   happy, happier, happiest

2   The endings –re, –st are added to the positive, and often the root vowel is modified. See 2.5.3.

   stor, større, størst   big, bigger, biggest

3   A different stem is used from that of the positive (irregular comparison). See 2.5.4.

   liten, mindre, minst   small, smaller, smallest

4   The words **mer, mest** are used with the positive, which inflects. See 2.5.5.

   kritisk, mer kritisk, mest kritisk   critical, more critical, most critical

2.5.2 Comparison with the endings –ere, –est

Most monosyllabic Norwegian adjectives add –ere to the positive in order to form the comparative and –est to the positive to form the superlative. Adjectives ending in –ere, –est include those whose indefinite declension is noted in 2.1.3.1–2.1.3.2, 2.1.4. Past participles ending in –en (2.1.3.2) –et (2.1.3.3) compare using **mer, mest** (2.5.5.1(b)).

2.5.2.1 *Many adjectives add* **–ere** *and* **–est**

Positive	Comparative	Superlative	Meaning
ny	**nyere**	**nyest**	new
sen	**senere**	**senest**	late
lav	**lavere**	**lavest**	low

Others include:

dyp, deep; **dyr**, expensive; **flink**, clever; **frisk**, healthy; **hard**, hard; **høy**, high; **snill**, kind; **sterk**, strong; **svak**, weak; **syk**, ill; **tykk**, thick; **tynn**, thin

A final unstressed –e (in the positive/basic form) is dropped before adding the endings:

stille	**stillere**	**stillest**	calm

2.5.2.2 *Most adjectives ending in* **–el, –en, –er** *drop the final* **–e** *of the stem*

See also 2.1.3.2.

Positive	Comparative	Superlative	Meaning
enkel	**enklere**	**enklest**	simple
sjelden	**sjeldnere**	**sjeldnest**	rare(ly)
mager	**magrere**	**magrest**	thin

If the basic form has a double consonant, there is usually a single consonant in the comparative and superlative:

sikker	**sikrere**	**sikrest**	safe
vakker	**vakrere**	**vakrest**	beautiful

But, as regards past participles in –en, see 2.1.3.3.

2.5.2.3 *Most adjectives ending in* **–m** *double the* **–m** *before adding* **–ere, –est**

See 2.1.3.2(c).

Positive	Comparative	Superlative	Meaning
dum	**dummere**	**dummest**	stupid

Others include:

stram, tight, taut; **øm**, painful; **slem**, mean

2.5.2.4 *Adjectives ending in –ig, –lig, –som take –ere, –st*

Positive	Comparative	Superlative	Meaning
viktig	**viktigere**	**viktigst**	important
tidlig	**tidligere**	**tidligst**	early
langsom	**langsommere**	**langsomst**	slow

Others include:

billig, cheap; **dårlig**, bad; **farlig**, dangerous; **hyppig**, frequent; **tidlig**, early; **vanlig**, common; **morsom**, amusing; **lønnsom**, profitable; **varsom**, careful

Note 1 – Adjectives in **–som** add an extra **–m** in the comparative, cf. 2.5.2.3 and Orthography 12.2.1.1.

Note 2 – The word **nær**, 'close, near', compares **nærmere**, **nærmest**.

2.5.3 **Comparison with the endings –re, –st plus modification of the root vowel**

The following adjectives form a small but frequently encountered group:

Positive	Comparative	Superlative	Vowel change	Meaning
lang	**lengre**	**lengst**	a → e	long
stor	**større**	**størst**	o → ø	big
ung	**yngre**	**yngst**	u → y	young
tung	**tyngre**	**tyngst**	u → y	heavy
få	**færre**	**færrest**	å → æ	few

(Note –est in the superlative.)

Note 1 – **Langt**, 'far' and **lenge**, 'for a long time' compare **lenger**, **lengst**.

Note 2 – The adjective **grov** 'coarse, rough' can also be inflected in this way (**grøvre, grøvst**), but it is far more common to inflect it according to 2.5.2.1 (**grovere, grovest**).

2.5.4 | Irregular comparison

2.5.4.1 | Different stems

The following adjectives (and adverbs) form their comparative and superlative by employing a different stem (so-called *suppletion*). They form a small but frequently encountered group.

Positive	Comparative	Superlative	Meaning	See also
gammel	**eldre**	**eldst**	old	
gjerne	**heller**	**helst**	willingly	
god/bra	**bedre**	**best**	good	2.1.5
ond/vond/				
dårlig/ille[*]	**verre**	**verst**	bad	2.5.2.4
liten	**mindre**	**minst**	little	2.1.3.4
mange	**flere**	**flest**	many	
mye	**mer**	**mest**	a lot	

[*] **dårligere, dårligst** is a frequent alternative.

2.5.4.2 | 'More – most'

The choice is: **mer – mest** or **flere – flest**.

(a) **Mer – mest** are used with non-count nouns. See 1.1.1.2(b).

Vil du ha mer kaffe?   Would you like more coffee?
Hun hadde mest innsikt.   She had most insight.

Vi vil se mer humor i showene.
We want to see more humour in the shows.

(b) **Flere – flest** are used with count nouns. See 1.1.1.2(a).

De må ha flere vikarer i skolene.
They must have more supply teachers in the schools.

Hver kvinne må få flere enn to barn.
Every woman must have more than two children.

Note 1 – While the distinction above is clear in the norm and in principle, in practice one frequently finds **mer** used with count nouns, especially in the spoken language:

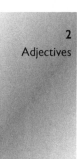

2

Adjectives

Det var mer kvinner enn menn der.

There were more women than men there.

Note 2 – The alternative forms **mere** and **fler** are possible after 2005:

mere akevitt, more aquavit; **enda fler problemer,** even more problems

Note 3 – **flere** also means 'several', 'a number of', 'various', 'different'. See 4.6.8.3. In a sense, it is an *absolute comparative*. See 2.5.11.

Mari sto der i flere timer.   Mari stood there for several hours.

Note 4 – If a comparison is implied when using **de fleste**, the noun following usually takes an end article:

de fleste delene av landet   most parts of the country

If no comparison is implied (i.e. if **de fleste** is an *absolute superlative*, see 2.5.12), the noun often has no end article:

De fleste biler har motoren foran.
Most cars have the engine at the front.

| **2.5.5** | *Comparison with* **mer(e), mest** |

Normally the forms **mer(e)** and **mere** are synonymous and interchangeable.

Positive	Comparative	Superlative	Meaning
presset	**mer(e) presset**	**mest presset**	pressured
flytende	**mer(e) flytende**	**mest flytende**	fluent
moderne	**mer(e) moderne**	**mest moderne**	modern

Note that in these constructions the adjective is inflected according to the indefinite declension and agrees with the word(s) it modifies:

Huset er mer bekvemt.
The house is more comfortable.

Stolene var noe mer bekvemme.
The chairs were somewhat more comfortable.

| 2.5.5.1 | *Adjectives comparing with* **mer(e), mest** |

108

Adjectives usually comparing with **mer(e)** and **mest** form a large and varied group, including most bi- and polysyllabic adjectives, such as:

(a) Most adjectives ending in –(i)sk (2.1.4.2 and 2.1.4.3):

Examples:

hatsk, malicious; **norsk**, Norwegian; **nordisk**, Nordic; **realistisk**, realistic; **et mer realistisk bilde**, a more realistic picture

(b) Past participles in –et and adjectives in –et(e) (2.1.4.6, 5.2.1.1(e), 5.3.12):

Examples:

ettertraktet, sought-after; **lukket**, closed; **sølete**, muddy; **den mest slurvete jobben**, the most slipshod job

(c) Present participles (2.1.5.1, 5.3.13, 5.2.1.3):

Examples:

fristende, tempting; **treffende**, appropriate; **et mer omfattende arbeid**, a more comprehensive work

(d) Many adjectives that do not inflect in their positive form (2.1.5). (This holds true also for (b) and (c) above: participles and adjectives in –et(e) do not inflect in their positive form.)

Examples:

avsides, remote; **gammeldags**, old-fashioned; **sexy**; **en mer felles politikk**, more of a joint policy

(e) Some adjectives that are derivatives, compounds or recent loans such as:

brannsikker, fireproof; **håpløs**, hopeless; **mer miljøvennlig mat**, more ecological food

---

| 2.5.5.2 | *Alternative methods of comparison* |

Some adjectives, particularly derivatives and compounds, are sometimes compared using **mer(e)**, **mest** and sometimes with inflexional endings:

kostbarere/mer kostbar, more costly; **morsommere/mer morsom**, more amusing

Such variation is, however, found only with some adjectives and not necessarily in the language of one person.

| 2.5.6 | *Adjectives deficient in the positive, positive and comparative, or superlative* |

| 2.5.6.1 | *No positive form* |

Some adjectives with a comparative in –re, superlative in –erst/–st and which denote place have no positive form, but are associated with an adverb or preposition. These adverbs or prepositions are given in brackets in the table below. See also adverbs of place 6.3.4.2.

Positive	Comparative	Superlative	Meaning

Place in relation to other elements and to the speaker:

Positive	Comparative	Superlative	Meaning
(bort(e))	**bortre**	**borterst**	(away), furthest away
(hit)	**hitre**	**hiterst**	(here), nearest

Place in relation to other elements and the centre:

Positive	Comparative	Superlative	Meaning
(inn(e))	**indre**	**innerst**	(in), innermost
(ut(e))	**ytre**	**ytterst**	(out), outermost
(midt)	**midtre**	**midterst**	(in the centre)

Place in vertical order in relation to something:

Positive	Comparative	Superlative	Meaning
(nede)	**nedre**	**nederst**	(down), at the foot of
(over)	**øvre**	**øverst**	(above), at the top
(under)	**undre**	**underst**	(below), at the bottom

Place in horizontal order in relation to something:

Positive	Comparative	Superlative	Meaning
(bak)	**bakre**	**bakerst**	(back), furthest back
(fram(me))	**fremre**	**fremst/forrest**	(forward), at the very front

Examples:

den fremre delen av skipet	the front of the ship
de indre delene av landet	the interior of the country
øverste ansvarlige	the person ultimately responsible

Note 1 – These comparative forms may not be used predicatively.

Note 2 – The words **borte, inne, ute, nede, framme** may be compared with **lengre** and **lengst**:

borte, away – **lengre bort**, further away – **lengst borte**, furthest away

| 2.5.6.2 | *Some adjectives exist only in the superlative form*

først, first; **mellomst**, middlemost; **nest**, next; **sist**, last; **ypperst**, most outstanding

Note that **sist** usually means 'last' in the sense of 'final'. 'Last' in the sense of 'latest, most recent' is often rendered by **senest**.

von Triers seneste film   von Trier's latest film
Kubricks siste film   Kubrick's last film

But this distinction is by no means clear-cut; **sist** can often be used instead of **senest**, compare:

de siste/seneste dagene, de siste/seneste årene, recent days/years

Takk for sist.   [*lit.*] Thank you for the last time.
[a phrase used when meeting someone again after having earlier been entertained by them (or even having met them).]

| 2.5.7 | *Adjectives that do not compare*

The following types of adjective do not normally possess a comparative or superlative form:

- Adjectives with an absolute or precise meaning

  allmektig, almighty; **barnløs**, childless; **død**, dead; **firkantet**, square; **gratis**, free; **gravid**, pregnant; **middelalderlig**, medieval; **norsk**, Norwegian

- Epistemic adjectives, i.e. those questioning whether a property is real or not, to what extent it is real and so on:

  ekte, genuine; **falsk**, false; **potensiell**, potential

- Compound adjectives with an amplifying prefix that already expresses a very high degree:

kjempestor, mega; **superhemmelig**, top secret; **ultraortodoks**, ultra-orthodox

Note – However, in practice, one can sometimes find these adjectives in the positive or superlative, especially when used figuratively:

Klassen var enda mer død enn vanlig.
The class (pupils) were even more dead/less communicative than usual.

Han er mer katolsk enn paven.
He is more Catholic than the pope (i.e. very narrow-minded).

2.5.8 | *The comparative is indeclinable*

The comparative formed with –ere/ –re retains the same form for both indefinite and definite irrespective of gender or number:

et eldre par, an elderly couple; **det eldre paret**, the elderly couple; **de eldre velgerne**, the older voters

See also indeclinable adjectives in –e, 2.1.5.1.(d).

2.5.9 | *Inflexion of the superlative*

2.5.9.1 | *Predicative use*

As with the positive form, when used predicatively, the superlative in –est/ –st may either be left uninflected (indefinite declension) or be inflected (definite declension):

Hans grøt er tykkest.
His porridge is thickest.

Min grøt er den tykkeste i Norge.
My porridge is the thickest in Norway.

2.5.9.2 | *Attributive use*

As with the positive form, when used attributively, the superlative is always inflected (definite declension):

den tykkeste grøten	the thickest porridge
det tykkeste treet	the thickest tree
de tykkeste vottene	the thickest mittens

2.5.9.3 –(e)st + –e

As with the positive form, when used attributively, superlatives whose uninflected form ends in –(e)st (2.5.2f.) add –e:

Det største problemet er veksten.
The biggest problem is growth.

2.5.9.4 *mest + present participle*

Superlatives formed using **mest** + present participle (2.1.5.1(a), 5.3.13) are uninflected because the present participle is never inflected:

den mest omfattende reformen   the most comprehensive reform

2.5.9.5 *mest + past participle*

With superlatives formed from **mest** + past participles (2.1.4.6(a), 5.3.12), the adjective is always inflected in the definite:

de mest ettertraktede kundene   the most sought-after clients
den mest snobbete gaten   the most snobbish street
de mest stjålne tyske bilene   the most stolen German cars

2.5.9.6 *No front article*

The superlative is used in some set expressions in the definite form without either front article or end article (often as an absolute superlative, 2.5.12).

i beste fall, at best; **i minste detalj**, in minute detail; **i nærmeste framtid**, in the near future

This is especially frequent with adjectives denoting place. See 2.5.6.

øverste hylle   the top shelf
nederste rille   the lowest shelf (in the oven)

Note – The superlative after **som** is generally used when a person or thing is compared with itself under different circumstances. This often corresponds to 'at its' in English:

Trafikken er som verst rundt sankthanshelga.
The traffic is at its worst over the Midsummer weekend.

2.5.10 *Expressing similarity, dissimilarity and reinforcement*

2.5.10.1 *like ... som*

Phrases with **like ... som** are used to link two elements that are similar.

Hun er like stor som storebroren sin.
She is as big as her older brother.

Piggfritt er like godt som piggdekk.
Tires without studs are as good as studded tyres.

2.5.10.2 *lik, ligne*

The adjective **lik** (–t, –e) and the verb **ligne/likne**, 'look like' are also used to express similarity.

Jeg er lik bror min.	I am like my brother.
Jeg ligner broren min.	I resemble my brother.

2.5.10.3 *enn*

In order to express dissimilarity, the particle **enn** 'than' can be used, often after an adjective in the comparative.

Vi tjener 20% mindre enn våre kolleger.
We earn 20% less than our colleagues.

Island spilte bedre enn England.
Iceland played better than England.

2.5.10.4 *ulik*

The adjective **ulik** (–t, –e) 'different, unlike' is also used to express dissimilarity.

Bergen er ulik andre norske storbyer.
Bergen is unlike other large Norwegian towns.

100 personer av ulikt etnisk opphav, kjønn og alder
100 individuals of different ethnic origin, gender and age

2.5.10.5 enda, mye

The words **enda**, 'even more', **mye**, 'much, far' may sometimes be used to reinforce the comparative.

En fredsløsning er enda fjernere.
A peace solution is even more remote.

Bueskyting er mye morsommere enn fotball.
Archery is much more fun than football.

2.5.10.6 aller

The word **aller**, 'very, by far, . . . of all' may be used to reinforce the superlative. See 6.2.7.1, Note.

Aller verst er situasjonen i Midtøsten.
Worst of all is the situation in the Middle East.

2.5.10.7 The more . . . the more'

Expressions with 'the more. . ., the more. . . ' are rendered in Norwegian by the bracketing expression **jo** + comparative, **desto** + comparative (or alternatively **jo . . . jo. . .** or **jo . . . dess. . .** or **dess . . . dess**)

Jo flere bøker som utgis, desto bedre.
The more books that are published the better.

2.5.11 The absolute comparative

When the second part of the comparison is not stated in Norwegian, the element of comparison may disappear in part or in whole. This is known as the absolute comparative as opposed to the more common relative comparative. English has no absolute comparative, and the Norwegian construction is often translated as 'rather X', 'quite Y'.

Relative comparative

Pengesummen han vant, var større enn forventet.
The sum of money he won was larger than expected.

Absolute comparative

Mannen hadde en større pengesum på seg.
The man had quite a large sum of money on him.

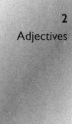

Other examples of the absolute comparative:

Hun har en mindre rolle i Peer Gynt.
She has a minor rôle in *Peer Gynt.*

Ingrid var en høyere polititjenestemann.
Ingrid was a senior police officer.

Vi har pakket for en lengre reise.
We have packed for quite a long trip.

Note that **en eldre kvinne**, 'an elderly woman' is not as old as **en gammel kvinne**, 'an old woman'. The absolute comparative is somewhat formal and only possible with a restricted set of adjectives.

2.5.12 The absolute superlative

The absolute superlative is used to indicate that something possesses a quality to a very high degree, without directly comparing it to anything else. The use of the superlative in this way is an exaggeration.

Relative superlative

Dette er den største bilen jeg noensinne har sett.
This is the biggest car I have ever seen.

Absolute superlative

De måtte møtes i største hemmelighet.
They had to meet in the greatest secrecy.

Note – Other examples of the absolute superlative in set phrases:

i høyeste grad, to the greatest extent; **i seneste laget**, a bit too late; **varmeste gratulasjoner**, warmest congratulations

The absolute superlative is rather formal and only possible with a restricted set of adjectives.

Chapter 3

Numerals

3.1 Forms of numerals

3.1.1 *Cardinal and ordinal numbers*

See 12.4.2 for advice about the use of figures and words.

Cardinal numbers			See section	Ordinal numbers	
0	null	zero, nought, nil, 'oh' nothing, love,			
1	én, ett	one	3.1.2	første	first
2	to	two	3.1.3	annen/annet/ andre	second
3	tre	three		tredje	third
4	fire			fjerde	
5	fem			femte	
6	seks			sjette	
7	sju/syv			sjuende/syvende	
8	åtte			åttende	
9	ni			niende	
10	ti			tiende	
11	elleve			ellevte	
12	tolv			tolvte	
13	tretten			trettende	
14	fjorten			fjortende	

15	femten		femtende
16	seksten		sekstende
17	sytten		syttende
18	atten		attende
19	nitten		nittende
20	tjue		tjuende
21	tjueen	3.1.2.1	tjueførste
22	tjueto		tjueandre
30	tretti/tredve		trettiende/tredevte
40	førti		førtiende
50	femti		femtiende
60	seksti		sekstiende
70	sytti		syttiende
80	åtti		åttiende
90	nitti		nittiende
100	(ett) hundre	3.1.4	hundrede
101	(ett) hundreogen		hundreogførste
1000	(ett) tusen	3.1.4	tusende
1001	(ett) tusenogen	3.1.4	tusenogførste
3 285	tretusentohundreogåttifem	Note 1	tretusentohundre-ogåttifemte
1 000 000	en million	3.1.5	en millionte
2 000 000	to millioner		
1 000 000 000	en milliard	3.1.5	

Note 1 – The word **og** forms part of a compound with no spacing. Cf. English 'and' as a separate word in e.g. 'two hundred and fifty'.

Note 2 – The word for 'one' is the only numeral to be inflected for gender: **én by, ett land**. The accent on the **e** and the double **tt** are to distinguish the (stressed) numerals from the (unstressed) indefinite articles **en, et**. (Officially, **ei** can be used with feminine nouns (see 1.1.2f) but it rarely is in writing.)

Note 3 – Numbers written in figures in Norwegian texts frequently have a space after the thousands where English has a comma. See 13.1.2.9(b):

Norwegian: **3 285**   English: 3,285

Note also that Norwegian **3,285** will normally translate into English as 3.285, i.e. Norwegian has a decimal comma where English has a decimal point (full stop or period).

Note 4 – Since 1951 tens have officially come before units: **femtiseks**, 56, though many Norwegians still say **seksogfemti**.

| **3.1.2** | *En, ett or ene?* |

| 3.1.2.1 |

(a) The choice of **én** or **ett** to translate the English word 'one' is determined by the gender of the noun that follows or is implied. See 1.1.2, 1.2.1, 1.9.1.

  én buss, one bus; **ett tog**, one train; **én av mine brødre**, one of my brothers; **ett av selskapets kontorer**, one of the company's offices

(b) However, when compounded in forms such as **tjueen, hundreogsekstien**, etc. **–en** tends to be used regardless of the gender of the noun that follows:

  femtien busser, fifty-one buses; **sekstien år**, sixty-one years

(c) In general counting, calculating and dates, **én** is used:

én, to, tre …	one, two, three …
én pluss to er tre	one plus two is three
nitten(hundreog)sekstien	nineteen sixty-one

(d) With time by the clock, **ett** is used:

Klokka er ett.	It's one o'clock.

  Toget har avgang kl 12:50 [ti på ett] fra plattform tre.
  The train departs at 12:50 from platform three.

3.1.2.2

When the English '(the) one' is used as a pronoun or an attributive adjective, the equivalent expression **den/det ene** is used.

Den ene av de to hadde en pistol.   One of the two had a pistol.

3.1.3 **To, tve–, et par**

3.1.3.1 **To–** and **tve–** in compounds

(a) The prefix **tve–** (no longer used to form new words) is found in some words to indicate **to:**

tvelyd, dipthong; **tvetydig**, ambiguous

(b) Otherwise **to–** is used as the first element in a compound:

tobent, bipedal; **todekker**, biplane; **tofeltsvei**, dual carriageway

3.1.3.2 **Et par**

Norwegian uses **et(t) par** in much the same way as English uses 'a pair (of)', 'a couple (of)', etc.:

et par sko	one pair of shoes
Han kommer om et par dager.	He's coming in a couple of days.
De ble et par i fjor.	They became a couple last year.

3.1.4 **Hundre, tusen**

3.1.4.1

Hundre and tusen are usually uninflected. When used as nouns, however, they have a plural in –er, and, especially when they denote 'abundance', an alternative and somewhat less formal plural in –vis:

i tusener/tusenvis av år	for thousands of years
i hundrer/hundrevis av år	for hundreds of years

Det var hundrevis av kamerabærende turister.
There were hundreds of camera-toting tourists.

As a rule of thumb, 'a hundred' is rendered in Norwegian by **hundre**, whereas 'one hundred' is **ett hundre**. Similarly, 'a thousand' is **tusen**, while 'one thousand' is **ett tusen**.

3.1.4.2

(a) Numerals between 1100 and 1999 in dates and prices are usually expressed in terms of **hundre**:

1500 kroner   **femtenhundre kroner**
(år) 1814   **attenhundreogfjorten/attenfjorten**

(b) When expressing year dates from 2000 to 2099, there is some variation, however:

2019   **tjue(hundreog)nitten/totusenognitten**

Most people use the longer form in formal writing while the shorter form occurs in speech.

3.1.5 | *Million, milliard, billion*

Million, milliard, billion are common gender nouns with a plural in –er. Norwegian **milliard** corresponds to 'billion' in modern English (i.e. 10^9) and Norwegian **billion** to 'trillion' (i.e. 10^{12}).

en million   one/a million

en omsetning på cirka ti milliarder
a turnover of approximately ten billion

3.1.6 | *Et dusin*

Although Norwegian **et dusin** corresponds to English 'a dozen', it is far less common in use. Where English uses 'a dozen' or 'dozens of' as an approximate value, Norwegian prefers **et titall** ('approximately ten') or **titalls** ('tens of') to fulfil this purpose. See also 3.2.2.1.

et dusin år senere	a dozen years later
et halvt dusin	half a dozen (3.4.2.1)
flere titalls butikker	several dozens of shops

3.1.7 Approximate numerical values

3.1.7.1 –tall

Norwegian often indicates an approximate value in excess of ten by adding the suffix –**tall** to a cardinal number. There will usually be an additional **et** before the numeral. See 3.2.2.1, 3.1.6.

et femtitall(s) personer   around fifty people, fifty-odd people

3.1.7.2 Noen og

Noen og is sometimes used with a cardinal number to indicate an approximate value in the same way as 'something' in English:

en kvinne på noen og førti år   a woman of forty-something

3.2 Cardinal numbers

3.2.1 Notes on the use of cardinal numbers

3.2.1.1 En ener, en toer, etc

Norwegian has special forms of the cardinal numbers up to twelve that are used as common gender nouns, i.e. **en ener, en toer, en treer, en firer,** etc. (plurals **enere, toere, treere,** etc.).

These and their compound forms in larger numbers are used to indicate:

(a) A numeral, i.e. 'a one', 'two threes':

Jeg kan ikke skille firerne hans fra syverne hans.
I can't tell his fours from his sevens.

(b) A start number, bus or tram number, number of a playing card, etc.:

Ta sekseren!   Take the number six.

(c) A position in a race, or some other form of ranking:

den evige toer   the eternal runner-up

3.2.1.2 *Stykk*

The noun **stykk** can be added after cardinal numbers, particularly in informal spoken language and when numbers are used without a following noun. Used in this sense, **stykk** has no English equivalent. In lists, **stykk** is sometimes abbreviated **stk**.

Vi har bestilt hundre stykk.   We ordered a hundred.

3.2.1.3 Frequency: *to ganger*, etc

To indicate frequency, **gang** (plural **ganger**) is used with a cardinal number:

en gang, once; **to ganger**, twice; **tre ganger**, three times, etc.

3.2.1.4 'Twofold', etc

(a) Multiplication can be indicated by adding the suffix –**dobbel(t)** to a form of the respective cardinal number. Used on its own, **dobbel(t)** corresponds to the English 'double'. Used as a suffix to cardinal numbers from three and upwards, it forms 'triple (treble)', 'quadruple', etc.

Det vil bli dobbelt så dyrt.
It will cost twice as much.

Hvordan tredoble vinduer hjelper.
How triple glazing helps.

en såkalt femdobbelt bypass-operasjon
a so-called quintuple bypass operation

123

(b) Multiplication is also expressed by **ganger: fire ganger fem er tjue,** 'four times five makes twenty' (3.2.7.1).

Note – 'single' may correspond to:

eneste	**hver eneste dag**	every single day
enkelt- in compounds:	**enkeltbillett**	single ticket
	enkeltrom	single room
alene- in compounds	**alenefar**	single dad

3.2.2 | Nouns formed with –tall

Neuter nouns may be formed by adding –**tall** to cardinal numbers. These nouns are used to express various meanings, as shown in 3.2.2.1f.

3.2.2.1 | Approximate number

et tjuetall skip   about twenty ships

Expressions indicating an indefinite number of tens, hundreds, thousands, etc. may be derived from these nouns by adding –**s** (see also 3.1.7.1):

titalls millioner dollar   tens of millions of dollars

3.2.2.2 | Decade or century

Han døde på (nitten(hundreog))nittitallet.
He died in the (nineteen) nineties.

på slutten av 1700-tallet
at the end of the eighteenth century

2000-tallet/tjuehundretallet
the twenty-first century

Note 1 – These nouns in –**tall** can take a genitive:

åttitallets beste film   the best film of the (19)80s

Note 2 – Centuries may also be expressed with **århundre:**

See also 3.1.4.2.

1800-tallet = det nittende århundre   the nineteenth century

3.2.3 | Age

There are a number of ways of expressing age:

Karoline er ti år (gammel).	Karoline is ten (years old).
Karoline er i tiårsalderen.	Karoline is (about) ten (years old).
Karoline er en tiåring.	Karoline is a ten-year-old.
Karoline er en tiårig jente.	Karoline is a ten-year-old girl.
Karoline, en jente på ti år	... Karoline, a girl of ten, ...
Hun har fylt ti.	She has had her tenth birthday.

3.2.4 | Temperature

Norwegians use the centigrade scale: 0°C (**Celsius**) = 32°F:

Termometeret viser –5°C/fem minusgrader/kuldegrader.
It's minus five (degrees) (23°F) on the thermometer.

Termometeret viser +15°C/femten plussgrader/varmegrader.
It's plus fifteen (59° F) on the thermometer.

I dag er det 0°C/null grader.
Today it is zero (32°F).

3.2.5 | Money

In Norwegian currency **100 øre = 1 krone**, though no coins in øre are in circulation any longer and amounts are rounded up or down to the nearest **krone**. In written price information, **kroner** are separated from øre by a comma.

100,–	**etthundre kroner**
100,50	**etthundre kroner og femti øre**

3.2.6 | Telephone numbers

The digits after the national dialling code are frequently expressed in speech in pairs:

0047–12 34 56	**null null førtisju tolv trettifire femtiseks**

3.2.7 | Mathematical expressions

3.2.7.1 | Differences in Norwegian and English mathematical symbols

Norwegian symbol	English	Norwegian
+	add to	**legge sammen, legge till**
=	equals	**er lik med/lik**
$4 + 5 = 9$	$4 + 5 = 9$	**fire pluss fem er (lik med) ni**
–	subtract from	**trekke fra**
$12–2 = 10$	$12–2 = 10$	**tolv minus to er (lik med) ti**
.	multiply by	**multiplisere med**
	times	**gange med**
$6 \cdot 3 = 18$	$6 \times 3 = 18$	**seks ganger tre er (lik med) atten**
:	divide by	**dele med/dividere med**
$25{:}5 = 5$	$25 \div 5 = 5$	**tjuefem delt på/dividert med fem er (lik med) fem**
$2^2 = 4$	$2^2 = 4$	**kvadratet av to er fire**
$10^3 = 1000$	$10^3 = 1000$	**ti opphøyd i tre/ti i tredje er (lik med) tusen**
$\sqrt{16} = 4$	$\sqrt{16} = 4$	**roten/kvadratroten av seksten er fire**
5 m^2	5 m²/5 sq.m.	**fem kvadratmeter**
5 m^3	5 m³/5 cu.m.	**fem kubikkmeter**
%	%	**prosent**
‰	‰	**promille**

3.2.7.2 | The decimal comma

Some other points to note are that Norwegian uses a decimal comma, **desimalkomma**, where English has a decimal point (13.1.2.9(a)) and a space or full stop to separate thousands and millions, etc. in numbers written in figures, not a comma as in English. See 13.1.2.9 (b).

3.2.7.3 *The sign ×*

Note also that the sign (in English used for multiplication: 10 × 2 = 20) is in Norwegian generally used only for the measurement of area: **200 × 45 mm**, '200 mm by 45 mm'.

3.3 Ordinal numbers

3.3.1 *Form*

3.3.1.1 *With front article*

Ordinal numbers are found with the front article or after a possessive or noun in the –s genitive form.

det første mennesket	the first human
det tredje rike	the Third Reich

3.3.1.2 *No front article*

The front article is often omitted before an ordinal in a noun phrase in the definite form:

første gang	the first time
nærkontakt av tredje grad	close encounters of the third kind

3.3.2 *Andre/annen*

Andre can be used for 'second'

den andre bilen jeg ser i dag	the second car I see today
den andre mars	the second of March
den andre verdenskrigen	the second world war

An alternative is **annen,** but this is mostly found in numerical expressions and dates, e.g. **annen mars,** and in certain set expressions: **annen verdenskrig** (note no determiner and no suffix/'end article').

3.3.3 | Enumeration

Notice that 'firstly', 'secondly', 'thirdly' = **for det første, for det andre, for det tredje.**

3.3.4 | Kings and popes

Ordinal numbers (frequently written in figures) are used in the names of kings, popes, etc.:

Harald 5./Harald den femte	(King) Harald V
Pave Johannes Paul II/den andre	(Pope) John Paul II

3.3.5 | Frequency

In contrast to English usage, Norwegian uses ordinal numbers to indicate frequency of occurrence.

en gang hver femte dag	once every five days

3.3.6 | Derivatives

Most fractions are formed from cardinal numbers (3.4.1). The following nouns are also derived from ordinal numbers. See also 3.2.2.2.

et årti/tiår	a decade
et århundre	a century
et årtusen	a millennium

3.3.7 | Differences from English

Note the following differences in the use of ordinals in Norwegian and English:

førsteside	the front page
Hva heter du til fornavn?	What's your first name?
(Hva er fornavnet ditt?)	

3.4 Fractions

3.4.1 The form of fractions

With numbers from one to twelve, the numerator in Norwegian fractions is a cardinal number, and the denominator is either an ordinal or a cardinal number to which is added the noun suffix –del (en del = 'a part', 'share').

¼ = **en firedel/fjerdedel**
¾ = **tre firedeler/fjerdedeler**
¼l. = **en firedels/fjerdedels liter**

In ordinals ending in –ende (3.1.1), the denominator may be either an ordinal ending in –ende or a cardinal number: **en åtte(nde)del**, 1/8; **tre ti(ende) deler**, 3/10; **en tjue(nde)del**, 1/20; etc.

3.4.2 'Half', 'one and a half', 'quarter'

3.4.2.1 'Half' = halv, –t, –e [adjective]

en halv time	half an hour Note word order
halve laget	half (of) the team
et halvt år	half a year/6 months
en og en halv måned	1½ months [*lit.* 'month']/6weeks
ett og et halvt år	1½ years/18 months
to og en halv måned	2½ months
Klokken er halv ti.	It's half past nine. See 3.6.1f.

Note also the alternative forms **halvannen måned**, '1½ months'; **halvannet år**, '1½ years'. The noun following **halvannen** is in the singular. **Halvannen** is perhaps becoming less common.

3.4.2.2 'Half' = halv, halvdel –en, halvpart –en, [noun]

These are non-neuter nouns that mean 'a/the half share of something'. They are most common in the definite form:

dele i to halve	cut in half
den siste halvdelen av løpet	the last half of the race

Halvparten av atten er ni.	Half of eighteen is nine.
over halvparten av kundene	more than half the customers

$3.4.2.3$ 'Half'= **halvt** [adverb]

halvt ironisk	half ironic
halvt i spøk	half-jokingly, half in jest
med halvt lukkede øyelokk	with half-closed eyes

$3.4.2.4$ 'A quarter'

'A quarter' may be rendered in Norwegian by **en fjerdedel** or **en/et kvart.** In many instances when followed by a noun these two alternatives are synonymous. Note that the use of **en** or **et** before **kvart** is governed by the gender of the noun following:

en fjerdedels mil	a quarter of a (Norwegian) mile
	[approx. 1½ English miles]
en fjerdedel av brødet	a quarter of the bread
tre fjerdedeler	three quarters
en kvart million	250,000
et kvart århundre	25 years
kvart på tre	a quarter to three (cf. 3.6)

But notice:

dele i fire deler	divide something into quarters

3.5 Dates

$3.5.1$ *Years*

$3.5.1.1$ *Compounds*

Years are most often written in figures in Norwegian. See 13.3. However, when written in full they appear as one word. **hundreog** may occasionally be omitted (see also 3.1.4.2(b)).

1984 = **nitten(hundreog)åttifire**   nineteen eighty-four
1295 = **tolv(hundreog)nittifem**   twelve ninety-five

Huset vil være ferdig nedbetalt i 2030 [tjue(hundreog)tretti/ totusenogtretti].
The house will be paid for in 2030.

For centuries, see 3.1.4.2.

3.5.2 | Months, weeks, days

3.5.2.1 | Months

(a) Months of the year do not have a capital letter in Norwegian unless they begin a sentence:

januar, februar, mars, april, mai, juni, juli, august, september, oktober, november, desember

(b) Months have common gender and do not possess a plural form.

en kald januar   a cold January

(c) As in English, the corresponding ordinal number is used to express the date in a particular month. Notice that Norwegian does not have an equivalent for 'th', 'rd' or 'st' in English dates or for the word 'of' before the month in English idiom.

3. [tredje] januar 2018   3rd [the third of] January 2018

(d) The preposition 'on' before dates in English has no equivalent in Norwegian. See 7.6.9.

Hun er født (den) 12. mai 1992.
She was born on the 12th of May 1992.

(e) Norwegian dates may be written in any of the following forms:

12.5.1992   12.05.1992   12.5.92   12.05.1992   1992–05–12

Note – 12/5–92 is also found but this usage is not recommended by Språkrådet.

3.5.2.2 *Days*

(a) Days of the week do not have a capital letter in Norwegian unless they begin a sentence:

mandag, tirsdag, onsdag, torsdag, fredag, lørdag, søndag

(b) Days of the week are common gender nouns and possess a plural form in –er. See 1.4.4.

Jeg hater mandager.   I hate Mondays.

3.5.2.3 *Weeks*

Norwegian diaries and calendars generally number the weeks of the year. They begin on Mondays:

År 2019 begynner uke 14 den 1. april.
In 2019 week 14 begins on 1st April.

3.6   Telling the time

3.6.1 *Clock time*

3.6.1.1 *'What is the time?'*

(a) There are, as shown in the diagram in 3.6.1 above, two important differences between the standard English and Norwegian ways of telling time by the clock:

1) 'Half past' an hour in English is always expressed in Norwegian as 'half (to)' the next hour, although no preposition is used in Norwegian.
2) Times between a quarter past the hour and a quarter to the hour are usually expressed in Norwegian as minutes before and after the half-hour.

Note that, in the examples that follow, the use of the word **minutt/er** is optional.

Hvor mye er klokka?	What time is it?
Hva er klokka?	What is the time?
Klokka/Den er ett.	It's one o'clock. (See 3.1.2.1 (d))
Klokka er ett (minutt) over ett.	It's one minute past one.
Klokka er kvart over fem.	It's (a) quarter past five.
Klokka er fem (minutter) på halv åtte.	It's twenty-five (minutes) past seven.
Klokka er halv seks.	It's half past five/It's five-thirty.
Klokka er åtte (minutter) over halv seks.	It's twenty-two (minutes) to six.
Klokka er tjue på seks.	It's twenty to six.
Klokka er kvart på seks.	It's a quarter to six.

Note – **Klokka/klokken** is often abbreviated **kl.**

(b) The word **en** is always omitted before **kvart** in expressions such as **kvart på fem**, **kvart over fire**, etc. (whereas **en** is not omitted before **kvart** in expressions that do not tell the time).

3.6.1.2

Some other useful expressions of time:

ved ett-tiden
cirka klokka ett   } around one (o'clock)
rundt ett

3
Numerals

Klokka er akkurat ett. **Klokka er presis ett.**	It is exactly one o'clock.

et døgn   a day = a 24-hour period
en halvtime   half an hour
fjorten dager   a fortnight

Chapter 4

Pronouns and determiners

4.1 Introduction

The class of pronouns comprises rather few words, in Norwegian as in English, but the pronouns occur very frequently, especially the personal pronouns. They are, therefore, important to learn.

Pronouns serve 'pro nouns', i.e. they function in place of a noun. Compare

Harry har kysset Gulla.   Harry has kissed Ginny.
Han har kysset henne.   He has kissed her.

In the second example, **henne** serves the same function as **Gulla** in the first; **henne** functions in place of the noun. Similarly, **han** serves the same function in the second sentence as **Harry** in the first, so **han** is also a pronoun.

It is not easy to delimit the class of pronouns exactly; in *NRG* from 1997, pronouns and determiners are treated as two different word classes. In this grammar, we treat pronouns and determiners in the same chapter, cf. 4.3.1 below.

4.2 Personal pronouns

4.2.1 *Case inflection*

The personal pronouns are the 'core examples' of pronouns. They are the only words in the written Norwegian language that retain a vestige of the Old Norse case distinction, i.e. a difference between nominative and accusative. This works in essentially the same way as in English; simplified, the nominative case is used when the pronoun serves as subject, the accusative otherwise (cf. 4.2.4.10 below). Compare:

Harry har kysset Gulla.   Harry has kissed Ginny.

The position after the non-finite verb can be filled by the object, but not by the subject, cf. 10.4. Thus, the word order makes clear that **Gulla** (Ginny) is the object, and it follows that **Harry** is the subject. If we replace the proper noun **Gulla** with a personal pronoun, this pronoun has to be in the accusative:

Harry har kysset henne.   Harry has kissed her.

In this example, not only does the word order signal that **henne** is the object, but the form of the pronoun does so too, because the accusative **henne** 'her' cannot serve as subject. The nominative form is **hun**, and only then can the pronoun serve as a subject:

Harry har hun kysset.   She has kissed Harry.
     (*Lit.* Harry she has kissed.)

In this example, the personal pronoun **hun** is in the nominative. It cannot serve as object. Therefore, **hun** must be the subject of the sentence, in this case the person doing the kissing. (The word order also indicates this; the object is not usually found in the position between finite and non-finite verb.) Consequently, Harry must be the person being kissed, in this example.

4.2.2 | *The actual forms*

The personal pronouns of Norwegian are:

	Nominative	Accusative
Singular		
1.	**jeg** I	**meg** me
2.	**du** you	**deg** you

3. *Masculine*	**han** he	**han/ham** him
3. *Feminine*	**hun** she	**henne** her
3. *Masculine/* *Feminine*	**den** it	**den** it
3. *Neuter*	**det** it	**det** it
Plural		
1.	**vi** we	**oss** us
2.	**dere** you	**dere** you
3.	**de** they	**dem** them

Pronouns are even more frequent in the spoken language than in written text. There are many differences between speech and writing when it comes to pronouns.

In the written language, shown in the table, the personal pronouns differentiate for case, with a couple of exceptions. First, the second person plural pronoun **dere** does not differentiate for case. It may thus be compared with the English 'you' (even if that pronoun does not show number either; **dere** is clearly plural).

Note – In the spoken language, most speakers do not have case inflection in the third person plural and the third person singular masculine, and some have no case inflection in the first person plural, some none in the second person singular. It is thus in the first person singular that the case distinction is most solidly anchored.

In the spoken language, a number of pronouns may sound rather differently. For example, instead of **han**, one may hear 'n; instead of **hun**, one may hear 'a, and instead of **du**, we may hear 'u:

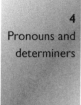
Nå kommer'n!	Here he comes!
Nå kommer'a!	Here she comes!
Nå slutter'u!	Now you quit!

4.2.2.2

Personal pronouns can be followed by a relative clause or a prepositional phrase, and this may be more common in Norwegian than in English:

Hun som står der, er Norges statsminister.
She who is standing there, is the Norwegian Prime Minister.

Spør han med den rutete skjorta.
Ask him with the chequered shirt.

Tenk på henne som løste det ondes problem.
Think of her who solved the problem of evil.

Especially in the spoken language, duplication of pronouns (10.9.5) is not uncommon:

Jeg tar litt mer kaffe, jeg.   *Lit.* I'll have a bit more coffee, I.

4.2.3 | Polite pronoun?

Traditionally, there has been a polite pronoun **De** – nominative **De**, accusative **Dem**, identical to the third person plural (as in German):

Vil De ikke ha en kopp kaffe?
Would you not like a cup of coffee?

Kan jeg be Dem komme fram og ta imot medaljen?
Can I ask you to step forward and receive the medal?

This pronoun is, however, not part of normal usage today. Some Norwegians may even react negatively – feeling that the use of **De** by the other party implies either an undesirable social distance or that the addressee is so old as to be antiquated.

In official correspondence, **De** is also seldom used these days, but it is not quite so stylistically 'marked':

Vi viser til Deres brev av 5. mai.
We refer to your letter dated May 5.

In newspapers, magazines and advertisements, one could find **De** well into the 1970s.

4.2.3.1 *Other forms of address*

It is possible to address adults (especially men), using their family name:

Kan du se på dette, Kristoffersen?
Can you have a look at this, Kristoffersen?

These days, this has an air of 'buddies' talk'.

4.2.4 *Notes on each pronoun and usage*

4.2.4.1 *Jeg 'I'*

This pronoun is used to refer to the speaker. It inflects for case (nominative **jeg**, accusative **meg**).

Jeg vil bli konge, keiser. [Ibsen, *Peer Gynt*]
I want to become king, emperor.

Jeg elsker Carmen, Carmen elsker meg.
I love Carmen, Carmen loves me.

Hvorfor er alle så sinte på meg som sa sannheten?
Why is everybody so mad at me who spoke the truth?

Note 1 – In written non-fiction, it is more common to use **jeg** in Norwegian than it is to use 'I' in English.

Note 2 – Notice the idiomatic expression **meg bekjent**, 'as far as I know'.

4.2.4.2 *Du 'you'*

This pronoun is used to refer to the other party in a dialogue. It inflects for case (nominative **du**, accusative **deg**). While English 'you' may be used for a single addressee or a crowd alike, Norwegian **du** is restricted to one addressee; if there are many, **dere** is used (cf. 4.2.4.8).

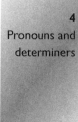

Hva skal du bli når du blir stor?
What do you want to be when you grow up?

Hva synes du, Ingebjørg?   What do you think, Ingebjørg?
Nå skal jeg vise deg noe.   Now I shall show you something.

Note 1 – In speech and informal writing, **du** may also be used with the same meaning as **man** 'one, they':

Det er ikke uvanlig å bli deprimert når du mister ektefellen.
It is not unusual to be depressed when you lose your spouse.

Perhaps this use of **du** in part reflects English influence, since **man** is more traditional in the written language. See 4.7 on indefinite pronouns.

Note 2 – **Du der** 'you there' may be used to address – rather bluntly – somebody the speaker does not know, especially if they are up to no good:

Hei, du der! Slutt å plage den stakkars hunden!
Hey you there! Stop pestering the poor dog!

Note 3 – **Du da** (*lit.* 'you then') may be used to address somebody the speaker does know, especially with a certain emotional load (endearment or irritation):

Du da ... Du trengte da ikke kjøpe en ny Porsche til meg.
Oh you ... You did not have to buy me a new Porsche.

Du da ... Du kan bare tie stille.
Oh you ... You can just keep quiet.

Note 4 – Notice the case in the idiomatic expressions **Du godeste**, 'My goodness'; **Kjære deg**, 'Dear you'. Notice also that Norwegian uses the possessive in **Din tosk**, 'You fool', and similar expressions, cf. 4.2.4.10 (c).

| 4.2.4.3 | *Han* 'he' |

The pronoun **han** is used:

(a) To refer to male persons

Der kommer Rolf. Han er travel.
There comes Rolf. He is busy.

Joseph blir sjokkert av det Orson forteller ham.
Joseph is horrified by what Orson tells him.

Legen min sa jeg burde drikke mindre, og han sa jeg burde trimme mer.
My doctor told me to drink less, and he said I should exercise more.

While the personal names in the first two examples indicate that reference would be made with **han**, the third example is different. **Rolf** and **Joseph** will refer to males by the conventions for Norwegian first names, while **legen min** can refer to a person of either sex. It is thus the sex of the doctor in question that makes the speaker use **han** in the third example.

(b) To refer to higher animals that are male:

Hva heter hunden din? Han heter Buster.
What is your dog called? He is called Buster.

Her er et bilde av isbjørnen Knut, som var veldig populær i Tyskland, idet han spiser frokost.
Here is a picture of the polar bear Knut, who was very popular in Germany, as he is eating breakfast.

In these examples, **han** is practically obligatory. The reason does not only have to do with the animals being 'higher', but also with familiarity. If somebody has never seen the dog Buster before, they might reasonably ask:

Hva heter den? What is it called?

The dog's owner, however, is unlikely to answer using **den**. Similarly, the example involving the polar-bear Knut above may be contrasted with the following:

Dette er bilde av en isbjørnhann idet den angriper teltet til to turister.
This is a picture of a male polar bear as it attacks the tent of two tourists.

When animals are less domesticated or 'lower' down the scale, **den** will be more normal. It would be strange to refer to the once familiar polar bear Knut with **den**, and it would be strange to refer to the unfamiliar aggressive polar bear with **han**. The fact that the attacking bear is referred to with an indefinite noun phrase, and thus is unfamiliar, is also relevant.

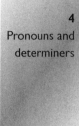

(c) Allegedly gender-neutral use:

At least until 1960, it was fairly generally accepted that **han** could be used as an allegedly gender-neutral pronoun. Compare the following quote:

> **Hvad gagner det et menneske om han vinner den hele verden, men tar skade på sin sjel?**
> For what is a man profited, if he shall gain the whole world, and lose his own soul? (Matthew 16, 26; 1930 version)

The Norwegian word **menneske** is inherently sex-neutral (unlike the English word 'man') and has neuter gender, and yet the masculine pronoun was chosen. Already in the 1978 version, however, we find:

> **Hva gagner det et menneske om det vinner hele verden, men taper sin sjel?**

The allegedly 'neutral' use of **han** is probably best avoided today. However, this poses a problem, inasmuch as Norwegians do not like to use the neuter pronoun about a specific human being. To say **det** 'it' about an adult may (if not in the biblical example above) almost seem offensive. See further 4.7 on 'evasion', and 1.2.4.1.

Han can also be used as a determiner, cf. 4.3.2.5 below.

Note – In North Norway, **han** can also be used with meteorological verbs, the way **det** is used in the rest of the country, cf. 4.2.4.6, 3.

4.2.4.4 *Hun* 'she'

This pronoun inflects for case (nominative **hun**, accusative **henne**). It is used to refer to:

(a) Female persons

> **Kjersti er en god kollega. Hun er omtenksom og vennlig.**
> Kjersti is a good colleague. She is considerate and friendly.

> **Eldbjørg har vært på hytta. Det var fint for henne.**
> Eldbjørg has been to the cabin. That was nice for her.

> **Har du sett sjefen i dag? Nei, hun er sjuk.**
> Have you seen the boss today? No, she is ill.

The third example differs from the previous two. Any Norwegian will know that the first names **Kjersti** and **Eldbjørg** refer to females; by contrast, **sjefen** can refer to a person of either sex.

(b) Female higher animals

Katta vår er kanskje vakker, men hun er ikke så snill.
Our cat may be beautiful, but she is not so well-behaved.

In this case, an alternative may be **den**, cf. 4.2.4.3(b), 4.2.4.5.

Note 1 – In the usage of some authors, boats and ships are also referred to with **hun**.

Note 2 – In the speech of many Norwegians, the division of labour between **han, hun** and **den** is different than in Bokmål. We may use Nynorsk (the other written standard of Norwegian, cf. the Introduction to this book), to represent these dialects. In Nynorsk, **han** and **ho** (= **hun**) are used to refer to entities of the masculine gender and feminine gender respectively, be they animate or inanimate. In other words, **den** is not used as a personal pronoun. **Han** can be used to refer both to a father and to a chair (**faren, stolen**), **ho** can be used to refer to both a mother and a book (**mora, boka**).

Hun can also be used as a determiner, cf. 4.3.2.5 below.

Note 3 – Recently, some language reformers have suggested introducing an additional personal pronoun to be used without reference to gender, e.g. **hen**; this pronoun has become fairly common in Swedish. In Norwegian, this suggestion has not gained much ground so far, but it remains to be seen how this will develop. (Some also wish to reserve **hen** for trans-persons.)

4.2.4.5 | *Den 'it'*

Den does not inflect for case. Both **den** and **det** can be used as inanimate pronouns in the third person singular (just as English 'it'); what distinguishes them is gender. **Den** is common (masculine and feminine), **det** is neuter.

Den is used as a pronoun:

(a) To refer to animals, especially lower or unfamiliar ones, and non-animates of non-neuter gender

Bildet viser en blåhval idet den svømmer forbi skipet.
The picture shows a blue whale as it passes our boat.

Se på den!   Look at it.
Turistene elsker den.   The tourists love it.

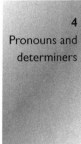

Her står farfars gamle stol. Den er faktisk ganske stygg.
Here is granddad's old chair. It is actually rather ugly.

Likte du ikke Sniffs nye roman? Nei, jeg mislikte den faktisk.
Didn't you enjoy Snoopy's new novel? No, I disliked it, actually.

(b) To refer to a person of unspecified sex

This is only found when the person is defined further, typically in a relative clause. In English, a possible translation will often involve using the plural:

Den som tror at nordmenn er født med ski på beina, kjenner nok ikke så mange nordmenn.
Those (*lit.* the one) who think that Norwegians are born with skis on their feet, probably do not know many Norwegians.

Den som har visjoner, bør oppsøke lege.
Those (*lit.* the one) who have visions should consult a doctor.

(c) In exclamations, **den** can be followed by a relative clause to indicate a wish:

Å, den som var på hytta nå.   Oh, I wish I were at the cabin now.
Å, den som var i England ...   Oh, to be in England ...

Note – Informally, one may also use **den** to refer to specific ideas, suggestions, questions:

Den var ikke dum!   That is not a stupid idea.

There are other uses of **den**, but they can be classified as determinative uses; see 4.3.1. and 4.3.2.1 below.

| 4.2.4.6 | **Det** *'it'*

The pronoun **det** 'it, that' is used in a variety of functions. While most often translated by English 'it', **det** has an even broader meaning. It can also be translated by 'there', 'that' or 'so':

Dette huset kjøpte vi i fjor. Det ligger ved sjøen.
This house we bought last year. It is close to the sea.

Nå er vi framme. Det var godt å høre!
Now we are there. That is good to hear!

Det dyrkes ikke hvitløk på Romerike.
They do not grow [*Lit.* It is not grown] garlic on Romerike.

Han er vanskelig, og det er hun også.
He is difficult, and so is she.

Det var få restauranter i Sandnes i 1965.
There were few restaurants in Sandnes in 1965.

Pronouns and determiners

Det 'it' can be used as a pronoun:

1) To refer to a non-animate, typically expressed by a preceding noun phrase, of neuter gender:

Der står huset vårt. Er det ikke fint?
There is our house. Isn't it nice?

Bordet står på låven. Det skal kastes.
The table is in the barn. It will be thrown away.

Note – If the preceding neuter noun denotes a human being, Norwegians tend to avoid the personal pronoun **det**. See 4.7.2.

2) To refer to a phrase or clause that in itself is genderless:

Å være eller ikke, det er spørsmålet.
To be or not to be, that is the question.

At du kunne ro så langt, det hadde jeg aldri trodd.
That you could row so far, that I would never have thought.

In 1) and 2), **det** may be said to refer to or represent a noun phrase (or something similar); in other words, **det** is used pronominally. Also, in 1 and 2, **det** may potentially be stressed.

However, there are a number of pronominal usages of **det** where this does not hold true. In types 3–6 below, there is no noun or noun phrase that could replace **det**, and to stress the pronoun would sound strange. This is where we talk of 'formal subjects', cf. also 10.3.2.

3) With meteorological verbs and some other verbs of perception:

Det snør ute.	It is snowing outside.
Det lysnet i skogen.	It got lighter in the forest.
Det bråker så fælt her.	It is so noisy here.
Det lukter av osten.	*Lit.* It smells of the cheese; The cheese stinks.

4) Preceding an infinitive construction or an at-clause:

Det er moro å arbeide.   It is fun to work.

Det var fint at du kunne komme.
It was good that you could come.

In such cases, the potential subject **å arbeide** may be turned into a real subject:

Å arbeide er moro.   To work is fun.
At du kunne komme, det var fint.   That you could come, was fine.

Especially the second example is rather formal; infinitives and at-clauses as subjects are often 'copied', using **det,** 'it' (especially in the spoken language):

Å arbeide, det er moro.   To work, that is fun.

At du kunne komme, det var fint.
That you could come, that was fine.

5) In cleft sentences (cf. 10.3.2.4):

Det var butleren som drepte lorden.
It was the butler who killed the lord.

Det var i biblioteket (som/at) liket ble funnet.
It was in the library (that) the body was found.

6) In existential sentences, where English uses 'there':

Det er mange sauer på New Zealand.
There are many sheep in New Zealand.

Det satt to katter på et bord.
There were two cats sitting on a table.

Det vokser et tre i Brooklyn.
A tree grows in Brooklyn (novel by Betty Smith)

In existential sentences (cf. 10.3.2.2, 10.7.3.4), **det** is often considered a mere place-holder. It cannot be replaced by a noun, and it cannot be stressed. The third example illustrates the fact that Norwegians do not like an indefinite subject sentence-initially.

In 1) – 3) and 5), Norwegian **det** can be translated into English 'it'. In type 6, by contrast, English uses 'there'. So does Danish, and some Norwegian dialects. Because of the Danish tradition that has influenced Bokmål (cf. the Introduction), **der** is not ruled out in such existential sentences:

Der er en lykke i livet som ikke kan vendes til lede.
There is a joy in life that cannot be turned to grief. [A. Øverland]

However, the use of **der** in these sentences is becoming rare in Bokmål.

7) To refer back to some non-neuter noun phrases:

Akevitt, det er tingen!   Aquavit, that's the thing!
Pannekaker, det er sunt.   Pancakes are good for you.

In these examples, the antecedent noun (phrase) does not have neuter gender, but **det** indicates that the semantics of the noun is mass-like. (Compare adjective agreement, 2.2.6.)

In fact, one can refer back to noun phrases of any gender and number with **det** if they do not have a specific referent (and thus typically are indefinite), and particularly if they are not the subject:

Jeg trenger en hammer og ei sag. Det kan du få låne av meg.
I need a hammer and a saw. *Lit.* That you can borrow from me. You can borrow that from me.

Vi hadde en terrier den gangen. Det har vi ikke nå.
We had a terrier back then. *Lit.* That we do not have now. We do not have it now.

Notice the difference between **det** and other pronouns in such examples:

Vi hadde en terrier den gangen. Den har vi ikke nå.
We had a terrier back then. *Lit.* That (same terrier) we do not have now. We do not have that one now.

Batman har en søt kjæreste. Det vil Robin også ha.
Batman has a cute girlfriend. *Lit.* That Robin wants too (i.e. a cute girlfriend). Robin wants one too.

Batman har en søt kjæreste. Henne vil Robin ha.
Batman has a cute girlfriend. *Lit.* Her Robin wants (i.e. Batman's girlfriend). Robin wants her.

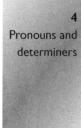

8) In impersonal passives (see 5.6.1.1 (c)):

Det arbeides mye.   A lot of work is going on.

Det blir oppført et nytt bygg.   A new building is being erected.

Det dyrkes ikke hvitløk i Nes.   Garlic is not grown in Nes.
(place-name)

9) Occasionally where it translates into English as 'so':

Du mener det?   You think so?

La oss håpe det.   Let's hope so.

This is particularly in combination with the words **også**, **òg** (and **med**), meaning 'too':

Vi dummet oss ut, men det gjorde de også,
We made fools of ourselves, but (then) so did they too.

Hun er pen, og det er han òg.
She is good-looking, and so is he.

10) In examples with a copula, **det** may serve as subject and refer to a person or thing identified by the subject complement.

Det er kona mi.   That is my wife.

Det er boka di.   That is your book.

11) To refer back to a verb phrase:

Harry ville drikke mer, men Hermine ville ikke det.
Harry wanted to drink more, but Hermione did not want that (i.e. to drink more).

Du bør gå, og det straks.
You had better leave, and that (i.e. your going) right now.

La oss gå hjem. Hvorfor det?
Let's go home. Why (Why so)?

12) To refer back to an adjective phrase:

Hermine er skoleflink, men det er ikke Ronny.
Hermione is good at school, but Ronny is not [*lit.* it].

Vennlig og snill, det er han ikke.
Friendly and kind, [it/that] he is not.

There are other uses of **det**, but they can be classified as determinative uses, see 4.3 below.

| 4.2.4.7 | **Vi** *'we'* |

Like its English equivalent, this pronoun usually refers to the speaker and a number of others, including or excluding the addressee. **Vi** inflects for case (compare **vi – oss**). As with the other pronouns, the accusative case is used when the pronoun is governed by a preposition or when it is object; see also 4.2.4.10.

Skal vi gå?   Shall we go?

Vi er fra politiet; la oss komme fram.
We are from the police; let us through. (excluding the addressee)

La oss komme oss ut herfra.
Let's get out of here. (including the addressee)

Note 1 – In journalese, **vi** can mean 'the reporter (on behalf of the newspaper and its readers)'; this usage is less common these days.

Note 2 – **Vi** can be used as a form of address.

Hvordan har vi det i dag?   How are we (you) today?
Har vi sovet godt?   Did we (you) sleep well?

This is an almost stereotypical nurse – patient interaction, and may be perceived as a little patronising.

Note 3 – Note the fixed expressions **oss imellom** 'between you and me'; **oss bekjent** 'as far as we know'.

Like many other personal pronouns, **vi** can also be used as determiner, cf. 4.3.2.4.

| 4.2.4.8 | **Dere** *'you (pl.)'* |

Dere is clearly plural (unlike English 'you', which may be either singular or plural; **dere** may thus be compared with American 'you guys'). **Dere** does not inflect for case.

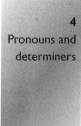

| Vil dere ha en kopp til? | Would you like another cup? |
| Vi tenker på dere. | We think of you. |

Like many other pronouns, **dere** can be used as a determiner, cf. 4.3.2.4.

4.2.4.9 De 'they'

This pronoun is used to refer to a plurality of participants irrespective of gender who are not present in the speech situation. **De** inflects for case (nominative **de**, accusative **dem**). The case distinction is rarer in the spoken language.

De ser på henne.	They look at her.
Hun ser på dem.	She looks at them.
Hun gav dem en tankevekker.	She gave them food for thought.

The personal pronouns in the first and second person normally refer to animates (since non-animates are unlikely to participate in the speech situation); the third person pronoun, by contrast, often refers to non-animates:

Hvor er brillene mine? De ligger under avisa.
Where are my glasses? They are under the newspaper.

Veiene på Vestlandet, de har da blitt mye bedre?
The roads in West Norway, they have improved (haven't they)?

De can also be used as a determiner, cf. 4.3.2.4.

Note 1 – In speech and informal writing, **de** may be used with the same meaning as **man** 'one, they' (see also 4.7.2):

De burde aldri ha lagt ned natt-toget til Stockholm.
They should never have withdrawn the night train to Stockholm./
The night train to Stockholm should never have been withdrawn.

Note 2 – **De** can also be used to refer back to a collective noun, even though this noun grammatically is in the singular. In the following example, the singular pronoun **det** (which may seem grammatically correct) would be very unlikely:

Politiet er nokså sikre, men de har ennå ikke sagt noe.
The police are fairly sure, but they have said nothing as yet.

The nominative is the case of the subject; the accusative is the case of the object (direct or indirect) and of other 'dependents', as when the pronoun is governed by a preposition (see also 4.2.1). Compare:

Jeg kjente henne igjen.	I recognised her.
Hun kjente meg ikke igjen.	She did not recognise me.
Hun så på meg.	She looked at me.

The nominative is also used as a 'vocative', i.e. to address others:

| **Kom, du, så går vi oss en tur.** | Come, let's go for a walk. |
| | (Come on, you...) |

While this is the main rule and very much like English, the choice of case is not always as straightforward as this.

Subject complements might perhaps be expected to occur in the nominative. As in English, however, they are normally in the accusative:

| **Hvem er det? Det er meg!** | Who is it? It is me! |

Hvis du var meg, hadde du da sagt ja?
If you were me, would you then say yes?

Using the nominative here is not common in written Bokmål. Some speakers will find it stilted or affected.

(a) In 'cleft sentences' (cf. 10.3.2.4), where a subject has been 'split', the nominative is recommended and common:

Det var du som sa at månen er en grønn ost.
It was you who said that the moon is made of (*lit.* is a) green cheese.

Compare:
Hvem sa at månen var en grønn ost? Det var deg.
Who said the moon is made of (*lit.* is a) green cheese? You did.

Det var han som gravde opp Osebergskipet.
He was the one (*lit.* it was he) who excavated the Oseberg Ship.

(Compare: **Det var ham.**)

Note – The accusative form can also be found in such examples, but this is traditionally considered wrong:

Tenk om det var deg som gikk barbeint i snøen.
Imagine it was you walking bare-foot in the snow.

(b) In emphatic, isolated use, English pronouns occur in the accusative, Norwegian in the nominative

Me, worried?	cf.	**Bekymret, jeg?**
Him, a murderer?		**Morder, han?**

(c) In certain exclamations where English has an accusative pronoun, Norwegian uses a possessive:

Oh, you fool!	**Å, (du) din tosk!**
Oh, you smart-alec!	**Å, (du) din luring!**
Oh, I am a fool!	**Å, jeg mitt naut!** [*Lit.* my cow/ox]

This usage is restricted to the first and second person singular. In the first person (as in the third example above), Norwegians use a personal pronoun in the nominative in addition to the possessive.

(d) In certain fixed cases of exclamations where English uses a possessive, Norwegian uses a personal pronoun in the nominative:

My goodness!	**Du godeste!**
Good grief!	**Du storeste!/Du store!**

The fixed character of **Du godeste, Du storeste** is also shown in that the adjective inflection is not the one we normally find for **god, stor** (which would be **beste, største**, respectively (cf. Adjectives 2.5.4.1, 2.5.3).

(e) In certain (almost fixed) cases of address, Norwegian uses a personal pronoun in the accusative:

Dear you!	**Kjære deg!**
Poor you!	**Stakkars deg!**

Note – In some cases, Norwegians these days accept the nominative:

Vi ser på de/dem som har gått i toget.
We watch those who have gone in the procession.

(Third person plural, much variation, both nominative and accusative are accepted; the nominative is spreading.)

After **enn** 'than', **som** 'as', the accusative is common:

Hun er flinkere enn meg.   She is more gifted than I am.
Vi er like smarte som dem.   We are as smart as they are.

4.3 Determiners

4.3.1 Pronoun or determiner?

The words **den, det** and **de** do not only have pronominal uses; they can also be used as determiners (see also 2.3.3.1):

Den gamle favorittstolen til farfar var faktisk ganske stygg.
The favourite old chair of granddad's was actually quite ugly.

Kaptein Ahab var besatt av den hvite hvalen.
Captain Ahab was obsessed with the white whale.

De mest innbitte skientusiastene håper at det fine været skal vare til påskeferien.
The most ardent skiing enthusiasts hope that the fine weather will last until the Easter vacation.

There is no noun that can replace **den, det, de** in the examples above; they do not function 'pro noun'. The third person plural **de** is telling. As a pronoun, it inflects for case (cf. 4.2.4.9); there is, for example, a contrast between **de** and **dem** in:

De tenker på oss, og vi tenker på dem.
They think of us, and we think of them.

However, consider the following examples:

De store hvalene lurte hvalfangerne.
The big whales outsmarted the whalers.

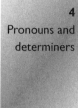
Hvalfangerne stirret på de store hvalene.
The whalers stared at the big whales.

There is no case inflection of **de** when the word is used determinatively. When used in this way, **de** does not stand in for any noun. This is one reason why *NRG* operates with a word-class called 'determiners'.

However, the distinction between pronouns and determiners is subtle. In fact, **de, den** and **det** are not alone in showing the 'dual usage' illustrated above. A number of other words can also be used either as a determiner or as a pronoun, e.g. **en** 'one', **alle** 'all':

Jeg kjenner en lærer.   I know a teacher.
          determinative

Jeg kjenner en som har gått Birkebeineren siden 1970.
          pronoun
I know one (person) who has done the Birkebeiner Race since 1970.

Alle mennesker behøver en god bok iblant.
determinative
Everyone needs a good book sometimes.

Alle behøver en god bok iblant.
pronoun
Everyone needs a good book sometimes.

In short, pronouns and determiners overlap. In this grammar, they are not treated as separate word classes; they appear in the same chapter and are seen as different uses of (the same) words.

4.3.2 | *Determinative use of third person pronouns*

4.3.2.1 | *Den*

(a) **Den** can be used determinatively (preceding a non-neuter noun phrase of common gender):

Dette er den fineste hoppbakken i verden.
This is the finest ski-jumping hill in the world.

Oppe på loftet fant hun den gamle anorakken.
Up in the attic she found the old anorak.

På den herregården var det et lite museum.
At that manor house there was a small museum.

Den as determiner has partly the same function as the suffixes **–en, –a,** and they are traditionally called 'front' and 'end' articles, or, in Norwegian, **bestemt foranstilt artikkel** respectively **bestemt etterhengt artikkel**.

(b) Normally, the noun following **den** will be definite:

Den grøten var god!   That porridge was delicious!

Den mannen som står der borte, er broren min.
That man standing over there is my brother.

Hun tenkte tilbake på den tida med glede.
She thought back on that period with pleasure.

However, in literary written language one can find quite a few examples of **den** followed by an indefinite noun:

I den natt da han ble forrådt, ...
On the same night in which he was betrayed, ... (I Corinthians 11:23)

Det er den eneste glede.   That is the only joy.

Also in a large number of set expressions, such as:

for den saks skyld ...	If it comes to that ...
for den del	
noe i den dur	something similar (colloquial)
Den røde plass	Red Square (in Moscow)
Den forbudte by	The Forbidden City (in Beijing)

If the noun phrase beginning with **den** contains an adjective (or is followed by a relative clause), an indefinite noun is also slightly more frequent. Thus, **den hopper** 'the jumper' is unlikely, but **den tyske hopper** 'the German jumper' is slightly more frequent, even if **den tyske hopperen** is by far the most common. (See also 2.3.4.1.)

Note 1 – A standard way of beginning jokes involves the use of **den** 'the one':

Har du hørt den om dansken, svensken og nordmannen som skulle svømme om kapp over Atlanterhavet?
Did you hear the one about the Dane, the Swede and the Norwegian who were to compete in swimming across the Atlantic?

Note 2 – Noun phrases consisting only of a determiner **den** and a noun are rather rare. Thus, **den mannen** 'the/that man', **den tida** 'the/that time' are rare, but they can be used to signal that the speaker and the addressee are in a close relationship and share a lot of knowledge, and that the speaker is trying to remind the addressee of this: **Den mannen, hva skjedde med ham?** 'That man, what happened to him?' Alternatively, **den tida**, etc. can be used for emphasis and contrast: **På den tida inntraff de første istidene,** 'At that period, the great ice ages occurred'. In that case, there is stress on the determiner.

Unlike English, Norwegian does not need an 'extra' word after the adjective in such examples as the following (see also 2.4.1.1):

> **Hvilken kjole liker du best, den blå eller den grønne?**
> Which dress do you prefer, the blue one or the green one?

> **Ikke før hadde hun vist ut en bråkmaker, så kom den neste.**
> No sooner had she expelled one trouble-maker than the next one turned up.

4.3.2.2 Det

(a) Just like **den, det** can be used determinatively. It will then usually precede a noun (a noun phrase) of neuter gender:

> **Der borte står det gamle huset hun vokste opp i.**
> Over there is the old house in which she grew up.

> **Det sorgløse livet vi drømte om, finnes ikke.**
> The carefree life we dreamt of does not exist.

Det has partly the same function as the suffix –**et** (cf. 4.3.2.1).

Normally, the noun following will be in the definite, but not necessarily:

> **Det gode liv er en drøm.**   The good life is a dream

The use of the indefinite noun here is normally rather formal. (See also 2.3.4.) The same rules apply as for **den**; see 4.3.2.1.

Note 1 – Noun phrases consisting only of a determiner **det** and a noun are rather rare: **det huset**, 'that house'. They are used in the same way as phrases consisting of **den** + noun. See 4.3.2.1(c) Note 2.

Note 2 – Some fixed expressions involve an indefinite noun: **Det hvite hus** 'The White House', **det ganske land** 'all the country', **det rene sludder** 'nonsense'. See 2.3.4.1.

Note 3 – **Det** may precede an adjective in the definite without a noun following, especially in literary or formal use: **det onde**, 'evil'. See 2.4.

(b) **Det** can also precede an **at**-clause or an infinitive construction:

Det å bli kalt populist tar jeg som et kompliment.
To be called a populist, I take that as a compliment.

Det at du tok feil da, betyr ikke nødvendigvis at du har rett nå.
The fact that you were wrong then does not necessarily mean that you are right now.

4.3.2.3 *De*

De can be used determinatively, preceding either a noun (phrase) or an adjective:

Der ser du de bøkene jeg har lett etter.
There you see those books I've been looking for.

De gamle klassikerne er ofte litt triste.
The old classics are often rather sad.

When used as a determiner, **de** does not have an accusative form, cf. 4.3.1.

4.3.2.4 *First and second plural pronouns in determinative use*

Vi 'we' can marginally be used as a determiner. In such cases, **vi** retains case inflection (unlike **han, hun, de**):

Vi nordmenn er dessverre ikke beskjedne og nøysomme lenger.
Sadly, we Norwegians are no longer modest and thrifty.

Snakker dere om oss nordmenn?
Are you talking about us Norwegians?

Also **dere** 'you (pl.)' can be used determinatively:

Dere gallere er rare!   You Gauls are strange!

| 4.3.2.5 | *Han* and *hun* as determiners

The personal pronouns **han** and **hun** are also used determinatively. While this has been frowned upon, traditionally, it seems to be spreading, although it is still informal or colloquial:

Hva heter *hun i Drammen*?
What is the name of her in Drammen?

Er *han snille der borte* faren din?
Is he the kind one over there, your dad?

Hun legen og han snekkeren.
She the doctor and he the joiner.

| 4.3.2.6 | *Proximal determiners:* **Denne, dette** *'this';* **disse** *'these'*

(a) These words are used as proximal determiners, and only rarely pronominally; they normally precede a noun (phrase). **Denne** and **dette** are used before a noun in the singular, **disse** before one in the plural. Usually, the noun is in the definite:

Denne jenta heter Aud.	This girl is called Aud.
Denne gangen måtte Boris gi opp.	This time, Boris had to give up.
Dette barnet ble født for tidlig.	This child was born prematurely.
Disse filmstjernene er de største.	These movie stars are the greatest.

Both **dette** and **denne** agree in grammatical gender with the noun following; **dette** is used before neuters, **denne** before non-neuters. (Compare **den** and **det**; **den** is used with non-neuters, 4.3.2.1, **det** with neuters, 4.3.2.2.) The difference between **denne, dette, disse** on the one hand and **den, det, de** on the other is that the former suggest proximity and the latter do not. (Compare the difference between 'this', 'these' and 'that', 'those' in English.)

Denne hunden heter Buster.	This dog is called Buster.

This will normally imply that the dog is close to the speaker (physically or mentally). By contrast, such proximity is not implied in the following:

Den hunden heter Rambo.	That dog is called Rambo.

Den is not so clearly proximal. In examples like this, **den** can be stressed in speech, if contrast is aimed for.

The same proximity contrast applies for **dette – det** and **disse – de:**

Dette barnet er mitt.	This child is mine.
Det barnet er ikke mitt.	That child is not mine.
Disse hundene er snille.	These dogs are kind.
De hundene er slemme.	Those dogs are mean.

While English has a contrast between 'those' and 'they', Norwegian uses **de** for both.

Denne (dette) can also indicate closeness in time:

Denne helga er kongen og dronningen i Harstad.
This weekend the king and queen are in Harstad.

Compare **denne uka,** 'this week' vs. **den uka,** 'that week'.

(b) It is possible to use an indefinite form of the noun after the determiners **denne, dette, disse** but, this is somewhat literary and unusual these days. No dog owner will say in a casual conversation **denne hund,** but, as with **den, det,** cf. 4.3.2.1 and 4.3.2.2, an adjective or a relative clause increases the possibility of using the noun in the indefinite, as does a formal style:

Det var meg en fornøyelse å få dele dette utsøkte måltid med Dem.
It has been a pleasure for me sharing this exquisite meal with you.

Denne forunderlige by som ingen forlater før han har fått merker av den.
This strange city [viz. Oslo] that nobody leaves before it has marked him (*lit.* he has been marked by it) – Hamsun

Å, disse plagede detektiver! Oh, those tormented detectives!

(c) The last of these three examples also illustrates the 'emotional load' that sometimes comes with **disse** (**denne, dette**), cf. **disse evinnelige forelesningene,** 'those eternal lectures'; **dette stadige maset ditt,** 'this continual nagging of yours'.

4.3.2.7

Typically, **denne, dette, disse** are used as determiners. In formal language, they can also be used as pronouns, however. They will then refer 'back' (to the left) in the text:

> **Utenriksministeren har hatt flere samtaler med sin russiske kollega Lavrov, og denne har sagt at Russland har et legitimt krav på Krim.**
> The foreign minister has had several talks with his/her Russian colleague Lavrov, and the latter (i.e. Lavrov) [*lit.* this] has said that Russia has a legitimate claim to Crimea.

> **Islands statsminister er gått av, og dette kom vel ikke som noen overraskelse.**
> The Prime Minister of Iceland has resigned, and this (i.e. the resignation) did not really come as a surprise.

To use **denne** to refer to persons is much more formal than to use **dette** to refer to events; the use of **dette** above can also be found in spoken language.

Compare:

> **Islands statsminister er gått av, og det kom vel ikke som noen overraskelse.**
> The Prime Minister of Iceland has resigned, and that (i.e. the resignation) did not really come as a surprise.

The sentence with **det** means practically the same thing as the one with **dette**, but it is less literary.

Also, **disse** 'these' can be used pronominally in this way, but that is formal and infrequent (even more so than using **denne** in this way):

> **Kongen av Ruritania har vært i kontakt med alle hertugene, og disse har forsikret ham om at de forblir lojale.**
> The King of Ruritania has been in touch with all the dukes, and the latter (*lit.* these) have assured him that they will stay loyal.

Notice, however, that there is also a decidedly less formal use of **denne, dette** without a following noun in examples like the following, when **dette** is used directly to point to the cod:

Her bad vi om god torsk – og så fikk vi dette!
Here we asked for good cod – and we got this!

4.3.2.8 Atypical uses of **denne, dette**

Denne can also be used as a determiner in front of a proper name. It will then signal a certain distance:

Hvem er denne Julie som Romeo mumler om?
Who is this Juliet that Romeo is mumbling about?

The implication is that the speaker has not heard about Juliet before (so here there is no 'proximal' meaning, unlike in 4.3.2.6). The connotation of distance may be quite strong:

Hva for slags menneske var egentlig denne Himmler?
What kind of human being was this Himmler, really?

By contrast, the use of **den** in the following example signals that the speaker knows or has heard about several Camerons, and now is picking out the right specimen:

Å, er det den Cameron?   Oh, it is that Cameron?

Dette can also be used when showing something or even somebody, not necessarily inanimate or of neuter gender:

Dette er kona mi.   This is my wife (Meet my wife).
Dette er god mat.   This is good food (This food is delicious).
Dette må ta slutt.   This has to stop.

4.3.2.9 Other determiners: **herre, derre, her, der**

In colloquial language, a determiner and a noun may be followed by **her**, 'here' or **der**, 'there', which then function as proximal determiners:

De øynene der – de minner meg om Bette Davis.
Those eyes there – they remind me of Bette Davis.

Dette huset her burde vi aldri ha kjøpt.
This house here, we should never have bought it.

4.4 Possessives

4.4.1 Introduction

These words include the following:

Non-neuter		Neuter	Plural	
min	min/mi	mitt	mine	my (mine)
din	din/di	ditt	dine	your (yours)
hans	hans	hans	hans	his
hennes	hennes	hennes	hennes	her (hers)
dens	dens	dens	dens	its
dets	dets	dets	dets	its
vår	vår	vårt	våre	our, ours
deres	deres	deres	deres	your, yours
deres	deres	deres	dere	their, theirs
sin	sin/si	sitt	sine	his/her/hers/ its/their/theirs

4.4.1.1

Traditionally, these words are called pronouns. However, they do not inflect for case, unlike the personal pronouns. The possessives also have a different distribution than personal pronouns:

Det er min bil.   That is my car.
Det er bilen min.   That is my car.

No noun can replace **min** in these examples, so the word does not serve 'pro noun', cf. 4.1.

The possessives **min, din, sin, vår** inflect for gender and number; personal pronouns do not.

Det er bilen min.	That is my car.	**4** Pronouns and determiners
Det er hytta mi.	That is my cabin.	
Det er huset mitt.	That is my house.	
Det er bøkene mine.	Those are my books.	

4.4.1.2

Feminine forms such as **mi, di, si** occur very infrequently in Bokmål (though not in speech). Very few people write **mi bok**, 'my book' or **Boka er mi**, 'The book is mine'. However, it is somewhat more frequent to use the special feminine forms **mi, di, si** immediately following the noun; **mi** is somewhat more commonly used in **boka mi** than in **mi bok** or **boka er mi**. To write *boka min is wrong; to write **boken min** is quite all right. Cf. 1.1.2, 1.2.3 on the feminine gender.

4.4.1.3

The third person singular inanimate possessives **dens, dets** are rare in practice. They are literary – **dets** even more so than **dens**. Possession is, after all, typically associated with humans (or institutions), and humans are seldom referred to with **det** (cf. 4.2.4.3(c), 4.7.2 and 1.2.4.1 Note 1).

The reflexive possessive **sin** is used to 'reflect', to refer to the subject. (Cf also 4.5.1.2–4.5.1.5 on **seg**.) Other possessives will not usually refer back to the subject.

Compare:

Kari liker sønnen sin.	Kari likes her (own) son.
Kari liker sønnen hennes.	Kari likes her (some other woman's) son.

Watson tok forstørrelsesglasset sitt.
Watson took his (own) magnifying glass.

Watson tok forstørrelsesglasset hans.
Watson took his (some other man's) magnifying glass.

Gry og Ola klemte sønnene sine.
Gry and Ola hugged their (own) sons.

Gry og Ola klemte sønnene deres.
Gry and Ola hugged their (some other people's) sons.

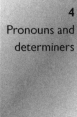

Notice, however, that **sin** may refer back to the 'logical subject' of an infinitive:

Per ba Ola fjerne bilen sin.
Per asked Ola to move his [Ola's] car.

Per ba Ola fjerne bilen hans.
Per asked Ola to move his (i.e. Per's) car.

While the possessive **sin** traditionally has had a reflexive function only (cf. 4.4.1), it has spread in Bokmål in recent years, replacing the traditional –s genitive (see also 1.8.1.7):

Det er Katrine sin bil.	That is Katrine's car
Det er jentene sine fotballer.	It's the girls' footballs

This usage has been frowned upon, but not so much any more. For many Norwegians, –s is not really felt to be an option, at least not in the spoken language, and particularly not with non-human possessors (see 1.8.1.7).

Note also that, with no noun following after a possessive, **sin** may be used contrastively, even by people who otherwise prefer –s:

Det er min brors bil, ikke din far sin.
That is my brother's car, not your father's.
(**Din fars** is possible here, but less used.)

4.4.1.4

Note that **deres** covers both the second and the third person plural; it can mean either 'your/s' or 'their/s'.

4.4.2 | *Preposed vs. postposed possessive*

There is a nuance in meaning and style between the construction where the possessive is preposed and that where the possessive is postposed. Thus, there is a difference between **huset mitt** and **mitt hus**, even if both translate into English as 'my house'.

The normal case, especially in the spoken language, is that the possessive is postposed (unlike English).

Vi elsker puslespillene våre. We love our puzzles.

If the possessive is postposed, the noun will occur in the definite, as above, but if the possessive is preposed, the noun will occur in the indefinite:

Vi elsker våre puslespill. We love our puzzles.

In the written language, there used to be a preference for a preposed possessive, presumably at least partly because Danish does not accept the construction with a postposed possessive. These days, a preposed possessive may seem literary, but not wrong.

Hytta vår ligger inne i skogen (normal). Our cabin is in the forest.
Vår hytte ligger inne i skogen. Our cabin is in the forest.

Out of context a preposed possessive can seem literary, but it is perfectly normal, even preferred, if a contrast is aimed for:

Deres hytte ligger ved sjøen, mens vår hytte ligger inne i skogen.
Their cabin is by the sea, while our cabin is in the forest.

Det er min sykkel, ikke din. That is my bike, and not yours.

In English, there are special emphatic possessives, sometimes described as possessive adjectives, such as 'yours, mine':

No, this one is mine; that one over there is yours.

Norwegian has no such special emphatic possessives:

Nei, denne er min; den der borte er din.

Note – In the spoken language, a postposed possessive can follow an indefinite noun if that noun denotes a close relative: **bror min,** 'my brother'.

4.4.3 | *Possessives that do not inflect*

While the possessives **min** 'my'; **din** 'your'; **sin; vår** 'our' agree in gender and number with their head noun, the third person possessives **hans** 'his'; **hennes** 'her'; **deres** 'your; their', by contrast, are not inflected for gender or number of the head noun.

Compare:

min hund, mitt dyr
min is used because the noun **hund** is non-neuter, **mitt** because the noun **dyr** is neuter.

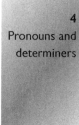
mine hunder, mine dyr
In both these examples, **mine** is used because the noun is in the plural.
There is no gender distinction in the plural.

hennes hund, hennes dyr
hennes does not show any inflectional contrast; it does not matter
whether the following noun is neuter or non-neuter, singular or plural.

Hans, hennes, like the English 'his, her' point to the 'logical gender' of the
relevant noun (the possessor):

Lærerne hennes roste alltid Hermine.
Her teachers always praised Hermione.

Dette var ikke hans store dag, tenkte Ronny.
This was not his finest hour [*lit.* his big day], Ron thought.

Legen var veldig sjarmerende, så han spurte om telefonnummeret hennes.
The doctor was very charming, so he asked for her phone number.

In this example, **hennes** is used even if the noun **lege**, 'doctor' itself does not
indicate a woman. Compare also:

**Cybill Shepherd spilte blondinen – jeg husker ikke hvem som
spilte bølla, men jeg husker smilet hans.**
Cybill Shepherd played the blonde – I cannot remember who played the
baddie, but I remember his smile.

The noun **bølle**, 'baddie' is (perhaps surprisingly) a feminine, if one has a
three-gender system; and yet, in this example, **hans** must be chosen, because
the speaker does remember the male actor, if not his name.

4.4.4 | *English uses a possessive, Norwegian does not*

In some cases where English uses a possessive pronoun, Norwegian does
not. For more details, see also 1.11.7. Typical examples include:

1) Nouns denoting body parts and articles of clothing:

Jeg har vondt i beinet/hodet.
I have pain in my leg/head (my leg/head hurts).

Han tok av seg genseren.
He took off his sweater.

A vernacular way of expressing 'possession' with body parts is by using a prepositional construction:

Signe tok tak i armen på Tor.
Signe got hold of Tor's arm [*lit.* the arm on Tor].

2) Nouns denoting close relatives:

Hun så på broren.
She looked at [her] brother.

Ragnhild og faren kom inn.
Ragnhild and [her] father came in.

3) 'Close/personal possession':

Hei, du må ikke glemme veska.
Hey, don't (*lit.* you must not) forget your bag.

Note 1 – Sometimes one finds Anglicisms in translation. Thus, Norwegian cashpoints display the 'Norwenglish' text **Sett inn ditt kort**. The idiomatic Norwegian expression should really be **Sett inn bankkortet**.

Note 2 – Sometimes, Norwegian uses a possessive pronoun alone where English has to use a longer circumlocution:

Vi har gjort vårt.   We have done our bit (our task).

Alle bidrar med sitt, og etterpå blir det kaffe og vafler.
Everybody will contribute with their stuff, and afterwards, there is coffee and waffles.

4.5   Reflexive (and related) pronouns

4.5.1 | *Reflexive* **seg**

4.5.1.1

If the object refers to the same person or entity as the subject, English can add 'myself, yourself, himself, herself', etc. In the first and second person, Norwegian does essentially the same.

I can shave myself, thank you.	**Jeg kan barbere meg selv, takk.**
You must not cheat yourself.	**Du må ikke snyte deg selv.**

In the third person, however, Norwegian has a pronoun specially desig-
nated for reflexive use:

Han barberte ham.
He shaved him (= shaved another man.)

Han barberte seg.
He shaved (himself). (The reflexive pronoun is not usually translated).

The following examples involve the verb **slå**, which can mean 'hit' or 'hurt'
among other things:

Han falt av sykkelen og slo seg.
He fell off the bike and hurt himself.

In this example, **seg** refers back to **Han** (only one person is involved).

Han bøyde seg fram og slo ham. He leaned over and hit him.

In this example, **ham** does not refer to the same person as **han** (two persons
are involved).

If we want to express that, unusually, a man has hit himself, we say

Han slo seg selv.   He hit himself.

This may be contrasted with the following example, in which a man hits
somebody else, and it is emphasised that the hitter did this on his own:

Han slo ham selv.   He hit him himself.

Selv serves an emphatic purpose here (cf. 4.5.3). The previous example and
the one below report the same action, but in the one below there is no
particular emphasis on the hitter carrying out the action on his own; this is
only stated as a matter of fact:

Han slo ham.   He hit him.

Compare also the contrast between the following:

Romeo elsker bare deg.   Romeo loves only you.
Boris elsker bare seg selv. Boris only loves himself.

4.5.1.3

Reflexive pronouns cannot be used as subjects; they will usually refer back to the subject:

Wiltersen meldte seg til tjeneste.
Weasley reported (himself) available for service.

Note, however, that in a subordinate clause, the reflexive pronoun refers back to the 'logical subject', and not necessarily to the grammatical one:

Wiltersen bad Malfang komme seg vekk og dra dit pepperen gror.
Weasley asked Malfoy to get lost and go where the pepper grows (i.e. to go to hell).

The 'logical subject' of the infinitive **komme** here is **Malfang** (although the grammatical subject of the main clause is **Wiltersen**), so **seg** refers to **Malfang**.

Less frequently, **seg**, typically combined with **selv** (4.5.3), can refer 'forwards':

Seg selv har han alltid stelt pent med.
He has always treated himself gently.

The rules for the reflexive vary somewhat in Norwegian dialects, and the rules of Bokmål are sometimes broken.

4.5.1.4

Using **seg** will often emphasise that the subject is somehow 'affected' by the action of the verb. Compare the following:

Hun fant seg en ny leilighet.
She found a new apartment for herself (and is affected by it).

Hun fant en ny leilighet (til oss).
She found a new apartment (for us) (and she need not be affected).

Kain slo Abel.	Cain hit Abel. (Cain need not be affected.)
Kain slo seg.	Cain hurt himself. (Cain is affected.)

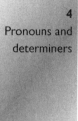

As noted, **seg** refers back to the subject (grammatical or logical). This means that **seg** is never used as a subject.

4.5.1.5

When used as a subject complement, **seg** cannot be used alone; it must be used with the intensifier **selv**:

Hun er ikke lenger seg selv.
She is no longer herself (she has changed).

Note – Fixed expressions with **seg** include:

i seg, i og for seg 'in isolation, per se, strictly':

Kortspill kan ikke i seg kalles noen moralsk trussel.
Card games cannot in themselves be called a moral threat.

I og for seg er det riktig at Margaret Thatcher ikke var så populær utenom England.
Strictly speaking, it is right that Margaret Thatcher was not so popular outside of England.

for seg 'separately':

I denne vanskelige saken må hver faktor betraktes for seg.
In this difficult matter, each factor must be considered separately.

4.5.2 | Obligatory reflexive after certain verbs

4.5.2.1

Some verbs require a reflexive pronoun, for example:

skamme seg, 'be ashamed'; **forelske seg,** 'fall in love'; **pådra seg (en sykdom),** 'catch (an illness)'

Thus, there is no verb **skamme/forelske** without a reflexive; it is not possible to **skamme/forelske** somebody else. See also 5.5.3.

Compare:

Jeg har pådratt meg en lei forkjølelse. I have caught a nasty cold.
Hun har pådratt seg en lei forkjølelse. She has caught a nasty cold.
* Hun har pådratt meg en lei forkjølelse.

4.5.2.2

Even for some verbs where the reflexive is not obligatory, the difference in
meaning between a verb with reflexive and the corresponding one without
can be quite considerable. Compare:

snyte seg 'sneeze, blow one's nose' vs. **snyte**, 'cheat'
ha seg 'enjoy oneself; have sex' vs. **ha**, 'have'
dra seg, 'be idle, do nothing' vs. **dra**, 'pull'. Compare also 5.5.3.

4.5.3 *Selv 'self'*

4.5.3.1

Selv (and the less used variant **sjøl**) translates '(it)self, (my)self' etc. It can be
seen as an intensifier; it often makes the meaning more emphatic; it 'under-
lines' the person in question. Compare:

Knytt skolissene dine.   Tie your shoelaces.

and

Knytt skolissene dine   Tie your shoelaces yourself.
selv.

Unlike English 'self', **selv** does not inflect for number:

Du kan gjøre jobben selv.   You can do the job yourself.

De vil bare klage; de vil ikke bidra selv.
They just want to complain; they do not wish to contribute themselves.

Also when fronted, **selv** is uninflected:

Selv kan jeg ikke gjøre noe i denne saken.
Myself, I cannot do anything in this matter.

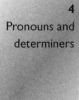

Pronouns preceding **selv** are typically in the accusative:

Du er og blir deg selv.   You are and will be yourself.

Note also that in examples like the one below, English 'myself', 'for myself' etc. will be worded differently in Norwegian:

For myself, I think that . . .   **Selv mener jeg at . . .**
Jeg for min del/part mener at . . .   Myself, I think that . . .

4.5.3.2

When preceding a definite noun, **selv** can be definite. In such cases, the meaning is rather like English 'very':

Det er selve grunnlaget for rapporten som nå blir trukket i tvil.
It is the very basis of the report that is now in question.

Etter tre timers prat kom selve problemet opp.
After three hours of chatting, the real problem came up.

4.5.3.3

Notice the fixed expressions:

Selveste 'no less than':

Den mannen var selveste paven.
That man was no less than the pope/the pope himself.

Det sier seg selv 'that goes without saying':

At alle burde lære norsk, sier seg selv.
It goes without saying that everybody ought to learn Norwegian.

4.5.4 *Hverandre* 'each other'

This pronoun is called reciprocal; there is a reciprocity going on in the action:

Bokserne slo hverandre.   The boxers hit each other.
Barna ertet hverandre.   The children teased each other.

The reciprocal pronoun is used more frequently in Norwegian than in English, because English omits 'each other' for some 'naturally reciprocal' situations:

| Romeo and Juliet kissed. | **Romeo og Julie kysset hverandre.** |
| They met at the station. | **De møtte hverandre på stasjonen.** |

Hverandre typically serves as object, direct (as in the examples above), or indirect, as in the following:

Torill og Beate gav hverandre gaver.
Torill and Beate gave each other presents.

Hverandre can be governed by a preposition:

Ronny og Harry så på hverandre.
Ron and Harry looked at each other.

Less frequently, **hverandre** can be found with inanimates:

Gassene har nøytralisert hverandre.
The gases have neutralised each other.

Note – Sometimes, a verb + **hverandre** can mean roughly the same thing as that verb + the reciprocal verb suffix –s (cf. 5.6.3.1):

De møtte hverandre – De møttes   They met.

Hverandre is a much more common way of expressing reciprocity than is –s, however.

4.6   Quantifiers

As the word indicates, quantifiers specify the quantity of what follows.

4.6.1 | Words meaning 'all'

4.6.1.1 | Introduction: **All, Alt, Alle** 'all'

These three words usually translate as English 'all', but they sometimes translate 'each' or 'every'. The very frequent words **alt** and **alle** can be used determinatively or pronominally; the infrequent **all** can only be used determinatively:

Alle nordmenn elsker da brunost?
Surely, all Norwegians love brown cheese?

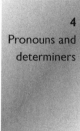

Alle tog står på grunn av politisk streik.
All the trains have stopped because of a 'political strike'.

Tønsberg var en liten by der alle kjente alle.
Tønsberg was a small town where everyone knew everyone.

All mat er god.   All food is good.
(Traditional reproach to children who have complained about the food).

All maten ble spist opp.   All the food was eaten.
Alt bråket har gjort meg lei.   All the noise has made me fed up.
Alt er som det skal.   Everything is as it should be.

If there is another determiner, **all/alle/alt** will come first (cf. 10.2.2.1(c)):

all den gode maten   all the good food
alle de fine jentene   all those fine girls

Sometimes, **alle** or **alt** will be used where English has 'each/every'. **Alle** used
by itself normally translates as 'everybody':

Hvorfor liker alle Angela?   Why does everybody like Angela?

Butikken er åpen alle dager unntatt søndager.
The shop is open every day except Sundays.

Note 1 – The fixed expressions **alt sammen, alt i hop** 'everything, alto-
gether'; **alle sammen** 'all (people) together'; **kjære alle sammen**, 'dear all'.

Note 2 – **Alle** can take a possessive –s, in which case it is mostly used
determinatively:

Det er alles ansvar å skape et godt samfunn.
It is everybody's responsibility to create a good society.

Alt and **all** cannot take a possessive –s.

4.6.1.2 Alle

Pronominal **alle** typically refers to all people (4.6.1.1). However, if the relevant noun can be inferred from the context, **alle** may refer to other entities:

Hvor er det blitt av sauene? De gresser bakom låven, alle sammen.
Where have the sheep gone? They are all [together] grazing behind the barn.

Hvorfor er det ingen romaner av Hovland her? Alle er utsolgt.
Why are there no novels by Hovland here? They are all sold out.

Alle can be followed by a noun in either the definite or the indefinite (plural); there can be a nuance in meaning.

Alle hunder eter kjøtt.	All dogs eat meat.
Alle jentene elsker fotball.	All the girls love football.

The former example with an indefinite noun applies to all dogs in the universe. The latter example with a definite noun is only a statement about all the girls in question. It applies to all members of a subgroup.

If **alle** is used as subject, the subject complement will be in the plural:

Alle virker sinte. Everybody seems angry.

4.6.1.3 Alt

Alt will invariably refer to things. It is often used determinatively, preceding neuters:

Alt melet trengs til kakene. All the flour is needed for the cakes.
Alt håp er ute. All hope is gone.

Donald, kjære nevø! Alt ditt er mitt, og alt mitt er mitt.
Donald, dear nephew! All that is yours is mine, and all that is mine is mine.

However, **alt** can also be used pronominally, meaning 'everything':

Det var en fin dag; alt gikk bra.
It was a nice day; everything went well.

Når alt kommer til alt, . . .
(*Lit.* When everything comes about.) At the end of the day, . . .

If **alt** is used as a subject, the subject complement will be in the neuter singular:

Alt føles meningsløst. Everything feels pointless.

Note that **alt** can be used even when referring back to a common gender noun if the noun is non-count. (Compare **det**, 4.2.4.6.)

Det var ikke noe honning igjen, for Brumm hadde spist opp alt.
There was no honey left, because Pooh had eaten everything (all of it).

Alt can be followed by a noun in either the definite or the indefinite singular. When it is followed by a noun in the indefinite, we are dealing with a general statement:

> **Alt øl inneholder vann.**   All beer contains water.

When followed by a noun in the definite, reference is made to a subgroup (cf. 4.6.1.2):

> **Alt ølet vi hadde, er borte**   All the beer we had is gone.

Note – **Allting** 'everything' can often be used as a synonym for **alt**, but **allting** is informal.

> **Alt/Allting er bra.**   Everything is fine.

However, **allting** is never followed by a noun, **alt** often is.

4.6.1.4 All

All used with a (feminine or masculine) count noun will often correspond to English 'every':

> **Du har all grunn til å være trist.**
> You have every reason to be sad.

4.6.1.5 Samtlige 'all, all of'

Unlike **alle**, **samtlige** is very formal. It is only followed by nouns in the indefinite plural.

> **Statsministeren har innkalt samtlige statsråder til et hastemøte.**
> The Prime Minister has called all ministers to an urgent meeting.

> **Samtlige fantastiske romaner vil bli inndratt.**
> All fantasy novels will be confiscated.

This word is rarely used as a pronoun.

4.6.1.6 Hele 'all', 'the whole', 'the entire'

Hele can be used as a determiner, normally followed by a noun in the definite singular.

Hele dagen satt Langbein og tenkte.
All day Goofy sat pondering.

Hele familien var i full sving.   All the family was in full swing.
Han sølte øl over hele meg.   He spilled beer all over me.

| 4.6.2 | *Words meaning* 'many, much'

The central words here are **mange**, 'many' and **mye**, 'much'. Mye is used before non-count nouns, **mange** before count nouns. Both can be used both pronominally and determinatively (Compare **noen** and **noe**, 4.6.3.).

| 4.6.2.1 | **Mye** '*much, a lot of*'

(a) **Mye** is used before mass nouns:

Det er mye trøst i en hund.
There is great consolation in a dog.

Det var ikke mye vann igjen i brønnen.
There was not much water left in the well.

Mye can also be used in front of a normally countable noun when that noun is used as if it were a non-count noun:

Cairn terrier er mye hund i en liten kropp.
The Cairn Terrier is a lot of dog in a little body.

Note – In informal language, **mye** can also occur before countables:

Der det er mye jenter, er det også mye gutter.
Where there are many [*lit.* much] girls, there will also be many [*lit.* much] boys.

(b) **Mye** can be used in front of adjectives in the neuter, and unlike English, Norwegian need not add a following word:

Det er mye godt å si om ham.
There are many good things [*lit.* much good] to say of him.

Mor mi har opplevd mye trist.
My mother has experienced a lot that is sad. [*lit.* much sad]

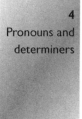

(c) **Mye** can also be used alone (pronominally), similarly to English 'a lot':

Her er det mye jeg har lyst til å si.
There are many things [*lit.* much] I'd like to say here.

Mye taler for at regjeringen må gå.
Many things [*lit.* much] indicate that the cabinet will have to step down.

4.6.2.2 *Mange 'many'*

(a) As its meaning indicates, **mange** is used before count nouns in the plural:

Mange nordmenn går på ski i påska.
Many Norwegians go skiing at Easter.

Dette har hendt mange ganger.
This has happened many times.

If a normally uncountable noun is treated as a countable, **mange** can precede it:

Det er mange øl som passer til pinnekjøtt.
There are many beers [i.e. kinds of beer] that go well with dried mutton rib.

(b) **Mange** can also be used before an adjective only, which will then be in the plural. Normally, the reference will be to people:

Dette gjorde mange unge frustrert.
This made many young (people) frustrated.

(c) **Mange** can also be used as a pronoun, usually referring to people:

Mange sier at Voldemort er underveis.
Many (people) say that Voldemort is on the move/coming.

Mange, whether alone or before an adjective only, can also refer to inanimates, if the noun is easily accessible from the context:

Veit du om noen hus som er til salgs nå? Ja, mange. Mange dyre og noen billige.
Do you know any houses that are up for sale now? Yes, a lot. Many expensive ones and some cheap ones.

(d) **Manges** is only found determinatively in set phrases:

etter manges mening   in the opinion of many

4.6.2.3 *(En) masse* 'lots of'

(En) masse is found primarily in front of non-count nouns and countable inanimate nouns. It is colloquial, especially without the determiner **en**:

Lammet har (en) masse ull. The sheep has plenty of wool.
Skrue har (en) masse eiendommer. Scrooge has lots of properties.

One can occasionally also find **masse** in front of countable animates:

Plutselig kommer (en) masse gutter løpende inn.
Suddenly, a lot of boys come running in.

4.6.3 **Noen, noe** 'some, somebody; any, anybody'

4.6.3.1 Usage and inflection of **noen**, etc

(a) These words can be used both determinatively and pronominally. With a determinative function, **noen** is used both with nouns in the singular and plural, **noe** normally only with non-count nouns in the singular. Like **ingen** (4.6.6.2), **noen** does not usually combine with a neuter in the singular. **Noen** and **noe** do not inflect for case, but for gender; **noe** can be considered the neuter of **noen**. Compare:

Det er ikke noe fly. That is no plane (neuter).
Det er ikke noen fugl. That is no bird (common gender)

The relation between **noen** and **noe** is complicated, however. In isolation, they will be interpreted as animate and inanimate respectively:

Det er noen utenfor. There is somebody outside.
Det er noe utenfor. There is something outside.

(b) When used as a determiner, **noen** is typically used with count nouns in the plural:

Da kom det noen gale vitenskapsmenn.
Then some mad scientists appeared.

Noen ganger skremmer du meg faktisk.
Sometimes you actually scare me.

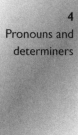

(c) If the sentence is negated, **noen** is commonly used with count nouns in the singular:

Dr. Frankenstein kjenner ikke noen forsker fra Ruritania.
Dr. Frankenstein does not know any scientist from Ruritania.

Again, combining **noen** with a plural noun is common:

Dr. Frankenstein kjenner ikke noen forskere fra Ruritania.
Dr. Frankenstein does not know any scientists from Ruritania.

(The alternative in the singular, **ikke noen forsker**, is used only if there has already been talk about one specific scientist.)

(d) As a pronoun, **noen** will normally refer to people (Compare **alle**, 4.6.1.2, **mange** 4.6.2.2):

Noen vil alltid klage.   Some (people) will always complain.
Det er ikke noen hjemme. There is nobody (*lit.* not anybody) home

If the relevant noun is easily inferred from the context, however, **noen** can also be used to refer to non-humans:

Liker du Bent Hamers filmer? Ja, jeg liker noen.
Do you like Bent Hamer's films? Yes, I like some [of them].

4.6.3.2 | *English 'some – any'*

Norwegian does not show any contrast quite like the English contrast between 'some' and 'any' (and related words, such as 'somebody', 'something'; 'anybody', 'anything'); normally, both these words translate with **noen**:

Are there any slices of bread left?	**Er det noen brødskiver igjen?**
Yes, there are some in the cupboard.	**Ja, det er noen i skapet.**
They do not know any enforcers.	**De kjenner ikke noen torpedoer.**
They only know some vicars.	**De kjenner bare noen prester.**

Noen can also be used to mean 'anybody whatsoever':

Barnet ville ikke dele faren med noen.
The child did not want to share its father with anybody.

Hun arbeidet hardere og bedre enn noen mann.
She worked harder and better than any man.

Note – In English, one may use 'some' to convey that the noun in question
has excellent qualities (or, ironically, the opposite):

That is some house you've got here!
She is some woman!

Norwegian uses **noe til, for en/ei/et, litt av en/ei/et** to express this:

Det er noe til hus du har her! For et hus du har her.
Hun er litt av ei dame/Hun er noe til dame/For ei dame.

Note – English 'any', meaning 'whatever', translates typically as **en, et**
(determinatively) **hvem, hva** (pronominally) **som helst**:

Do you have a book? Any book will do.
Har du ei bok? Hvilken som helst bok går bra.

Ask any passer-by in Cleveland . . .
Spør en hvilken som helst forbipasserende i Cleveland . . .

Anybody could have done this job.
Hvem som helst kunne gjort denne jobben.

They are willing to pay us anything.
De er villige til å betale oss hva som helst.

4.6.4 **Noe** *'some, something; a part of; a little'*

4.6.4.1

This word is used as both determiner and pronoun. It is used before neuter
nouns, and before non-count nouns, regardless of gender:

Har du noe mel å låne bort?   *Neuter, non-count*
Have you any flour I could borrow?

Det er ikke noe hus.   *Neuter, count*
That is no house.

Har du noe ull?   *Common, non-count*
Have you any wool?

Noe can also be used before count nouns, if they are treated as non-count:

Det er noe terrier i denne hunden. There is some terrier in this dog.

Noe can be used before adjectives:

Det er noe rart med denne bilen.
There is something odd (wrong) with this car.

Er det noe nytt?	Is there any news?
Noe så ergerlig!	(Oh) how annoying!

Pronominally, **noe** can be used alone:

Noe er galt.	Something is wrong.
Er det noe?	Is something the matter?

Note – **Noe** can also be used to mean 'slightly', 'a little':

Argumentasjonen virket noe enkel.
The argument seemed slightly simplistic.

4.6.4.2

Noenting is a near-synonym of **noe**, but **noenting** is informal.

Jeg har ikke hørt noe.	I have not heard anything.
Jeg har ikke hørt noenting.	I have not heard anything.

While **noe** can precede a noun, **noenting** cannot. **Noenting** can, however, precede an adjective, even if this is rare:

Jeg har ikke hørt noenting nytt, jeg.
Me, I have not heard anything new/any news.

4.6.5 Somme 'some'; somt, 'something'

See also 2.2.2.3.

Somme kjerringer er slike.
Some womenfolk/wives are like that.

Somme sier at kvinner er fra Mars og menn fra Venus.
Some say that women are from Mars and men from Venus.

Somt er bra, somt er dårlig.
Something is good, something is bad.

Somme can be used as both pronoun and determiner, **somt** only as a pronoun. Both are rare in present-day Bokmål. **Noe/n** is used instead.

4.6.6 | **Ingen** *'nobody', 'no', 'none'*

4.6.6.1

This word can be used both as a pronoun and as a determinative.

Ingen likte Sniffs nye roman.
Nobody liked Snoopy's new novel.

Ingen barn er like.
No children are alike.

Ingen trær vokser inn i himmelen.
No tree (*lit.* trees) will grow into the sky, i.e. there is a limit to everything.

When used as a pronoun, **ingen** is normally used of people (like **alle**, 4.6.1.2, **mange** 4.6.2.2, **noen**, 4.6.3.1 (d)), but not necessarily:

Ingen liker å få høre sannheten.
Nobody likes to be told the truth.

Det er ingen hjemme.   There is nobody home.

Av alle biler jeg har hatt, har ingen vært verre enn denne.
Of all cars that I have owned, none has been worse than this one

When **ingen** is used as a subject, there is some vacillation over whether the agreeing complement should be in the singular or plural:

Ingen er bare snill.   Nobody is only kind.
Ingen av dem er bare snille.   None of them is only kind.

4.6.6.2

Used as a determinative, **ingen** can precede (feminine or) masculine nouns in the singular or, in the plural, nouns of any gender – **ingen jente** (fem sg);

ingen gutt (masc sg); ingen jenter (fem pl); ingen gutter (masc pl); ingen jorder (neut pl).

Ingen does not combine with a neuter in the singular, however. If the noun following is clearly a neuter singular, ikke noe will be used instead. Thus, we find ingen mann, 'no man' (masculine or common), but ikke noe tre, 'no tree' (neuter). Note that ikke noen mann is also perfectly possible; i.e. the construction with ikke noen (noe) can be used in all genders and both numbers.

Note – An alternative to ikke noe is intet (intet tre), but this is rather literary and rarely used these days.

4.6.6.3

If an object (or a complement) begins with ingen (or intet), it will have to occur before the non-finite verb, if there is one.

> **Hun har ingenting sett og ingenting hørt.**
> She has seen nothing and heard nothing.
> *Object before non-finite verb*

> **Vi har ingen sommer hatt.**
> We have had no summer.
> *Object before non-finite verb*

If the object begins with ikke, by contrast, it can occur after the non-finite verb, in the 'normal' object position cf. 10.7.3.2.

> **Hun har ikke sett noe og ikke hørt noe.**
> She has seen nothing and heard nothing.
> *Object after non-finite verb, normal word order*

An object or a potential subject beginning with ingen (etc.) will not occur after an adverbial:

> **Hun skrev ingenting ned**. Cf. **Hun skrev ikke ned noe.**
> She wrote nothing down.

4.6.7 | Hver 'each', 'every'; enhver 'each, any'

4.6.7.1

Hver translates into English as both 'each' and 'every'. If used determinatively, it inflects for gender according to the noun it precedes (common gender hver, neuter hvert). It only precedes nouns in the singular.

Hver eneste dag tenkte Geoff på Katya.
Every single day Geoff thought about Katya.

Hvert år kommer det nye epler.
Each year there are new apples.

De tok to epler hver.
They took two apples each.

Hver tar sin, så tar jeg min.
Each takes his/hers, so I take mine.

The neuter of **hver** is **hvert**:

Etter hvert kast drakk dartspilleren litt øl.
After each throw the dart player drank a little beer.

Notice the idiom:

etter hvert   in time, gradually

4.6.7.2

Enhver (neuter **ethvert**) is less used, and somewhat formal. **Enhver** is used as a pronoun and as determiner, **ethvert** in practice only as a determiner:

Det må enhver kunne forstå.
That everybody should be able to understand.

For enhver ansvarlig samfunnsborger er dette uakseptabelt.
For any responsible citizen, this is unacceptable.

Dette kan ethvert barn forstå.
This any child can understand.

Note – **for enhver pris**, at any cost; **noe for enhver smak**, something for every taste.

4.6.8 | *Other quantifiers*

4.6.8.1 | *Få 'a few', færre, færrest*

Få is fewer than **noen** (4.6.3), by its meaning. Determinatively, it is used with count nouns:

Her er noen få utvalgte klassikere.
Here are a few select (*lit.* chosen) classics.

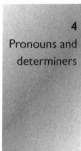
Det var få professorer som brydde seg om studentene den gangen.
There were few professors caring for the students in those days.

When the relevant noun is not readily available from the context, i.e. when få is used pronominally, it will normally refer to people:

Mange er kalt, men få er utvalgt.
Many are called, but few are chosen.

Færre, færrest are the comparative and superlative of **få.**

Få and **færre** can be used pronominally:

Få vil lese boka; færre vil betale for det.
Few want to read the book; (even) fewer are willing to pay for it.

Unlike **færre, færreste** requires another determiner.

De færreste er egentlig onde.   Only very few are really evil.

4.6.8.2 | *Litt, lite* 'a little', *mindre* 'less', *minst* 'least'

The words **litt, lite** 'a little' can both serve as quantifiers:

Vil du ha litt kaffe?	Would you like some coffee?
Ja, jeg tar litt, jeg.	Yes, I'll have a little.
Det er litt kaffe igjen.	There is a little coffee left.
Det er lite kaffe igjen.	There is little coffee left.

There will be less coffee left if **lite** is used than if **litt** is used.

Litt can also be used adverbially, meaning 'a little, slightly'

Vent litt!   Wait a little!

Both **litt** and **lite** are historically related to the adjective **liten** 'little, small', but **litt** has become an independent word; only **lite** can be seen as the neuter of **liten** today (cf. 2.1.3.4).

Also **mindre**, 'less' and **minst**, 'least' can quantify:

Dessverre drikker han mindre kaffe enn øl.
Sadly, he drinks less coffee than beer.

Hun drikker minst akevitt.
She drinks the least acquavit.

Notice that **minst** can also mean 'at least':

Hun drikker minst halvannen liter vann om dagen.
She drinks at least 1.5 litres of water per day.

4.6.8.3 *Flere* 'several', *flest*

Flere (also **fler**) and **flest** may be considered the comparative and superlative forms respectively of **mange**.

Det er flere som synger i kor, enn som spiller fotball.
More (people) sing in a choir than play football.

Flere statsråder vurderer et opprør.
Several ministers are considering a revolt.

De fleste blir tankefulle når døden nærmer seg.
Most (people) become pensive when death approaches.

De fleste bilene hadde bulker.
Most of the cars had dents.

De (aller) fleste biler har bulker.
Nearly all cars have dents.

Flere cannot be used after **de**, while **fleste** can only be used after **de**.

Joanna har flere beundrere enn Phil.
Joanna has more admirers than Phil.

Notice that **flest** can follow its noun:

Nordmenn flest var ikke så begeistret for Trump.
Most Norwegians were not very enthusiastic about Trump.
Compare: **De fleste nordmenn** ...

4.6.8.4 *Translating English 'more', 'most'*

(a) 'More' and 'most' with count nouns translate as **flere, flest, de fleste**:

Jeg kan ikke spise flere kaker.
I cannot eat any more cakes.

Jeg har mange CD-plater, men han har flest.
I have many CDs but he has most.

De fleste mennesker liker kysten.
Most people like the seaside.

(b) 'More' and 'most' with non-count nouns translate as **mer, mest, det meste**:

Vi bør spise mer frukt og grønnsaker.
We should eat more fruit and vegetables.

Kjøkkenet får mest sol om våren.
The kitchen gets most sun in the spring.

– Er det noe øl igjen? – Vi har drukket det meste.
'Is there any beer left?' 'We have drunk most of it.'

4.7 | Indefinite pronouns and evasion strategies

4.7.1 | Indefinite pronouns: Man, ens and others

Man, en, 'one' are sometimes referred to as indefinite pronouns, as they have a rather general meaning. The personal pronouns **du**, 'you (sg.)' and **de**, 'they' can also be used as indefinite pronouns in informal language. See 4.2.4.2, Note 1 and 4.2.4.9, Note 1 respectively.

4.7.1.1 | Man, 'one'

Man is restricted to the nominative; it can only be used as subject:

Man skal ikke plage andre.   One should not bother others.

For øvrig kan man gjøre hva man vil.
Apart from that one may do as one pleases.

Slikt noe gjør man da ikke!   Such things are not done!

If one needs a corresponding non-nominative, **seg** can be used:

Man bør vaske etter seg.   One should clean up after oneself.

| 4.7.1.2 | *En*, 'one' |

En is mostly found in the nominative:

En viser til Deres brev av 5. mai.
We/One refer to your letter dated May 5.

However, **en** is not restricted to the nominative. It can be found as an object (direct or indirect), and, rarely, after prepositions:

Det kan gi en hjemlengsel å drikke lunkent øl.
It may make one homesick to drink lukewarm beer.

Det er fint å ha en kjæreste som tenker på en.
It is nice to have a sweetheart that thinks of you (*lit.* one).

As with **man**, the reflexive **seg** combines with the indefinite pronoun **en**:

En bør vaske etter seg.   One should clean up after oneself.

Note – The determiner/indefinite article **en** (**ei**, **et**) is dealt with in 1.11.

| 4.7.1.3 | *Folk* |

Informally, the noun **folk** 'people' may be used pronominally:

Sett brødet på benken, så kan folk ta det de vil ha.
Put the bread on the bench, and then one (*lit.* people) may take what one wants (they want).

I nyere tid har man/folk blitt enige om at honning er sunt.
More recently, one/people agree that honey is good for you.

If **folk** is used as a subject, its subject complement is normally in the plural, cf. 2.2.3.1.

| 4.7.2 | *Personal pronouns and 'evasion'* |

In a number of instances, one may feel uncertain about pronominal usage in the third person singular, typically because one does not know the sex of the person referred to. (In English, this is well known from the debate on 'he', 'they', in examples such as 'the reader – he'.) In such instances, there are various 'evasion' (or avoidance) strategies. Consider the following:

Tjuven har tatt seg inn gjennom vinduet. *Han eller hun* har så stjålet hele kakefatet.
The thief has got in through the window. He or she has then stolen the entire plate of cakes.

Politiet var i kontakt med bakeren, men *denne* valgte ikke å anmelde forholdet til å begynne med.
The police have been in touch with the baker, but the latter chose not to press charges to begin with.

Seinere satte bakeren kakefatet inn med lim, slik at det ville feste seg til hendene på tjuven. Etter det var det lett for politiet å finne *vedkommende*.
Later, the baker glued the plate of cakes, so that it would stick to the thief's hands. After that, it was easy for the police to find the person concerned.

Det er ikke så lett å være student i dag. *De* er utsatt for så mange press og forventninger.
It is not so easy to be a student today. They are exposed to so many pressures and expectations.

Det er ikke lett å være lærer, heller. *Man/en/du* har så ulike studenter.
It is not so easy to be a teacher, either. One has/You have so many different students.

Vedkommende, han eller hun and denne are rather formal and mostly used in written language. De, man, en are not so stylistically marked; du is rather informal and perhaps best avoided in writing. See also 4.7.1.

If a person has been referred to with a neuter noun, 'evasion' becomes particularly acute, since to use the neuter pronoun det about a person seems offensive (4.2.4.3(c)). Such cases are rather rare, since nouns for human beings are typically non-neuter, but here are two examples:

Vitnet ble bedt om å komme fram, og hun tok plass i vitneboksen.
The witness was asked to step forward, and she took her place in the witness box.

Der kommer postbudet, og han smiler fra øre til øre.
There comes the postie, and he is smiling broadly.

An exception is the word **barn**, 'child', which may be referred to with **det**.
See also 1.2.4.1 Note 1.

4.8   Interrogative pronouns

4.8.1   *Hva 'what', hvem 'who'*

4.8.1.1

The indeclinable pronouns **hva** and **hvem** can usually be translated by
English 'what' and 'who' respectively, and are used in questions and interrogative clauses:

Hva har du tenkt å gjøre nå?	What do you intend to do now?
Hva tenker du på?	What are you thinking about?
Hvem blir president?	Who will be president?
Hvem smilte Smilla til?	Who did Smilla smile at?

Hva and **hvem** are of neuter and common gender respectively:

Hva er godt?	What is good?
Hvem er god?	Who is good?

The interrogatives **hva, hvem** may introduce subclauses. If **hvem** or **hva** are
the subject of the clause, they must be followed by **som**:

Jeg veit hvem jeg tror på.   **hvem** is object
I know who I believe in.

De så hva som hendte.   **hva** is subject
They saw what happened.

See also 9.4.1.2.

Jeg veit ikke hva jeg skal ha på meg på festen.
I do not know what to wear at the party.

Hva hun kan si, slutter aldri å forbause meg.
What she can say, never ceases to amaze me.

Gjør hva du vil! Gå hvor du vil!
Do what you want! Go where you want!

Note – There are many dialectal variants of these pronouns. Instead of **hva**, one may hear e.g. **kva, ka, å, hått**, instead of **hvem, kem, ken, kven, håkken**.

Hva is not used determinatively. English 'what' in determinative use can be translated **hva for en (ei, et, noen)** or **hvilken (hvilket, hvilke)**:

Which hand do you want? **Hvilken/hva for en hånd vil du ha?**

See 4.8.4.1–4.8.4.3.

4.8.1.2

Note that **hvem** can also be used when picking out animates, as in the following example, where English has 'which':

Begge bryterne var sterke, men hvem av dem vant?
Both the wrestlers were strong, but which of them won?

If the interrogative is immediately followed by an **av**-phrase, it is more common to use **hvilken**, etc. in the written language:

Hvilken/hvem av bryterne kommer til å vinne?
Which one of the wrestlers is going to win?

English uses 'one' after 'which', whereas Norwegian does not use **en**, 'one' after **hvem** or **hvilken**.

Hva can also be used to indicate that one has not heard what the speaker said, comparable with English 'I beg your pardon'.

Note – Placed finally, **hva** can be used in a manner resembling English tag questions.

Det var noe til scoring, hva? That was some goal, wasn't it/eh?

4.8.1.3 'Whichever'

English 'whatever, whoever' can usually be translated with **hva (som) enn**, **hvem (som) enn**:

whatever it may take **hva som enn måtte kreves**
whoever he may be **hvem han enn måtte være**

4.8.1.4

Notice the following fixed expressions:

Hva verre er ...	And then, something worse ...
Hva mer er ...	And besides ...
Hva meg/det angår ...	As far as I/that is concerned ...

Hva can be used to mean approximately the same thing as **det som**:

Etter hva vi nå vet ...	According to what we now know ...
Etter det som vi nå vet ...	According to what we now know ...

4.8.2 *Position of interrogatives*

The interrogatives are often placed at the front of a sentence, but if there are several interrogatives, not all can come first:

Hva sa hvem på seminaret?   Who said what at the seminar?

In the spoken language in particular, one may find echo-questions where interrogatives do not come first:

A: Tristan og Isolde, du liksom. Jeg så Tristan kysse Julie på seminaret! B: Tristan kysset *hvem* på seminaret?
A: Tristan and Isolde, my foot. I saw Tristan kiss Juliet at the seminar!
B: Tristan kissed *who* at the seminar?

Such questions can express surprise, even incredulity.

If, in a question, **hva** or **hvem** is governed by a preposition, it will still usually not be preceded by that preposition (cf. 'Prepositional stranding', 7.1.3.3).

Hva tenker du på?	What are you thinking about?
	(Extremely unlikely: **På hva tenker du?**)
Hvem var du forelsket i?	Who were you infatuated by?

4.8.3 **Translating English** *'whose'*

In present-day Norwegian, there is no straightforward equivalent to English 'whose', as in 'Whose is this?'. (The word **hvis** in this sense is found in older literature (**Hvis er dette?**), but it is now obsolete.) The normal expression today is:

Hvem er dette sitt? Or: **Hvem sitt er dette?**

Hvis is obsolete also in determinative use. 'Whose money is this?' will by twenty-first-century authors not be rendered as **Hvis penger er dette?** The normal way of asking this today would be:

Hvem sine penger er dette?
Hvem eier disse pengene?

In English, 'whose' may also introduce a relative clause:

Stapleton, whose dog scared poor Sir Charles, was a crook.

Again, hvis used to be possible:

Stapleton, hvis hund skremte stakkars Sir Charles, var en skurk.

But again, hvis is now obsolete – if less so in this function than as an interrogative. In order to translate from English, some circumlocution may be required:

Stapleton, som eide den hunden som skremte stakkars Sir Charles, var en skurk.

A politician whose name everybody knows...
En politiker alle kjenner navnet på ...

4.8.4 | Hvilken, hva for en 'which'

4.8.4.1 | Determinative use

Masc./Fem.	Neuter	Plural
hvilken	**hvilket**	**hvilke**
hva for en	**hva for et**	**hva for noen**

English can use 'what' followed by a noun (determinatively), as in 'What food do you like?', 'What plans do we have?'. In Bokmål, one does not normally combine **hva** + noun, but there are several ways of constructing such questions, e.g. by means of **hvilken, hvilket, hvilke; hva for en/noen** + noun. **Hva for en** is used less in writing than **hvilken** (**hvilket, hvilke**). There is no genitive form in –s.

Hva for en, hvilken are typically used with count nouns (or non-count nouns used as countables).

> **Hvilken tegneserie liker du best?** (masc.)
> Which cartoon do you like the most?

> **Hva for (en) tegneserie liker du best?**

> **Hvilken bok vil du ha?** (fem.)
> Which book do you want?

> **Hva for (ei/en) bok vil du ha?**

> **Hvilket hus bor Langbein i?** (n.)
> Which house does Goofy live in?

> **Hva for et hus bor Langbein i?**

> **Hvilke elever ønsket å komme i hvilke hus?** (pl.)
> Which pupils wanted to come into which houses?

> **Hva for (noen) elever ønsket å komme i hvilke hus?**

Hva for en, hva for noe are very often 'split':

> **Hva liker du for noen biler, da?** What cars do you like, then?

English 'what' can also be used to mean 'what kind of', corresponding to Norwegian **hva for slags**, as in:

> **Hva for slags bil kjører du?** What (kind of) car do you drive?

4.8.4.2 | *In exclamations*

Whereas English uses 'what' in exclamations, such as 'What a day!', **for en (et)** is the normal Norwegian translation. Compare:

What a day! **For en dag!**

> **Å, for en strålende morgen** . . .
> Oh, what a wonderful morning . . .

> **For en idrettsmann han er, Bjørndalen.**
> What an athlete he is, Bjørndalen.

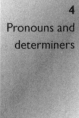

It is also possible to use **hvilken**, but this is more literary:

Hvilken idrettsmann han er, Bjørndalen.
What an athlete he is, Bjørndalen.

4.8.4.3 | *Pronominal use*

Hvilken, hva for en are not only used determinatively; they can also serve a pronominal function:

Hvilken vil du ha?   Which one do you want?
Hva for et foretrekker du?   Which one do you prefer?

In the spoken language, one may often find **hva for noe** where the written language would prefer **hva**:

Hva er det du sier for noe?   What is that you are saying?
Hva er det for noe?   What is that?

Note – The question words **hvorfor**, 'why'; **hvordan**, 'how' are seen as adverbs in this grammar, see 6.2.2.5 and 6.3.5 respectively. On this point, we differ from *NRG*.

4.8.4.4 | *In relative clauses:* **som** *or* **hvilket?**

The use of **hvilket** to introduce relative clauses is mainly obsolete, but not in examples like the following, in which **hvilket** refers back to the whole event denoted by the main clause:

USA protesterte heftig mot den russiske invasjonen, hvilket vel ikke var uventet.
The USA objected strongly against the Russian invasion, which was not unexpected.

Hun bestemte seg for å bli veganer, hvilket gledet hennes far.
She decided to become a vegan, which delighted her father.

Alternatively, **noe som** can be used:

USA protesterte heftig mot den russiske invasjonen, noe som ikke var uventet.
The USA objected strongly against the Russian invasion, which was not unexpected.

Hun bestemte seg for å bli veganer, noe som gledet hennes far.
She decided to become a vegan, something which delighted her father.

Note that **som** alone cannot be used in such cases.

Both **hvilket** and **noe som** in these constructions are fairly formal. A less formal construction here is just to coordinate (**USA protesterte, og det var ikke uventet; Hun ble veganer, og det gledet hennes far.**)

4.9 Other pronouns and determiners

4.9.1 Begge, både *'both'*

4.9.1.1

Norwegian has two words that translate as English 'both', **både** and **begge**. Both are indeclinable. When English 'both' is followed by 'and', in co-ordinations, Norwegian uses the conjunction **både** (cf. 9.2.2.3).

Både laks og torsk er godt.	Both salmon and cod taste good.
Livet er både vondt og godt.	Life is both good and bad.

Både broren og søstera var sure.
Both the brother and the sister were grumpy.

4.9.1.2

When English **both** can be replaced by 'the two, both of them', Norwegian uses **begge**, which is a pronoun:

Begge skulle seinere bli enda surere.
Both would later become even grumpier.

Jeg er glad i begge, likevel.
I am fond of (them) both, nevertheless.

Begge can be used determinatively (**både** cannot):

Begge søsknene var sure. Both siblings were grumpy.

Vil du ha honning eller syltetøy? Takk, begge deler!
Would you like honey or jam? Thank you, both (things), (please)!

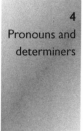

If combined with other pronouns/determiners, **begge** comes first:

I løpet av dagen har *begge de andre* imamene våre sykmeldt seg.
In the course of the day, both our other imams have called in sick.

4.9.1.3

Note, however, **de begge**, which can only be used when no noun follows (and usually about people), versus **begge de**, which may be used whether a noun follows or not:

Vi har snakket med dem begge.	We have talked to them both.
Begge de hestene har vunnet mye.	Both horses have won a lot.
Begge de har vunnet mye.	They have both won a lot.
Han passet begge de hestene.	He looked after both the horses.

Begge can take the possessive –s, and is then typically used before a noun, even if it can also be used alone:

Det er i begges interesse å unngå rettssak.
It is in the interest of both (parties) to avoid a trial.

Den er begges. It belongs to them both.

Note: **oss begge, de begge, dere begge** alongside **begge oss, begge dere.**

4.9.2 **Samme** *'same'*

This word is mostly used determinatively, and it can only be used in a definite noun phrase. It can be followed by an indefinite or a definite noun, and it can, but does not have to, be preceded by a determiner. For example, **samme dag, samme dagen** and **den samme dagen** all mean 'the same day'. However, **samme dagen** is slightly colloquial; **samme dag** is somewhat literary, **den samme dagen** is perhaps the 'neutral' option.

Samme can be used with nouns irrespective of gender and number:

Den samme hesten vant.	The same horse won.
De samme hestene vant.	The same horses won.

Det var (det) samme året som vi ble gift.
That was the same year as we got married.

Samme can be used with count nouns (above) and with non-count:

Det er samme hat som kommer til uttrykk her.
It is the same hatred that is expressed here.

Note – the idioms **samme for meg**, I don't care', **samme ulla** [*lit.* the same wool] 'the same kind'

De er av samme ulla.   They are cut from the same cloth.

4.9.3 **Annen** *'other'*

4.9.3.1

This word agrees in gender, number and definiteness, with the noun to which it is juxtaposed:

Common	Neuter	Definite/Plural
en annen mann	**et annet hus**	**den andre mannen**
		det andre huset
		andre menn
		de andre bøkene

Trans. another man, another house, the other man, the other house, other men, the other books

4.9.3.2

Annen can be used pronominally, but it can also be used determinatively:

Henrik og en annen vant.   Henrik and another won.
Henrik og en annen gutt vant.   Henrik and another boy won.

Note – The alternative feminine form **anna** and the alternative neuter form **anna** are both very rare in Bokmål.

Used after another determiner, **annen** may often correspond to English 'else' or 'different':

Det var noe annet jeg ville snakke med deg om.
There is [*lit.* was] something else I wanted to talk to you about.

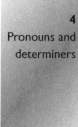

Og nå over til noe helt annet.
And now for something completely different.

Used after another pronoun/determiner, **annen** and **andre** can take a possessive –s (**annet** cannot):

Det var en annens glass du nettopp tømte.
It was another's glass you just emptied.

Det er alltid de andres feil.
It is always the others' (somebody else's) fault.

Andre can (unlike **annen**) also take a possessive –s without a preceding determiner:

Andres barn har han alltid funnet feil ved.
Other people's children he has always found fault with.

Note the fixed expressions:

Den enes død, den andres brød.
One man's death is what another man lives by.

På den ene side, på den annen side.
On the one hand, on the other hand.

<hr>

4.9.3.3

Translating English 'another' can sometimes be difficult. Note the following:

When English 'another' combines with expressions of quantity, Norwegian uses **en . . . til**, 'one more' or **enda en . . .** , 'another one . . .':

I had to wait another half an hour.
Jeg måtte vente en halvtime til/Jeg måtte vente enda en halvtime.

The English idiom 'one another' usually translates as **hverandre** (cf. 4.5.4):

They like one another a lot.   **De liker hverandre godt.**

4.9.4 | Egen 'own'

The neuter of **egen** is **eget** (**–n** is dropped before the neuter suffix **–t** in **eget** as in **annet**, but nowhere else), the plural/definite is **egne**. It can serve as an 'intensifier':

Dette er vår egen hytte/bil.	This is our own cabin/car.
Dette er vårt eget hus.	This is our own house.

Dette er våre egne nyskrevne tekster.
These are our own recently written texts.

Note – There is also an adjective **egen** (neuter **egent**), which means 'peculiar, difficult, stubborn': **Han virker nokså egen** 'He seems rather difficult.'

4.9.5 | Sånn, slik 'such'

These words are near-synonyms, but **sånn** is much more used in Bokmål and often perceived as being less formal than **slik**. They are difficult to classify, grammatically, but they can be used adverbially: **Ikke gjør det sånn/ slik!** 'Don't do it like that!'

However, they can also be used determinatively, and then they typically inflect for gender and number:

En sånn bil bør vi ha.	Such a car we should have. (masc.)
Ei sånn klokke vil jeg ha.	I want such a watch. (fem.)
Et sånt hus ønsker jeg meg.	Such a house I wish. (neuter)
Sånne biler og klokker er fine.	Such cars and houses are fine. (pl.)

Slike jenter, det vil gamle Norge ha.
Such girls, that is what old Norway wants! (Bjørnson) (pl.)

Sånn and **slik** are used only in the indefinite singular and plural (not in the definite singular).

In principle, **sånt** is the neuter of **sånn**:

Et sånt samfunn vil vi ikke ha.	Such a society we do not want.

In practice, however, **sånn** as determinative is often used uninflected also in the neuter, though this is not recommended in writing:

Vi kan ikke ha et sånn samfunn.   We cannot have such a society.

When used predicatively, **sånn** does not inflect for number or gender:

De er sånn (*sånne).   They are like that.
Barnet er sånn (*sånt).   The child is like that.

Chapter 5

Verbs

5.1 Introduction

5.1.1 Every sentence has a finite verb

The verb is central in Norwegian grammar, for two reasons. Firstly, every complete Norwegian sentence must contain at least one finite verb. By 'finite verb', we understand those verb forms that can 'finish' the sentence, namely the present tense, the past tense and the imperative (see also 10.3.3). Here, then, are three complete Norwegian sentences:

Nora kjøper makroner.	Nora buys macaroons.
Nora kjøpte makroner.	Nora bought macaroons.
Kjøp makroner, Nora!	Buy macaroons, Nora!

If, by contrast, there is no 'finite' verb form (as in a newspaper headline, e.g. **To drept i bilulykke**, 'Two killed in car accident'), we do not speak of a sentence. One finite verb alone may be sufficient to speak of a sentence, as in the imperative **Skyt!**, 'Shoot!'. Secondly, although Norwegian, like English, is fairly 'poor' in terms of inflection, the verb is richer in inflection than most other word classes.

5.1.2 Actions and states

Verbs usually denote actions and states, in Norwegian as in English. Compare e.g. **danse**, 'dance'; **hoppe**, 'jump'; **kjøpe**, 'buy'; **slå**, 'hit', all denoting actions, and **hete**, 'be called'; **være**, 'be'; **synes**, 'think, feel', denoting states. The examples are given in the infinitive which, just as in English, is normally used as the 'look-up form' (citation form) of the verb in grammars and dictionaries (see also 5.2.1.1(a)).

5.1.3 | Tense

Norwegian verbs inflect for tense. If a word shows tense inflection, it must be a verb, and practically every verb can be inflected for tense. The basic tense opposition is, as in English, the one between the present and the past tense. Compare **danser** ('dances', present) – **danset** (past); **hopper** ('jumps', present) – **hoppet** (past); **kjøper** ('buys', present) – **kjøpte** (past); **heter** ('is called', present) – **hette** (past); **er** ('is', present) – **var** (past).

The reason for the labels 'present' and 'past' is that these forms typically anchor the sentence to the current situation and a previous or somehow non-current situation respectively. Cf. 5.3.3–5.3.5. Compare the following examples:

> **Theresa May er statsminister nå som jeg skriver dette.**
> Theresa May is Prime Minister now as I'm writing this.   *Present*

> **Harold Wilson var statsminister i 1965.**
> Harold Wilson was Prime Minister in 1965.   *Past*

> **Hermine kysser Ronny nå.**
> Hermione kisses (is kissing) Ron now.   *Present*

> **Gulla kysset Harry i går.**
> Ginny kissed Harry yesterday.   *Past*

5.1.4 | No inflection for person or number

Norwegian verbs do not inflect for number or person, i.e. in contrast to English, agreement for number and person is not an issue for the verb. A verb has the same inflection no matter what its subject is:

> **Han danser.**   He dances.
> **Vi danser.**   We dance.
> **Du danser.**   You (singular) dance.
> **De danser.**   They dance.

5.1.5 | Periphrastic tenses

As in English, there are 'periphrastic tenses'. These are constructions with both a main verb and an auxiliary that serve a function roughly analogous to that of the inflectional verb forms present and past. The periphrastic tenses include the present perfect (**hun har danset**, 'she has danced'), the past perfect (**hun hadde danset**, 'she had danced') and others. There is both an inflection on the (finite) auxiliary and a non-finite main verb (a supine). See further 5.3.6 and 5.3.7.

5.1.6 | Mood and voice

While tense (dealt with further in 5.3) may be thought of as the central inflectional category for Norwegian verbs, mood (5.4) and voice (5.6, also known as 'diathesis') are also relevant. The category of aspect is not expressed inflectionally; there is (as in Swedish and Danish) nothing in Norwegian quite like the English distinction between 'he sings' and 'he is singing'.

5.2 Conjugations

Conjugations are verbal inflection classes. They do not carry meaning in quite the same way as e.g. tense does. While the contrast between **hun danser**, 'she dances' and **hun danset**, 'she danced' may carry meaning, there is usually no difference in meaning between different inflection classes. Consider an English example: Americans may say they 'snuck', the English may insist on 'sneaked'; there is no further difference in meaning involved. This does not mean, however, that weak and strong inflection classes are totally insignificant. For some reason, such errors are often noticed, even if they seldom create problems communicatively.

Note – In fact, there are links between conjugation and meaning when it comes to the transitive – intransitive 'verb pairs' and the fact that modals inflect in a rather special way. Cf. 5.5.2.1 and 5.4.2.1 below.

5.2.1 | Principal parts

5.2.1.1 | Introduction

(a) Norwegian dictionaries and grammars will normally represent the verb by its infinitive (the 'look-up form', see also 5.3.1.1). If more verb forms are listed, then it is traditional to list the four principal parts:

infinitive, present, past and supine. The present and the past are the most informative of these four, in that, if we know them, we have a good chance of predicting the rest of the paradigm (the list of inflected verb forms).

Here are two examples from the largest conjugation (inflection class):

Infinitive	Present	Past	Supine	
danse	**danser**	**danset**	**danset**	dance
		dansa	**dansa**	
hoppe	**hopper**	**hoppet**	**hoppet**	jump
		hoppa	**hoppa**	

(b) There is quite a lot of variation available in Norwegian orthography (cf. Introduction and 12.2), and the past tense and supine of **danse** illustrate this. Writers may choose whether to write **danset** or **dansa**. If they write **danset**, they are also advised to write **hoppet**.

(c) The *stem* is a construct of the grammarian, not an actually occurring verb form. The stem is that part of the verb (marked in italic below) to which inflexional suffixes are added. In the infinitive, for example, an –e is usually added to the stem:

dans+e	Weak class I	dance
kjøp+e	Weak class II	buy
skriv+e	Strong	write

There are some verbs whose stems end in a vowel, and no vowel is added to form the infinitive of such verbs:

spå	Weak class III	prophesy

The stem of a verb is identical to its imperative: **Dans! Kjøp! Skriv! Spå!**

(d) In addition to the principal parts, there are other members of the verb paradigm. The imperative is the most clearcut member, but the participles are often included.

Imperative	Present participle	Past participle
dans!	**dansende**	**danset**
hopp!	**hoppende**	**hoppet**

(e) It is a moot point whether we need to distinguish between the supine and past participle in Norwegian Bokmål. These two are more often than not identical, and many grammars treat both together as 'past participle'. If a distinction is made, as in this grammar, the term *supine* is used to refer to the indeclinable verb form that combines with forms of the auxiliary verb **ha**, 'have' (and **få**, 'get'). This may, for example, result in a present or past perfect:

Jeg har *malt* huset.	I have painted the house.
Han har *svidd* kjøttet.	He has burnt the meat.
Jeg fikk *malt* huset.	I had the house painted.
Donald hadde *ødelagt* mye.	Donald had destroyed a lot.

See further 5.3.6 and 5.3.7.

(f) The *past participle* can help form passives. See also 5.3.1.2, 5.6.1.2(b) and (c).

Huset ble malt i 1982.	The house was painted in 1982.
Huset er ødelagt.	The house is ruined.

Like an adjective, the past participle can also function as an attributive modifier of a noun. In that case, the past participle is inflected:

Han liker ikke *malte* jenter.	He does not like painted girls.
Det *ødelagte* huset står tomt.	The ruined house is empty.

Since **malte, ødelagte** differ from **malt, ødelagt,** we use two different labels here, but the two are clearly close.

(g) The *present participle* is most often used as an adjective (2.1.5.1(a)), but there are also nouns that look like present participles. See also 1.4.5.1(c), 5.3.13.1.

Boka er et *sviende* oppgjør.   *Adjectival use*
The book is a scathing criticism.

En handelsreisendes død   *Nominal use*
Death of a salesman (play by Arthur Miller)

The present participle can also be used verbally, however:

De ble *stående* tause sammen.
They were standing silent together.

(h) The *infinitive* functions either as a verb together with an auxiliary, or as a noun; in the latter function, it is preceded by the 'infinitive marker' å 'to'. See 5.3.1.5 and 5.3.1.6.

Vi skal synge gamle sanger.   We shall sing old songs.
Å synge er hyggelig.   To sing (Singing) is nice.

(j) The simple tenses, namely present and past, are marked on the verb itself; usually by an inflectional suffix (ending), cf. **han spiller,** 'he plays' vs. **han spilte,** 'he played'.

5.2.1.2 | Classes

(a) Strong and weak

The detailed classification of verbs can differ between grammars. However, the major distinction is between strong and weak verbs. The past tense of weak verbs has a syllabic suffix added to the stem; the past tense of strong verbs does not. Thus, weak verbs have more than one syllable in the past tense; strong verbs usually do not. With very few exceptions, strong verbs display a vowel change from the infinitive to the past and weak verbs do not.

Compare **danse,** 'dance' versus **drikke,** 'drink':

danse (infinitive) – **danset** (past)   weak
drikke (infinitive) – **drakk** (past)   strong

Essentially the same distinction can be made in English; for example, 'dance' is a weak verb, compare 'dance (infinitive) – dance*d*', while 'drink' is a strong verb, compare 'drink – dr*a*nk'. Compare the Norwegian verbs above. While it is fairly common in English grammars to refer to strong and weak verbs as 'irregular' and 'regular' respectively, this is not common practice in Norwegian grammar. While English has only one weak class vs. many strong ones, Norwegian has several classes of both weak and strong verbs.

(b) Main classes

Here is a first overview of the main classes we operate with in this grammar:

Class	Infinitive	Present	Past	Supine	Meaning
Weak I	**danse**	**danser**	**danset**	**danset**	dance
Weak IIa	**kjøpe**	**kjøper**	**kjøpte**	**kjøpt**	buy
Weak IIb	**bygge**	**bygger**	**bygde**	**bygd**	build
Weak III	**nå**	**når**	**nådde**	**nådd**	reach
Strong	**skrive**	**skriver**	**skrev**	**skrevet**	write

By classifying the verbs in this way, we try to systematise what might otherwise seem a bewildering variety. The major division is into three conjugations of weak verbs (I, II, III) and one of strong verbs. See 5.2.2–5.2.6 for further details.

(c) Weak classes

As the table in (b) above shows, weak verbs can be further classified on the basis of their past tense suffix.

Class I has the suffix –et added to the stem. Class I verbs also stand out from the rest in that their past tense and supine are invariably formally identical. Compare the class I verb **danset** (past) = **danset** (supine) with the class III verb **nådde** (past) ≠ **nådd** (supine).

Class III stands out by its past tense suffix –dde and by having monosyllabic infinitives and monosyllabic present tense forms; in contrast, class I and II verbs have infinitives and present tense forms of more than one syllable. By and large, it is therefore easy to recognise members of class III.

Class II verbs select either the suffix –te or the suffix –de in the past tense (and –t respectively –d in the supine). Compare **kjøpte** and **bygde**. The suffix –te is found if the final stem consonant is either unvoiced (as **p** is) or if it is **l, n, r**; we call this 'class IIa'. The suffix –de is usually found after stems ending in –**v**, –**g** or a diphthong; we refer to this as 'class IIb'. (See 5.2.3.2.)

(d) Weak and strong – number and frequency

Weak verbs are much more numerous than are strong ones. By one estimate, in a good dictionary there are 4,800 weak verbs and only some 200 strong ones. On the other hand, many strong verbs are among the most frequently occurring verbs in the language. Some strong verbs are so frequent in everyday language that it is good to learn their inflection by heart. Among the weak classes, class I has the most members and class III the fewest. Subclass IIa is much larger than IIb. While weak verbs are subdivided on the basis of their suffix (cf. above), strong verbs are subdivided on the basis of their vowel change (cf. below).

(e) Predicting forms

The present participle is formed in the same way for all verbs, whatever class they belong to; the suffix –ende is added to the stem. Compare **dansende, kjøpende, byggende, nående, skrivende.**

Excepting those verbs that have only one syllable in the infinitive, i.e. verbs from weak class III and some strong ones, the infinitive is also formed in the same way for all verbs, by adding the suffix –e to the stem. Compare **danse, kjøpe, bygge, skrive.** See also 5.2.2.3.

The infinitive and the present participle tell us less about the rest of the paradigm (they are inflectionally less informative) than the present and the past. If we see an infinitive **fjære** 'to feather', we cannot be quite sure of its past tense (compare **bære**, 'carry' – **bar** vs. **lære**, 'learn; teach' – **lærte**). If, by contrast, we see a past tense **fjæret**, the supine of this verb must be **fjæret**, its infinitive must be **fjære** and its present tense **fjærer** (i.e., it must be a weak class I verb).

The distribution between the classes in general, and between weak classes I and II in particular, can be difficult for the foreign learner. This is especially so if we only have the orthography and the infinitive to go by, cf. **fjære, bære, lære** above.

Things are not usually quite so difficult, however; many generalisations can be made on the basis of the form (shape) of the verb. In general, 'birds of a feather go together': A verb will often inflect like another verb with which it rhymes.

Weak class III verbs stand out from the other weak classes both in the infinitive and the present tense (cf. (c) above). If we know that **spå**, 'foretell, prophesy' (infinitive) is weak, then we can predict the present, past and supine straightaway (**spår** – **spådde** – **spådd**). Orthographically, class III verbs also stand out in the past tense by the suffix –dde. If we meet the past tense form **klådde**, 'groped', the verb must be a class III verb. If we know that the verb is a weak one, the supine suffix –dd also tells us the verb belongs to class III.

If the verb has three consonants stem-finally (e.g. **plystre**, 'whistle'), it can only belong to class I. If the infinitive ends in –**ere**, that verb can only belong to weak class IIa. Such verbs are numerous; examples include **inkludere**, 'include' and **multiplisere**, 'multiply', compare the past tenses **inkluderte, multipliserte**. If a weak verb has two consonants stem-finally, then it will probably belong to class I, cf. **vinke**,'wave' – **vinket, rappe**, 'nick, pinch' – **rappet**. This is only a rule of thumb, but useful.

If the verb has only one consonant in the end of the stem, i.e. if its vowel is long in speech, then it will probably belong to class II. Compare **slepe**, 'drag, pull' – **slepte** and **like**, 'like' – **likte**. This is, again, a rule of thumb.

Alternatively, a verb with two consonants in the end of the stem can be strong. However, it cannot belong to class III, as the stem of members of that class will invariably end in a vowel.

If we encounter the past tense of a verb, the rest of the paradigm is usually quite easy to deduce. If the past tense ends in –**et**, the verb belongs to weak class I; if it ends in –**dde**, the verb belongs to weak class III, and if the past tense ends in –**te** or –**de**, to IIa and IIb respectively.

Classes have little communicative effect. If, for example, a learner were to inflect the verb **slepe**, 'pull, drag' wrongly and produce the erroneous *slepet instead of the correct **slepte**, the chances are that a Norwegian will understand anyway.

| 5.2.1.3 | *Generalised suffixes*

Here is a general pattern of suffixes for Norwegian verbs. Number refer to conjugations. We omit a number of exceptions.

Infinitive: vowel (always), usually –**e** (weak classes I and II + most strong verbs)

Present tense: –**r** (always), usually preceded by –**e** (weak classes I and II + most strong ones)

Past tense: –**et** (weak class I), –**te** (weak class IIa), –**de** (weak class IIb), –**dde** (weak class III), no suffix (strong)

Supine: –**et** (weak class I), –**t** (weak class IIa), –**d** (weak class IIb), –**dd** (weak class III and some strong verbs), –**et** (most strong verbs), –**tt** (some strong verbs)

Present participle: **–ende** (always)

Imperative: No suffix, identical to stem

Past participle: Usually like the supine (cf.5.3.12.2)

5.2.2 | Class I

5.2.2.1 | Frequency

This is the largest of the verb classes in Norwegian, containing 55% of all verbs at a rough estimate. Here are some examples:

kaste, throw; **hamre**, hammer; **snorke**, snore

It also attracts most new verbs, for example

jobbe, work; **shoppe**; **surfe**; **seive**, store/save on a computer

New verbs that have an infinitive in –ere (a stem in –er) follow class IIa, however. See 5.2.3.2.

5.2.2.2 | Main paradigm

Infinitive	Present	Past	Supine	Meaning
danse	**danser**	**danset**	**danset**	dance
hamre	**hamrer**	**hamret**	**hamret**	hammer
kaste	**kaster**	**kastet**	**kastet**	throw
snorke	**snorker**	**snorket**	**snorket**	snore

Further examples include: **hviske**, whisper; **bue**, yell boo; **lee**, rug, move; **smigre**, flatter; **kjøle**, 'cool' cool and many others

5.2.2.3 | Form

The infinitive equals the stem + –e (as with other weak classes except III). The present tense equals the stem + –er (again, as with other weak classes except III). The past tense and the supine equal the stem + –et or –a.

Class I verbs have a characteristic identity of form (syncretism) between the past and the supine. This is not found in the other classes. Compare the class I verb **danset** (past) = **danset** (supine) with the class III verb **nådde** (past) ≠ **nådd** (supine) or the class II verb **kjørte** ≠ **kjørt**.

Note – An alternative to the suffix –et, though much less used in writing, is –a. Thus, **danset** is much more frequent in written Bokmål than **dansa**. In speech, by contrast, **dansa** is much more frequent than **danset**.

5.2.3 | *Class II*

5.2.3.1 | *Frequency*

This class contains roughly 1,900 of the 4,800 verbs in *Bokmålsordboka*, so it is fairly large. However, the majority of the members (approximately 1,500 of those 1,900) are made up of verbs whose infinitive ends in –ere. These verbs are usually of Latin (or Neoclassical) origin, e.g. **multiplisere**, 'multiply'; **reagere**, 'react'. The class is productive; for example, when Norwegians started using the verb **eskalere**, 'escalate', the past tense form became **eskalerte**.

5.2.3.2 | *Form*

Infinitive	Present	Past	Supine	
IIa				
kjøpe	**kjøper**	**kjøpte**	**kjøpt**	buy
like	**liker**	**likte**	**likt**	like
reagere	**reagerer**	**reagerte**	**reagert**	react
IIb				
kreve	**krever**	**krevde**	**krevd**	demand
lage	**lager**	**lagde**	**lagd**	make, produce
bygge	**bygger**	**bygde**	**bygd**	build

Some members of this class have a stem ending in a diphthong **ei** or **øy**; they belong to IIb.

veie	veier	veide	veid	weigh
greie	greier	greide	greid	manage
sløye	sløyer	sløyde	sløyd	gut (fish)
drøye	drøyer	drøyde	drøyd	linger, be slow

Note 1 – Verbs with a stem ending in the diphthongs **ai, au** are few, but tend to belong to class I:

praie	praier	praiet	praiet	get to stop
snaue	snauer	snauet	snauet	cut very short

Note 2 – Many, but not all, verbs of class IIb can alternatively inflect according to class I, but then *only* with the suffix –**et** and not –**a**. For example, for **kreve**, 'demand', there is, as well as **krevde**, an alternative past tense form **krevet** (but not **kreva**); on the other hand, for **leve**, 'live' there is only **levde** (and not *levet).

Members of this class typically have a stem ending in one or two consonants. Like class I verbs, class II verbs have the infinitive suffix –**e** and the present tense suffix –**er**. Class II verbs select either the suffix –**te** or the suffix –**de** in the past tense. Compare the past tense forms of **kjøpe** 'buy' and **bygge** 'build', **kjøpte** and **bygde** respectively. The suffix –**te** is found if the final stem consonant is either unvoiced (as are **p, k**, for example) or if it is **l, n, r** (even though the latter are actually voiced). The suffix –**de** is usually found after **v, g** (both voiced) or the diphthongs **ei, øy**. Compare **krevde, lagde, greide** with **kreve, lage, greie**. If the verb takes –**te** in the past tense, it will take –**t** in the supine. We call this subclass IIa. If the verb takes –**de** in the past tense, it will take –**d** in the supine; we call this subclass IIb. In *Bokmålsordboka* there are approx. 1,750 members in IIa, approx. 80 members in IIb.

Note 3 – An exception is **love**, 'promise'; its past tense can be **lovte** (or **lovde** or **lovet**).

(b) Before a suffix that begins with a consonant, a double consonant in the stem is usually reduced to one, orthographically, cf. **bygge** vs **bygde** above. Compare also:

Infinitive	Present	Past	Supine	Meaning
IIa				
felle	**feller**	**felte**	**felt**	fell, make fall
trykke	**trykker**	**trykte**	**trykt**	press, print
IIb				
tygge	**tygger**	**tygde**	**tygd**	chew
dømme	**dømmer**	**dømte**	**dømt**	judge

This rule is not specific to class II, cf. 12.2.1.1.

(c) We have based our classification of weak verbs on suffixes. However, some few weak (usually class II) verbs display vowel alternation in addition to suffixes, e.g.

Infinitive	Present	Past	Supine	Meaning
telle	**teller**	**talte**	**talt**	count
smøre	**smører**	**smurte**	**smurt**	spread (e.g. butter)

See further 5.2.5.1.

5.2.4 Class III

5.2.4.1 Frequency

This is the smallest of the weak classes. It has some 70 members of the 4,800 verbs in *Bokmålsordboka*. It is probably not productive any more. If these days verbs are borrowed whose stem end in a long vowel in the 'donor' language, e.g. 'boo' from English – so that the verb might seem to fit into class III – Norwegians tend to insert an –e and assign the verb to class I (**bue** – **buer** – **buet** – **buet**).

5.2.4.2 Main paradigm

Infinitive	Present	Past	Supine	Meaning
sy	**syr**	**sydde**	**sydd**	sew
spre	**sprer**	**spredde**	**spredd**	spread
spa	**spar**	**spadde**	**spadd**	dig with a spade

The stem ends in a stressed vowel. The infinitive is identical to the stem. The suffixes are –r (present), –dde (past), –dd (supine). In speech, the vowel is long in the infinitive and present but short in the past and supine. Here are some further examples:

bla, 'turn the page'; **kle**, 'dress; suit'; **fri**, 'propose (to marry)'; **glo**, 'stare'; **bo**, 'live'; **snu** 'turn'; **spy**, 'vomit'; **snø**, 'snow'; **flå**, 'flay'

The normal supine suffix is –dd, but note the very frequent verb **ha**, 'have':

ha	**har**	**hadde**	**hatt**	have

5.2.5 Irregular weak verbs

5.2.5.1 Vowel change

Some weak verbs display a vowel change in the past tense. While there are many patterns of vowel change in the strong verbs, the weak verbs have a more restricted set. Examples include the modals (cf. 5.4.2) and the following rather mixed bag:

Infinitive	Present	Past	Supine	
telle	**teller**	**talte**	**talt**	count
fortell	**forteller**	**fortalte**	**fortalt**	tell, say
selge	**selger**	**solgte**	**solgt**	sell
smøre	**smører**	**smurte**	**smurt**	oil; spread (butter)
spørre	**spør**	**spurte**	**spurt**	ask
gjøre	**gjør**	**gjorde**	**gjort**	do
velge	**velger**	**valgte**	**valgt**	choose

These verbs have the same vowel in the infinitive and present, and a different one in the past and the supine.

5.2.5.2 No present tense suffix

Some very frequent verbs do not take a present tense suffix. Apart from the modals, this group includes:

Infinitive	Present	Past	Supine	
gjøre	**gjør**	**gjorde**	**gjort**	do
spørre	**spør**	**spurte**	**spurt**	ask
vite	**vet**	**visste**	**visst**	know

Note also that the very frequent strong verb **være**, 'be' does not take a present tense suffix, cf. 5.2.6.7.

5.2.5.3 Modals

The verbs that express modality (cf. 5.4.1) are by and large weak and irregular.

Infinitive	Present	Past	Supine	
tørre	**tør**	**turde**	**turt**	dare
ville	**vil**	**ville**	**villet**	would

kunne	kan	kunne	kunnet	could
måtte	må	måtte	måttet	must
burde	bør	burde	burdet	ought to
skulle	skal	skulle	skullet	should

Unlike English modals, these verbs have all their principal parts. (Though some of the non-finite forms listed above, e.g. the supine **burdet**, are rather literary and infrequent.)

Note – An alternative form to **tørre** is **tore**, to **turde** is **torde**.

5.2.6 | Strong verbs

Strong verbs have no syllabic past tense suffix (cf. 5.2.1.2(a) and (b)):

Infinitive	Past		
like	**likte**	enjoy	weak
skrike	**skrek**	scream, yell	strong

5.2.6.1 | Frequency

Roughly 200 of the verbs in *Bokmålsordboka* are strong; 4,800 are weak. Thus, there are fairly few strong verbs compared to weak ones. However, many strong verbs are of high frequency, and some are indispensable in daily speech, e.g. **være**, 'be'; **bli**, 'become'; **ta**, 'take'; **få**, 'get'.

5.2.6.2 | Form: General remarks

(a) Most strong verbs have stems ending in a consonant, and their infinitives have a consonant stem + –e. The present tense of these verbs ends in –er, the supine usually in –et. Compare:

Infinitive	Present	Past	Supine	
skrive	**skriver**	**skrev**	**skrevet**	write
skyve	**skyver**	**skjøv**	**skjøvet**	push
springe	**springer**	**sprang**	**sprunget**	run
bære	**bærer**	**bar**	**båret**	carry

Note – Excepting the past tense, then, these strong verbs have basically the same suffixes as weak class I (**danse**); however, they

217

usually have a vowel shift and they cannot take –a as an alternative in the supine.

(b) Verbs like **skrive** – with the vowel **i** (long in speech) in the stem and **e** (or **ei**) in the past tense – constitute one of the largest strong subclasses. Also, verbs like **skyve** – with the vowel **y** in the stem and **ø** (or **øy**) in the past tense – make up a large strong subclass. Cf 5.2.6.3f. below.

(c) The norm for strong verbs that have a bisyllabic infinitive is that their supine is bisyllabic too; cf. the table above. However, a fair number of such verbs have a supine that would seem to belong to a weak verb of class III. For example, while **snyte**, 'cheat', inflects largely as **skyve** (present **snyter**, past tense **snøt**), the supine of **snyte** is **snytt** (and not *****snøtet**). Similarly, while **slite**, 'struggle', inflects largely as **skrive**, its supine is **slitt** (not *****slitet**). The supine **bydd** may be used whether the verb **by**, 'bid', 'offer' is inflected as strong (past tense **bød/bøy**) or weak (past tense **bydde**) – both options are in fact within the norm.

(d) The majority of strong verbs have a consonant-final stem, cf. the examples above. Thus, for most strong verbs, the infinitive is bisyllabic. There are, however, also a number of strong verbs whose stem ends in a vowel, i.e. verbs whose infinitive is monosyllabic. These verbs look like verbs in weak class III (**spå**) – with the exception of the past tense:

Infinitive	Present	Past	Supine	
svi	**svir**	**svei**	**svidd**	scorch
gli	**glir**	**glei**	**glidd**	slide
fly	**flyr**	**fløy**	**flydd**	fly
by	**byr**	**bøy**	**bydd**	bid, offer

The normal supine for verbs like these ends in –**dd**. For some verbs of very high frequency, however, the supine suffix is –**tt**. Compare **bli** 'become'; **dra**, 'go, pull'; **slå**, 'hit'; **gå**, 'go, walk'; **ta**, 'take', the supine of which is **blitt, dratt, slått, gått** and **tatt** respectively. Many of these verbs also have an 'unexpected' consonant past tense suffix, cf. (f) below.

(e) There is no syllabic suffix for the past tense of strong verbs, and yet some strong verbs have a consonant suffix in the past tense. Compare **finne – fant** 'find'; **falle – falt** 'fall'. These verbs, then, stand out among strong verbs in having a past tense suffix added to their stem, but this suffix is not a syllabic one. It is only verbs with stems in –**n**, –**l** that have such a suffix. Examples include **binde – bandt** (pronounced /bine – bant/), 'bind'; **forsvinne – forsvant**, 'disappear'; **vinne – vant**, 'win', holde – **holdt**, 'hold'; smelle – **smalt**, 'make a bang'; gjelde – **gjaldt**, 'apply to'.

(f) For some highly frequent verbs, we also find 'unexpected' consonantal suffixes in the past tense:

ta 'take' – **tok; be** 'ask' – **bad; stå** 'stand' – **stod; dra** 'drag, pull' – **drog; gå** 'go' – **gikk; få** 'get, receive'– **fikk; gi** 'give' – **gav**

Except for –k/kk, these consonants are not obligatory in writing (and not heard in speech). Thus, the alternative past tense forms of **be, stå, dra, gi** are **ba, sto, dro, ga** respectively.

Note – From an historical point of view, these verbs once had a bisyllabic infinitive (e.g. **take/tage, bede, stande, drage**). At least partly because of their high frequency, these infinitives came to be reduced; the second syllable was lost.

(g) Almost all strong verbs have a past tense vowel that differs from that of the infinitive and present (which is always the same). Some strong verbs display yet a third vowel in the supine.

Strong verbs can be subdivided into groups according to the vowels in the stem of the principal parts. The following lists may not be exhaustive, but they show how many verbs are inflected. The first three subgroups are the largest ones in terms of members. While we have listed all forms for all verbs below, even native writers may in practice be uncertain about some of them.

(h) Just as for the weak verbs, a rule of thumb is that 'birds of a feather flock together': strong verbs usually inflect like the verbs they rhyme with.

5.2.6.3 *Strong verbs I: i–e (ei)–e*

Infinitive	Present	Past	Supine	Meaning
Bisyllabic infinitive and supine				
drite	**driter**	**dret**	**dretet**	shit (vulgar)
drive	**driver**	**drev**	**drevet**	drive, drift
gripe	**griper**	**grep**	**grepet**	catch

klive	kliver	kleiv	klevet	step, climb
knipe	kniper	knep	knepet	pinch
pipe	piper	pep	pepet	chirp
rive	river	rev	revet	tear, demolish
skri(de)	skri(de)r	skred	skredet	glide
skrike	skriker	skrek	skreket	shout
skrive	skriver	skrev	skrevet	write
snike	sniker	snek	sneket	sneak
stige	stiger	steg	steget	climb, step
svike	sviker	svek	sveket	betray
vike	viker	vek	veket	retreat

Bi– or monosyllabic infinitive, monosyllabic supine

bite	biter	bet	bitt	bite
grine	griner	gren	grint	weep, sob
hvine	hviner	hven	hvint	shriek
kvine	kviner	kven	kvint	shriek
skite	skiter	skjet	skitt	shit (vulgar)
slite	sliter	slet	slitt	struggle
li(de)	li(de)r	led	lidd	suffer
ri(de)	ri(de)r	red	ridd	ride
skinne	skinner	skein	skint	shine
stri(de)	stri(de)r	stred	stridd	fight (figurative)

Only monosyllabic infinitive, monosyllabic supine

bli	blir	ble	blitt	be, become
gli	glir	gled	glidd	glide
gni	gnir	gned	gnidd	rub
svi	svir	sved	svidd	scorch, smart
vri	vrir	vred	vridd	twist

Most of the verbs in this group are listed with the past tense vowel **e**, but have **ei** as an alternative. For example, the most common past tense form of **drive** is **drev**, but **dreiv** is a possible alternative. However, for the verbs listed with **ei** in the table, **e** is not an alternative. (The verbs **lide** has the alternative supine form **lidt**.)

If the verb is monosyllabic in the infinitive, it will have the supine suffix –dd, cf. **svi** – **svidd**. Note the exception, the extremely frequent verb **bli**, whose supine is **blitt**. (Compare the extremely frequent weak verb **ha**, 5.2.4.2.)

| 5.2.6.4 | *Strong verbs II:* **y–ø(øy)–ø**

Infinitive	Present	Past	Supine	Meaning
Bisyllabic infinitive, bisyllabic supine				
fly	**flyr**	**fløy**	**fløyet**	fly
fryse	**fryser**	**frøs**	**frosset**	freeze [intr.], be cold
klype	**klyper**	**kløp**	**kløpet**	pinch, nip
klyve	**klyver**	**kløv**	**kløvet**	split, cleave
krype	**kryper**	**krøp**	**krøpet**	creep
lyve	**lyver**	**løy**	**løyet**	tell a lie
ryke	**ryker**	**røk**	**røket**	smoke [intr.]
Bisyllabic infinitive, monosyllabic supine				
bryte	**bryter**	**brøt**	**brutt**	break
flyte	**flyter**	**fløt**	**flytt**	float
lyde	**lyder**	**lød**	**lydt**	sound
nyse	**nyser**	**nøs**	**nyst**	sneeze
nyte	**nyter**	**nøt**	**nytt**	enjoy
skyte	**skyter**	**skjøt**	**skutt**	shoot
skryte	**skryter**	**skrøt**	**skrytt**	boast
smyge	**smyger**	**smøg**	**smøget**	slink
snyte	**snyter**	**snøt**	**snytt**	cheat
stryke	**stryker**	**strøk**	**strøket**	stroke, delete
tyte	**tyter**	**tøt**	**tytt**	ooze, seep

Note – Alternative forms of the verbs meaning 'lie' are in the infinitive **ljuge** and **lyge**, in the present **ljuger** and **lyger**.

Most of the verbs in this group are listed with the past tense vowel ø, but have øy as an alternative. For example, the most common past tense form of **bryte** 'break' is **brøt**, but **brøyt** is a possible alternative. However, for those verbs that are listed with **øy** in the table, **ø** is not an alternative. Note also that for the verbs **lyde, skryte** there is no alternative with **øy**.

5.2.6.5 Strong verbs III: i/e/y–a–u

Infinitive	Present	Past	Supine	Meaning
Bisyllabic infinitive, bisyllabic supine				
binde	binder	bandt	bundet	bind, tie
brekke	brekker	brakk	brukket	break
briste	brister	brast	brustet	burst
dette	detter	datt	dettet	fall
drikke	drikker	drakk	drukket	drink
finne	finner	fant	funnet	find
finnes	finnes	fantes	funnes	exist
fornemme	fornemmer	fornam	fornemmet	perceive
forsvinne	forsvinner	forsvant	forsvunnet	disappear
sitte	sitter	satt	sittet	sit
slippe	slipper	slapp	sluppet	avoid, let fall
spinne	spinner	spant	spunnet	spin, purr
sprekke	sprekker	sprakk	sprukket	burst, crack
springe	springer	sprang	sprunget	run
sprette	spretter	spratt	sprettet	jump; split
stikke	stikker	stakk	stukket	prick, sting, run away
svinne	svinner	svant	svunnet	vanish
synge	synger	sang	sunget	sing
synke	synker	sank	sunket	sink [intr.]
tvinge	tvinger	tvang	tvunget	force, compel
vinne	vinner	vant	vunnet	win
Bisyllabic infinitive, monosyllabic supine				
brenne	brenner	brant	brent	burn [intr.]
gjelde	gjelder	gjaldt	gjeldt	apply to, be valid
knekke	knekker	knakk	knekt	chip
smelle	smeller	smalt	smelt	make a bang
renne	renner	rant	rent	run, flow

| 5.2.6.6 | Strong verbs IV: a–o–a |

Infinitive	Present	Past	Supine	Meaning
dra	drar	dro(g)	dratt	pull
fare	farer	for	fart	travel
gale	galer	gol	galt	crow
gnage	gnager	gnog	gnagd	gnaw
grave	grave	grov	gravd	dig
jage	jager	jog	jagd	chase
sverge	sverger	svor	sverget	swear
ta	tar	tok	tatt	take

For **gale, gnage, grave, jage, sverge,** the strong form in the past tense is not obligatory and somewhat literary. The verbs **gale** and **sverge** more often inflect like class I verbs, **gnage, grave, jage** like class IIb. On the consonant insertion in **drog, tok,** cf 5.2.6.2(f).

| 5.2.6.7 | Strong verbs V: e/æ-a–å |

Infinitive	Present	Past	Supine	Meaning
bære	bærer	bar	båret	carry
skjære	skjærer	skar	skåret	cut
stjele	stjeler	stjal	stjålet	steal
svelte	svelter	svalt	sveltet	starve [intr.]
være	er	var	vært	be

The verb **være** is highly irregular, by 'dropping' the **v** and by having no suffix in the present tense. **Svelte** is very rare; **sulte** (weak, class I) is the preferred variant.

| 5.2.6.8 | *Strong verbs VI: no change* |

Infinitive	Present	Past	Supine	Meaning
falle	**faller**	**falt**	**falt**	fall
hete	**heter**	**het**	**hett**	be called
hogge	**hogger**	**hogg**	**hogd**	chop
holde	**holder**	**holdt**	**holdt**	hold
komme	**kommer**	**kom**	**kommet**	come
løpe	**løper**	**løp**	**løpt**	run
sove	**sover**	**sov**	**sovet**	sleep
gråte	**gråter**	**gråt**	**grått**	weep

These verbs stand out by having no stem vowel change. Note that **falle** and **holde** have a suffix –t added in the past tense, compare 5.2.6.2(e) above. **Hete, hogge** and **løpe** can alternatively inflect as weak class II verbs.

| 5.2.6.9 | *Strong verbs VII: others* |

Infinitive	Present	Past	Supine	Meaning
ete	**eter**	**åt**	**ett**	eat
ligge	**ligger**	**lå**	**ligget**	lie (be down)
legge	**legger**	**la**	**lagt**	put, lay
si	**sier**	**sa**	**sagt**	say
slå	**slår**	**slo**	**slått**	hit
slåss	**slåss**	**sloss**	**slåss**	fight

5.3 The use of the verb forms

| 5.3.1 | **The infinitive – major uses** |

| 5.3.1.1 | The 'look up form' (citation form) |

The infinitive is not a tense; it does not locate the verb in time. For its form, see 5.2.1.1(c) and 5.2.1.3. The infinitive is the form used to 'represent' the verb in dictionaries, and so important for the learner. If, we wonder, say, what the Norwegian verb **knydde** means, we can guess that it must be the past tense of a weak verb class III (cf. 5.2.1.2 (e), 5.2.4.2). We must then look up the infinitive **kny** in order to learn that this verb means 'grumble, object'.

5.3.1.2 *Passive infinitive*

Practically all verbs have an (active) infinitive, just as they have a present or past tense. For some few verbs, mainly modals, the infinitive is marginal, however (5.2.5.3).

The infinitive can take the passive suffix –s:

Kan dette fikses?   Can this be fixed?

Tintin skulle skytes, men ble berget i grevens tid.
Tintin was to be shot, but was saved in the nick of time.

Note 1 – Since there is a passive infinitive, the infinitive without –s can also be referred to as the active infinitive.

Note 2 – Not all verbs have a passive infinitive.

5.3.1.3 *Verbal and nominal use*

There are two major uses of the infinitive in Norwegian (as in English), viz. the verbal one, where it is combined with another verb, typically an auxiliary, and the nominal one, where it does not combine with another verb, and is usually preceded by å, 'to':

Hun kan danse hele natta.   She can dance all night. (verbal)
Å danse er gøy.   Lit. To dance is fun. (nominal)

On verbal use, see further 5.3.1.5 below, on nominal use, see 5.3.1.6. The word å, 'to' can be classified as a subjunction, cf. 9.3.3.

5.3.1.4 *Infinitive as imperative*

There is an additional, 'minor' use of the infinitive; it can be used as if it were an imperative, especially when combined with a negative adverbial and in child-directed speech:

Nei, ikke plage hunden,   No, [do] not pester the dog,
  Petter!   Petter!
Sitte pent nå, Buster!   Sit nicely, Buster (dog's name)!
Aldri snakke med mat i munnen!   Never talk with your mouth full.

Examples such as these are rare in standard, written prose. Standard written prose is rarely directed to children, and it is an unsuited medium for orders of the kind conveyed in these examples. Such orders are not so rare in speech, however.

Note – In cases like these, the infinitive is used as if it were a finite verb form. One may perhaps think of this as ellipsis of a subject and an auxiliary (**Nei, du må ikke plage hunden, Petter. Du må sitte pent nå, Buster!**).

5.3.1.5 *Verbal use of the infinitive with and without **å***

The following types of two-verb constructions involve the infinitive without å 'to':

(a) The modal (and semi-modal) auxiliaries: **burde**, 'ought to, should'; **få**, 'be allowed to; had better'; **kunne**, 'be able'; **la**, 'let', **måtte**, 'have to, must'; **skulle**, 'should'; **tore/tørre**, 'dare'; **ville**, 'would'. See 5.4.2.1.

Castafiore kan synge.	Castafiore can sing.
La meg komme fram.	Let me pass.
Vi skal reise til Bergen.	We are going to Bergen.
Du får gjøre det, du.	You had better do it.

(b) Verbs which serve as modal equivalents and are followed by a negation, such as **behøve**, 'need to'; **bruke**, 'usually (do)'; **forsøke**, 'attempt to'; **love**, 'promise to'; **orke**, 'be able to'; **pleie**, 'usually do', **våge**, 'dare to'; **tenke**, 'intend to' – and a number of others.

Without negation, these verbs usually take an å-infinitive:

Vi pleier å spise torsk til jul.	We usually eat cod for Christmas.
Behøver du å tenke deg om?	Do you need to think about it?

A negative adverbial, such as **ikke**, 'not'; **aldri**, 'never' typically allows dropping å:

Du behøver da ikke (å) skrike.	Surely you don't need to shout.
Vi pleier ikke (å) spise kalkun.	We do not usually eat turkey.

Han bruker da aldri (å) svare sånn.
He does not usually answer like that.

In the examples without a negative element, å cannot be dropped; in those containing a negation, å can (but does not have to) be dropped. Apart from this, it is not entirely straightforward when å can be dropped and when it must not. There is some variation.

Note – After some verbs, including **forsøke, prøve** 'try', **å** can be dropped, even in the absence of negation, though this is not so common:

Haddock forsøkte (å) gjøre som Tintin sa.
Haddock tried to do as Tintin said.

Hun prøvde (å) tvinge oss ut.
She tried to force us out.

(c) The infinitive can be used in 'object and infinitive constructions' (also known as 'accusative with infinitive'). See 10.10.2.2. Here the noun or pronoun is the grammatical object of the finite verb in the main clause, but it may at the same time be thought of as the subject of the infinitive. This construction is found after the verbs **be**, 'ask'; **la**, 'let' and a number of others denoting perception, such as **se**, 'see'; **høre**, 'hear'; **kjenne** 'feel'.

Tintin bad Haddock snakke.   Tintin asked Haddock to talk.

Hun kjente steinen gnage i skoen.
She felt the stone chafe in her shoe.

(d) Infinitive in 'subject and infinitive' constructions (10.10.2.3):

Alma ble hørt synge den kvelden. Alma was heard singing that night.
Marilyn ses danse hver tirsdag.   Marilyn is seen dancing every Tuesday.

This is a rather literary use.

| 5.3.1.6 | *Nominal use of the infinitive* |

The infinitive frequently functions as a noun. In such cases, it is normally preceded by **å** 'to'. Like a noun, the infinitive can fill a syntactic function alone or be part of a phrase filling such a function.

(a) Infinitive (with complements) as subject:

Å *arbeide* er morsomt, men vi skal ikke bare ha det gøy i livet.
To work is fun, but we should not only have fun in this life.

Å *gå søndagstur* er sunt.   To go for a Sunday walk is healthy.

See also 2.2.1.4(b).

If there is an infinitive subject, the predicative adjective is in the neuter (**morsomt, sunt** above, cf. 2.2.1.4). Often, the pronoun **det** 'it' is found as an anticipatory, formal subject in addition to the postponed, potentialsubject potential subject, viz. the infinitive phrase:

Det	**er**	**morsomt**	**å arbeide.**
It	is	fun	to work.
Formal			*Potential*
subject			*subject*

Det er sunt å gå søndagstur.   It is healthy to go for a Sunday walk.

Both constructions – **Å arbeide er morsomt** and **Det er morsomt å arbeide** – are perfectly grammatical. However, the former is more literary; the spoken language has a preference for the construction with **det** as a formal subject. (The spoken language prefers not to use long subjects sentence-initially, cf. 10.7.3.4, 10.9.1.3).

Note – If the infinitive is represented by a pronoun, this pronoun will also be in the neuter.

Å arbeide, *det* er morsomt.   *Subject function*
Lit. To work, it is fun/Working is fun.

Liker du å lage mat? Ja,
***det* elsker jeg.**   *Object function*
Do you like cooking? Yes, I love it.

(b) Infinitive (with complements) as object. See 10.3.4.1.

Hun elsker *å arbeide*.   *With a noun as object*
She loves working.
(Cf. **Hun elsker arbeidet sitt.**   She loves her work.)

Jeg foretrekker *å spille badminton sammen med far*.
I prefer to play badminton together with dad.

Cf. **Hun foretrekker *badminton*.**   *With a noun as object*
She prefers badminton.

(c) As subject complement:

Å leve, det er *å elske*.   To live, that is to love.

Kunsten er *å arbeide hardt*, men ikke for lenge.
The trick is to work hard, but not too long.

(d) As object complement:

Det kaller jeg *å dumme seg ut*.
That I call making a fool of oneself.

While (a)–(d) show the infinitive fulfilling a syntactic function by itself, there are also cases in which it is part of a phrase fulfilling such a function. For example, the infinitive can be:

1) Preceded by a preposition. In such cases, the phrase is often an adverbial or an object. See 10.2.6.

Han gikk *uten å si et ord*	He left without saying a single word.
Sjefen tenker *på å si opp*.	The boss considers resigning.

While English can have a 'gerund' in '–ing' in such cases, Norwegian has no exact equivalent (cf. 5.3.2.3). Norwegian can have a preposition immediately before an infinitive; English cannot, cf. 7.1.3.6.

2) Preceded by a preposition after many adjectives:

Elgen er *god til å svømme*.	The elk/moose is good at swimming.
Hermine er *glad i å lese*.	Hermione is fond of reading.

3) Preceded by a preposition after nouns:

Draco er en *kløpper til å lyve*.	Draco is an ace at lying.

Note – With prepositional expressions indicating intention, **for** å should be used, not only å:

Harry er kommet *for å redde oss*.
Harry has come (in order) to save us.

Dette er viktig *for å motvirke frykt*.
This is important to counteract fear.

4) Infinitive qualifying a noun, pronoun or adjective as attribute:

Kunsten *å myrde*.	The art of murdering.
	(short story by Cora Sandel)
Hun har noe *å fortelle oss*.	She has something to tell us
Denne boka er tung *å lese*.	This book is a heavy read.

5.3.2 | *The infinitive in English and Norwegian and the English gerund*

5.3.2.1 | English infinitive = Norwegian infinitive

The use of the infinitive in the two languages is often identical:

(a) In two-verb constructions. See 5.3.1.5.

You really must come.
Du må faktisk komme.

(b) In adjectival constructions

It is not easy to be a rock star.
Det er ikke lett å være rockestjerne.

(c) In object and infinitive constructions. See 10.10.2.2.

She told him to go to hell.
Hun bad han dra til Bloksberg.

(d) As subject

Å feile er menneskelig; å tilgi er guddommelig.
To err is human, to forgive divine. [Alexander Pope]

Note that, if two infinitives are co-ordinated, the preference in Norwegian is for no subjunction å before the second infinitive (even if it may be included):

We enjoy eating and drinking well.   **Vi liker å spise og drikke godt.**

5.3.2.2 *English infinitive = Norwegian full clause*

(a) With object and infinitive constructions, verbs like 'want', 'wish', 'allow' are used (cf. 5.3.1.5(c):

Why do you want me to go?
Hvorfor vil du at jeg skal dra?

I'm hoping for that crook to be caught soon.
Jeg håper (at) den skurken snart blir tatt.

Note – The subjunction at may sometimes be omitted, cf 10.8.4.1.

However, Norwegian sometimes allows for object and infinitive in such cases, compare 5.3.1.5(c) above.

(b) After 'wait for', 'long for', 'count on', 'rely on':

Were they waiting for the grass to grow?
Ventet de på at gresset skulle gro?

Can we count on you to explain the niceties of English?
Kan vi regne med at du forklarer finessene i engelsk?

(c) After an interrogative:

Dupont had no idea who to ask.
Dupont ante ikke hvem han skulle spørre.

He asked her what to do next.
Han spurte henne hva som så skulle gjøres.

Note the passive infinitive in the last example.

(d) After 'too' + adjective, or adjective + 'enough':

It was too dark for us to see anything.
Det var for mørkt til at vi kunne se noe.

It was dark enough for us to give up honourably.
Det var mørkt nok til at vi kunne gi opp med æren i behold.

(e) After 'had better':

You had better hurry up!
Det er best (at) du skynder deg!

5.3.2.3 *Norwegian has no gerund (or verbal noun)*

Unlike English, which has a gerund in "The proof of the pudding is in *the eating*," or "It's no use *crying* over spilt milk", Norwegian has an infinitive or a full clause in instances such as the following:

(a) English infinitive or gerund = Norwegian infinitive

He began to read/reading.	**Han begynte å lese.**
Do you intend to leave/leaving today?	**Har du tenkt å dra i dag?**
I prefer to travel/travelling by train.	**Jeg foretrekker å ta toget.**
It's no use crying over spilt milk.	**Det er ingen vits i å gråte over spilt melk.**

Also after verbs meaning 'continue', 'finish', 'give up', 'avoid', 'escape', 'want', 'need':

It has stopped raining.	**Det har sluttet å regne.**
We can't avoid hurting him.	**Vi kan ikke unngå å såre ham.**

(b) English gerund = Norwegian full clause

He went to bed, having first taken his medicine.
Han gikk og la seg etter at han først hadde tatt medisinen sin.

(c) English possessive + gerund = Norwegian full clause

His persistent meddling annoys me.
At han alltid må blande seg, ergrer meg.

She died without our knowing it.
Hun døde uten at vi visste om det.

(d) English preposition + gerund = Norwegian preposition + infinitive

After having eaten lunch, we went for a walk.
Etter å ha spist lunsj gikk vi en tur.

(e) English preposition + gerund = Norwegian preposition + å-phrase

Everybody praised Martin for having written such a fine book.
Alle roste Martin for å ha skrevet ei så fin bok.

It is perhaps more common, especially in the spoken language, to turn this into a full clause. In that case, the subject has to be inserted again:

Everybody praised Martin for having written such a fine book.
Alle roste Martin for at han hadde skrevet ei så fin bok.

The city of Oxford is renowned for being home to many famous scholars.
Byen Oxford er kjent for å huse mange berømte forskere.

Or:

Byen Oxford er kjent for at den huser mange berømte forskere.

5.3.3 | The present tense

For form, see 5.2.1.1 and 5.2.1.3. The present tense is used by and large as in English.

The five main uses of the present tense in Norwegian listed below must not be thought of as entirely separate. (There is a connection between what usually holds true and what holds true eternally, for example.) Furthermore, there are many and varied uses of the present tense in Norwegian (as in English). Note in particular that 'right here and right now' is only one of many. (The use of the past tense is more restricted.)

Note – Sometimes when English uses the present tense, Norwegian will use the past. Cf 5.3.5.5.

5.3.3.1 Instantaneous present

The emphasis is on what is happening here and now. While these are cases in which the justification for the label 'present' is very clear, such cases do not constitute the majority of examples with the present tense.

Zlatan *skyter* **– og det er mål!**	Zlatan shoots – and it's a goal!
Hva *gjør* **du?**	What are you doing?
Jeg *sitter og leser* **avisa.**	I'm sitting reading the newspaper.

5.3.3.2 State present

The emphasis is on the general and timeless:

Gud *er* **Gud om alle mann var døde.**
God is God even if all men were dead. (hymn)

Stavanger *ligger* **ved Nordsjøen.**
Stavanger is situated on the North Sea.

Vann *koker* **ved 100 grader Celsius.**
Water boils at 100 centigrade.

5.3.3.3 Habitual present

The emphasis is on regular repetition over a period:

Linda og Phil *reiser* **til Frankrike hver vår.**
Linda and Phil go to France every spring.

Grammatikktimene *begynner* **klokka ni.**
The grammar classes start at 9 o'clock.

Kaptein Haddock *liker* **whisky.**
Captain Haddock likes whisky.

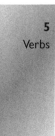

5.3.3.4 Future action

This is perhaps especially common with **bli**, **være**, verbs of motion and phrases involving a distinct marker for future time (5.3.8.1), but we should stress that the simple present is the normal way to express future time reference in Norwegian:

I morgen ettermiddag *blir* det regn.
Tomorrow afternoon there will be rain.

Vi *reiser* til Zürich om fjorten dager.
We shall go to Zürich in a fortnight.

Når du engang *kommer* neste sommer, skal vi atter drikke vin.
When you come next summer, we shall drink wine again. (pop song, deLilos)

The third example illustrates that, when the futurity is introduced in a subclause in the present tense, the main clause may contain a verb in a 'periphrastic' 'future tense' construction 5.3.8.3ff. This is quite common.

5.3.3.5 Historic (dramatic) present

The present may also be used about past events:

(a) To create a dramatic illusion of 'now' in a narrative about the past. This is often the case in storytelling or literary works:

I høst var vi ute på fiske. Lenge var det stille, og ingenting skjedde. Men så, plutselig *rykker* det kraftig til.
Last autumn we were out fishing. For a long time, it was quiet, and nothing happened. But then, suddenly, there is a mighty tug.

I 1865 var Ibsen fortsatt en nokså ukjent person, men dette *endrer* seg brått med *Peer Gynt*.
In 1865 Ibsen was still a fairly unknown figure, but with *Peer Gynt*, this changes suddenly.

(b) When the result of an action in the past is important, especially when relating to a book or work of art; when the action described somehow is still valid:

Jonas Lie *beskriver* familielivets gleder og sorger.
Jonas Lie depicts the joys and sorrows of family life.

Platon *legger* vekt på menneskets medfødte intellekt, mens Aristoteles *legger* vekt på erfaringen.
Plato emphasises the intellect that man is born with, while Aristotle emphasises experience.

While Jonas Lie, Plato and Aristotle are long gone, their descriptions or ideas are here described as being somehow still with us.

5.3.4 | *The present tense in English and Norwegian and the English progressive (or continuous) tense*

5.3.4.1 | *Differences in usage*

By and large, the use of the present tense is the same in the two languages (see 5.3.3), but there are some minor differences:

(a) Present in Norwegian = past in English:

This is found in combination with the past participle, when an action is completed in the past, but the (tangible) result of the action remains:

Peer Gynt er skrevet av Ibsen.
Peer Gynt was written by Ibsen.

Stavanger domkirke er bygd på 1100-tallet.
Stavanger Cathedral was built in the 12th century.

Note – It is possible to use the past in Norwegian in such cases, but it may have a certain 'distancing' effect, cf. 5.3.5.1.

Bjørger ble skrevet av Knut Hamsun under et annet navn, før han ble den Knut Hamsun vi nå kjenner.
Bjørger was written by Knut Hamsun under a different name, before he became that Knut Hamsun we now know.

Stavanger domkirke ble bygd på 1100-tallet.
Stavanger Cathedral was built in the 12th century.

A common example of Norwegian present vs. English past is the use of the present tense with **være født**, 'be born' when people are still alive:

Når er du født?	When were you born?
Hun er født i 1960.	She was born in 1960.

If the past tense is used with **født,** the normal implication is that the person is dead:

Charles Dickens ble født i 1812.   Charles Dickens was born in 1812.

Note – One may, however, use the past without there necessarily being such an implication, but there will still be a 'distancing' effect:

Jeg ble født på et sjukehus som nå er gjort om til kontorer.
I was born in a hospital that has now been converted to offices.

(b) Present in Norwegian = present perfect in English when the action is
    continuing:

Dette er første gangen jeg spiser haggis.
This is the first time I have eaten haggis.

Dette er første gangen jeg har spist haggis.
[would imply that the eating is over]

Present in Norwegian = periphrastic future in English when there is a
time marker:

Det blir regn til kvelden.	There will be rain this evening.
Vi har gjester på søndag.	We'll have guests on Sunday.

This does not mean that Norwegian cannot have a periphrastic future:

Det skal bli regn til kvelden, sier de.
There will be rain this evening, they say.

Vi skal ha gjester på søndag.   We'll have guests on Sunday.

| 5.3.4.2 | *Norwegian near-equivalents of the English present progressive* |

The English present progressive, which expresses a limited but not necessarily complete process that is in progress (at a given time), can be rendered in different ways in Norwegian:

(a) Simple present tense. See 5.3.3.1–5.3.1.5.

Hvor går du?	Where are you going?
Nå flyr vi over Bergen.	We are now flying over Bergen.

(b) Two verbs in the present or past co-ordinated (linked) by **og**, 'and'. The former verb in such examples is typically one of location, the latter typically one of action. The sense of location/posture in the first verb can have become slightly weakened.

Han sitter og leser avisa.   He is (sitting) reading the newspaper.

Gustav ligger på sofaen og tenker på mat.
Gustav is lying on the couch, thinking of food.

In the grammatical literature, cases like these are often referred to as 'pseudo-coordination'. They differ from standard examples of co-ordination in a number of ways. For example, the two co-ordinated verbs in pseudo-coordination cannot change places, as the verbs in an ordinary coordination usually can:

Han sitter og leser. – *Han leser og sitter.

The latter of these two examples is odd, even ungrammatical, as indicated by the asterisk. This is unlike 'ordinary'/'genuine' co-ordination:

Hun synger og danser.   She sings and dances.
Hun danser og synger.   She dances and sings.

The most common 'first' verbs in such pseudo-coordinations are **ligge**, 'lie' (see also 5.8.2.1); **sitte**, 'sit' (5.8.2.2); **stå**, 'stand' (5.8.2.3).

(c) **holde på å** + infinitive fulfills the same function as English 'be involved in/ be in the process of'. There is emphasis on the action being in progress:

Han holder på å lage middag.   He is busy cooking dinner.
Romeo og Julie holder på å dø.   Romeo and Juliet are dying.

Da vi kom, holdt de på å lage mat.
When we came, they were busy cooking.

However, **holde på å** can sometimes mean 'be on the point of/about to':

Vi holder på å dø her ute.   We are about to die/dying out here.

This is perhaps more common in the past tense:

Læreren holdt på å røpe hemmeligheten.
The teacher was about to divulge the secret.

Kaffen holdt på å koke over.
The coffee was just about to boil over/nearly boiled over.

This does not mean that the teacher divulged the secret or that the coffee boiled over, only that he respectively it came close to doing this.

(d) **drive og + verb:** The combination of the verb **drive**, the conjunction **og** 'and' and a verb can give a progressive or continuative result, and is typically combined with verbs denoting actions.

Tor Arne driver og skriver på en artikkel.
Tor Arne is (in the process of) writing a paper.

Svein drev og leste da jeg banket på døra hans.
Svein was reading when I knocked on his door.

This construction has a somewhat colloquial flavour.

(e) **være og + verb:** The combination of the verb **være**, 'be', the conjunction **og**, 'and' and a verb can give a progressive result, and is typically combined with verbs denoting actions. Note, however, that this construction always implies that the action is carried out somewhere else.

Far er og ser etter sauene.
Father is (away) looking for/after the sheep.

Ragnhild er og besøker mor.
Ragnhild is (away) visiting mum.

Note – Two other related and rather colloquial constructions are **se og +** verb and **ta og +** verb. They are clearly related to the pseudo-coordinations and they have an aspectual function, but not one akin to that of the English progressive. They are rather used to denote inchoativity, the starting of an event:

Ta og skrell potetene!   Peel the potatoes.
Se og kom deg ut!   Get out!

Note – The English progressive may also be used in a 'continuative' sense. In that case, an idiomatic Norwegian translation may involve repeating the verb form preceded by **og**, 'and'. For example, 'David is always talking' may be translated **David prater og prater.**

5.3.5 | The past tense

For form, see 5.2.1.2 and 5.2.1.3.

Terms and main use

(a) The past tense ('preterite') in Norwegian (**preteritum**, in older grammars **imperfektum**), is typically used to express a completed action at a point of time in the past. Thus, the Norwegian past tense is used largely as its English equivalent:

Norge var i union med Danmark fram til 1814.
Norway was in a union with Denmark up to 1814.

I går regnet det hele dagen.
Yesterday there was rain all day long.

Past events are often perceived to be more 'distant' than events taking place now; similarly, the past tense often has a 'distancing' effect compared to the present tense.

As in English, the main difference between the past tense and the present perfect (5.3.6) is that the latter typically signals some kind of 'current relevance' for the action denoted. The distinction can be quite important:

Det var krig mellom Norge og Sverige i 1814.
There was war between Norway and Sweden in 1814.

Det har vært krig mellom supporterne i to år nå.
There has been war between the supporters for two years now.

In the first example, one would normally infer that the war is past history; in the second, that the war is still going on.

(b) The past tense can be used with a phrase that also signals a point in the past, i.e. a time marker, often a time adverbial (10.7.3.1, 10.8.2.2.(a)):

I fjor dro vi til Frankrike.   Last year we went to France.

Note – *I fjor har vi dratt til Frankrike, with a definite time adverbial combined with the present perfect, would normally be considered unacceptable, as indicated by the asterisk (cf. 5.3.6.1).

The time marker may be understood in a longer narrative text, just as in English; thus, it is not necessary to specify again and again in the text below that the action takes place before Easter last year:

Da vi kom til Zürich før påske i fjor, tok vi inn på det vanlige hotellet vårt. Heldigvis rakk vi middagen. Det var kalvelever på menyen.

As we arrived in Zürich before Easter last year, we arrived at our usual hotel. Fortunately, we made it for dinner. There was calves' liver on the menu.

Main uses of the past in Norwegian in addition to the one already surveyed include repeated action (5.3.5.2), polite use (5.3.5.3), unreal situations (5.3.5.4) and first impressions (5.3.5.5).

5.3.5.2 | Repeated action

The past tense can be used to express a repeated action in the past (in the same way as the present is used to express a repeated action, cf. 5.3.3.3); English can use 'used to/would':

Da de var gift, kranglet og skrek de hver eneste dag.
When they were married, they would quarrel and scream every single day.

Da jeg var student, spiste jeg ertesuppe uten kjøtt annenhver kveld.
When I was a student, I would eat pea soup without meat every other night.

Note – It is also possible to use **bruke** or **pleie**, 'usually do, used to' + å + infinitive in order to give a sense of repeated action:

Da de var gift, pleide de å kaste blomsterpotter på hverandre.
When they were married, they used to throw flower-pots at each other.

Da brukte naboen å be dem dempe seg.
Then their neighbour would ask them to calm down.

Bruke å is less common than pleie å.

5.3.5.3 | Politeness – with the modal auxiliary

(a) The past tense of a modal auxiliary (5.4.2) can be used to convey an additional note of politeness or caution in requests:

Kunne du løfte kofferten for meg?	Could you lift the trunk for me?
Kunne du sende meg saltet?	Would you pass the salt (please)?

There is absolutely nothing wrong with

Kan du løfte kofferten for meg?   Can you lift the trunk for me?

However, this latter question may be understood as a direct question about physical ability.

Even in suggestions, this past tense use of a modal auxiliary conveys a note of caution, of indirectness:

Skulle vi invitere onkel Ebenezer til julemiddagen?
Should we invite Uncle Ebenezer for Christmas dinner?

Kunne du være så snill å gi meg et råd?
Could you please give me a piece of advice?

This wording is more cautious than the alternative with the modal in the present tense:

Skal vi invitere onkel Ebenezer til julemiddagen?
Kan du være så snill å gi meg et råd?

(b) It is easier to answer 'no' when the modal is in the past tense. This 'distancing effect' of **kunne, skulle**, compared to present tense **kan, skal**, is perhaps due to the fact that the past, by its nature, is 'more distant' from the current reality than is the present. If we actually wish to ask about somebody else's ability to carry out an action now, the present tense is the natural choice:

Kan den lille dama virkelig løfte 200 kilo?
Is that little woman really able to lift 200 kg?

Note – It is also possible to choose a combination of past modal, an infinitive **ha,** 'have' and a supine:

Kunne du (ha) løftet kofferten for meg?
Skulle vi (ha) invitert onkel Ebenezer?

This injects a further note of politeness or caution. See also 5.4.2.3.

5.3.5.4 | *Unreal situations*

As the past is 'more distant' than the present, the past tense can have a modal sense; it can be used to indicate a hypothetical situation:

Om jeg var en rik mann, . . .
If I were a rich man, . . . (Tevje's song from *Fiddler on the Roof*)

Om jeg var deg, hadde jeg gitt meg et takknemlig kyss nå.
If I were you, I'd give me a grateful kiss now.

This use of the past to express unreal situations is – especially outside of conditional subclauses and with other verbs than **være** 'be' – rather infrequent, but still much more frequent in Norwegian than in English. The past perfect (**Om jeg hadde vært en rik mann/deg. . .**) is a more frequently used alternative (see also 5.3.7.4).

5.3.5.5 First impressions or feelings

In some impersonal expressions describing first impressions or feelings, the past tense is used in Norwegian where English would use the present tense:

Det var synd!	That is a shame!
Dette var god kaffe!	This is good coffee!

(This may be said after the first sip, when there is still a lot of coffee left.)

Det var godt nytt.	This is good news.
Det var en annen ting. . .	There is another thing. . .

5.3.6 The present perfect

5.3.6.1

Here are two initial examples of the present perfect:

Vi har vært i Oslo.	We have been to Oslo.
De har/er gått.	They have gone.

For form, see also 5.1.5. For use with the negative, see 10.7.3.2.

This construction is traditionally called 'the perfect'. We shall use more recent terminology, as reflected in *NRG*. The more recent term indicates that there is a perfective auxiliary **ha**, 'have' that is found in the present tense inflection (**har**).

The present perfect typically indicates 'current relevance' (cf. also 5.3.5.1); that an action completed in the past is still relevant to a present situation;

there is thus a link between the past and the present. The point of time for the past action may be indeterminate, but the point of reference is usually the present. This is rather similar to English.

Bestefaren min har vært sekretær.
My granddad has been a secretary.

This sentence would typically indicate that the speaker's granddad is still alive, and that his being a secretary is somehow relevant now. Compare, by contrast, the past near-equivalent:

Bestefaren min var sekretær.   My granddad was a secretary.

This sentence is more naturally understood as a piece of information about the speaker's late grandfather. This interpretation is not obligatory (compare also 5.3.4.1). But also in the following example, the granddad's having been a secretary is less relevant:

Bestefaren min var sekretær fram til han gikk av med pensjon, men nå skriver han ikke lenger ei linje.
My granddad was a secretary until he retired, but now he does not write a line any more.

5.3.6.2

There is a clear link between 'current relevance' and another important use of the present perfect; namely, that it often indicates recent past:

Nå har mjølka kokt over.   Now, the milk has boiled over.

Kom med en gang, doktor! Petter har hogd seg i beinet.
Please come at once, doctor! Petter has chopped his own leg.

Using the past tense in these examples is not impossible, but it would give a 'distancing' effect.

An action may have gone on for years. If the verb is combined with an indeterminate adverbial of time, we still prefer the present perfect:

Tore har bodd i Tromsø i mange år.
Tore has lived in Tromsø for many years.

5.3.6.3

Typically, the present perfect is formed with the auxiliary **ha,** 'have' + the supine:

Kari har sunget	Kari has sung.
Kari har danset.	Kari has danced.
Kari har gått.	Kari has left.
Felicia har forsvunnet.	Felicia has disappeared.

This option is always available in Norwegian. Alternatively, however, the present perfect for some verbs – those denoting (self-)movement or transition – can be formed with **være,** 'be'. Examples include **gå,** 'go'; **forsvinne,** 'vanish'; **komme,** 'come; **bli,** 'become':

Kari er gått.	Kari is gone.
Felicia er forsvunnet.	Felicia has disappeared.
Grete er blitt sjuk.	Grete has fallen ill.

Note 1 – This 'second option' is apparently becoming less common.

Note 2 – The choice of auxiliary **ha/være** in the past perfect follows the same principles, see 5.3.7.

5.3.6.4 *Time adverbial*

The time adverbial found together with the present perfect will typically be vague and include the present (cf. time adverbials with the past tense):

Jeg har bodd her *lenge*.	I (have) lived here for a long time.
***Nå* har du kanskje lest nok?**	Now, you may have read enough?

Erna har vært statsminister *i to år*.
Erna has been prime minister for two years.

This latter point illustrates a contrast between the past and the present perfect in Norwegian. The present perfect does not combine with adverbials that denote past time excluding the present:

Jeg var her *i fjor*.	I was here last year.
Hunden bjeffet *i går*.	The dog barked yesterday.
***Jeg har vært her i fjor.**	
***Hunden har bjeffet i går.**	

The latter two examples, with the combination of present perfect and adverbials denoting the past, would usually not be accepted, as indicated by the asterisk (but see 5.3.6.11 for the 'inferential perfect').

Note – Past tense:

Jeg bodde her lenge; Erna var statsminister i to år.
This would normally imply that the speaker no longer lives here, respectively that Erna is no longer prime minister.

5.3.6.5 *Inclusive present perfect*

With a suitable adverbial, the present perfect may indicate that an action has taken place and is still taking place:

De har vært gift i mange år.
They have been married for many years [and are presumably still married].

cf. **De har vært gift.**
They used to be married [but are presumably no longer married].

See also 5.3.6.7.

5.3.6.6 *Repeated or customary action*

The present perfect may express a repeated or customary action.

Jeg har spist havregrøt til frokost siden 90-tallet.
I have eaten porridge for breakfast since the 90s.

Han har oppført seg som en tosk så ofte han har fått sjansen.
He has behaved like a fool whenever he got the opportunity.

Norwegians may also use **har pleid** (less frequently **brukt**) + infinitive to emphasise a sense of customary action, cf. 5.3.5.2, Note.

Det har pleid/brukt å gå fint for oss.
Things have usually gone well for us.

5.3.6.7 *Two events in the future*

The present perfect may express the relationship between two events in the future when one completed action precedes another. See 5.3.8.5.

Når jeg har vasket opp, kan vi drikke kaffe.
When I have done the dishes, we can have coffee.

Har vi bare fått fiskekaker først, klarer vi alt.
If we only get fish-cakes first, we shall be up for anything.

5.3.6.8 *Norwegian present perfect = English future perfect*

The present perfect is often used in Norwegian where English would use the future perfect. See 5.3.9.

Når du kommer fram til Bodø, har nok jeg reist videre.
When you get to Bodø, I shall have left.

5.3.6.9 *Norwegian present perfect = English past tense*

This is used when some action completed in the past has a connection with the present. (Cf. 5.3.6.1.)

Hvor har du lært norsk?   Where did you learn Norwegian?
[The knowledge of Norwegian still exists.]

Hvem har skrevet *Peer Gynt*   Who wrote *Peer Gynt?*
[The play still exists and is read/performed.]

In the above examples, the simple past is also available, alternatively.

This use of the present perfect in Norwegian is especially frequent in questions and negative statements, in particular if the sentences include **aldri**, 'never' and **noensinne, noen gang**, 'ever':

Har dere sovet godt i natt?   Did you (pl.) sleep well tonight?

Nei, det har jeg aldri tenkt på før.
No, I never thought of that before.

Har du noen sinne hørt maken til tull?
Did you(sg.) ever hear such nonsense?

Jeg har aldri sett en hei eller hørt havet.
I never saw the moor nor ever heard the sea. (Emily Dickinson)

These examples are sometimes referred to as 'experiental'. English can have the simple past or the present perfect in many experiential sentences; Norwegians usually prefer the present perfect.

5.3.6.10	*Norwegian present perfect = English present*

This is found when the English present is used idiomatically to express a past action:

Jeg har glemt hva han heter.	I forget what he's called.
Jeg har hørt de skal skilles.	I hear that they are getting divorced.

5.3.6.11	*Inferential use*

The present perfect does not normally combine with time adverbials that locate the action in the definite past. ***Elgen har gått forbi i går**, 'The moose has gone by yesterday' seems as unacceptable as its counterpart would in English (cf. 5.3.6.4). However, an exception is illustrated in the following examples:

Her har det gått en elg i går.   A moose has been round here yesterday.

Natt til i går har så morderen listet seg inn i huset.
The night before last the murderer has then sneaked into the house.

The examples are possible if, say, hunters are looking at moose droppings or a detective is reconstructing the stages in a crime.

5.3.7	**The past perfect**

The past perfect is traditionally referred to as the 'pluperfect' (Norwegian **pluskvamperfektum**). More recent grammars tend to prefer the term 'past perfect', and hopefully the label is easier. Compare **har sunget**, 'has/have sung' (present perfect) vs. **hadde sunget,** 'had sung' (past perfect). Like the present perfect, the past perfect is usually formed with the supine preceded by **ha**, 'have', but it can alternatively be formed with **være** for some few verbs (denoting transition and movement, cf. 5.3.6.3):

Cf.

Kari hadde sunget.	Kari had sung.
Kari hadde danset.	Kari had danced.
Kari hadde/var gått.	Kari was gone.
Siv hadde/var forsvunnet.	Siv had disappeared.
Sindre hadde/var blitt sjuk.	Sindre had been taken ill.

For use with negative elements, see 10.7.3.2.

The Norwegian past perfect may (like its English equivalent) be used about an action in the past which has taken place before another action expressed by the past tense:

Etter at Kari hadde sagt dette, brast Per ut i gråt.
After Kari had said this, Per started crying.

Før vi kom, hadde han satt over kaffen.
Before we came, he had put the coffee kettle on.

| 5.3.7.2 | *Result*

The past perfect may be used about the result of a completed action:

Da hadde mjølka kokt over.   By that time the milk had boiled over.

This is perhaps not so much a distinct function as, again, 'past in the past', cf. 5.3.7.1.

| 5.3.7.3 | *Inclusive past perfect*

The past perfect may indicate that an action had taken place and at some point in the past was still taking place (cf. 5.3.6.5):

Kampen hadde vart i fire minutter da målmannen ble utvist.
The match had lasted for four minutes when the goalie was sent off.

| 5.3.7.4 | *Conditional or unreal sense*

Like the past (5.3.5.4), the past perfect may be used modally; it may have a conditional sense, for example indicating an unreal situation:

Hvis Hank Williams ikke hadde drukket så mye, hadde han kanskje levd lenger.
If Hank Williams had not drunk so much, he might have lived longer.

Hadde jeg vært deg, hadde jeg ikke bedt henne ryke og reise.
If I had been you, I would not have told her to bugger off.

This use of the past perfect is quite common. This may be seen as a modal use (rather than a temporal one). In such examples, the past perfect may be used about the future, given a suitable adverbial:

Hadde ikke toget til Stavanger gått så tidlig i morgen, kunne vi sitte oppe lenge i kveld.
If the train for Stavanger did not leave so early tomorrow morning, we could sit up a long time tonight.

The use of the past perfect in such cases is, as the third example indicates, perhaps even more usual in the conditional subclause than in the main clause.

5.3.8 | The future

There is no inflectional form of the verb in Norwegian (or English) specifically to indicate the future. When Norwegians speak about actions that are to take place in the future, they often do so in the present tense (cf. 5.3.3.4):

I 2050 er hun 90 år.	In 2050, she will be 90 years old.
Neste fredag drar jeg til Bergen.	Next Friday I shall go to Bergen.

While the present may be the most frequent choice in speech, there are several constructions that typically are used to express future more specifically, including **skal** + infinitive, **vil** + infinitive, **kommer til å** + infinitive, cf. 5.3.8.2f.

5.3.8.1 | Present tense to express future

See also 5.3.3.4.

(a) In these examples, we often find a time adverbial:

Jeg kommer snart.	I will come soon.
Toget går om fem minutter.	The train leaves in five minutes.

(b) A time marker is not always necessary, especially not with the verbs **bli**, 'be'; **få**, 'have'; **komme**, 'come':

Blir det regn?	Will there be rain?
Får du tid til å gjøre det?	Will you have time to do it?

Note – The combination of **tenke**, 'intend' in the present perfect and an infinitive (with å) indicates future intention:

Tore har tenkt å skrive enda en flott artikkel.
Tore is planning writing another brilliant paper.

Less frequently, one may find the combination of **tenke** in the simple present combined with an å-infinitive:

Hun tenker å sette potetene.   She intends to plant the potatoes.

(c) In both temporal clauses (10.8.2.2(a)) and conditional clauses (10.8.2.2(b)), the present tense is (as in English) often used to indicate the future:

Så snart arbeidsdagen er slutt, går jeg på kino.   *Temporal*
As soon as the working-day is over, I go to the movies.

Om det er kaldt i jula, drar vi ikke til Eina.   *Conditional*
If it is cold in Christmas, we do not go to Eina.

5.3.8.2 | *Komme til å + infinitive*

(a) A very frequent way of expressing futurity is through the construction **komme til å + infinitive**:

Det kommer til å snø til helga.	There will be snow this weekend.
Denne boka kommer til å bli en flopp.	This book will be a flop.
Liverpool kommer til å vinne.	Liverpool will win.

Komme til å + infinitive is used to indicate futurity, and it is perhaps more 'neutral', freer from modal overtones, than the alternatives **skulle** 'should' or **ville** 'would' + infinitive. It is, therefore, well suited to combine with non-personal subjects in cases where the speaker does not take any responsibility for the statement. **Det kommer til å snø** may seem more 'neutral' than **Det vil/skal snø**. (**Det skal snø** might, for example, indicate that the speaker has some particular reason for his belief that there will be snow.)

(b) The construction **komme til å** + infinitive is probably most frequent when **komme** is in the present tense. However, it is also found in the past tense:

Jeg visste at Buster kom til å bli glad når jeg kom hjem.
I knew that Buster (dog's name) would be happy when I got home.

Ingen kunne ane at katta kom til å bli overkjørt neste dag.
Nobody could foresee that the cat would be run over the following day.

(c) Likewise, **komme til å** may also be found with **komme** in the infinitive, although this may be less frequent:

Du kan komme til å angre på de orda.
You might come to regret those words.

Note – In the past tense, there is another meaning available of **kom til å** + infinitive, namely 'happened to do' the action described by the infinitive unintentionally, even by accident.

Dessverre kom jeg til å velte kaffekoppen.
Unfortunately, I happened to knock over the coffee cup.

This use of **kom til å** + infinitive is normally found only with subjects denoting humans and higher animals (animate subjects).

5.3.8.3 *Skal* + *infinitive*

This construction can be used to indicate future; it can have a modal sense too (5.4.2.2). Unlike **komme til å** + infinitive, **skal** + infinitive, especially when used with a human subject, may indicate a firm intention of carrying out the action at some point in the future:

Nå skal jeg gå hjem og finne fram skiene.
Now I shall go home and take out my skis.

When the subject is not human, **skal** can often indicate simple futurity, i.e. it may be merely temporal:

Toget skal gå ganske snart.   The train will leave fairly soon.

Det skal bli så godt å komme vekk litt.
It will be so nice to get away a bit.

For **ville, vil** + infinitive, see 5.4.2.4.

5.3.8.4 *Skulle* + *infinitive*

This construction can be used to indicate the future in the past, i.e. something viewed as future from a point of reference in the past:

I går sa han at han skulle ringe meg i dag.
Yesterday he said that he would call me today.

Jeg skulle akkurat til å ringe, og så stod du der!
I was just about to ring, and then you were there!

This construction can also be used modally, to signal obligation, even if **burde** + infinitive may be the more common option (cf. 5.4.2.2(a), 5.4.2.6.)

Du skulle ikke si sånne ting.   You should not say such things.

5.3.8.5 *Present perfect*

The present perfect occasionally indicates an action taking place before another action in the future. See 5.3.6.7.

Når vi har vært i København, drar vi videre til Paris.
When we have been to Copenhagen, we shall go on to Paris.

Tror du du har lest dokumentene før møtet?
Do you think you will have read the documents before the meeting?

5.3.9 *The future perfect*

The 'future perfect' can be realised by **skal ha (vil ha)** + supine or **kommer til å ha** + supine. It expresses a state or action lasting up to a point in time in the future. See present perfect, 5.3.6.

Innen 2030 skal vi ha prøvd alle skiene som fins i verden.
By 2030 we shall have tested all the skis that exist in this world.

Før Ole Einar gir seg, kommer han til å ha gått mer skiskyting enn noen annen.
Before Ole Einar quits, he will have done more biathlons than anybody else.

5.3.10 | *The future of the past*

5.3.10.1

The 'future of the past' can be realised by **skulle**, 'should', **ville**, 'would' + infinitive. It often expresses a future state or action in relation to a point in time in the past and is often used in indirect speech:

Så hyggelig at du kom – jeg skulle akkurat sette over kaffen.
How nice that you came – I was just about to put the coffee on.

Faktisk skulle Gustav dø bare noen uker seinere.
In fact, Gustav would die only a few weeks later.

5.3.10.2

Sometimes, this construction can have a modal function; the following example is not about the past, but about the present:

Nå ville jeg ta opp en kinkig sak.
Now I would like to raise a difficult issue.

Compared to **Nå vil jeg ta opp en kinkig sak**, the speaker appears more hesitant, less actively willing, when **ville** is used. (Again, the past indicates 'distance', cf. 5.3.5.3(d).) While this construction is often used about the past, it is not restricted to the past:

Skulle han ringe igjen i morgen, må du bare be han kontakte meg.
If he should call again tomorrow, just you ask him to contact me.

Skulle det dukke opp flere lik, er det bare å ringe.
If any more bodies should turn up, just call. (film title)

See also 5.3.8.2 on the construction with **kom til å**.

5.3.11 | *The future perfect of the past*

5.3.11.1

The 'future perfect of the past' is realised by **skulle** (**ville, burde**) + **ha** + supine of the main verb. It expresses a state or action lasting between two points in time, both in the past. It is often found in indirect speech. This construction is also used in conditional expressions.

Hun skulle (ha) reist med morgenflyet, men så ble hun sjuk.
She should have left by the morning plane, but she was taken ill.

Du skulle (ha) tenkt deg om før du sa noe så dumt.
You should have thought twice before saying something so stupid.

5.3.11.2

The non-finite auxiliary verb **ha**, 'have' is not obligatory in all cases, as indicated by the parentheses above. Omitting **ha** is typical of the spoken language, but is acceptable in writing too. However, there are cases where **ha** cannot be left out:

Hun så seg omkring ... Hvor kunne han ha gått?
She looked around ... Where could he have gone?

Here, **ha** cannot be left out, as the verbal construction deals with actual possibility (not with intention or obligation).

5.3.12 *The past participle*

5.3.12.1

First, remember the distinction between supine and past participle (5.2.1.1(e)): The supine is indeclinable, and it is used after the auxiliary verb **ha** to form the present perfect (5.3.6) and the past perfect (5.3.7), while the past participle is used after the auxiliary **være** (and **bli**) in a passive or adjectival manner.

5.3.12.2

The main rule for the past participle is fairly easy. For weak verbs, the base form of the past participle is identical to the supine, the indeclinable form. For strong verbs, there may be a difference, but only rarely.

Han har kastet avisene.   He has thrown away the newspapers.
Supine, weak class I

Avisene er kastet.   The newspapers are thrown away.
Participle

De har trykt boka.	They have printed the book. *Supine, weak class II*	**5** Verbs
Boka er trykt.	The book is printed. *Participle*	
De har skutt monsteret.	They have shot the monster. *Supine, strong*	
Monsteret ble skutt.	The monster has been/is shot.	

(a) As the examples show, the participle does not inflect for number when used in a passive construction with **være** or **bli**. However, the past participle can be used as an adjective, both predicatively and attributively. When used attributively, and especially as an element in compounds, it takes on the inflections associated with an adjective:

de kastete/kastede/kasta avisene	the discarded newspapers
det forkastede forslaget	the rejected proposal
den trykte versjonen	the printed version
de skadeskutte monstrene	the shot and wounded monsters

(b) The suffix –**ede** can only replace –**ete** in the definite/plural of participles of weak class I.

(c) The past participle can also be used as an adjectival noun (typically denoting people), and then also takes on the inflections of the adjective:

brev til en ukjent	letter to a stranger
I drømme ser han de ukjente.	In his dreams, he sees the unknown.
De drepte kommer aldri tilbake.	The dead [*lit.* killed ones] will never return.

5.3.13 The present participle

The present participle is formed by adding –**ende** to the verb stem, cf. **stå – stående**, **syng – syngende** (cf. 5.2.1.1(g)). It does not inflect. Some verbs do not have a present participle (e.g. the modals).

5.3.13.1 | Use

The present participle has a number of uses.

(a) It can be used in the same way as an adjective
Attributively (see 2.1.1):

frittgående høns	free-range hens
en levende beskrivelse	a vivid (*lit.* living) description

Predicatively (2.1.1):

Romanen er gripende.	The novel is moving.
Denne filmen var spennende.	This film was exciting.

(b) It can be used in the same way as a noun:

Hvis en reisende en vinternatt ...   If a traveller one winter night ...

Dette gjelder ikke bare for troende.
This does not only apply to believers.

Participles used as nouns usually indicate people.

(c) In an adverbial function (6.1.1):

Ronny kan være slående ufølsom.
Ron can be particularly insensitive.

Boka var overraskende svak.
The book was surprisingly poor.

(d) As a verb, e.g. after **komme**, come; **gå**, go; **bli**, remain:

Han gikk nynnende nedover vegen.
He walked down the road whistling.

Vi ble sittende stumme etter slikt dumt snakk.
We remained sitting speechless after such silly talk.

5.3.14 | **Renderings of the English present participle in Norwegian**

For translations of the other English ' –ing' forms, see 5.3.1.6 and 5.3.2.3.

5.3.14.1 | *Norwegian uses two verbs*

For pseudo-coordination, see also 5.3.4.2(b).

Eivor sat reading for hours.	**Eivor satt og leste i timevis.**
They stood watching the train.	**De stod og så på toget.**

5.3.14.2 | *Norwegian uses a finite verb and an infinitive*

See also 5.3.2.3.

Do you like skiing?	**Liker du å gå på ski?**
We went on ice-fishing.	**Vi fortsatte å pilke.**

5.3.14.3 | *Norwegian uses an object and infinitive construction*

See also 10.10.2.2.

I heard her cursing.	**Jeg hørte henne banne.**

5.3.14.4 | *Norwegian has a full clause; English has a contracted sentence*

See also 5.3.2.3.

Asking him to come back later, she returned to her work.
Hun bad ham komme tilbake seinere, og gikk tilbake til arbeidet.

5.4 Mood and modality

5.4.1 | *Introduction*

5.4.1.1 |

Mood and modality relate to the attitude of the speaker to the activity expressed by the verb; whether, for instance, the speaker considers the content of the sentence to be true (or based on hearsay, or desirable). In terms of inflection, there are two 'living' members of the mood category, viz. the imperative, e.g. **kast,** 'throw'; **syng,** 'sing', and the indicative, e.g. **kaster, synger,** 'throws, sings'; **kastet, sang,** 'threw, sang'. The indicative is much more used and fairly uninformative: All it tells us is that the imperative has not been chosen. The imperative, by contrast, tells us that the speaker sees some action as desirable.

Besides these two, there are remnants of a subjunctive (optative), mostly restricted to certain set phrases, e.g. **Lenge leve kongen,** 'Long live the king', cf. 5.4.3. While the term 'mood' is restricted to inflection in this book, the term 'modality' is not.

5.4.1.2

Modality can be signalled periphrastically, by various modal auxiliaries or constructions:

> **Mistenkte *skal ha* truet avdøde tidligere på dagen.**
> The suspect is reported to have threatened the deceased earlier that day.

This sentence does not only state that the suspect threatened the deceased, but also that this statement is built on second-hand evidence. This is shown by the use of **skal ha truet.** (See also 'inferential use', cf. 5.3.6.11.)

5.4.1.3

As in English, one may also use the past tense and the past perfect modally. Consider:

> **Om jeg ble rik, hadde jeg kjøpt nytt hus til mor mi.**
> If I became rich, I'd buy a new house for my mother.

The past tense **ble** and the past perfect **hadde kjøpt** do not locate the action in the past; rather, they underline the hypothetical character of the statement.

Note – **Om jeg blir rik, kjøper jeg nytt hus til mor mi** is also a sentence that signals a hypothetical scenario. Yet the idea of becoming rich is not quite so hypothetical as when the past is used. (The past is perceived as more 'distant' (5.3.5.1), i.e. unlikely.)

5.4.1.4

A third main way of signalling modality is by means of various adverbial phrases:

Hva gjør John Ole nå? Å, han arbeider _sikkert_.
What is John Ole doing now? Oh, he is surely working.

Mistenkte kom _visstnok_ med trusler mot avdøde.
The suspect allegedly made threats to the deceased.

The adverbs **sikkert,** 'surely' and **visstnok,** 'allegedly, probably' tell us that the speaker is not sure, but is making a suggestion or a guess.

5.4.1.5 Modal auxiliary verbs

Modal auxiliary verbs (5.4.2) are used together with the main verb in the infinitive (or with **ha, få** + a supine):

Vi skal reise til Eina i juleferien.
We shall go to Eina (place-name) in the Christmas vacation.

Du må gå nå.   You must go now.

Sometimes, modals can be used without an infinitive:

Jeg må på do.   _Lit._ I must on loo, i.e.
                                   I must go to the loo.

When modals are used without an infinitive, there is usually an adverbial of direction – typically denoting direction to a certain place:

Vi skal til Eina nyttårsaften.
Lit. We shall [go] to Eina (place-name) on New Year's Eve.

5.4.1.6 Modal forms

These comprise the indicative, the imperative (5.4.4) and, marginally, the subjunctive (5.4.3):

Eldbjørg _drikker_ kaffe nå.   Eldbjørg is drinking coffee now.
       Indicative

***Spis* opp maten din nå!**   Eat your food now.
Imperative

Søren *ta* den oppblåste tufsen.   Damn that pompous fool!
Subjunctive

Conditional constructions

The past perfect can be used to signal a conditional.

Om jeg ikke hadde hatt ti tommeltotter, ville jeg blitt tømrer.
If I didn't have ten thumbs, I'd have become a carpenter.

Vi kunne reist mer, om vi ikke hadde hatt hund.
We could have travelled more, if we had not had [the] dog.

See 5.3.7.4.

5.4.2 | Modal auxiliary verbs

5.4.2.1 | *Form*

These verbs can express mood when used together with the infinitive of the main verb.

Infinitive	Present	Past	Supine	Meaning
skulle	skal	skulle	skullet	shall, will
kunne	kan	kunne	kunnet	be able
ville	vil	ville	villet	will, want to
måtte	må	måtte	måttet	must, have to
burde	bør	burde	burdet	should, ought to
tore*	tør	torde	tort	dare, is probably
la	lar	lot	latt	let
(få	får	fikk	fått	may, be allowed to, must)

*For alternative forms of **tore**, see 5.4.2.7.

5.4.2.2 | **Skulle**

(See also 5.3.8.3f. and 5.3.9f. on uses denoting the future.) Note the following uses of **skulle** (present tense **skal**):

(a) Necessity, duty, obligation:

Du skal ikke lyve.   You shall not lie.

(b) Opinion, assumption, possibility:

Skulle dette være morsomt?   Was this supposed to be funny?

(c) As a sign that the statement is built on indirect information:

Bobby Fischer skulle visstnok være ganske vanskelig.
Bobby Fischer was supposed to be fairly difficult.

(d) As a sign of conditionality:

Det skulle være interessant å høre hvorfor dødsstraff er så bra.
It would be interesting to hear why capital punishment is so good.

5.4.2.3 *Kunne*

Kunne (present tense **kan**) 'could, can, be able to' has many uses, including
the following:

(a) Possibility

Kan du komme?   Can you come?/Is it possible for you to come?

The past tense **kunne** would here be more indirect, in some contexts more
polite.

(b) Ability

Jeg kan gå på skøyter.   I can skate.

Here, the past tense **kunne** would be about ability only; there is no politeness involved.

(c) Permission

Kan jeg låne bilen din i kveld?   May I borrow your car tonight?

Again, a past tense **kunne** would signal an indirect question, increased
politeness.

(d) Concession

Det kan nok stemme.   That may be right.

The past tense here might indicate a restraint on the concession:

Det kunne nok stemme, om det ikke var for at ...
That might have been right, if it were not for the fact that ...

Note – When used as a main verb, **kunne** indicates ability, typically in a language or a field of knowledge:

Arne kan islandsk. Arne knows Icelandic.
Åshild kan fotball. Åshild knows (everything about) football

5.4.2.4 *Ville*

Ville (present tense **vil**), 'would, want' has many uses, including the following:

(a) Subject's wishes

Vil du ha en kopp kaffe? Would you like a cup of coffee?
Nå vil vi ha snø! Now we want snow!
Jeg vil at du går nå. I want you to leave now.

There is a difference between **vil**, which often indicates wish, and **skal**, which may come closer to 'neutral' futurity:

Vil du være med på kino? Would you like to go to the cinema with me/us?
Skal du på jobb? Are you going to work?

The use of **vil** is not necessarily 'strong' or 'direct' (unlike English):

Jeg vil mye heller spille fiolin. I would much rather play the violin.

(b) To denote futurity, although this is less common than in English:

Toget vil stoppe på Årnes i dag. The train will stop at Årnes today.

(c) As a sign of conditionality:

Det ville være interessant å høre hvorfor dødsstraff er så bra.
It would be interesting to hear why capital punishment is so good.

5.4.2.5 *Måtte*

Måtte (present tense **må**), 'must, have to' has many uses, including the following:

(a) Compulsion, necessity. In positive expressions, the verb means 'must', 'have to', 'be forced to':

Jeg må dessverre gå nå.   Unfortunately, I have to go now.
Det må være løgn.   That has to be a lie.

Geitosten må være i kjøleskapet.
The goat cheese must be in the fridge.

In negative expressions **må ikke** is ambiguous. It can mean either 'It is not necessary that X should . . .' or 'It is necessary that X should not . . .'.

Du må ikke synge om du ikke vil.
You don't have to sing if you do not want to. (It is not necessary that . . .)

Du må ikke angripe broren din med øks.
You must not attack your brother with an axe.
(It is necessary that you do not. . .)

(b) In fixed expressions, for wishes, possibilities, concessions:

Det må jeg si!   I say!
Gid hun lenge lenge leve må!   Long may she live.
Måtte det vare!   May this last!
Det må så være.   That may well be.

5.4.2.6 *Burde*

The past tense form **burde** 'ought to' is often perceived as more polite and tentative than the present **bør**; some writers avoid the present of this verb. **Burde** can be used in verbal constructions to indicate:

(a) Suitability or strong recommendation

Du burde lese denne boka.   You should read this book.
Man bør ikke plage andre.   One should not pester others.

English 'should' indicating suitability will often translate as **burde/bør**:

Kristin burde/bør finne en annen mann enn Erlend.
Kristin should find another man than Erlend.

(b) Assumption, possibility

Han bør ha kommet hjem nå.
He should have come home by now.

5.4.2.7 Tore/tørre

The normal meaning of **tore/tørre** (past tense **turte/torde**) is 'dare':

Den vesle gutten turde ikke legge seg.
The little boy dared not go to bed.

Si det en gang til om du tør.   Say that again if you dare.

In literary language, the verb may be used as a modal to denote possibility or assumption:

Saken turde være foreldet.   The case would seem outdated.

5.4.2.8 La

La 'let' has a number of uses, some modal:

(a) Permit, give leave to

Læreren lot barna leke.   The teacher let the children play.
La legen komme fram!   Let the doctor pass!

Note – In constructions with **La oss**, 'Let us' + infinitive, the listener may either be included in the 'we-group' or not. **La oss komme oss av gårde**, 'Let us get off' is an example where the listener clearly is included. In **La oss komme forbi**, 'Let us pass', the listener is clearly excluded.

(b) Refrain from changing ('leave/let be')

La bøkene være, barn.   Leave the books alone, children.
La osten stå i kjøleskapet.   Let the cheese stand in the fridge.

(c) Commission, undertaking

Christian 4. lot oppføre en ny hovedstad.
Christian 4. had a new capital built.

While (a)–(c) are all cases of the 'object and infinitive' (10.10.2.2), (c) is a more literary and formal use.

5.4.2.9 Få

If **få** is used non-modally, it usually means 'receive, get':

Harry fikk gaver fra en anonym beundrer.
Harry received gifts from an anonymous admirer.

However, like English 'get', **få** can also be used meaning 'get somebody to do something':

Eldbjørg får meg til å le.   Eldbjørg makes me laugh.

In its more modal functions, **få** can indicate:

(a) Permission

Får jeg gå på kino med Maud?   May I go to the movies with Maud?
Du får gjerne ta litt kake.   You had better take/may take some cake.

(b) Necessity, weak compulsion

Dere får gjøre det, dere.   You (pl) had better do it, you had.
Du får ordne opp i rotet   You (sg) had better sort out the mess.

(c) 'Get to'

Vi får se Klee-utstillinga i Zürich.
We shall get to see the Klee exhibition in Zürich.

When combined with the supine, **få** has a somewhat different function than when it is combined with the infinitive. While **Kari får ordne opp i rotet** (infinitive) means that Kari had better sort out the mess, **Kari fikk ordnet opp i rotet** (supine) means that Kari actually sorted out the mess. Similarly, **Du får gjerne ta litt kake** means that 'you' may well take some cake, while **Du fikk gjerne tatt litt kake?** implies that 'you' managed to take some more cake (I suppose).

| 5.4.2.10 | *Har å* 'be obliged to' |

Har å resembles English 'have to' formally, and both convey a kind of modality, but they do not mean quite the same thing. English 'have to' can denote any kind of 'necessity', social or simply physical; Norwegian **ha å** is only used about social necessity. It is very strong and rather formal:

Studentene har å etterkomme skriftlige instrukser.
The students are obliged to follow written instructions.

har å + infinitive is little used outside the present tense.

5.4.3 | *The subjunctive*

As to form, the subjunctive is identical to the infinitive. Unlike the imperative, the subjunctive (**konjunktiv, optativ**) is not a 'living' member of the mood category or of Norwegian verb inflection. If a new verb enters the language, it is unlikely ever to be used in the subjunctive. Nevertheless, the subjunctive is found in certain fixed expressions:

Lenge leve kongen!   Long live the king!

Herren velsigne deg og bevare deg.
The Lord bless you and keep you (Numbers, 6).

Faen ta deg!   Damn you! (vulgar)

Note – While the subjunctive by and large has long been relegated to fixed expressions, it has had a slightly more important role in swearing. Only the third example above occurs in 'normal' spoken language.

The role that the subjunctive played has, to a large extent, been taken over by other constructions, involving modal auxiliaries or adverbs:

Forhåpentligvis får kongen leve lenge.
Hopefully, the king will have a long life.

5.4.4 | *The imperative*

5.4.4.1

(a) The imperative is a member of the mood category. It is used for commands (cf. the older term **bydeform**, 'the form used for ordering'). When new verbs enter Norwegian, there will normally be an imperative available. Once Norwegians have started using the verb **seive** 'save on a computer' (cf. English 'save'), the imperative **seiv** can be used:

Seiv manuskriptet før du slutter for dagen.
Save the manuscript [on your computer] before quitting for the day.

Formally, the imperative is identical to the verb stem (cf. 5.2.1.1(c)). Thus, it ends in a stressed vowel in Class III verbs (and some strong ones); for all other verbs, it ends in a consonant (but see (c) below).

(b) In writing, imperative sentences can be marked with an exclamation mark, but often they are not:

Pass deg!   Look out!

Gå ikke over vegen før bussen har kjørt.
Do not cross the road before the bus has left.

For use with the negation **ikke**, see 10.10.1.1, Note 2.

(c) Not all verbs have an imperative. For example, the modals do not, and it is highly unusual to find the imperative of verbs denoting actions over which the subject cannot have control (e.g. **gjelde**, 'apply, hold', **forekomme**, 'happen', and passive s-verbs). Also, many Norwegians avoid imperative of verbs whose stem end in a consonant sequence that they find difficult to pronounce. Thus, many writers avoid the imperative of **sykle**, 'cycle', **åpne**, 'open' as they do not like words ending in –**kl**, –**pn**. Instead, circumlocutions will be used (e.g. **Vær så snill å åpne**, 'Please open').

5.4.4.2 Use of the imperative

(a) The imperative is typically associated with commands and orders, but it may also be used to express wishes or pieces of advice. Usually, a subject in the second person (singular or plural) may be inferred:

Kom hit!	Come here!

Sometimes, a subject is explicitly expressed, for example to 'soften' the command:

Kom hit, gutten min.	Come here my boy.

Insertion of the subject does not always 'soften'; it may clarify who the addressee is, or show a contrast:

Sitt ned, Asbjørn.	Sit down, Asbjørn.

Bare rydd, du, så skal jeg vaske opp så lenge.
Just you tidy up, and I'll do the dishes in the meantime.

The imperative may also be 'softened' by adding a 'please', but this is not as obligatory as in English:

Vær så snill og kom hit!	Come here, please.
Kom hit, (så) er du snill	Come here, please.

(b) While many examples of the imperative may be seen as commands, there are examples that cannot:

Tilgi oss vår skyld.	Forgive us our sins. (Lord's Prayer)

Note – The imperative can be used in impolite utterances, as in English (e.g. **Dra til helvete!** 'Go to hell!'). However, the imperative is not necessarily less polite than other means of expression. **Kom hit!**, 'Come here!' is a less offensive way of asking the hearer to come than the simple present indicative **Du kommer hit!**, which is best avoided in polite interaction between adults.

5.4.5 | Conditional constructions

A further means of signalling modality is to use one of the common kinds of conditional construction found in 5.4.5.1–5.4.5.3.

5.4.5.1 | Conditional clause

See also 10.8.2.2(b), 10.8.3.2.

Om ikke grammatikere var så rare, ...
If grammarians were not so strange ...

Hvis månen hadde vært en gul ost, hadde jeg kjøpt en liten bit.
If the moon had been a yellow cheese, then I would have bought a small piece.

5.4.5.2 | Question clause expressing condition

The conditional can also be expressed by using question word order (see 10.8.5.2) as English may do on occasions.

Kommer hun, så går jeg.   If she comes, I go.

Hadde du ikke lagd så gode vafler, hadde jeg ikke spist så mange.
Had you not made such good waffles, then I would not have eaten so many.

5.4.5.3 | Imperative clause expressing condition

See also 5.4.4.2.

Et opp silda, så skal du få dram.
You eat your herring, then you'll get a tot.

5.5 Transitive, intransitive and reflexive verbs

5.5.1 Introduction

5.5.1.1 Transitive, intransitive, ditransitive

(a) As traditionally described, transitive verbs take a direct object, intransitive ones do not:

Koalaen fortærer maten. The koala devours/is devouring the food.
(**fortære** is transitive, **maten** its direct object)

Elvis lever. Elvis lives.
(**leve** is intransitive, there is no object)

The verb **fortære** requires an object; **leve** is seldom used with one.

(b) However, the transitive – intransitive distinction is rarely so straightforward. The verbs **male**, 'paint', and **spise**, 'eat' usually take an object:

Jeff malte bilder med kommersiell appell.
Jeff painted pictures with commercial appeal.

Koalaen spiser bare én eneste plante.
The koala eats one plant only.

Yet these verbs may be used without an object, especially if that object can be recovered from the context:

Vi skal male fra ni til ett i morgen.
We shall paint from nine to one tomorrow.

Når jeg spiser, lar jeg mobiltelefonen være.
When I eat, I put aside my mobile phone.

Similarly, the verbs **sove, danse** 'sleep, dance' are usually intransitive, but they can combine with an object (especially if this object is related to the verb):

Far min sover alltid godt om natta.
My father always sleeps well at night. *Intransitive, typical*

Barnet sov de uskyldiges søte søvn.
The child slept the sleep of the innocent. *Transitive, atypical*

Kari og Arve danser sjelden.
Kari and Arve rarely dance. *Intransitive, typical*

Kari og Arve danset bryllupsvals.

Kari and Arve danced their wedding waltz.　　*Transitive, atypical*

(c) This does not mean that the distinction between transitive and intransitive is without merit. Some verbs do combine with an object more easily than others, at least partly because of their meaning. It is part of the meaning of the verb **fortære**, 'devour' that there is both somebody devouring and something being devoured, while for **sove**, 'sleep' it is implied that somebody is sleeping, but not really that there is a 'product'.

(d) Typically, transitive verbs take a passive suffix or combine with other kinds of 'periphrastic passives' (cf 5.6.1.2(b),(c)) more easily than intransitives. For example, the transitive **spise**, 'eat' may well be found with a passive –s, as in **Muskatnøtt bør ikke spises rå i store mengder.** 'Nutmeg should not be eaten raw in large quantities', the intransitive **dø**, 'die' is practically never found in the passive. See further on the passive 5.6.

(e) While the transitive verbs in the examples above all combine with a direct object only, a further distinction is sometimes drawn between 'monotransitive' and 'ditransitive' verbs. Ditransitive verbs – such as **gi**, **forære**, 'give' – do not take only a direct object, but also an indirect one:

Romeo forærte Julie blomster.　　Romeo gave Juliet flowers.

Å lese M.H. Olsen har gitt meg mange gleder.

Reading M. H. Olsen has given me many pleasures.

(f) While ditransitive verbs are typically used with two objects, they may combine with only the direct one, especially if the other can easily be inferred:

Å lese kjendis.no har gitt få gleder; å lese M.H. Olsen har gitt mange.

To read kjendis.no (a web-site on celebrities) has provided few pleasures; to read M.H. Olsen has provided many.

The set of ditransitive verbs is much smaller than that of transitives. Besides **gi** and **forære**, it includes **vise**, 'show'; **forklare**, 'explain'; **donere**, 'donate'; **tilby**, 'offer'; **foreslå**, 'suggest'; **love**, 'promise'; **etterlate**, 'leave'; **låne**, 'lend'; **rekke**, 'reach/give'; **sende**, 'send', **si**, 'say'. Thus, certain meanings are often associated with ditransitives.

(g) The indirect object can alternatively be expressed by means of a prepositional phrase, just as in English.

Romeo gav blomster til Julie.	Romeo gave flowers to Juliet. (7.3.5.4, Note 2, 10.3.4.1(b)).

5.5.2 | Transitive and intransitive verbs

5.5.2.1 | Related pairs

Transitive and intransitive verbs sometimes occur in pairs with similar meanings and forms. In many cases, the transitive verb is a weak one, the intransitive a strong one (and in some cases, there is a relation of causation):

Transitive			*Intransitive*		
brenne	*weak*	burn	**brenne**	*strong*	burn
felle	*weak*	fell	**falle**	*strong*	fall
sette	*weak*	place, set	**sitte**	*strong*	sit
henge	*weak*	hang	**henge**	*strong*	hang

Compare:

Bonden brente høyet.	The farmer burnt the hay.
Høyet brant.	The hay burnt.
Hun hengte fra seg genseren.	She hung up her sweater.
Genseren hang over stolen.	The sweater hung over the chair.

Note – To many Norwegians, this is difficult. Thus, **Hun hang fra seg genseren** is often heard and seen.

In some cases, both related verbs are weak:

Transitive	*Intransitive*
vekke 'wake up'	**våke** 'stay awake'
	våkne 'wake up'
slukke 'extinguish'	**slukne** 'be extinguished'

5.5.2.2 | Either transitive or intransitive

Most Norwegian verbs may be used either with or without an object:

Fredager spiser vi fiskesuppe.	On Fridays, we eat fish soup. [tr.]
Ikke forstyrr! Mor spiser.	Do not disturb! Mother's eating. [intr.]

However, for many verbs there is a preference for transitivity or intransitivity. Cf. 5.5.1.1.

Transitive or intransitive in English

The transitive–intransitive distinction is somewhat more important in Norwegian grammar than in English. Sometimes, English will employ one and the same verb where Norwegian has two related verbs to make the distinction

They *sank* the ships.	**De senket skipene.**
	senke – senker – senket – senket (tr., weak)
Titanic *sank*.	**Titanic sank.**
	synke – synker – sank – sunket (intr. strong)

See also 5.5.2.1 above.

Sometimes English can use one and the same verb where Norwegians will use two completely different verbs (5.8.1.7):

Mother grows potatoes.	**Mor dyrker poteter (dyrke**, tr.)
The potatoes are growing.	**Potetene vokser (vokse**, intr.)
The mother fed the child.	**Mora matet ungen.**
He feeds on chocolate only.	**Han spiser bare sjokolade.**

Reflexive plus verb

(a) Reflexive verb constructions are formed using reflexive pronouns (see 4.5.1). The reflexive pronoun may then be considered the object of the verb. The action 'reflects' back on the subject (as the pronoun refers back to the subject), so that the subject is often 'affected' by the action (cf. 4.5.1.4).

Transitive, 'normal' object
I 'Rio Bravo' barberer Angie Dickinson Dean Martin.
In 'Rio Bravo' Angie Dickinson shaves Dean Martin.

Transitive, reflexive pronoun as object
Peter barberte seg to ganger om dagen.
Peter shaved [himself] twice a day.

(While Angie Dickinson presumably is not 'affected' by the shaving, Peter is.)

Transitive 'normal' object	Reflexive pronoun as object
Han kastet bladet.	**Keeperen kastet seg og tok ballen.**
[**bladet** = object]	[**seg** = reflexive object]
He threw the magazine.	The goalie dived and caught the ball.
Hun gjemte boka.	**Barnet gjemte seg.**
[**boka** = object]	[**seg** = reflexive object]
She hid the book.	The child hid (itself).

(b) While the relation in meaning between e.g. the transitive **barbere** 'shave' and the reflexive **barbere seg,** 'shave oneself' is fairly straightforward, there can be a considerable difference in meaning between the simple verb and its reflexive counterpart, as **snyte – snyte seg** and **slå – slå seg** illustrate (see also 4.5.2.2):

Kjeltringen snøt oss alle.	The crook cheated us all.
Bestefar snøt seg.	Granddad blew his nose.

5.5.3.1 Transitive normal or reflexive

Most transitive verbs may be used with a 'normal' object or with a reflexive object:

Frisøren vasket kunden.	**Frisøren vasket seg.**
The hairdresser washed the customer.	The hairdresser washed (himself).

5.5.3.2 Only reflexive

Some verbs are only found together with the reflexive pronoun (and never intransitively or with any other object, cf. 4.5.2.1). These include:

befatte seg med, 'concern oneself with'; **begi seg,** 'go, travel'; **forelske seg,** 'fall in love'; **forkjøle seg,** 'catch a cold'; **forspise seg,** 'overeat'; **gifte seg,** 'marry'; **innfinne seg,** 'turn up'; **skynde seg,** 'hurry'; **utspille seg,** 'take place'.

As the examples indicate, many of the verbs have a prefix in **for–**, **be–**, but not all.

5.5.3.3 Reflexive in Norwegian, but not in English

(a) Often, a verb used with a reflexive object in Norwegian corresponds to one without a reflexive in English:

Tintin reiste seg.	Tintin rose/got up.
Jeg føler meg faktisk dårlig.	Actually, I feel sick.
Julenissen bør skynde seg.	Santa Claus had better hurry.
Bør Donald og Dolly gifte seg?	Should Donald and Dolly get married?

A number of these verbs indicate bodily movement or grooming:

legge seg, lie down; **nærme seg**, approach; **røre seg**, move; **barbere seg**, shave; **gre seg**, comb. Others include **anstrenge seg**, make an effort; **avholde seg**, abstain; **beklage seg**, complain; **forestille seg**, imagine; **forandre seg**, change; **gifte seg**, marry; **glede seg**, look forward to; **grue seg**, fear; **oppføre seg**, behave; **te seg**, behave; **trekke seg**, withdraw; **vise seg**, appear.

(b) Norwegian allows for considerable freedom with the reflexive construction. For instance, a normally intransitive verb can be used with a reflexive pronoun and an adverbial to indicate movement (compare English 'way'):

Hun danset seg forbi vaktene.
She danced her way past the guards.

Han mumlet seg inn i våre hjerter.
He mumbled his way into our hearts.

5.5.3.4 Reflexive or –s form

In some cases, an alternative to the reflexive form is an intransitive –s form of the verb (cf. also 5.6.3.2):

Herrene samler seg rundt sigarene.
The gentlemen gather around the cigars.

Herrene samles rundt sigarene.

| 5.6.1.1 | *Active and passive, subjects and agents*

(a) In an active sentence, there may be both a subject and an object. The subject is often identical to the agent (the party carrying out the 'action'):

Brit Bildøen beskriver sorgen.   Brit Bildøen describes the grief.
Subject   *Object*

In a corresponding passive sentence, there cannot be both a subject and an object. The object from the active sentence becomes the subject in the passive sentence, the subject of the active construction will be expressed by means of a prepositional phrase (if at all, see also (b) below and 5.6.2.2).

Sorgen beskrives av Brit Bildøen.   The grief is described by Brit
Subject   Bildøen.

The two sentences may be seen as roughly synonymous. In both, **Brit Bildøen** is doing the describing; **Brit Bildøen** is the agent in both. However, the focus differs in the two sentences. The active sentence is more naturally used if **Brit Bildøen** is already the topic (what we are talking about); the passive sentence is perhaps more naturally used if we are already talking about the grief. See also Topicalisation 10.7.2.

(b) In a passive sentence, the grammatical subject is not the agent; it is infrequent, in actual use, to express the 'agentive' **av**-phrase. The reason for using the passive is often that the speaker wishes to omit the agent. The agent may be unknown or obvious, or the speaker may wish to focus on the action itself:

Dørene lukkes.
The doors are closing.

Frokosten serveres mellom 6 og 10.
Breakfast is served between 6 and 10.

Faktisk snakkes det mye fransk i Canada.
Actually, French is spoken a lot in Canada.

(c) Norwegian also allows for so-called impersonal passives. They have no agent or any straightforward English equivalent. The verb stem in such constructions is often intransitive, but not necessarily:

Nå skal det danses.	There will be dancing now.
Her skal det slaktes.	*Lit.* Here there will be butchered; Here butchering will be done.
I dag skal det arbeides.	*Lit.* Today there will be worked; Today some work will be done.

Here there is no agent, but neither is there a 'full' grammatical subject, only the 'dummy pronoun' **det** (cf.4.2.4.6, 8).

5.6.1.2 Three kinds of passive

In Norwegian, there are several ways of expressing a content roughly corresponding to the English 'passive'. (There are more ways in English as well, cf. 'Dumbledore was killed' and 'Dumbledore got killed'.) The three main kinds of passive in Norwegian include one strictly inflectional (a) and two periphrastic ones (b–c).

(a) The –s passive (–s is added to the active form of the verb, see 5.6.1):

Dørene stenges.	The doors are closing/being closed.
Sorgen beskrives av Bildøen.	The grief is described by Bildøen.

(b) Forms of **bli** + past participle (i.e. periphrastic forms. For forms of the past participle, see 5.3.12.1f):

Dørene blir stengt.	The doors are closing/being closed.
Sorgen blir beskrevet av Bildøen.	The grief is described by Bildøen.

(c) Forms of **være** + past participle (i.e. periphrastic forms. For forms of the past participle, see 5.3.12.1):

Dette problemet har vært oversett.
This problem has been overlooked.

Denne sorgen har vært beskrevet av Bildøen.
This grief has been described by Bildøen.

Note – In spoken language, the –s passive is usually avoided outside of the infinitive. Apart from (b) and (c), other modes of expression may be chosen, such as **de, man** etc. + an active verb:

De stenger dørene.   They are closing the doors.

5.6.1.3 *Choice of the passive form*

It is not always easy to say why one of the types above will be or should be chosen, but there are some general rules of thumb.

(a) The –s passive (For more detail see 5.6.2 below)

The present tense s-passive tends to be found in written rules and regulations and texts giving guidance or instruction.

Fårikål serveres rykende varm.
Mutton-and-cabbage is served piping hot.

Tablettene tas tre ganger om dagen.
The tables are taken three times a day.

It can also be found in texts that do not give instruction, however:

4500 syklister skades i trafikken årlig.
4,500 cyclists are injured in traffic annually.

The infinitive –s passive is often used with a modal verb (cf 5.6.1.2, Note):

Ved å bruke hjelm kan disse skadene reduseres betydelig.
By using a helmet these injuries can be reduced substantially.

Note the construction with **det** and the –s passive:

Det snakkes om et nyvalg.   There is talk of a new election.

Det eksporteres store mengder gass.
A large amount of gas is exported.

(b) The **bli** passive

This has a wide area of use, especially where a single, concrete action or an action in the past is involved. In speech, it is the most widely used form.

Mange biler blir stjålet hvert år.
A lot of cars get stolen every year.

En betydelig mengde dyrearter blir utryddet.
A considerable number of species of fauna are being eradicated.

Huset ble solgt for en million kroner.
The house was sold for a million kroner.

It is preferred with the verb **ville**:

Det er tatt mange prøver og disse vil bli analysert.
A lot of samples have been taken and these will be analysed.

Ville + –s passive is usually understood as volitional:

Jeg vil undersøkes av lege!
I want to be examined by a doctor!

(c) The **være** passsive

This has a more restricted area of use, often denoting a state or continuing action.

Gjerningsmannen er pågrepet.
The perpetrator has been arrested.

Tre personer er skadet i ulykken.
Three people have been injured in the accident.

Flyet er forsinket. Mange passasjerer er rammet.
The flight has been delayed. Many passengers have been affected.

With many verbs denoting description, evaluation or reference, the **være** passive is used in the same way as the **bli** passive, e.g. **anse**, 'consider'; **betrakte**, 'regard'; **hevde**, 'claim'; **nevne**, 'mention'; **skrive**, 'write'.

5.6.2 | The –s passive

5.6.2.1 | The form of the **–s** passive

See table below.

	Infinitive	Meaning	Present	Past	Supine
Weak I	**kastes**	be thrown	**kastes**	–	–
Weak IIa	**kjøpes**	be bought	**kjøpes**	**kjøptes**	–
Weak IIb	**bygges**	be built	**bygges**	**bygdes**	–
Weak III	**sys**	be sewn	**sys**	–	–
Strong	**gripes**	be invited	**gripes**	**(?greps)**	–

(a) As the infinitive and the present –s forms are identical, formally, it is a moot point whether to distinguish between them. In the infinitive and the present, a suffix –s can be added to the active verb form. This holds true for most verbs, regardless of inflection class.

(b) In the past tense, only verbs belonging to weak class II (and a few strong ones) can take a suffix –s. There is some individual variation. Fairly few will use past –s passives like **kjøptes**, and even fewer use **greps**.

(c) The verb **løfte**, 'lift' belongs to weak class I, so there will be no past –s passive available. The verb **lese**, 'read' belongs to weak class II, for which a past –s passive often is available:

Infinitive active	**løfte**	**lese**
Infinitive passive	**løfte–s**	**lese–s**
Past active	**løftet**	**leste**
Past passive: available?	–	**leste–s**
Present active	**løfter**	**leser**
Present passive = infinitive passive	**løfte–s**	**lese–s**

(d) For a few frequent verbs whose stem ends in a vowel (i.e. of class III and some strong ones), there is variation between –s and –es. For example, corresponding to the actives **få**, 'get' and **se**, 'see' (strong), both **fås** and **fåes**, both **se** and **sees** are found. In such cases, –s is the safe option; it is always acceptable.

5.6.2.2 *The –s passive: use*

(a) Here are some examples of the use of the –s passive:

Jula må feires.	Christmas must be celebrated.
Gavene skal kjøpes.	The gifts will be bought.
Grisene slaktes.	The pigs are slaughtered.

This is not the most frequent passive construction in the spoken language, but, as it shows up in a specific passive suffix, peculiar to the Nordic languages, it catches the eye.

The –s passive is more common in the infinitive – following an auxiliary – than in the present, especially in the spoken language. As with the other passive constructions, the agent is downtoned, for example because it is unknown or immaterial (cf. 5.6.1.1 (b)). In the examples above, the focus is not on who is doing the celebrating, buying or butchering. The point is that these actions be carried out.

(b) Frequently, the –s passive emphasises the action of the verb. Time may be less relevant; an –s passive often indicates repeated rather than single action.

Frokosten serveres i første etasje.
Breakfast is served on the ground floor.

Slike forseelser straffes med bøter.
Such misdemeanours are punished with fines.

As in some other uses of the present tense, the statement holds generally, 'timelessly', cf. 5.3.3.2.

(c) A present tense –s passive can be used to indicate an instruction or even a command:

Xylofon skrives med x.
Xylophone (the word) is (to be) written with an x.

Hunder holdes i bånd i parken.
Dogs are (to be) kept on a lead in the park.

This instructional use of the present tense –s passive has become somewhat less common. (It is not found in new cookbooks, for example). Still, in the infinitive, in combination with a modal, the –s passive is quite frequent, even in the spoken language:

Xylofon skal skrives med X.
Xylophone (the word) should be written with an x.

Hunder skal holdes i bånd her.
Dogs are to be kept on a lead here.

Noen burde beskyttes mot seg sjøl.
Some people should be protected against themselves.

5.6.3 | Other uses of the suffix –s

While the main use of the suffix –s in Norwegian verbs is to express the passive, this is not the only option. Thus, an –s may express:

1 The passive:	**Boka leses.**	The book is read.	See 5.6.2.3.
2 The reciprocal:	**De møtes.**	They meet.	See 5.6.3.1
3 The deponent:	**Vi trives her.**	We like it here.	See 5.6.3.2.

5.6.3.1 | The reciprocal

An –s verb may indicate reciprocity, in which case the subject both carries out an action and is the object of it. These verbs usually have a plural subject:

Anne og Kari slåss. Anne and Kari fight.

The simplex verb **slå** means 'hit'. In the example, Anne hits Kari, but Anne is also hit by Kari. Kari hits Anne, but she is also hit by her. Reciprocal –s verbs ending in –s are not inflected forms of a verb (the way –s passives are), but distinct words: The –s is an integral part of the reciprocal verb. But other verbs without –s usually correspond to these: cf. **slå – slåss**, 'hit'; **se – ses**, 'see'.

Here are some other examples of reciprocal –s verbs:

Søsknene treffes bare til jul. The siblings only meet for Christmas.
De møttes på pubben. They met in the pub.

Reciprocal –s verbs may often be paraphrased with the same verb + the pronoun **hverandre** 'each other' (see 4.5.4):

Anne og Kari slår hverandre.
Anne and Kari are hitting each other.

Søsknene treffer hverandre bare til jul.
The siblings only meet for Christmas.

De møtte hverandre på pubben.
They met each other in the pub.

Other reciprocal verbs include **enes**, 'agree', **forenes**, 'unite', **forsones**, 'reconcile', **råkes** 'meet', **skilles**, 'divorce', **samles**, 'gather', **ses**, 'meet'.

Other —s verbs, including deponents: Passive form but active meaning

Some —s verbs have a more active meaning. They are a mixed lot, and may not correspond to a verb without an —s at all:

Buster trivdes godt i Stavanger.
Buster liked it in Stavanger.

Angie synes Vladimir er primitiv.
Angie thinks Vladimir is primitive.

There is no verb *trive, *syne corresponding to **trives**, 'like it', **synes**, 'think', and **trives, synes** do not have a passive meaning, but are similar in meaning to the active (reflexive) **like seg** and the active **mene** respectively. Such verbs – active in meaning, passive-like in form – are traditionally called deponents.

Deponent verbs also include **lykkes**, 'succeed', **mislykkes**, 'fail', **eldes**, 'grow old', **ferdes**, 'go', 'travel', **vantrives**, 'be unhappy', **minnes** 'recall', **skjemmes**, 'be ashamed'.

However, there are also some —s verbs that correspond to a verb without an —s, formally, but where the difference in terms of meaning is so considerable that we may speak of two distinct verbs. Examples include **finnes**, 'exist' versus **finne**, 'find' and **omgås**, 'mix socially' versus **omgå**, 'evade (rules)'.

Det finnes mange skjulte skatter som ikke blir funnet.
There are many hidden treasures that are never found.

Most deponent verbs are intransitive (but **minnes** and **synes** are transitive).

5.7 Compound verbs

5.7.1 Introduction

5.7.1.1

One kind of compound verb is where a verb is prefixed by a particle. In some of these compounds, the particle (an adverb or preposition) forms an integral and inseparable part of the verb and remains attached to it in all circumstances. This kind of compound is known as *inseparable* (Norwegian fast sammensatte verb, 11.2.2.14). With very few exceptions, such verbs inflect in the same way as the uncompounded verb:

stå – står – stod – stått, stand
påstå – påstod – påstått, claim

$\boxed{5.7.1.2}$

In other examples, the particle may become separated from the verb under some circumstances and in certain forms of the verb. This kind is known as a *separable compound* (**løst sammensatte verb**). The difference between separable and inseparable does not have to correspond to any major difference in meaning. For example, **gjennomgå** or **gå gjennom** can both mean 'teach, read closely, lecture':

Torodd gjennomgår klassiske verk.   *Not separated*
Torodd is lecturing on classical works.

Torodd går gjennom klassiske verk.   *Separated*
Torodd is lecturing on classical works.

However, often there is a difference in meaning. If so, it is typically the more 'abstract' sense that is associated with an inseparable verb, the more 'concrete' one with a separable verb (see also 5.7.3). In the more concrete sense 'walk through', for example, only **gå gjennom** is possible (and not **gjennomgå**):

Eventyrerne gikk gjennom Gobi-ørkenen.
The adventurers walked through the Gobi Desert.

Compare:

Mekanikeren ser over motoren.
The mechanic checks the engine.

Bremsesvikten ble dessverre oversett.
The brakes failure was unfortunately missed.

Han er så høy at han så over henne.
He is so tall he looked over her.

Blondinen bare overså bølla.
The blonde simply ignored the thug.

5.7.2 | Inseparable compound verbs

Inseparable compound verbs (11.2.2.14) include the following.

5.7.2.1 | Verbs compounded with nouns

Examples include **sultestreike**, 'hunger strike', **grisebanke**, 'beat to a pulp' (colloq.), **planlegge**, 'make a plan', **øvelsesskyte**, 'practise shooting' and many others. Noun-verb compounds may be the most common compounded verbs. These include many temporary compounds. See also 11.2.2.6.

5.7.2.2 | Verbs compounded with adjectives

fullføre, complete; **godkjenne**, approve; **småle**, laugh a little, smile; **bråsnu**, turn abruptly

Note – Some adjective + verb combinations may be kept integral or separated for stylistic reasons. In the latter case, the adjective will take on agreement in number and gender as usual, as a word in its own right:

Reingjør og sett bort verktøyet.   Clean and stow away the tools.
Gjør verktøyet reint straks!   Clean the tools at once.

See also 11.2.2.10.

5.7.2.3 | Verbs compounded with other verbs

lekeslåss, playfight; **kosekrangle**, bicker in a friendly way

The analysis of these first elements is a vexed issue; for this book, we choose a simple analysis.

See also 11.2.2.9.

5.7.2.4 | Verbs compounded with other word-like elements

tredele, trisect; **selvdø**, die of natural causes

Some verbs compounded with adverbs or prepositions

> **gjennomføre**, carry out; **utpeke**, appoint; **avgjøre**, decide; **framstille**, present

This is a large group of verbs. See also 5.7.1.1, 5.7.3–5.7.5, and 11.2.2.14.

5.7.2.6 *Verbs compounded with certain prefixes*

It can be quite difficult to decide whether the first element below is a prefix or more word-like. The lists below do not comprise all possible first elements.

(a) Unstressed prefixes include:

be–	**betale**	pay, pay for
er–	**erkjenne**	realise
for–	**forklare**	explain

(b) Stressed prefixes include:

an–	**ansette**	appoint
bi–	**bisette**	inter
fore–	**forelese**	lecture
mis–	**mistenke**	suspect
sam–	**samtykke**	agree to
u–	**uroe**	worry, bother
unn–	**unnslippe**	manage to avoid, break free
van–	**vanskjøtte**	mismanage

5.7.2.7

A number of compound verbs only exist in the integral form:

> **forvrenge**, distort; **underkjenne**, reject

These include cases where the second part of the verb does not exist as an independent verb:

> **innlemme**, incorporate; **avbilde**, depict

In other words: There is no *lemme, and so no *lemme inn either.

5.7.3 | Separable compound verbs

These comprise two main groups; those that are usually separated into verb and particle (5.7.3.1), and those that are found in both a separated and an integral form (5.9.4f.). See also 11.3.8.

5.7.3.1 | Always separated

Certain verbs are always separated except in the present and past participles, where the tendency towards inseparable forms is clear. Compare:

Han vil reise bort (*bortreise).	
Han reiste bort (*bortreiste).	
Han har reist bort.	He has gone away. (supine)
*Han har bortreist.	
Han er bortreist.	He has gone away. (past participle)
Hun har kjent deg igjen.	She has recognised you. (supine)
Du er gjenkjent.	You are/have been recognised. (past participle)
et gjenkjennende blikk	a look of recognition (present participle)
Sildeoljefabrikken er nedlagt.	The herring oil factory is closed.
oppsøkende journalistikk	investigative journalism

While Sildeoljefabrikken er lagt ned is also possible, *Søkende opp journalistikk is not.

Note the difference between the participle and the supine:

De har lagt ned sildeoljefabrikken.
They have closed the herring oil factory

5.7.4 | Separable or inseparable forms – stylistic differences

5.7.4.1

In many cases, the separated and integral forms are very close in meaning. The separated forms are then usually preferred except in rather formal usage. Compare **legge ned**, 'lay (sth.) down':

Hilde la bøkene ned.	Hilde laid the books down.
Russland nedla veto.	Russia exercised her veto.

While **Russland la ned veto** is also possible, *__Hilde nedla bøkene__ is not, as indicated by the asterisk. There are many other examples of this; see also 5.7.1.2 (gå gjennom/gjennomgå).

Despite such stylistic differences, it is more common to compound in the participles (see also 5.3.12 and 5.7.3.1):

Elektrikeren brøt av forbindelsen.
The electrician cut the connection.

en avbrutt ledning	a broken cable
Hun avbrøt direktøren.	She interrupted the director.
en avbrutt tankerekke	an interrupted chain of thought

5.7.5 | *Separable or inseparable forms – semantic differences*

5.7.5.1

Certain Norwegian verbs have separated and integral forms with different meanings (cf. English: 'take over' and 'overtake'). In such cases, the separated form usually has a literal meaning (physical or concrete), the corresponding integral form a figurative meaning:

Separated = Literal	*Integrated = Figurative*
Bussjåføren satte mjølkespannet av i vegkrysset.	**Styret avsatte administrerende direktør.**
The bus driver set the milk churn down at the crossroads.	The board fired the CEO.
De gikk over veien.	**Dette overgår mine forventninger.**
They crossed the road.	This surpasses my expectations.
Han streket under feilen.	**Hun understreket betydningen av å holde sammen.**
He underlined the mistake.	She emphasised the importance of sticking together.

Sometimes the semantic difference is so great as to warrant regarding the two forms as two distinct verbs:

Beinet gikk tvert av.	**Statsråden avgikk i går.**
The leg broke off.	The minister resigned yesterday.

5.7.6 | Separable verbs – the position of the particle

5.7.6.1 | Verb + particle juxtaposed

See also 10.2.3, 10.3.4.3, 10.6.1. The two parts of a separable verb, i.e. verb + particle, are usually juxtaposed in a clause or sentence:

Strek under det viktigste.	Underline what is most important.
Jeg tar på meg penklær.	I am putting on formal clothes.

5.7.6.2 | Verb + particle not juxtaposed

(a) In a main clause with simple verb and a clausal adverbial. See 10.4.2.1(e).

Jeg kjenner ikke igjen min gamle hjemby.
I don't recognise my old home-town.

Metallbein går sjelden tvert av.	Metal legs rarely break.

(b) In many cases where the subject follows the verb in a main clause:

Kjente Anna igjen Vronskij?	Did Anna recognise Vronskij?
Gikk beinet virkelig tvert av?	Did the leg really snap?

(c) In imperatives constructed with a clausal adverbial:

Kast ikke bort instruksjonsheftet!
Do not throw away the instruction booklet.

(d) When a 'light', unstressed object pronoun intervenes:

Jeg tar dem på.	I put them on.
Jeg kjenner deg igjen.	I recognise you.

5.8 Some problem verbs

In this section some problems of a more lexical nature are briefly outlined.

5.8.1 Translation into Norwegian of some problem verbs

These notes illustrate only some common problems. They are not dictionary definitions.

5.8.1.1 Arrive/leave

1 arrive [of people], **ankomme, komme**

They arrive on Monday. **De kommer på mandag.**

2 arrive [of trains, boats, planes, etc.], **ankomme**

The boat gets in today. **Båten ankommer i dag.**

3 leave [intransitive], **reise, dra, gå**

They left early. **De gikk tidlig.**

4 leave [transitive], **la . . . være, etterlate**

Leave your sorrows at home.
La sorgene være igjen hjemme.

The late NN leaves four children.
Avdøde NN etterlater seg fire barn.

5.8.1.2 Ask

1 enquire, **spørre**

She asked him about the problem. **Hun spurte ham om problemet.**

2 ask [someone to do something], **be**

She asked him to come. **Hun bad ham komme.**

3   ask [questions], **spørre, stille spørsmål**

The police asked many questions.   **Politiet stilte mange spørsmål.**

5.8.1.3 *Change*

1   alter, **forandre, endre**

The law was changed recently.   **Loven ble nylig forandret.**

2   change one's mind, **ombestemme seg**

Gunnar changed his mind.   **Gunnar ombestemte seg.**

3   exchange [sth. for sth. else], **skifte, bytte**

Time to change clothes?   **På tide å skifte klær?**

4   change money, **veksle**

She changed her kroner into Euros.   **Hun vekslet kronene til euro.**

5.8.1.4 *Drive*

1   drive a vehicle [i.e. sit behind the wheel], **kjøre**

Kari drove the bus into the garage.
Kari kjørte bussen inn i garasjen.

2   travel [i.e. be driven], **dra**

We drove to Norway.   **Vi dro til Norge.**

3   to provide the power for something, **drive**

The engine is driven by steam.   **Maskinen er drevet med damp.**

4   cause a change, **gjøre**

She drove him crazy.   **Hun gjorde ham gal.**

5.8.1.5 *Feel*

1   feel [transitive], **kjenne/føle**

Suddenly he felt the pain.   **Brått kjente/følte han smerten.**

2 feel [intransitive], **kjenne/føle seg**

He felt tired.   **Han kjente/følte seg trøtt.**

3 feel [deponent], **kjennes/føles**

It feels sad.   **Det kjennes trist.**

5.8.1.6 Go

1 go by vehicle, **dra/reise**

We are going to Trondheim.   **Vi reiser/drar til Trondheim.**

2 go [especially on foot or in the sense of 'leave'], **gå**

We really must go now.   **Vi må faktisk gå nå.**

He walked all the way.   **Han gikk hele veien.**

5.8.1.7 Grow

1 grow [intransitive], **vokse**

Corn grows in the USA.   **Det vokser mais i USA.**

2 grow [transitive], **dyrke**

People grow corn in the USA.   **De dyrker mais i USA.**

3 increase in size, **øke**

The GNP has grown.   **BNP har økt.**

5.8.1.8 Know

1 know [facts], **vite**

Do you know what he is called?   **Veit du hva han heter?**

2 know [people], **kjenne**

Do you know her?   **Kjenner du henne?**

3 know [languages, specialisms], **kunne**

Do you know French?   **Kan du fransk?**

4   know, be aware of, **kjenne til**

Do you know any hotels in Sandnes?
Kjenner du til noen hoteller i Sandnes?

5.8.1.9 *Live*

1   dwell, reside, **bo**

He lives in Bergen.   **Han bor i Bergen.**

2   be alive, **leve**

Ibsen lived another four years.   **Ibsen levde enda fire år.**

5.8.1.10   *Put*

1   place horizontally, **legge**

Put the book on the table!   **Legg boka på bordet!**

2   place upright, **sette**

Put the bottle on the table!   **Sett flaska på bordet!**

3   insert into, **putte, legge**

Put the money in your wallet.   **Putt/Legg pengene i lommeboka.**

5.8.1.11   *See*

1   see, **se**

Can you see that beetle?   **Kan du se den billa?**

2   meet, **treffe, møte**

Did you see Mr Smith?   **Traff/møtte du herr Smith?**

3   realise, **skjønne, forstå**

I see what you mean.   **Jeg skjønner/forstår hva du mener.**

1 movement, stoppe, stanse

She stopped the car.

Hun stoppet/stanset bilen.

The car stopped. Bilen stoppet/stanset.

2 cease doing, slutte

She stopped eating.

Hun sluttet å spise.

5.8.1.13 Think

1 hold an opinion, synes

She thinks the book is good.

Hun synes boka er god.

2 ponder, tenke

She sat thinking about it.

Hun satt og tenkte på det.

3 intend, tenke på

She is thinking of buying a new car.

Hun tenker på å kjøpe ny bil.

4 believe, tro

Nobody thinks that this is true.

Ingen tror at dette er sant.

5.8.1.14 Want

1 want [to do], ville

I want to go home.

Jeg vil gå hjem.

2 want [to have], ville ha, ønske seg

I want a new pair of skis.

Jeg vil ha/ønsker meg nye ski.

5.8.2 Other Norwegian equivalents of the English verb to be

In addition to være, 'be', at least five Norwegian verbs are regularly used to translate different senses of the English verb 'to be'.

5.8.2.1 *Ligge*

This verb, normally translated 'lie', is used of objects, places and towns lying horizontally (see also 5.3.4.2):

Boka ligger på bordet.	The book is on the table (lying face down, for example)
Kniven ligger på benken.	The knife is on the bench.
London ligger ved Themsen.	London is (situated) on the Thames.

5.8.2.2 *Sitte*

This verb, normally translated 'sit', is used of objects that are fixed in position (see also 5.3.4.2):

Briller skal liksom sitte på nesa.
Specs are supposed to be on your nose.

Lokket sitter fast.	The lid is stuck.

5.8.2.3 *Stå*

This verb, normally translated 'stand', is used of objects that stand vertically, and when 'is' etc. indicates 'is written' (see also 5.3.4.2):

Boka står på hylla.	The book is (standing) on the shelf.
Gyngestolen står på verandaen.	The rocking-chair is on the porch.
Dette står i Bibelen.	This is to be found in the Bible.

5.8.2.4 *Finnes*

In order to indicate existence or non-existence **finnes** is often used.

Finnes det en kvinne, en slik som jeg vil ha?
Does a woman exist, such a one as I want? (pop song, deLillos).

Det fantes ikke en eneste fornuftig tanke i hele boka.
There was not one single sensible thought in the entire book.

5.8.2.5 | *Bli*

In order to indicate transition (change of state), **bli** 'become' is used rather than **være**:

Hva ble utfallet av avstemningen?
What was the result of the vote?

Hvis det blir snø, ...   If there is snow, ...

Chapter 6

Adverbs

6.1 Introduction

6.1.1 Adverbs as a word class

This word class is anything but homogeneous. It is a class where words have traditionally been put that have little in common as regards their form, function or both. One common feature here is that many adverbs form attributes:

Arbeidet var _meget_ kjedelig.　　　　　　　　*Attribute to adjective*
The work was very boring.

Det er viktig at _nettopp_ guttene utfordres.　　*Attribute to noun*
It is important that the boys in particular are challenged.

6.1.2 Classification

6.1.2.1 In this grammar

Words that can be compared, such as **høyt**, 'highly'; **langt**, 'far'; **dårlig**, 'badly', and which traditionally are treated as adverbs, are in this book discussed under Adjectives (2.5.2.f).

6.1.2.2 In Norsk referansegrammatikk (NRG)

The authors of *NRG* have reclassified adverbs so that many words traditionally found in this word class (**her, der, borte**, etc.) are regarded as prepositions. Here, we deviate and follow the more traditional solution.

6.2 Meaning and function

6.2.1 Introduction

6.2.1.1

In adverbial use, adjectives in –t and those in –(l)ig have two main functions in the sentence. They are normally used as adverbials of manner or place, or as uptoners qualifying adjectives or adverbs. See also 10.3.6.1 and 6.2.7.1.

Adverbials of manner

Sov *godt*!
Sleep well!

***Samtidig* kommer det *stadig* nye opplysninger.**
At the same time, new information is constantly coming in.

Uptoners

Blomstene var *utrolig* vakre.
The flowers were incredibly beautiful.

6.2.1.2

As shown by the examples below, an adverbial can modify a verb, an adjective, another adverb, a clause or a noun phrase or prepositional phrase:

Ungene vokser *fort*.
The youngsters are growing rapidly.

De opptrådte *veldig* dumt.
They behaved very stupidly.

***Trolig* omkom rundt 60 mennesker.**
Probably about 60 people died.

Det har pågått i *nesten* et år.
This has been going on for almost a year.

Briller ble oppfunnet i Italia *allerede* på 1200-tallet.
Eyeglasses were invented in Italy already in the thirteenth century.

6.2.1.3

Adverbs can be divided into several categories as regards meaning and use. Traditionally, adverbs have been categorised as adverbs of time, manner, place or degree and as modal or clausal adverbs. (cf. 6.2.2).

Adverbs may, however, also be categorised according to their function, as *adjuncts, conjuncts* and *disjuncts*.

(a) *Adjuncts* (typically adverbs of time, manner, place and degree) usually form an integral part of the structure of the clause, whereas conjuncts and disjuncts are peripheral to the clause structure.

Hun likte det *ille*.	She took this badly.
Han er *utrolig* tålmodig.	He is incredibly patient.

(b) *Conjuncts* establish a connection between a clause or phrase and a previous part of the same sentence or sequence.

Han er svært syk, men *likevel* røyker han.
He is very ill but nevertheless he smokes.

Det bør *følgelig* støttes av staten.
It should consequently be supported by the state.

(c) *Disjuncts* express the speaker's attitude or evaluation.

Dessverre har han vært mye syk.
Unfortunately, he has been ill a lot.

Han får *høyst sannsynlig* verdensrekorden.
He will in all likelihood get the world record.

6.2.2 Adverbs classified by meaning

The following paragraphs provide examples of some of the most common adverbs and adverbials. The lists are by no means exhaustive.

6.2.2.1 Time: answering the questions ***Når?*** 'When?'; ***Hvor lenge?*** 'How long?'; ***Hvor ofte?*** 'How often?'

aldri, never; **allerede**, already; **alltid**, always; **da**, then; **ennå**, still; **etterpå**, after(wards); **innimellom**, occasionally; **fremdeles**, still; **før**, previously; **først**, first; **iblant**, sometimes; **igjen**, again; **lenge**, for a long time; **noensinne**, ever; **nylig**, recently; **nå**, now; **ofte**, often; **siden**, ago, since; **sist**, last; **straks**, immediately; **sjelden**, seldom; **tidvis**, from time to time; **vanligvis**, usually

Point in time:	**nå**, **da**, **før**, etc.
Frequency:	**aldri**, **ofte**, **alltid**, **sjelden**, etc.

6.2.2.2 *Manner: answering the question* **Hvordan?** *'How?'*

bra, well; **fort**, quickly; **ille**, badly; **nøye**, carefully; **ugjerne**, unwillingly; **sakte**, slowly; **slik/sånn**, in this/that way; **vel**, well

6.2.2.3 *Place: answering the question* **Hvor?** *'Where?/Where to?'*

See also 6.3.4.2. For adverbs of location and movement, see 6.4.1.

annetsteds, elsewhere; **ditover**, over there; **der**, **dit**, there; **frem** **(/fram)**, **fremad**, forwards; **halvveis**, halfway; **hjemme**, at home; **her**, **hit**, here; **nedenfra**, from below; **overalt**, everywhere; **sammen**, together; **tilbake**, back; **utendørs**, outdoors; **utenlands**, abroad

6.2.2.4 *Degree: answering the question* **Hvor mye?** *'To what extent?'*

See also 6.2.7.1.

altfor, too; **ganske**, rather; **helt**, completely; **høyst**, extremely; **litt**, (a) little; **mest**, mostly; **mye**, a lot; **nesten**, almost; **omtrent**, approximately; **overmåte**, exceedingly; **svært**, very; **særdeles**, particularly; **temmelig**, rather; **veldig**, very; **ytterst**, extremely

6.2.2.5 *Cause: answering the question* **Hvorfor?** *'Why?'*

altså, therefore; **derfor**, which is why; **nemlig**, viz.; **følgelig**, consequently

6.2.3 Adverbs classified by function

The heterogeneity of adverbs is most apparent with regard to their different functions. While some adverbs are semantically independent, for example the adverbs of manner (adjuncts) in 6.2.2.2, others need a context in order for their meaning to be established.

Compare:

> **Plutselig slo flammene opp. Derfor ble politiet tilkalt.**
> Suddenly the flames flared up. At that the police were called.

Plutselig modifies the action of the verb; it tells us *how* the flames flared up; it is an adjunct (6.2.1.3). **Derfor** refers back to a previous statement which establishes the *reason* why the police were called; it is a conjunct (6.2.1.3). In 6.2.4–6.2.6 the main types of adverbs are classified by their function.

6.2.4 | *Pronominal adverbs*

As in the case of pronouns, the meaning (or reference, in technical terms) of these adverbs is determined by their context. They may be:

6.2.4.1 | Anaphoric (referring back)

The adverb refers to the linguistic context in which it is used:

> **– Han ble drept i Tromsø. – Der har jeg aldri vært.**
> "He was killed in Tromsø.'" "I have never been *there*."

> **I april var det fint vær. Og *da* var det påskeferie også.**
> In April, the weather was good. And *then*, it was the Easter holiday too.

> **Bilen er på verksted. Derfor går jeg til jobben.**
> The car is at the garage. *That is why* I am walking to work.

6.2.4.2 | Deictic

The adverb refers to the external, non-linguistic context:

> **De kommer *hit* på besøk.** They are coming *here* on a visit.
> **Nå jobber han igjen.** *Now* he is working again.

6.2.4.3

Whereas pronouns replace nouns, pronominal adverbs replace prepositional phrases:

Bilen	**stoppet**	*foran huset.*
Noun		*Prepositional phrase*
The car	stopped	in front of the house.

Den	**stoppet**	*der.*
Pronoun		*Pronominal adverb*
It	stopped	there.

6.2.4.4 Relative

These introduce a relative clause.

Det er stedet *der* faren min vokste opp.
It is the place *where* my dad grew up.

6.2.4.5 Interrogative

Notice that interrogative adverbs introduce both direct and indirect questions, i.e. both main and subordinate clauses. As a result, the word order varies. See also 10.7.4, 10.8.1.2.

Main clause	*Subordinate clause*
Hvor er vi?	**Jeg vet ikke *hvor* vi er.**
Where are we?	I don't know *where* we are.
Når kom du hjem?	**Jeg vet ikke *når* jeg kom hjem.**
When did you get home?	I don't know *when* I got home.

6.2.4.6 Indefinite

Vi fant dem ikke *noensteds.*
We couldn't find them *anywhere.*

Aldri *noensinne* har jeg sett maken.
I have never *ever* seen the like.

6.2.5 Clausal adverbs

These adverbs (conjuncts or disjuncts) modify the clause as a whole rather than a particular word or phrase in the clause. For their position in the clause, see 10.5.2.

Clausal adverbs include:

- Adverbs formed by adding –vis to adjectives ending in –lig, –ig. See 6.3.2.2.

  Når står du *vanligvis* opp?　　When do you *usually* get up?

- Some other adverbs:

  altså, therefore; **dessverre**, unfortunately; **gjerne**, willingly; **ingenlunde**, by no means; **ikke**, not; **jo**, **nok**, **vel**, (for translations, see 6.5.1.4); **kanskje**, perhaps; **knapt**, scarcely

Paragraphs 6.2.5.1–6.2.5.3 illustrate the major types of clausal adverbs.

6.2.5.1 | *Negations (and equivalents)*

Negations are sometimes regarded as modal adverbs. See 6.3.4.3. The most common negating adverb is **ikke**, 'not'. The dated near-synonym **ei** is only found in fixed expressions: **Ei blott til lyst**, 'Not merely for pleasure'. **Ikke-** is also used in compounds: **en ikke-røyker**, 'a non-smoker'; **ikke-vold**, 'non-violence'.

aldri, never; **ikke**, not; **neppe**, scarcely; **umulig**, not possibly

Det er *knapt* 15° i rommet.　　It is *scarcely* 15° in the room.
Det kan *umulig* være sant.　　That cannot *possibly* be true.

6.2.5.2 | *Modal adverbs*

These show the speaker's attitude to the statement, degree of certainty, involvement or reservation. They include:

jo, **nok**, **vel**, (for translations, see 6.5.1.4); **naturligvis**, naturally; **sannelig**, truly

Han har *sikkert* rett.　　He's *certainly* right.
Vi kan *dessverre* ikke komme.　　*Unfortunately*, we can't come.

$\boxed{6.2.5.3}$ *Conjunctional adverbs*

These adverbs are conjuncts and link clauses in a similar way to coordinating and subordinating conjunctions. See also 9.1.4.2. However, a clause beginning with a conjunctional adverb has inverted (FV–S) word order. See also two-part constructions in (e) below. Conjunctional adverbs also occur within a clause:

Dette er vi *altså* helt enige i.
We *therefore* totally agree to this.

Jeg lærte *dessuten* å spille piano.
What is more, I learnt to play the piano.

The main relationships expressed using conjunctional adverbs are:

(a) Adversative (Opposition)

derimot, on the other hand, by contrast; **enda**, still; **imidlertid**, however; **(al)likevel**, nevertheless

Det er *likevel* større arbeidsledighet i andre deler av landet.
There is, *however,* greater unemployment in other parts of the country.

(b) Consecutive (Consequence or inference)

altså, consequently; **derfor**, therefore; **følgelig**, accordingly; **så, således**, so, then

Det er ikke *derfor* jeg skriver.   That's not *the reason* I write.

(c) Copulative (Linking)

dessuten, moreover; **heller**, just as well; **likeså**, equally; **og, også**, also; **videre**, moreover

Videre har hun publisert bøker og artikler.
Moreover, she has published books and articles.

(d) Explicative (Explanation or motivation)
jo, **nemlig** (for translations, see 6.5.1.4)

Det er *nemlig* han som har gjort det.   He is the one who did it, in fact.

(e) Notice two-part constructions of the type; **så vel . . . som**, 'both . . . and'; **enten . . . eller**, 'either . . . or'; **verken . . . eller**, 'neither . . . nor'; **dels . . . dels**, 'partly . . . partly', (see 9.2.2.3).

Han skriver bøker som både barn og voksne liker.
He writes books that both children and adults like.

6.2.6 | Adverbs focussing on all or part of the clause

6.2.6.1

These adverbs emphasise or restrict a clausal element by making its significance in the statement more precise. The two most important adverbs are **bare**, 'only' and **også**, 'also'. They focus on either the subject, complement, object, verb or adverbial:

		Focus on:
Bare Malin fulgte med.	Only Malin came along.	*subject*
Malin er bare ulykkelig.	Malin is just unhappy.	*complement*
Vi traff bare Malin.	We only met Malin.	*object*
Malin synger bare.	Malin just sings.	*verb*

Malin slo bare med venstre hånd.
Malin only hit with her left hand.

Også Malin fulgte med.	Malin also came along.	*subject*
Vi traff også Malin.	We also met Malin.	*object*
Malin synger også.	Malin sings too.	*verb*
Også i går sang Malin.	Yesterday too, Malin sang.	*adverbial*

Other clausal adverbials of this type include **kun**, 'only', **til og med** and the rarely used **endog, sogar** meaning 'even':

Kun fiske med stang og håndsnøre er tillatt.
Only fishing with rod and line is allowed.

Note – **Selv** as an adverb is found only before a noun phrase:

Selv turisthotell er billigere å drive enn sykehus.
Even hotels are cheaper to run than hospitals.

6.2.7 | Adverbs qualifying the adjective/adverb phrase

6.2.7.1 | Uptoners and downtoners

A number of adverbs, particularly those denoting degree or kind, are used as uptoners or downtoners.

(a) Uptoners (or amplifers) are used to strengthen the meaning of adjectives or other adverbs:

meget, very; **svært**, extremely; **veldig**, very

Colloquial uptoners include some words that have lost their original sense:

enormt, enormously; **forferdelig**, frightfully; **fryktelig**, awfully; **grådig**, (informal) really; **kolossalt**, hugely; **sabla** (very informal), extremely; **uhyre**, tremendously; **ubeskrivelig**, indescribably; **voldsomt**, terribly;

Det var grådig spennende.	It was extremely exciting.

Note – The use of aller with superlatives:

Den aller siste flaska ble åpnet.	The very last bottle was opened.

In colloquial Norwegian, prefixes such as brå–, dritt–, døds–, gørr–, kjempe–, mega–, stor–, super– are sometimes added to adjectives as uptoners (see affixoids 11.4.1):

Det var kjempemorsomt å hoppe tau med barna mine.
It was great fun to do skipping with my children.

Han er gørrlei av å trene hver dag.
He is totally fed up of training every day.

(b) Downtoners (or diminishers) weaken the meaning of adjectives or other adverbs:

litt	a little, not very
Hun ble litt irritert over det.	She was a little irritated by it.

(c) Other adverbs qualify the adjective to a less high degree: **ganske**, 'quite'; nokså, 'rather'; temmelig, 'fairly'

Skadene ble temmelig omfattende.
The damage was rather extensive.

6.3 Form

6.3.1 Introduction

From a formal point of view, Norwegian near-equivalents to English adverbs can be broadly divided into three main groups:

In English, there is usually a formal difference between an adjective such as 'nice' (used attributively as in 'a nice car') and the corresponding adverb 'nicely' (used as an adverbial, 'swimming nicely'). The Norwegian facts are somewhat different: When used adverbially, the adjective will typically occur in the neuter form, cf. **en fin bil**, 'a fine car'; **et** *fint* **hus**, 'a fine house'; **svømme** *fint*, 'swim well'. Thus, while English grammars must distinguish between adverbs and adjectives, newer Norwegian grammars tend to say that what we find in adverbial functions is the adjective in the neuter. In such cases, the 'adverbs' – or rather adverbials – are usually derived from adjectives and from indeclinable adjectives in –(l)ig (e.g. **temmelig**, 'rather'), and are usually formed by adding the suffixes –t (e.g. **varsomt**, 'carefully') or –vis (e.g. **heldigvis**, 'luckily') or by using the present participle as an adverbial of degree (e.g. **utelukkende**, 'solely'). Adverbs compare in the same way as the adjectives from which they derive, see 2.5. See also 6.3.2f., 6.2.1, 6.1.1.

| 6.3.1.2 | Simple forms

This group comprises adverbs that are simple and invariable in form (e.g. **her**, 'here'; **da**, 'then'). Some of these historically were derivatives (e.g. **aldri**, 'never'; **sjelden**, 'rarely'). See also 6.3.4.

| 6.3.1.3 | Historical compounds

This group comprises adverbs that historically were compounds (e.g. **alltid**, 'always'; **derfor**, 'therefore'; **ennå**, 'still'). See also 6.3.5.

| **6.3.2** | **Adverbs derived from adjectives**

| 6.3.2.1 |

(a) Words used in adverbial function can be formed from adjectives, and in principle all adjectives in the neuter may serve in the function associated with adverbs.

Adjective Common gender	Adjective Neuter	Adverbial function
fri = free	**fritt** = free	**fritt** = freely
cf.	**et fritt samfunn** a free society	**å velge fritt** to choose freely

Adjectives ending in –(l)ig (2.1.4.1) do not add –t in either their adjectival or adverbial function:

cf.	**et lykkelig liv** a happy life	**De levde lykkelig.** They lived happily.

(b) Common gender forms of the adjective that have stems already ending in –t do not add the ending –t (2.1.4.5):

Adjective in adverbial function

et absolutt flertall
an absolute majority

Det er absolutt nødvendig.
It's absolutely necessary.

en perfekt løsning
a perfect solution

perfekt løst
perfectly resolved

The adverb and the neuter singular form of the adjective are, therefore, as a rule identical. For this reason, it is important to distinguish between them, especially when translating into English.

Compare the following:

et vakkert hus
vakkert = adjective, neuter form

a beautiful house

Huset ligger vakkert.
vakkert = adverbial function

The house is beautifully situated.

6.3.2.2

Some adjectives in –(l)ig form adverbs by adding –vis ('way, manner'):

nødvendigvis, necessarily; **rimeligvis**, probably; **sannsynligvis**, in all likelihood; **vanligvis**, ordinarily

−vis can also be added to a noun to form an adverb:

delvis, partially; **eksempelvis**, for instance; **forholdsvis**, relatively; **gradvis**, gradually

−vis can, however, also form quantifiers (**hundrevis**), cf. 3.1.4.1.

6.3.2.3

Present participles (5.3.1.3) may also be used adverbially:

et *blendende* **hvitt lys**	a blinding white light
en *flunkende* **ny bygning**	a brand-new building
en *klinkende* **klar avtale**	a crystal-clear contract

6.3.2.4

Past participles (5.3.1.2) may also be used adverbially:

Mange unge klappet *begeistret.*
A lot of youngsters clapped enthusiastically.

6.3.3 | Other adverbs which historically are derivatives or compounds

6.3.3.1 | Forms in −e

bare, only; **ganske**, rather; **gjerne**, gladly; **ikke**, not; **kanskje**, perhaps; **neppe**, scarcely

Den filmen vil jeg gjerne se.   I would really like to see that film.

This group includes a number of adverbs of place:

borte, away; **hjemme**, at home; **inne**, in; **nede**, down; **ute**, out

Den som taper hjemme mot Norge, kan ikke ha spilt bra.
Anyone who loses at home against Norway cannot have played well.

6.3.3.2 Forms in −(e)s, −ledes, −lunde

These are added to compounds.

aldeles, absolutely; **fremdeles**, even now; **særdeles**, particularly

en aldeles utmerket ferieuke på hytta
a quite wonderful week's holiday at the cabin

annerledes, different; **således**, like this, for this reason; **noenlunde**, reasonably

Vi kan således ikke si noe.   For this reason, we cannot say anything.

6.3.3.3 Forms in −messig

The suffix **−messig** is added to nouns to form adjectives (11.3.1.2(k)) that are very often used adverbially.

Hvordan sikre at kontroller blir gjort regelmessig?
How to ensure that checks take place regularly?

Others include:

lovmessig, legal; miljømessi, g, **miljømessig,** environmentally;
regelmessig, regularly; **uforholdsmessig**, disproportionately

6.3.3.4 Forms in −sides

avsides, apart; **hinsides**, beyond; **jevnsides**, alongside

Det er hinsides all fornuft.   It is beyond any common sense.

6.3.3.5 Forms in −steds, −sinne

etsteds, somewhere; **ingensteds**, nowhere; **noensinne**, ever

det beste vi noensinne har prestert
the best we have ever achieved

6.3.4 | Simplex adverbs

6.3.4.1 | Adverbs of time

These include:

da, then; **ennå**, still; **nå**, now; **straks**, immediately

Han ble straks arrestert.   He was immediately arrested.

6.3.4.2 | Adverbs of place

These include:

der, there; **her**, here; **hjem**, home; **frem**, forwards

Jeg vil ikke reise hjem.   I don't want to go home.

6.3.4.3 | Modal adverbs

These words express the attitude of the speaker to what is said (see also 6.5.1.4):

aldri, never; **ikke**, not; **jo**, after all; **nok**, probably

Hans mor likte jo aldri jentene han tok med hjem.
His mother after all never liked the girls he brought home.

6.3.4.4 | Conjunctional adverbs

These words join two clauses together, and some of them may perhaps also be considered compounds:

altså, therefore; **imidlertid**, however; **også**, also; **dog**, however, yet (formal)

Jeg tenker, altså er jeg.   I think, therefore I am.

6.3.5 | Compound adverbs

Some Norwegian compound adverbs are:

altfor, too; **alltid**, always; **altså**, therefore; **derfor**, consequently;
derimot, on the other hand; **deretter**, after that; **dertil**, for that,

besides; **dernest**, after that; **enda**, still; **ennå**, hitherto; **hvorfor**, why; **især**, especially; **likeså**, likewise; **(al)likevel**, nevertheless; **nettopp**, just, exactly; **også**, also; **overalt**, everywhere; **riktignok**, admittedly, indeed; **tilbake**, back; **visstnok**, probably

6
Adverbs

Compounds formed from an adverb and a preposition include compounds ending in the following:

–ad	**innad**, inwards; **oppad**, upwards
–av	**derav**, hence
–etter	**deretter**, subsequently; **heretter**, henceforth
–for	**altfor**, too; **derfor**, therefore; **hvorfor**, why
–fra	**derfra**, thence; **herfra**; from here
–imot	**derimot**, by contrast; **bortimot**, approximately; **oppimot**, drawing close to
–med	**dermed**, consequently; **hermed**, hereby
–om	**derom**, about that; **herom**, about this
–over	**bakover**, backwards; **fremover**, ahead; **innover**, inwards; **oppover**, upwards; **utover**, across
–på	**derpå**, subsequently
–til	**dertil**, thereto; **hittil**, so far; **inntil**, up to; **opptil**, near to
–ved	**derved**, thereby; **herved**, hereby

6.3.6 | Other frequent adverbials

A distinction should be made between adverbs and adverbials (10.1.1, 10.2.5, 10.3.6). Adverbs can be defined formally and functionally and, with a few exceptions, are single-word units. While adverbials may have the same function in the clause as adverbs, they are purely functional units with wide variations in their internal syntactic structure. Many frequently used adverbials in Norwegian are prepositional phrases or coordinated adverbials (adverb + coordinating conjunction + adverb).

Examples of prepositional phrases as adverbials:

for det meste, mostly, generally; **i alle fall/iallfall/ihvertfall**, in any case; **i det hele tatt**, everything considered; **under alle omstendigheter**, in any case

Examples of coordinated adverbials:

av og til, now and again; **først og fremst**, primarily; **her og nå**, here and now; **i og for seg**, in itself; **titt og ofte**, time and again; **nå og da**, now and then; **att og fram**, to and fro (*lit.* back- and forwards)

6.4.1 *Location and motion towards*

6.4.1.1 *Forms of adverbs expressing location and motion towards*

A small number of adverbs denoting place (6.2.2.3, 6.3.4.2) have two distinct forms. One form is used with verbs indicating location, rest or movement *within* a specific area (**være**, 'be'; **bo**, 'live'; **finnes**, 'be'; **sitte**, 'sit'; **stå**, 'stand'; **ligge**, 'lie'; **bli**, 'stay', etc. See also 7.2.2). A different form is used with verbs indicating motion, whether actual or imagined, *towards* another place (**reise**, travel; **fare**, travel; **gå**, 'go'/'walk'; **komme**, 'come'; **løpe**, 'run'; **ringe**, 'phone'; etc.). Adverbs of this type are:

Location	Motion towards
her, here	**hit**, (to) here
der, there	**dit**, (to) there
hjemme, at home	**hjem**, home

Examples:

Vi er *her* hver mandag.	We are here every Monday.
Vi kommer *hit* hver mandag.	We come here every Monday.
De er *ute* på reise.	They are off travelling.
De skal *ut* på reise.	They are going off travelling.

6.4.1.2 *Motion away from a place and to a place*

These adverbs are compounds. See also 7.4.3.

From a place	To a place
bortefra, away from	**bortover**, across to
hjemmefra, (away) from home	**hjemover**, homewards
inne(n)fra, from the inside	**innover**, inwards
ute(n)fra, from the outside	**utover**, outwards
Jeg flyttet tidlig hjemmefra.	
I left home at an early age.	

Note – Perhaps unexpectedly, **nedenfra**, 'from below' means the opposite of **ned fra**, 'down from', and **ovenfra**, 'from above' means the opposite of **opp fra**, 'up from'.

6.5 Translating adverbs

6.5.1 Translation from Norwegian

6.5.1.1 Allerede

1 already:

De er allerede gått.   They have already left.

2 as early as:

Supermann ble tegneseriehelt allerede i 1938.
Superman became a comic strip hero as early as 1938.

3 even:

Allerede som barn var han annerledes.
Even as a child he was different.

6.5.1.2 Først

1 first:

Først besøkte vi Håkon.   First we visited Håkon.

2 not until, only:

Først ved 17-tiden kom de.   They did not arrive until 5 o'clock.

6.5.1.3 Gjerne, heller, helst

(a) Gjerne

1 willingly, readily, by all means, with pleasure, likes to:

– Drikker du øl? – Ja takk, gjerne!
"Do you drink beer?" "Yes, with pleasure!"

Det dramaet vil jeg gjerne se.
I would like to see that play.

2 (just as) well:

De kan like gjerne gi opp.
They might just as well give up.

3 as a rule:

Hun tok gjerne bilen til jobben.
She generally took the car to work.

(b) **Heller** is the comparative form of **gjerne** and corresponds to English 'rather', 'prefers to':

Han vil heller ha vin enn øl.
He would rather have wine than beer.

(c) **Heller** can be used after a negative, usually in the same way as English 'neither', 'not either', etc. Sometimes it is used together with **vel** as a discourse particle. See 6.5.1.4(d).

De vil ikke lyve, og det vil vel ikke jeg heller.
They do not want to lie and neither do I.

(d) **Helst** is the superlative form of **gjerne** and corresponds to 'preferably', 'rather':

Helst ville han slippe å komme.
He would prefer not to have to come.

6.5.1.4 *Jo, nok, vel, nemlig, visst*

When unstressed, these modal adverbs are employed as modal particles or discourse particles, so as either to introduce some degree of probability or uncertainty or to seek agreement on the part of the listener (modal particle), or else to mark links in the text or between the text and its context (discourse particle).

Note that, when stressed, **nok** = 'enough', 'sufficient'; **vel** = 'well'.

For **jo** as an interjection, see 8.2.

These adverbs correspond to a wide variety of English expressions.

(a) **Jo** indicates that the speaker expects the listener to agree with or to share knowledge of what he is saying. **Jo** corresponds broadly to English phrases such as 'you know', 'you see', 'of course':

Der er han jo!   Why, there he is!

Det er jo i morgen de skal komme.
It is tomorrow they are coming, as you know.

(b) Whereas **jo** implies 'as you already know', **nemlig** provides new
information of which the listener has previously been unaware. It has
the sense of 'as I am now telling you by way of explanation'. In many
instances, **nemlig** corresponds to the same kind of English phrases as
jo– 'you understand', 'you see', etc. – but the sense is quite different, as
the following contrasting examples indicate:

Du får komme i dag, i morgen er jeg nemlig i Stavanger.
You'll have to come today, as I'm in Stavanger tomorrow, you see.

Du får komme i dag, i morgen er jeg jo i Stavanger.
You'll have to come today. As you know, I'm in Stavanger tomorrow.

Nemlig can also mean 'namely', 'that is to say', 'in fact':

Vi kom litt senere – nemlig ved 20-tiden.
We arrived a little later, that is about 8 pm.

(c) **Nok** often injects a note of doubt or uncertainty, in some cases
conciliation or regret. It corresponds to English phrases such as
'probably', 'I expect', 'I daresay', 'to be sure', etc.

De kommer nok.   They will come I expect.
Han er nok ikke interessert i dette.
He is probably not interested in this.

Har du mistet mobilen din? Ja, jeg har nok det.
Did you lose your mobile phone? Yes, I suppose I did.

(d) **Vel** generally expresses a hope, expectation or desire that the listener
will agree, and as such corresponds to English phrases such as 'surely',
'I suppose', 'it's true', 'admittedly'. It may simply strengthen a statement
(like **jo**) or express conciliation (like **nok**).

Du fikk vel min e-post?   You got my email, I hope?
Ja, vi må vel håpe det.   Yes, we have to hope so, I suppose.

(e) **Visst** has two meanings:

1. Probably, most likely:

Det er visst sant.   That is probably true.

2. Certainly, for sure:

Visst var Fridtjof Nansen en sammensatt personlighet.
Fridtjof Nansen was certainly a complex personality.

Note that when **visst** is used as in meaning 2, which is rather rare these days, it will typically occur before the finite verb.

6.5.1.5 Langt, lenge

(a) **langt** = far (distance, neuter of the adjective **lang**):

Hvor langt er det til Mars?   How far is it to Mars?

(b) **lenge** = long (time):

Hvor lenge skal poteter koke?   How long should you boil potatoes?

6.5.2 Translation into Norwegian

This section outlines some common ways of rendering frequently encountered English adverbs in Norwegian.

6.5.2.1 'So'

The English adverb 'so' is rendered in various ways in Norwegian:

(a) In comparative expressions = **så**.

It is not so common.   **Det er ikke så vanlig.**

(b) Pronominal adverb, referring back = **det**. See 4.2.4.6.

"Is he married?" "I think so."   **– Er han gift? – Jeg tror det.**
I told you so.   **Jeg sa det til deg.**
So did I.   **Det gjorde jeg også.**

(c) As an uptoner = **svært** (**så** or **meget**):

It is so kind of you.   **Det er svært vennlig av deg.**
She is so kind.   **Hun er så vennlig.**

(d) As a conjunction:

- expressing purpose = **slik at, sånn at**:

  The programme is designed so that the Prime Minister will get to meet the voters.
  Programmet er laget slik at statsministeren skal få møte velgerne.

- expressing result = **så**:

  So I left.   **Så jeg dro.**

6.5.2.2 'Then'

'Then' is rendered by **da** or **deretter** (or **så**) in Norwegian depending on the meaning.

(a) **Da, dengang** = 'at that time', 'at that moment', 'on that occasion', 'in that case':

I thought so then and I think so now.
Det trodde jeg da, og det tror jeg nå.

(b) **Deretter** = 'after that', 'subsequently'

First, we had a coffee, then we went out.
Først drakk vi kaffe, deretter, så gikk vi ut.
Først drakk vi kaffe. Så gikk vi ut.

6.5.2.3 'Too'

(a) When 'too' qualifies an adjective or adverb and expresses an excessive degree of something, it is rendered in Norwegian by **for** or **altfor**:

The regulations are too complicated.
Regelverket er altfor komplisert.

Don't walk too fast! **Gå ikke for raskt!**

(b) When 'too' means 'also', 'as well', it is rendered by **også (og)**:

She got a new car, too. **Hun fikk en ny bil også.**

6.5.2.4 'Whenever', 'wherever'

English	Remarks	Norwegian	Example
'Whenever'	= 'at any time you like'	**når som helst,** **når … enn**	1
'Whenever'	= 'no matter when' = 'every time (that)'	**hver gang**	2
'Wherever'	= 'anywhere you like'	**hvor som helst**	3
'Wherever'	= 'no matter where' + clause = 'everywhere (that)' + clause	**hvor … enn**	4
'Wherever?'	= 'Where on earth?'	**hvor i all verden?**	5

1 'When should I come?' 'Whenever you like.'
   – Når skal jeg komme? – Når du (enn) vil.

2 Pinoccio gets a long nose whenever he tells a lie.
   Pinoccio får lang nese hver gang han lyver.

3 **De er så rike at de kan reise hvor (som helst) de vil.**
   They are so rich they can travel wherever they like.

4 **Kom frem, hvor enn du er!**
   Come out wherever you are!

5 **Hvor i all verden har du lært deg det?**
   Wherever did you learn that?

6.5.2.5 *'However'*

While 'however' in the sense of 'nevertheless' is rendered by **imidlertid, likevel, dog,** Norwegian also has a number of other ways of rendering English idioms with 'however'.

English	Remarks	Norwegian	Example
'However'	= 'no matter how' + adjective or adverb	**hvor … enn**	1, 2
'How ever?'	= 'How on earth…?'	**hvordan i all verden?**	3
'However you wish'	= 'in whatever way you wish'	**hvordan … enn, uansett**	4

1 However much I want to, I dare not do it.
   Hvor gjerne jeg enn vil, tør jeg ikke gjøre det.

2 However intelligent he may be, he cannot spell properly.
   Hvor intelligent han enn måtte være, kan han ikke stave rett.

3 How on earth could the Nobel Committee give him the prize?
   Hvordan i all verden kunne Nobelkomiteen gi ham prisen?

4 However you look at it, prices are rising.

Hvordan man enn snur og vender på det, stiger prisene.

Uansett hvordan man ser på det/snur og vender på det, . . .

Note that **uansett** can also translate 'anyway':

Jeg gjør det uansett. I will do it anyway.

Chapter 7

Prepositions

7.1 Introduction

7.1.1 *Prepositions and their meaning*

7.1.1.1

Prepositions describe relations; they often locate one entity (a 'participant') relative to another (a 'landmark') in space. For example, in **Kari ligger i senga,** 'Kari is in bed', the preposition **i,** 'in' describes the relation between **Kari** and **senga,** 'the bed' – she is located relative to the landmark, the bed. In **Knut sitter ved det gamle spisebordet,** 'Knut is sitting at the old dining-table', **ved,** 'at' describes the relation between **Knut** and **det gamle spisebordet.**

7.1.1.2

However, things are often not so simple. Prepositions can involve temporal relations; locating events in time, as in **Kari synger i kveld,** 'Kari is singing tonight'; **Beate kommer om åtte dager,** 'Beate will come in eight days'. They can involve more complex abstract relations, as in **Arve er glad i Kari,** 'Arve is fond of Kari'; **Siri var sint på Unni,** 'Siri was angry with Unni'. In such examples, it may be hard to explain the choice of prepositions, precisely because the relation is more abstract. Why should Norwegians say **glad i, sint på,** when the English say 'fond of', 'angry with'? Such questions are difficult; the use of prepositions is a stumbling block in learning many foreign languages. Still, some prepositions are extremely frequent, and that means that it is sensible to spend some time on learning some central patterns.

Also, Norwegian is a language where location and position matters. This shows not only in the posture verbs (cf. 5.3.4.2(b), 5.8.2), but also in prepositional usage. There are more compound prepositions in Norwegian than in English, and they are used more frequently.

7.1.2 Morphology

Prepositions are not inflected; they are indeclinable. Prepositions can be morphologically simplex, such as **i**, 'in', **på**, 'on', and the most frequent ones are. They can also be morphologically complex, such as **utenfor**, 'outside of', cf. **ute** and **for, innenfra**, 'from the inside' cf. **inne**, 'in' and **fra**, 'from', cf. 7.4 below and 11.2.2.16. However, the term preposition also commonly covers multi-word units such as **i stedet for**, 'in place of', 'instead of', **på grunn av** *lit.* 'on grounds of', 'because'. While these are not words, but groups of words, they fulfil the same function as single-word prepositions, and they are dealt with in 7.5 below. Compare **Boka blir ferdig om fire uker**, 'The book will be finished in four weeks' vs. **Boka blir ferdig i løpet av fire uker**, 'The book will be finished within four weeks'. Some prepositional word groups can even be discontinuous, e.g. **for . . . siden**, 'ago': **Det var for tre dager siden**, 'That was three days ago', see 7.5.16.

7.1.3 Syntax

7.1.3.1

As their name indicates, prepositions are usually preposed; they are in front of the complement (the phrase they are governing), cf. **ved det gamle spisebordet**, 'at the old dining table'.

7.1.3.2

Sometimes, prepositions can be postposed in Norwegian. This often involves fixed expressions, e.g. **oss imellom**, 'between ourselves, between you and me'; **Jorden rundt (på åtti dager)**, 'Around the world (in 80 days)', but not necessarily; the construction has some productivity, cf. e.g. **aficionados imellom**, 'between aficionados'.

Prepositions can also be found 'stranded', long after their complement, in so-called 'prepositional stranding', as in **Hva tenker du på?**, 'What are you thinking of?'. While prepositional stranding in formal English may raise some eyebrows, it is widely accepted in Norwegian, where, in many cases, the 'non-stranded' alternative is less conventional. This holds in particular for hv-questions (10.7.4.2) – **På hva tenker du?** would seem strange, for example. Also for fronted prepositional objects (prepositional phrases where the preposition belongs particularly closely together with the verb), the 'non-stranded' alternative is rare; 'In God we trust' may be good English, a Norwegian translation is **Gud stoler vi på** (or **Vi stoler på Gud**), never *På Gud stoler vi. Compare also 'This is the plane with which they travelled' and **Dette er flyet som de reiste med**; it would be impossible to put the preposition **med** immediately before **som**.

Prepositions 'govern' the words following (or, rarely, preceding); syntactically, prepositions are the heads of prepositional phrases. In these phrases, they can be followed by:

(a) noun phrases: **Knut sitter** *ved det gamle spisebordet.*

(b) pronouns (or pronoun phrases): **Ola tenker** *på dem*, 'Ola is thinking of them.'

(c) infinitive constructions: **Erna hadde håpet** *på å få et resultat*, 'Erna had been hoping for a result'; **Trine hadde drømt** *om å bli hørt*, 'Trine had dreamt of being heard.'

(d) clauses: **Jonas er lei** *for at det drøyer sånn*, 'Jonas is sorry that this is taking so much time'.

(e) prepositional phrases: **Monsteret kom fram** *fra bakom skapet*, 'The monster came out from behind the cupboard'

(f) nothing, i.e. they can stand alone: **Vil du sitte** *på*? *Lit.* 'Do you want to sit on', i.e. 'Do you want a ride?' **Hun gikk nettopp** *opp*, 'She just went up'.

In this last case (f), the prepositions have traditionally been called adverbs, and the two classes are sometimes difficult to distinguish, but we stick to more recent analyses on this point.

All prepositions can combine with noun phrases and pronouns. If their complement is a pronoun, it will be in the accusative: **Hun ser på meg** (not *jeg), 'She looks at me', **Du ser på henne** (not *hun), 'You look at her'. See 4.2.1.

By contrast, not all prepositions can combine with both infinitives and clauses. Prepositions that do not have a temporal meaning do not combine with a clause. Thus, **bak**, 'behind' does not combine with either clauses or infinitives, because it typically has a spatial meaning only. Conversely, **etter**, 'after' combines with both infinitives and clauses; it has a temporal meaning. Not all temporal prepositions are so general, however; for example, **før**, 'before' can combine with clauses (without an **at**), but not with infinitives.

Noun phrase	Clause	Infinitive
på taket	**stoler på at du går**	**tenker på å feire jul**
on the roof	trusting that you will go	thinking of celebrating Christmas
etter jul	**etter at du gikk**	**etter å ha tenkt over saken**
after Christmas	after you left	after having thought the matter over
før middag	**før du går**	(none)
before dinner	before you leave	
bak huset	(none)	(none)
behind the house		

This picture is simplified, however, and some prepositions (e.g. **med, uten**) are mainly used with other meanings. For glosses and further information on each, cf. 7.2.

The construction of preposition and infinitive/**at**-clause is thus markedly different from English, as the table above shows. (Norwegian has no gerund, cf. 5.3.1.6, 5.3.2, 5.3.2.3.) In English, one cannot combine prepositions with 'that'-clauses so freely. However, often inserting 'the fact' before 'that' will facilitate the translation. Compare: **Hun tenker på at han gikk**, 'She thinks about (the fact) that he left'; **Hun er sint for at han gikk**, 'She is angry at the fact that he left'.

Note – Many grammars use the label 'subjunction' rather than 'preposition' in such examples as **siden du gikk, innen jeg dør.** See also 9.1.4.2.

7.2 Prepositions and adverbs

7.2.1 The relation to adverbs

The delimitation between adverbs and prepositions can be difficult. See also 6.1.2.2.

7.2.2 A derivational relationship

7.2.2.1

A number of prepositions are closely related to a word that ends in –e:

inn – inne	in (for both words)
ned – nede	down (for both words)
opp – oppe	up (for both words)
ut – ute	out (for both words)

Typically, the word without –e (**inn, ned, opp, ut**) can govern a following phrase; the word with –e cannot. Thus, **ned trappa/veien** 'down the stairs/ the road' is an acceptable Norwegian phrase, while **nede** cannot govern a following noun (phrase); i.e. it is typically used 'intransitively'.

The word without –e indicates direction; the word with –e indicates absence of direction. Thus, **gå ned** can be translated as 'descend', **gå nede** can be translated as 'walk on a level lower than where we are', for example.

Note – This holds true also for a number of adverbs. See 6.4.1.1.

Compare:

Ola var ute, men gikk inn. Så nå er han inne, inntil han går ut igjen.
Ola was out(side), but went in. So now he is in(side), until he goes out again.

Hunden la seg ned, men den ble ikke liggende nede.
The dog lay down, but it did not stay lying down.

Since they denote absence of direction, words ending in –e may well combine with **være**, 'be', cf. e.g. **Hun er nede**, 'She is down' (physically or emotionally). The corresponding word without –e denotes direction, and so does not combine with **være**. Conversely, verbs of motion do not usually combine with words in –e. (Unless the situation is conceptualised from 'the outside', as in **Han kunne se folk gå der nede på stien**, 'He could see people walking down there on the footpath').

The relation between words with and without –e holds also for a couple of words that traditionally have not been treated as prepositions, but as adverbs (but recall from 7.2.1 that the distinction is tricky):

fram – framme	forward
hjem – hjemme	home
Får jeg følge deg hjem?	Can I follow you home?
Hjemme var han en tyrann.	At home, he was a tyrant.

| 7.2.2.2 | *Motion away from a place and to a place* |

These prepositions are compounds. They include among others:

From a place		*To a place*	
bortefra	away from	**bortover**	across to
inne(n)fra	from the inside	**innover**	inwards
ute(n)fra	from the outside	**utover**	outwards

Note – Perhaps unexpectedly, **nedenfra**, 'from below' means the opposite of **ned fra**, 'down from', and **ovenfra**, 'from above' means the opposite of **opp fra**, 'up from'.

7.3 Notes on some common simplex prepositions

| 7.3.1 | *av* |

| 7.3.1.1 |

This preposition, related to English 'of', 'off', can be used to locate participants with respect to some landmark, cf. **Finn gikk av sleden**, 'Finn got off the sled'. While such 'concrete' examples are rare with this preposition, they indicate a basic function of **av**, namely to denote place of origin, source or starting-point. Thus, **av** can be used to indicate the material which something is made of, e.g. **ei fjøl av tre**, 'a board made of wood'; **en blanding av sorg og lettelse**, 'a mixture of grief and relief'. **Av** can signal cause, as in **Terry logret av glede**, 'Terry wagged his tail with joy'. (While the wagging is not 'made of' joy, it has its origin in joy, as the board has its origin in wood.) Related to the notion of source, **av** is often found before the 'agent' in passives (cf. 5.6.1.1, 10.7.3.3), corresponding to English 'by', cf. **Oswald ble drept av Ruby**, 'Oswald was killed by Ruby'; **Finnegan's Wake er kjøpt av mange, men lest av få**, '*Finnegan's Wake* has been bought by many, but read by few'. **Av** can also signal 'part of', partitivity (and is also then related to origin or source), as in **halvparten av alle nordmenn**, 'half of all Norwegians'.

7.3.1.2

Like English 'by', **av** can be used to denote permanent properties, as in **Knut er blyg av naturen**, 'Knut is shy by nature'; **Bjørg er lærer av yrke**, 'Bjørg is a teacher by profession'; like English 'of', **av** can be used to introduce the 'source' of an action (sometimes unspecified) in constructions such as **Det var fint gjort av deg**, 'That was well done of you'; **Det var pent av Ragnhild**, 'That was good of Ragnhild'.

7.3.2 bak

This preposition is mostly used locationally, and usually translates as 'behind', cf. **Øksa står bak døra**, 'The axe is behind the door'. **bak** is not used temporally.

7.3.3 blant

This preposition usually translates as 'among': **Blant de mistenkte er det mange uskyldige**, 'Among the suspects many are innocent'. Note the expression **blant annet/andre**, 'among other things/others': **Det er mye godt med Danmark – silda, blant annet**, 'There are many good things about Denmark, – the herring, among other things'. Like English 'among', **blant** is normally followed by a noun (or pronoun) in the plural, not the singular.

7.3.4 etter

7.3.4.1

Etter, typically translated with 'after', can be used locationally, but, like its English counterpart, it will then imply succession: **Etter politibilen kom ambulansen**, 'After/Behind the police car came the ambulance'. (In this function, etter can often be replaced by **bak** 'behind': **Bak politibilen kom ambulansen.**)

7.3.4.2

In its more common temporal meaning, **etter** also implies succession, cf. **Etter middagen blir det småkaker**, 'After dinner there will be pastries', and often translates 'after' or 'since': **Etter Guernica var det klart hva som ville komme**, 'After Guernica it was clear what was to come'. Succession, following, is reflected also in that **etter** can mean 'according to, by' – **gå etter boka**, 'go by the book' (follow the rules), **evangeliet etter Matteus**, 'the gospel according to Matthew'. Also, there is a kind of 'incomplete following' when **etter** can indicate a longing, a search for, in which case it often translates as English 'for': **Politi og hjelpemannskap har lett etter de uheldige turistene**, 'Police and rescue teams have been searching for the unfortunate tourists'; **Romeos lengsel etter Julie**, 'Romeo's longing for Juliet'.

7.3.5 for

7.3.5.1

This preposition has a multitude of functions, but it is seldom locational, though it can be used when X covers Y, cf. **holde en hånd for munnen**, 'keep a hand in front of your mouth'; **holde tann for tunge** (proverbial) *Lit.* 'keep tooth before tongue', i.e. 'be silent'. Related to this 'cover' meaning is the 'concealment' meaning of **for**, as in **Leonore hadde hemmeligheter for kjæresten**, 'Leonore kept secrets from her sweetheart'. Some combinations of **for** and temporal expressions, e.g. **værvarselet for i morgen**, 'the weather forecast for (covering) tomorrow' and **for øyeblikket**, 'for the moment' are perhaps also relatable to this 'cover' meaning.

7.3.5.2

for most often translates as 'for' in English, and it will often mean 'for the benefit of (directed at)', as **Merlene Ottey løp for Slovenia**, 'Merlene Ottey ran for Slovenia'; **mumle for seg selv**, 'mumble to oneself'; **et hjem for foreldreløse**, 'a home for orphans'. If X is directed at Y, this often means that Y is taken into consideration, as in some usages with adjectives, cf. **Per er stor for alderen**, 'Per is tall for his age'.

7.3.5.3

for can also mean 'instead of, in exchange for' as in **Bjørn var reserve for Kjell**, 'Bjørn was a stand-in for Kjell', and this is quite common with prices, e.g. **90 kroner for en øl**, '90 crowns for a beer'; **noe for noe**, 'quid pro quo'. It can also mean 'in favour of' (and is then the opposite of **mot**, 'against'), as in **Mange amerikanere er veldig mot abort og veldig for dødsstraff**, 'Many Americans are strongly opposed to abortion and strongly in favour of the death penalty'.

7.3.5.4

The combination **for å** typically signifies intention (English '(in order) to'): **Du må knuse noen egg for å få omelett**, 'You have to break eggs (in order) to make an omelette'. Cf. also **for at**, as in **Kokken knuste noen egg for at vi skulle få omelett**, 'The chef cracked some eggs so that we could have an omelette'.

Note 1 – There is also another word (a conjunction) **for**, indicating cause: **Han lo, for hun var så morsom**, 'He laughed, for she was so droll/funny'.

Note 2 – While English uses 'for' to signal indirect objects, Norwegian typically uses **til**: 'Robert painted a picture for Patty', **Robert malte et bilde til Patty**. This is linked to the fact that English uses 'for' also followed by the names of specific persons – 'a gift for Mum', **en gave til mor**. Cf. also 'For somebody so dumb, you are surprisingly smart', **Til å være slik en tosk er du overraskende smart**. On the other hand, in some other constructions, Norwegian uses **for** where English has 'to', e.g. to indicate the point of view of a person: **For meg ser dette merkelig ut**, 'To me this looks strange'.

7.3.6 | foran

This preposition typically translates as 'in front of': **Traktoren stod foran låven**, 'The tractor was parked in front of the barn'; **Foran toget gikk det en elg midt i skinnegangen**, 'In front of the train an elk was walking in the middle of the tracks'.

7.3.7 | forbi

In its locational sense, this preposition translates as English 'past', cf. **Vera kjørte forbi åstedet**, 'Vera drove past the crime scene'. Like English 'past', it can also have a metaphorical meaning: **Alt er forbi**, 'Everything is over'.

7.3.8 | før

This preposition usually translates as 'before'. Used locationally, it will imply succession: **Før ambulansen kom politibilen**, 'Before/In front of the ambulance came the police car'. In its more common, temporal use, **før** also implies succession: **før solnedgang**, 'before sunset', **Før du sovner**, 'Before you fall asleep' (novel by Linn Ullmann). Used without any complement, **før** can mean 'earlier, before': **Det burde vi ha tenkt på før**, 'That we ought to have thought of before'.

7.3.9 | fra

7.3.9.1

In its directional sense, **fra** translates as 'from', and denotes place of origin or 'source': **Hvalfangerne kom hjem fra Sør-Georgia**, 'The whalers came home from South Georgia', **Fra Narvik går det tog til Kiruna**, 'From Narvik there are trains for Kiruna'. **Fra** can also be used of source in a less concrete sense: **Vi er fra Gerhardsen-epoken**, 'We are from the Gerhardsen era' (i.e. 1945–1965). In its temporal use, **fra** also denotes 'starting-point', as in **I Norge regner vi vikingtida fra 800 til 1000**, 'In Norway we take the Viking Age to be between 800 and 1000', or 'origin', as in **Her er ei låt fra 80-tallet**, 'Here is a tune from the 80s'. Similarly, in **et smil fra Julie**, 'a smile from Juliet'; **en gave fra Moriarty**, 'a gift from Moriarty', we also find the 'source' or 'origin' meaning of **fra**.

Note – While English can use 'from' to signify the source material, as in 'a boat made from wood', Norwegian cannot – **en båt laget av tre** (cf. 7.3.1.1).

7.3.9.2

In combination with some verbs, **fra** is better translated as 'out' or 'off': **Vi må si fra**, 'We must speak out'; **Hun kan ikke komme fra**, 'She cannot get away', **Maskinen er koblet fra**, 'The machine is turned off'.

7.3.10 *gjennom*

7.3.10.1

In its spatial sense, **gjennom** usually translates as 'through'; **I dag skal vi gå gjennom skogen**, 'Today we shall walk through the woods'; **en reise gjennom vakker natur**, 'a journey through beautiful countryside'. **gjennom** can also be used temporally, as in **norsk litteratur gjennom tidene**, 'Norwegian literature through the ages'; **Musene klarte seg gjennom vinteren**, 'The mice made it through the winter'. Like English 'through', **gjennom** must then be combined with a phrase indicating a longer period of time (*gjennom klokka 12.00.00 is impossible).

7.3.10.2

Sometimes, **gjennom** is used in a more figurative sense, indicating means, cf. **gjennom en kombinasjon av bestikkelser, trusler og vold**, 'through ('by way of') a combination of bribery, threats and violence'.

7.3.11 *hos*

This preposition typically locates somebody with somebody else (in the home of the 'landmark'): **Mette er på besøk hos besteforeldrene**, 'Mette is visiting her grandparents (at their place)', **hos Jane**, 'at Jane's'. **Hos** may not have a clear-cut English equivalent, but often 'at' will do.

7.3.12   i

7.3.12.1

This preposition is related to English 'in'. The highly versatile and frequent preposition **i** can locate a participant X inside a container-like landmark Y, as in **Veden er i uthuset,** 'The fire-wood is in the outhouse'; **De er i kirken nå,** 'They are in church now'. In such cases, **i** usually translates as English 'in' (cf. preceding examples), occasionally 'at, on' (cf. the following examples): **Vennligst betal i kassen,** 'Please pay at the check-out'; **Vi satte oss i sofaen,** 'We sat down on the sofa'.

7.3.12.2

When used temporally, **i** does not often correspond to English 'in', but rather to 'for' (cf. 7.6.6): **Ola skal arbeide i åtte timer** does not mean that Ola will begin work in eight hours' time, but that he will work for eight hours – i.e. for an eight-hour period. Compare also **Vi har vært i Trøndelag i tre uker,** 'We have been in Trøndelag for three weeks'; **I hele mitt liv har jeg aldri hørt noe så dumt,** 'In my entire life, I have never heard anything so stupid'. In all these examples, the notion of 'containment' is found, as in **i dag,** 'today', **i januar,** 'in January'. (Cf. also 7.6.6 on temporal uses).

In some cases where English uses no preposition in temporal usage, Norwegian has **i**, cf. 'Monday next week', **mandag i neste uke.**

Typically, **i** will be used if the landmark denotes a period that is perceived as having some duration.

7.3.12.3

Notice also **i** used with body parts, as in **jeg har vondt i hodet** *lit.* 'I have pain in the head', i.e. 'I've got a headache'; **hun tok ham i hånda,** 'she took him by the hand'; **professoren klødde seg i håret,** *lit.* 'the professor scratched herself/himself in the hair', i.e. 'scratched her/his head'. (In such examples, the use of **i** implies a fairly solid contact; for a very brief contact, **på** would be preferred, as that preposition can be used for 'superficial contact'.

7.3.12.4

The distinction between **i** and **på** 'at, on' can be problematic in many cases. See also 7.3.19. Typically, **i** is used when the landmark is seen as a 'container', it is used with 'volumes', internally, **på** when the landmark is seen as a surface or a point, from the outside:

På with surface, point	I with volume, container
på veggen	**i skapet**
on the wall	in the cupboard
på stolen	**i sofaen**
on the chair	on the sofa
på nettet	**i datamaskinen**
on the web	on the computer

The choice can involve a difference in meaning:

på landet	**i landet**
in the country(side)	in the country (e.g. Germany)
på gården	**i gården**
on the farm	in the yard
båten på vannet	**svømmeren i vannet**
the boat on the water	the swimmer in the water
hår på brystet	**vondt i brystet**
hair on the chest	pain in the chest
et smussmerke på glasset	**vann i glasset**
a dirty mark on the glass	water in the glass

7.3.13	med

This preposition typically translates as 'with, along with; including', cf. **Der kommer Gullhår med de tre bjørnene**, 'There's Goldilocks with the three bears', or 'by means of': **Han åpnet døra med en hårspenne**, 'He opened the door with a hair pin'; **Med vondt skal vondt fordrives** (proverb) *Lit.* 'With evil, evil is to be driven away', i.e. 'You fight fire with fire'. In combination with verbs, there can also be an inclusion sense to **med**, as in **Alle skal med**, *Lit.* 'Everyone shall with', i.e. 'Everybody is to be included'; **Hun kom med**, 'She came along/joined in'. Note that the inclusion sense is also found in **fra** *og med* 1. januar til *og med* 31. desember, which includes the dates at either extreme. fra 1. januar could be understood as 'as of January 2'.

Note – There is also an idiom **til og med** 'even' as in **Til og med dr. Watson ble lei av Holmes**, 'Even Dr Watson got fed up with Holmes'. This is not a preposition.

7.3.14 | mellom

This preposition often translates as 'between, through', and it is used in a fairly concrete sense, cf. **Ballen gikk mellom beina på målmannen**, 'The ball went through the goalie's legs'; **Mellom Asia og Europa ligger Bosporus-stredet**, 'Between Asia and Europa is the Straits of Bosporus'. It can also be used temporally: **Butikken er åpen mellom 10 og 17**, 'The shop is open between 10 and 17'. Notice also **mellom oss**, 'between you and me'; **mellom barken og veden** (*lit.* between the bark and the wood), 'between the devil and the deep blue sea'.

7.3.15 | mot

This preposition, often translated as 'towards' or 'against', typically has a sense of movement. **mot** can locate participants moving towards a landmark, as in **Napoleons styrker gikk mot Moskva**, 'Napoleon's forces went towards Moscow'; **Slåsskjempene gikk mot hverandre**, 'The fighters moved towards each other'. There is not always any movement, cf. **Kassene stod mot hverandre**, 'The boxes stood against each other'. The meaning 'sceptical of, negative to', as in **Åslaug var mot norsk EU-medlemskap**, 'Åslaug was against Norwegian EU membership', is related. In such cases, **mot** is the opposite of **for** (cf. 7.3.5.3).

However, confusion can arise in that the directional sense of **mot** also sometimes indicates an aim: **Jonas og Trygve arbeider mot et felles mål**, 'Jonas and Trygve are working towards a common goal/aim' will normally be understood as saying that Jonas and Trygve are working for the same goal.

7.3.16 | nær

This preposition translates as 'near; close to': **Hotellet ligger nær sentrum**, 'The hotel is close to the centre'; **Bilen gjorde nær 200 km/t**, 'The car did almost 120 mph'. It is typically used in a concrete, locational meaning.

7.3.17 om

This preposition is seldom used spatially, except when meaning 'via': **De måtte fly om København**, 'They had to fly via Copenhagen'. **Om** is often used temporally, however, and then translates either as 'at', cf. **om natta**, 'at night', or as 'in', cf. **om en time**, 'in an hour'; **om fire dager**, 'in four days'. In the spatial case, **om** typically combines with definite noun phrases. **Om** can also signal a topic, as English 'about', cf. **en artikkel om bunader**, 'an article about/ on folk costumes'; **en bok om juleskikker**, 'a book about Christmas customs'.

Note – There is also another word **om**, a subjunction meaning 'if' (9.3.2.2): **Om jeg var deg . . .**, 'If I were you. . .'

7.3.18 over

While English has a difference between 'over' and 'above', 'under' and 'below', there is no such difference in Norwegian. **Over** typically translates as English 'over' or 'above', as in **Helikopteret svever over rullebanen**, 'The helicopter is hovering over the airfield'; **En general er over en korporal**, 'a general is above (ranks above) a corporal'. Like its English counterpart, **over** can mean 'past', cf. **Sveriges gullalder var over**, 'Sweden's Golden Age was over'. As in English, **over** can mean 'via, by way of', as in **dra til Fargo over Chicago**, 'go to Fargo via Chicago'. Both in its spatial and its temporal use, **over** can mean 'on the other side of': cf. **De bor over elva**, 'They live on the other side of (above) the river'; **over helga**, 'after the weekend'.

7.3.19 på

7.3.19.1

This very frequent and multi-faceted preposition often corresponds to 'on', 'at'. It typically locates a participant on top of a physical object, at a point or on a surface: **Kjelen står på ovnen**, 'The kettle is on the stove'; **Fuglene sitter på ledningen**, 'The birds are sitting on the wire'. However, the 'participant' may be located on a vertical plane, as in **Bildet henger på veggen**, 'The picture is hanging on the wall', in which case 'contact' may be the key point about **på**.

For some time, **på** has been taking over some of the 'territory' of some other prepositions. Thus, it may now be more common to write **på kjøkkenet** than **i kjøkkenet**, 'in the kitchen', more common to write **lytte på** than **lytte** til, 'listen to', **på ettermiddagen** than **om ettermiddagen**, 'in the afternoon'. In such cases, there is usually some tolerance. (After all, Norwegians are used to linguistic variation, cf. Introduction).

7.3.19.2

Used temporally, **på** can – in a manner similar to its spatial function – locate an event 'at a point', cf. **på onsdag**, 'on Wednesday'; **på nyttårsaften**, 'on New Year's Eve'. **På** does not, therefore, usually combine with a noun denoting a longer period of time, so *på november and *på 1965 are out; the idiomatic preposition is **i**. **på kvelden**, 'in the evening'; **på våren**, 'in spring' are acceptable, but not quite as traditional as **om kvelden, om våren** (7.3.17).

7.3.19.3

På can be used with expressions containing measurement, numerical information: **ei jente på ti år**, 'a girl of ten'; **lønn på 180000 (kroner)**, 'a wage of 180,000 (kroner)'; **et skip på 100000 tonn**, 'a ship of 100,000 tons'.

På is not infrequently used to signal 'belonging', comparable to English 'of', cf. **taket på huset**, 'the roof of the house'; **halen på ulven**, 'the tail of the wolf' (see also 1.8.1.6, 7.7.3.5). What belongs to X is often also a quality or characteristic of X, and **på** is common after nouns denoting quality or characteristic, such as **fargen på øynene**, 'the colour of her/his eyes'; **størrelsen på skoene**, 'the size of the shoes'; **smaken på suppa**, 'the taste of the soup'.

På can often combine with noun phrases of manner: **på den måten, på det viset**, 'in that way'.

7.3.19.4

In combination with verbs of physical contact, **på** often indicates a more superficial, briefer kind of contact (since an object then is reduced to a point, as it were). Thus, there is a difference between **Gry løftet sekken**, 'Gry lifted the sack' and **Gry løftet på sekken**. If the lifting is complete and successful (say, if Gry is lifting the sack high above the ground and holding it there for a long time), the expression with **på** is unlikely. If the lifting is incomplete, say, Gry managed to lift the sack only for a short time, or lifted it off the ground only to move it a few centimetres further along the floor, the expression with **på** is more likely. Compare **Christine tok Øystein og** gikk, 'Christine took Øystein and left'; and **Christine tok på Øystein og gikk,** 'Christine touched Øystein and left'. Only the former implies that Christine had 'control' of Øystein, in some sense, and that he went along (or even was carried along); only the latter implies superficial touching.

Note – The effect of adding **på** after a verb may sometimes be comparable to that of the progressive aspect in English. Compare **Knut leste boka ferdig,** 'Knut read the book through' vs. **Knut leste på ei bok,** 'Knut was reading a book'; *Knut leste på ei bok ferdig is simply not grammatical.

7.3.19.5

In a number of cases, **på** will be translated by 'in': **på landet,** 'in the countryside'; **på hotellet,** 'in the hotel'; **på soverommet,** 'in the bedroom'. Some of these combinations are fixed, one cannot say **i landet** in Norwegian meaning 'in the countryside'. Sometimes, however, a different conceptualisation, a different point of view, will lead to choosing another preposition, even if the 'meaning' otherwise may seem unchanged.

Compare: **Vi er på badet,** 'We are in the bathroom' vs. **Vi er i badet,** which can mean not only 'We are in the bathroom', but perhaps even more likely 'We are in the bath (i.e. bath-tub)'. With **i,** the point of view is more 'internal', 'inside' a container.

Many nouns denoting institutions typically combine with **på** (**på skolen, på sjukehuset, på universitetet**), but not all (**i kirken, i banken**), and sometimes there is variation (**i/på radioen**). (For translations, see 7.3.19.6).

7.3.19.6 | på or i with place

The division of labour between **i** and **på** can be tricky, cf. also 7.3.12.4, but in the typical case, **i** is used with 'containers', **på** with 'points and surfaces'. Thus, the names of larger Norwegian cities typically take **i** (**i Bergen, i Oslo**), while smaller, and thus more 'point-like', towns (especially inland) can combine with **på** (**på Hamar, på Kongsvinger**). In the latter case, however, there is again some variability depending on conceptualisation (cf. 7.3.19.5); compare **Vi skal møtes på Kongsvinger,** 'We'll meet in Kongsvinger' vs. **En venn av meg bor i den fineste gamle trevillaen i hele Kongsvinger,** 'A friend of mine lives in the finest old wooden villa in all Kongsvinger'. In the former case, Kongsvinger is conceptualised as a point, in the latter as a 'container'.

However, this only applies to the names of towns and cities in Norway. Names of towns outside Norway are always preceded by **i**, even if they are small (**i Kineton, i Charlottenberg**). For other geographical locations, the main rule applies; **i** is used if the landmark is seen as a 'container', as districts and countries usually are, cf. **i Sussex**, 'in Sussex'; **i Belgia**, 'in Belgium', whereas **på** is used with points and surfaces, **på Zürich-sjøen**, 'on Lake Zürich'. Islands are conceived of as 'points', e.g. **på Island**, 'in Iceland'; **på Grønland**, 'in Greenland', but exceptions occur if they are very large and nations in themselves, cf. **i Australia**. Compare **i Europa**, 'in Europe' vs. **på Kontinentet**, 'on the Continent'.

Names of rivers, also abroad, can be subject to the same kind of variation (in line with the main rule) as in the **Kongsvinger** example. If conceptualised as surfaces, they can combine with **på**, if conceptualised as containers with **i**:

Det er mye trafikk på Hudson-elva.
There is a lot of traffic on the Hudson River.

Det har vært mye fisk i Hudson-elva.
There has been a lot of fish in the Hudson River.

Note also the following examples:

På:

på arbeid, at work; **på hotellet**, at the hotel; **på jobben**, at work; **på kino**, at the cinema; **på konsert**, at a concert; **på kontoret**, at the office; **på radio**, on the radio; **på restaurant**, at a restaurant; **på sjukehuset**, in/at the hospital; **på skolen**, at school; **på universitetet**, at/in the university

I:

i banken, at the bank; **i kirken**, at church; **i kjelleren**, in the cellar; **i leiligheten**, in the apartment; **i museet**, at the museum

Either **i** or **på**: **butikken** 'the shop'; **kjøkkenet**, 'the kitchen'; **teateret**, 'the theatre'; **soverommet**, 'the bedroom' – English 'at, in'

Perhaps confusingly, names of regions in Norway combine with **på** if they end in –**landet** (or –**rike**, –**møre**, cf. **på Sørlandet, på Ringerike, på Sunnmøre**). Other names of regions tend to combine with **i** (**i Trøndelag, i Nord-Norge, i Valdres**). With street names, we usually find **i**, cf. **i Storgata**, 'on the main street', **i Trondheimsveien**.

In some cases, **på** contrasts with **av** (cf. English 'on/off'), cf. **slå på radioen**, 'switch the radio on'; **slå av radioen**, 'switch the radio off'.

7.3.20 | rundt

This preposition often translates as 'around': **rundt hjørnet**, 'around the corner'. Like English 'around', it can also have the meaning '–ish', 'roughly': **Hun sang i rundt ti minutter,** 'She sang for roughly ten minutes'.

7.3.21 | til

7.3.21.1

In its simple locational sense, **til** denotes a direction and corresponds to English 'to'. Cf. **Vi dro til Oslo,** 'We went to Oslo'; **toget til Bergen,** 'the train to Bergen'. In this case, **til** is so to speak the counterpart of **fra,** indicating not a starting-point, but an end-point.

7.3.21.2

til is often used to signal possession, comparable to English 'of' (cf. 7.7): **Der er huset til Roald og Eva** 'There is the house of Roald and Eva'. Thus: **Dette er synspunktene til Putin** *lit.* 'These are the views/points of view to Putin' is most naturally interpreted as 'these are Putin's views, not 'these are the views to be presented to Putin'. In these two examples, **til** could be replaced by **–s** (**Roald og Evas hus, Putins synspunkter,** cf. 1.8.1), but this would be less natural if we are dealing with non-human 'possessors', especially if they are not expressed by proper names, e.g. **buret til papegøyen,** 'the parrot's cage'. (**Papegøyens bur** is possible, but very formal.)

7.3.21.3

In temporal expressions, **til** will often mean 'until, till, 'by": **De danset til sola rant,** 'They danced till the sun went up', or 'before': **Dette må være gjort til fredag,** 'This must be done by/before Friday'. As in its spatial function, temporal **til** has the meaning of end-point. Therefore, **til fredag** may be interpreted as 'before Friday'; contrast the quite unequivocal **Butikken har oppe til og med fredag,** 'The shop is open up to and including Friday' (cf. 7.3.13, 7.6.13).

| 7.3.21.4 |

Related to its directional sense, **til** can mean 'made for': **utstyr til trening**, 'equipment for training'; **fisk til middag**, 'fish for dinner'; **til å bli gal/kvalm av**, 'so as to drive you mad/make you queasy'.

| **7.3.22** | *under* |

| 7.3.22.1 |

While English distinguishes between 'over' and 'above', 'under' and 'below', there is no such difference in Norwegian (cf. 7.3.18); **under** will typically correspond to either 'under' or 'below'. Cf. **Hunden ligger under bordet**, 'The dog is lying under the table'; **Alt er vel under dekk**, 'All is well below deck'.

| 7.3.22.2 |

Under is not often used temporally, but it can be used in the sense of 'during', cf. **under møtet**, 'during the meeting'; **under krigen**, 'during the war'.

| **7.3.23** | *ut* |

This preposition will usually translate as English 'out', but English 'out' can also be translated as **ute**, cf. 7.2.2.1. **Kari gikk ut døra**, 'Kari went out of the door'. It can also be used temporally: **Billetten gjelder ut januar**, 'The ticket is valid throughout January' (i.e. until February).

| **7.3.24** | *ved* |

| 7.3.24.1 |

The locational sense of **ved** roughly translates as 'by', 'at the side of, next to'. Compare **Hammerfest ligger ved Nordishavet**, 'Hammerfest is situated on the Arctic Ocean'; **Han stod ved hennes side,** 'He stood by her side'; **De satte seg ved bordet,** 'They sat down at the table'.

7.3.24.2

Ved is also used in some temporal expressions, typically not very precise ones, e.g. **ved midnatt,** 'at midnight'; **ved sjutida,** 'around seven'. The meaning of close approximation is also found in some locational uses, such as **Kari traff rett ved målet,** 'Kari hit past the goal/target', which means that Kari did not score, but she came close. Note also **ved denne anledningen,** 'on this occasion'.

7.3.24.3

Ved can also be used to signal means, instrument: **Han ble valgt ved å appellere til folks verste instinkter,** 'He was elected by appealing to people's worst instincts'; **Han skadet sin egen sak ved at han alltid var så uhøflig,** 'He damaged his own cause through always being so impolite'. Cf. also **ved hjelp av** 'by means of' – **Ved hjelp av en hårnål åpnet Askepott dørlåsen,** 'By means of a hairpin Cinderella opened the lock' (7.5.14).

Note – There are some dialects where **med** is used more at the expense of **ved** (and vice versa).

7.4 Some morphologically compound prepositions

7.4.1

7.4.1.1

Unlike their English counterparts, Norwegian prepositions form compounds frequently. For example, **bak,** 'behind' and **på,** 'on' can form a compound preposition **bakpå,** as in **Bakpå sykkelen satt jeg,** 'At the back of the bicycle, I sat'; **inn,** 'in' and **med,** 'with' can form a compound preposition **innmed,** as in **Buster ligger innmed ovnen,** 'Buster lies near the oven'.

In fact, the majority of Norwegian prepositions are morphologically compound. They open for a quite nuanced description of the location of an object by means of a single word. Compare for example **Pakka ligger bakpå sykkelen,** 'The package is at the back of and on top of the bicycle'; **Hunden ligger bakmed sykkelen,** 'The dog lies behind and close to the bicycle'; **Hunden ligger innmed sykkelen,** 'The dog lies close to the bicycle'; **Kniven lå innunder sykkelen,** 'The knife was close to and under the bicycle'; **Heroinet var inni sykkelen,** 'The heroin was in/within the bicycle'.

Note – Norwegian has a relatively fine-calibre system for specifying location and position. The compound prepositions support this, as does the differentiation **inn – inne,** etc. 7.2.2.1. Also, Norwegians use verbs of position and posture extensively (5.3.4.2(b), 5.8.2).

7.4.1.2

Many compound prepositions have a fairly 'concrete' meaning, and the group of compound prepositions is large. However, many of them are infrequent (a case in point being **bakpå**), perhaps more so in writing than in speech (e.g. **innmed** is rare in writing). This grammar concentrates on writing and on frequent patterns, so we deal briefly with the compound prepositions. A couple of groups merit special mention, though.

7.4.2 | *Compound prepositions beginning with i– 'in–'*

7.4.2.1

These include **gjennom** vs. **igjennom, blant** vs. **iblant, mellom** vs. **imellom, fra** vs. **ifra, mot** vs. **imot.** On the whole, there is little significant difference in meaning between the members of each pair. For example, **fra** and **ifra** are often interchangeable. **Vi kommer ifra Oslo,** 'We are coming from Oslo' can be replaced by **Vi kommer fra Oslo** with little (if any) change of meaning.

7.4.2.2

However, if the complement is preposed (cf. 7.1.3.2), the word beginning with **i–** has to be used. Thus, one can write **mellom venner,** 'between friends' or **imellom venner,** but only **venner imellom,** not *venner mellom.

Also, there is a tendency to use the word beginning with **i**– if the preposition has no complement. Thus, whereas there is no clear preference in **Hun gikk i/gjennom isen**, 'She went through the ice', there is a preference for **Hun gikk igjennom**, although **Hun gikk gjennom** is also acceptable.

7.4.3 | Compound prepositions with –en– (–a–)

These include **innenfor** 'within'; **utenfor** 'outside'; **østenfor** 'to the east of'; **sønnenfor**, 'to the south of' and others. These prepositions usually have a moderately 'transparent' meaning. Thus, **innenfor** relates to **innen**, 'within' and **for**, 'for', but it hardly ever means anything approaching **for**; sometimes, however, it can overlap in meaning with **innen**. Compare **Innen/ Innenfor Høyre er meningene delte**, 'Within the Conservative Party, opinions are divided', **Dette må bli gjort innen/*innenfor 48 timer**, 'This must be done within 48 hours'.

Note – As an alternative to –en–, –a– can be found, i.e. **innafor, utafor**, are possible, but this is rare in writing.

7.5 Some common multi-word prepositions

Multi-word prepositions are units that function fairly similarly to single-word prepositions. English examples include 'in spite of', 'in the course of'. Below are fifteen such highly frequent units in Norwegian (7.5.1–7.5.15). Their semantics is not as intricate as that of the simplex prepositions, so we deal with them more briefly.

7.5.1 | i ferd med, 'about to'

This phrase typically occurs after the verb **være**, 'be':

Harry og Ronny var i ferd med å lykkes da Draco plutselig dukket opp.
Harry and Ron were about to succeed when Draco suddenly turned up.

This particular construction is often used where English would use a gerund:

Signe er i ferd med å bli bedre etter uhellet.
Signe is getting better after the accident.

7.5.2 | i forbindelse med, *'in connection with'*

**De som ikke tilhører Den norske kirke, har rett til fri i inntil
to dager per år i forbindelse med høytider i vedkommendes
religion.**
Those that do not belong to the Church of Norway are entitled to up
to two days a year off, in connection with holidays in the religion of said
person/s.

I forbindelse med skilsmissen var det mye rart som skjedde.
Related to/In connection with the divorce, many strange things
happened.

This complex preposition is fairly formal.

7.5.3 | i forhold til, *'compared to, in relation to'*

Mette er sterk i forhold til broren sin.
Mette is strong compared to her brother.

I forhold til det forrige utkastet ditt er dette en forbedring.
Compared to your previous draft this is an improvement.

Note – This particular phrase has perhaps become too popular in Norwegian in recent years; there is even a derogatory term '(i)**forholdisme**', used
to criticize its over-use, as in **Her er informasjon i forhold til pris**, 'Here is
information about price', more traditionally **Her er informasjon om pris**.

7.5.4 | i form av, *'in the shape of, in the guise of'*

Da dukket redningen opp i form av en snill svensk reiseleder.
Then rescue turned up in the guise of a kind Swedish travel guide.

Stortinget har gjort sitt i form av en ny lov.
Parliament has done its share in the shape of a new law.

7.5.5 | i henhold til, *'according to'*

I henhold til norsk rett er utmarka åpen for alle.
By Norwegian law, the wilderness is accessible to everybody.

This complex preposition is fairly formal.

7.5.6 i likhet med, *'like'*

I likhet med Gygrid hjelper Molly Wiltersen Harry.
Like Hagrid, Molly Weasley helps Harry.

7.5.7 i løpet av, *'during, in the course of'*

I løpet av sommeren vil alle tog bli kontrollert på nytt.
During the summer/This summer all trains will be checked again.

I løpet av arbeidet med avhandlinga om Hamsun ble hun lei.
In the course of the work with the dissertation on Hamsun she got fed up.

7.5.8 i motsetning til, *'in opposition to, unlike'*

I motsetning til Ibsen var Bjørnson en polemiker og debattant.
Unlike Ibsen, Bjørnson was a polemicist and debater.

7.5.9 i stedet for, *'instead of'*

Hva spiser dere i stedet for ribbe på juleaften?
What do you eat instead of pork ribs on Christmas Eve?

Du burde gå i stedet for å ta bilen.
You ought to walk instead of taking the car.

Note – An alternative version of this particular phrase is a simplex **isteden-for** (written in one word). Notice also the 'intransitive' in examples like **Vi valgte torsk i stedet**, 'We chose cod instead'.

7.5.10 i tillegg til, *'in addition to, besides'*

I tillegg til å skrive godt har Knausgård utseendet med seg.
In addition to writing well, Knausgård is good-looking.

Vi sier de skal arbeide hardt, men i tillegg til det er det lurt å ha flaks.
We tell them to work hard, but in addition to that, it is smart to be lucky.

Note the 'intransitive' in e.g. **Jeg tar brød i tillegg**, 'I'll have bread on the side'.

7.5.11 på grunn av, 'because of'

Lukket på grunn av glede.
Closed because of joy (note on shop-door in Oslo on 8 May, 1945)

Ble han valgt på grunn av russerne?
Was he elected because of the Russians?

7.5.12 som følge av, 'as a consequence of'

Foreningen med Sverige under én konge var oppløst som følge av at kongen hadde opphørt å fungere som norsk konge.
The union with Sweden under one king was dissolved as a consequence of the fact that the [Swedish] King had ceased to function as Norwegian king.

Som følge av luftforurensningen i Oslo blir mange syke.
As a consequence of the air pollution in Oslo many become ill.

This particular multi-word unit is formal. Less formal ways of expressing the last example would be **På grunn av luftforurensningen i Oslo . . .** or **Fordi det er luftforurensning i Oslo . . .**

7.5.13 til tross for, 'in spite of, despite'

Til tross for svakere krone reiser nordmennene mye utenlands.
Despite a weaker Norwegian krone, Norwegians travel abroad a lot.

Hun er en god sjef til tross for det.
She is a good boss in spite of that.

Note – 'In spite of' can also translate as **På tross av** or **Trass i**. Notice also **Tross alt**, 'despite everything', which is much used.

7.5.14 ved hjelp av, 'by means of'

Båttyven ble knepet ved hjelp av radarsporing.
The boat-thief was caught by means of radar tracking.

ved siden av, *'next to, in addition to'*

Ved siden av Sigrid Undset og Knut Hamsun var faktisk Trygve Gulbranssen en av de mest leste forfatterne.
Next to Sigrid Undset and Knut Hamsun, Trygve Gulbranssen was actually among the most read authors.

De studerer, og så har de jobb ved siden av.
They study, and they have a job on the side.

| 7.5.16 | *Discontinuous prepositional word groups*

| 7.5.16.1 |

There are some discontinuous prepositional word groups, sometimes called 'parenthetical', because they enclose the complement. These include the following two used temporally:

For . . . siden, 'ago'
For to uker siden innså Serafin at hamsteren lengtet etter en kamerat.
Two weeks ago, Serafin realised that the hamster was longing for a buddy.

For . . . skyld, 'for Xs sake'
De gikk Besseggen for utsiktens skyld.
They walked Besseggen for the sake of the view.

Hun gjorde det for din skyld.   She did it for your sake.

Fra . . . av, 'from . . . on'
Fra den dagen av drakk både mann og kone i Hellemyren.
(Amalie Skram)
From that day on both man and wife in Hellemyren drank.

Fra mandag av er det forbudt å studere grammatikk.
As of Monday, it is forbidden to study grammar.

| 7.5.16.2 |

There are also cases where two prepositions, conjoined, have a meaning worth noting. These include **fra og med** (7.3.13), **til og med** (7.3.13), and:

I og med, 'as, through, because of'

I og med at de kaster råtne tomater på oss, er de nok ikke imponert.
As they are throwing rotten tomatoes at us, they are probably not impressed.

I og med denne gullmedaljen er Marit vår beste skiløper gjennom tidene.
Through this gold medal Marit is our best skier ever.

7.6 From English to Norwegian – prepositions of time

Prepositional usage is often easier, relatively speaking, with 'concrete' locational meanings. Prepositions are frequently also used with temporal meanings (7.1.1.2), however, and these are often perceived as more difficult by learners. So, we shall compare English and Norwegian here. Sections 7.1–7.5 had Norwegian prepositions as their starting-point; in this section, we take English as our point of departure. Only temporal meanings are discussed. In section 7.7, we look at another classical problem, viz. how to translate English 'of'. (For a third difficulty, the distinction between **i** and **på**, see 7.3.12.4 and 7.3.19.6.)

7.6.1 English 'after'

In its temporal use, English 'after' typically translates as Norwegian **etter**:

after lunch	**etter lunsj**
after the war	**etter krigen**

7.6.2 English 'around'

In its temporal use, English 'around' often translates as Norwegian **rundt** (cf. 7.3.20):

around midnight	**rundt midnatt**
They will be here around four.	**De skal være her rundt fire.**

(An alternative is often **omkring**.)

7.6.3 | English 'at'

In some cases, when English 'at' combines with a specific point of time, no preposition is needed in Norwegian:

| at twelve o'clock | **klokka tolv** |
| at exactly one o'clock | **nøyaktig klokka ett** |

Note the following translations:

at the moment	**for øyeblikket**
at midday	**ved middagstider**
at night	**om kvelden/om natta**
at that time	**på den tida**
at this time	**på denne tida**
at this stage	**på dette stadiet**

(For 'at' in locational uses and the distinction på/i, cf. 7.3.12.4 and 7.3.19.6.)

7.6.4 | English 'between'

Used temporally, English 'between' typically translates as Norwegian **mellom**:

| between 2 and 4 p.m. | **mellom 14 og 16** |

7.6.5 | English 'during'

English 'during' can usually be translated **i løpet av** (7.5.7), sometimes with **i** as a possible alternative:

During next week, Ruritania will be invaded.
I løpet av neste uke vil Ruritania bli invadert.
I neste uke vil Ruritania bli invadert.

During the conversation Ron fell asleep.
I løpet av samtalen sovnet Ronny.

When followed by a noun that includes in its meaning an extended period of time, **under** may be a viable alternative in Norwegian:

> The seven dwarves fell asleep during the meeting.
> **De sju dvergene sovnet under/i løpet av møtet.**

Using **under** is not possible before a quantifying expression, unless it is used in the entirely different meaning of 'less than', in which case another preposition is also used:

> **Hun vant kampen på under to minutter.**
> She won the match in less than two minutes.

7.6.6 | English 'for'

7.6.6.1

English 'for' can be used when temporal duration is intended; how long something has lasted. In such cases, **i** is common in Norwegian:

> They have been married for six years now.
> **De har vært gift i seks år nå.**

> Hermione looked at Harry for 15 minutes.
> **Hermine så på Harry i 15 minutter.**

However, when the sentence contains the negation **ikke**, 'not' (or a word similar in meaning such as **knapt**, 'barely'; **aldri**, 'never'), **i** is rarely used, **på** often is:

> Hermione has not seen Harry for 15 minutes.
> **Hermine har ikke sett Harry på 15 minutter.**

> For a week, Amundsen's dogs had barely been given anything to eat.
> **Amundsens hunder hadde knapt fått mat på ei uke.**

7.6.6.2

When the period of time is conceived of as more 'point-like', 'for' often translates as **for**:

for the first time	**for første gang**
a room for the night	**et rom for natta**

This may be related to the 'cover' meaning of **for**, cf. 7.3.5.

Note – for Christmas   **til jul**

7.6.7 English 'from'

Often, this preposition translates as **fra,** also in its temporal meaning:

> From July 1, orange juice is prohibited in Ruritania.
> **Fra 1. juli er appelsinjus forbudt i Ruritania.**

> With effect from July 1, orange juice is prohibited in Ruritania.
> **Fra og med 1. juli er appelsinjus forbudt i Ruritania.**

7.6.8 English 'in'

7.6.8.1

English 'in' can be used when something is going to happen in the future, and then translates into Norwegian as **om:**

> In two weeks, the prohibition against orange juice will be effected.
> **Om to uker vil forbudet mot appelsinjus tre i kraft.**

> In a year's time, people will buy flats on the moon.
> **Om et års tid vil folk kjøpe leiligheter på månen.**

7.6.8.2

However, English 'in' can also be combined with nouns to describe the duration of events, typically with quantifying expressions. In such cases, **på** is often used in Norwegian (and **om** never is):

> Jane did her homework in an hour.
> **Jane gjorde leksene på en time.**

> Can you play 'Tiger Rag' in less than one minute?
> **Kan du spille 'Tiger Rag' på mindre enn ett minutt?**

See also 7.3.19.2.

Note the difference between **på en time** and **i en time**:

Kari gjorde lekser i en time.   Kari did homework for an hour.

While **Kari gjorde lekser i en time** does not imply that the action of doing homework is completed, **Jane gjorde leksene på en time** implies that the homework was completed (the landmark is conceived of as a point).

7.6.8.4

When referring to a specific period in the past, 'in' often translates as **på**:

in the 90s	**på 90-tallet**
in those days	**på den tida**

Note the combination with seasons and months:

in autumn, in spring	**om høsten, om våren**
in July	**i juli**

7.6.9 | **English 'on'**

When combined with names of days, 'on' typically translates as **på**:

On Friday we are leaving for Copenhagen.
På fredag drar vi til København.

never on a Sunday	**aldri på en søndag**

(For 'on' in locational uses and the distinction **på/i**, cf. 7.3.12 and 7.3.19.)

When English 'on' is used with dates, Norwegian often has no preposition:

He was born on the 25th of December
Han er født 25. desember

Though **på** can be used:

How to avoid a birth on the 17th of May?
Hvordan unngå fødsel på 17. mai?

7.6.10 English *'over'*

If English 'over' is used with a phrase specifying duration, Norwegian will often use **i**:

Scrooge has been saving money over a long period of time.
Skrue har spart penger i en lang periode.

With the meaning 'through', Norwegian can have **gjennom** (7.3.10):

Over the years, things have changed here.
Gjennom årene har ting endret seg her.

The English word 'over' can also be used in the sense of 'more than', in which case it typically translates as Norwegian **over**:

The war lasted for over four years after that.
Krigen varte i over fire år etter det

7.6.11 English *'past'*

If 'past' combines with a specific point of time, Norwegian uses **over**:

It's five past four.   **Klokka/den er fem over fire.**

(See 3.6.1 on telling the time)

If there is no complement, Norwegian can also use **forbi**:

Those days are past.   **Den tida er forbi/over.**

7.6.12 English *'since'*

Often, this preposition translates as **siden**:

Since 1985 this has been a tradition.
Siden 1985 har dette vært tradisjon.

Nobody has seen Lord Lucan since 1974.
Ingen har sett Lord Lucan siden 1974.

With nouns denoting events, **etter** may be more common in Norwegian:

Since the accident nobody has seen him.
Etter ulykken har ingen sett ham.

7.6.13 English 'through'

When used temporally, English 'through' often translates as **gjennom**, especially if followed by a plural noun (phrase), cf.

| through the ages | **gjennom tidene** |

If the noun phrase following is in the singular, **i løpet av** (7.5.7) is often a better translation, cf. 'through this last year' **i løpet av dette siste året.**

Note that where American English uses 'through' to mean 'up to and including', Norwegian uses **til og med**, cf. 7.3.13.

7.6.14 English 'till (until)'

This preposition usually translates as **til**:

| Please stay till Monday. | **Vær så snill å bli til mandag.** |
| Jane waited until Tarzan woke up. | **Jane ventet til Tarzan våknet.** |

7.6.15 English 'to'

With specific points of time, 'to' will often translate as **på** (cf. 3.6 on telling time):

| It's five to four. | **Klokka/den er fem på fire.** |

Note the expressions:

| today, tomorrow | **i dag, i morgen** |

7.6.16 English 'towards'

When used with landmarks of time, 'towards' will usually translate as **mot**:

| towards the end of the vacation | **mot slutten av ferien** |

Towards Christmas he became depressed.
Mot jul ble han deprimert.

7.6.17 English 'a'

English may use the word 'a' in expressions of frequency. This may not be a preposition, but its Norwegian translations are. Often, a viable (if perhaps slightly formal) equivalent is **per,** cf. 'eight times a day'; **åtte ganger per dag,** 'seven days a week'; **sju dager per uke.** If **per** is used, the noun following has to be indefinite. If other prepositions are used, the noun has to be definite: **Åtte ganger om dagen, sju dager i uka.** In such cases, **om** can be used with **dagen,** 'the day' or **natta,** 'the night', while **i** will be the usual choice for many other periods of time, cf. **åtte ganger i døgnet,** 'eight times every 24 hours'; **tre ganger i minuttet,** 'three times a minute'.

7.6.18 *Translating other temporal expressions into Norwegian*

Note the following expressions:

today	**i dag**
yesterday	**i går**
tomorrow	**i morgen**
the day before yesterday	**i forgårs**
in a week	**om ei uke**
next week	**(i) neste uke**
next autum	**neste høst, til høsten**

The word **neste** is just as confusing as English 'next'.

this afternoon	**i ettermiddag**
this morning	**i morges**
tonight	**i kveld**
in the morning	**om morgenen**
at night	**om natta**
in the evenings	**om kveldene, på kveldene**
on Wednesday	**på onsdag**
during the weekend	**i helga**
the weekend (to come)	**til helga**

in the 20th century	**i det 20. århundre,** **på 1900-tallet**	**7** Prepositions
in 2011	**i 2011**	

7.7 English 'of'

There are many possible translations of English 'of'. They include using:

7.7.1 The –s genitive

The –s genitive, cf. 1.8.1.1. Such cases typically involve relations of possession:

Frankrikes historie	the history of France
Sovjetunionens leder	the leader of the Soviet Union
kjærlighetens makt	the power of love

7.7.2 Compound noun

Compound noun, often used with 'part-of' relations between inanimates:

bordbeinet	the leg of the table
hustaket	the roof of the house
artikkelforfatteren	the author of the article

Unlike the examples in 7. 7.1, we cannot say that the table 'possesses' the leg or the house the roof. A compound can also often be used when the English 'landmark' denotes a material:

a house of cards	**et korthus**

7.7.3 Preposition in Norwegian

7.7.3.1 av

Av can be used when the landmark denotes material or origin (7.3.1.1):

pilspisser laget av stein	arrowheads made of stone
født av britiske foreldre	born of British parents

Av can also be used when there is a part-whole (partitive) relation involved; sometimes also with relations of possession:

et flertall av velgerne	a majority of the voters
store deler av Norge	large parts of Norway
eieren av hytta	the owner of the cabin

7.7.3.2 *fra*

When English 'of' is combined with a landmark denoting geographical origin and the preceding noun is not a title, Norwegian will usually have **fra** (7.3.9):

trollmannen fra Oz	the wizard of Oz
rottefangeren fra Hameln	the pied piper of Hameln

7.7.3.3 *i*

I is often used when the 'landmark' denotes a field of knowledge:

en professor i norsk	a professor of Norwegian
kunnskaper i grammatikk	knowledge of grammar

I is also used if the landmark is a place-name and the 'participant' has some permanent function, some title, in that place:

statsministeren i Belgia	the prime minister of Belgium

7.7.3.4 *over*

Over is often used when the preceding noun is some kind of collection of knowledge, such as a list, a map, a survey:

en liste over Norges monarker	a list of Norway's monarchs
et kart over Frankrike	a map of France
en oversikt over terriere	a survey of terriers

7.7.3.5 på

På is often used with numerical information (cf. 7.3.19.3):

en lønn på 500 000	a salary of 500 000
en forsinkelse på to døgn	a delay of two days and nights

På is often used to denote visible relations between objects or concrete participants:

taket på huset	the roof of the house
mannskapet på *Apollo 13*	the crew of *Apollo 13*

7.7.3.6 *til*

Til is often found when the 'landmark' denotes people, and there may be a relation of possession (cf. also 7.3.21.2, 7.7.1 and 7.7.3.1):

mora til barnet	the mother of the child
huset til en venn	the house of a friend

However, **til** can also be used in some other cases, sometimes when English can use 'leading up to':

årsaken til ulykken	the cause of the accident

7.7.3.7 No preposition

In some cases where English uses 'of', Norwegian uses no preposition or other grammatical word. This is often the case with quantifying expressions (1.5.4):

en kopp te	a cup of tea
fem kilo poteter	five kilos of potatoes
et stort antall feil	a large number of mistakes
alle innbyggerne	all of the inhabitants

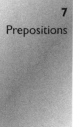

It is also typically the case when English 'of' is followed by a place-name:

byen Drammen   the town of Drammen
Kongedømmet Danmark   the kingdom of Denmark
Nord-Norge   the north of Norway

(Note that the last example also involves compounding.)

Note also the absence of preposition with times, dates, months:

Vi møttes den 10. desember.
We met on the 10th of December.

Kan du huske sommeren 2015?
Do you recall the summer of 2015?

Chapter 8

Interjections

8.1 Introduction

The class of interjections contains such words as

Ja, Yes; **Au**, Ouch; **Søren**, Blimey; **Å**, Oh; **Jøss**, Jeeze; **Morn**, Good morning; **Hurra**, Hooray

Interjections belong primarily to the spoken language, and less to formal written language. They do not inflect. They are not integrated in sentences and they can constitute an utterance on their own.

Hurra! Norge slo Sverige i kokke-VM!
Hooray! Norway beat Sweden in World Master Chef!

If found in a sentence, interjections are usually set apart by the use of the comma:

Ja, det kan du nok si.   Yes, you may say that.
Au, det svir!   Ouch, it stings!

Since interjections are not syntactically integrated and do not inflect, there is not a whole lot to say about their grammar in the strictest sense. Some interjections can take part in word formation, however. Corresponding to **ja**, **au** and **morn**, for example, we find **jada**, **auda**, **mornda/morna**. Also, from the point of view of interaction, it is good to know the function of basic *response particles*.

8.1.3

Interjections are a varied group, including response particles and reactions in conversation (**ja**), words of greeting (**Morn**), words of emotion (**Au, Søren, Hurra**), onomatopoetic words (**nøff**, 'oink'), and swearwords (**jøss**), among others. Words of greeting, saying goodbye, of politeness in interaction and words of emotion are the words the learner really needs. Onomatopoetic words and swearwords are not so necessary.

Note – In recent years, many speakers of Norwegian have adopted a number of interjections from English, such as: **Yes! Wow!** Not all of these are used by all Norwegians, however. (While **yes** can also be used as an interjection in Norwegian, 'no' cannot.)

8.2 Response particles: Ja, jo, nei

8.2.1 *Ja, nei*

The interjections **ja**, 'yes' and **nei,** 'no' correspond well to their English counterparts.

Har du vært i Frankrike?	**Ja, det har jeg/Nei, det har jeg ikke.**
Have you been to France?	Yes, I have/No, I have not.
Liker du sild? Ja/ Nei.	Do you like herring? Yes/no.
Skal du lese Knausgård i sommer?	**Ja, det skal jeg/ Nei, det skal jeg ikke.**
Will you read Knausgård this summer?	Yes, I will. No, I will not.

8.2.2 *Uses of ja, nei, jo*

(a) In addition to **ja**, 'yes', however, Norwegian has the additional response particle **jo**, also translated by English 'yes'. **Jo** is used when the preceding question contains a negative:

Likte du ikke fotballkampen? Jo, det gjorde jeg.
Didn't you enjoy the football game? Yes, I did.

Har du aldri vært i Frankrike? Jo, men det er lenge siden.
Have you never been to France? Yes, but that was a long time ago.

To answer these questions with **Ja** is unidiomatic and may create confusion. When faced with a question without a negative element, the choice is normally between **ja** and **nei**; when faced with a question containing a negative, we normally have a choice between **jo** and **nei**.

(b) The use of **ja, jo** and **nei** is not restricted to questions. They can all be used to indicate disagreement or agreement after non-questions:

Ja, 'yes' indicates agreement with a preceding statement not containing a negative:

– Gene Tierney var jammen pen. – Ja, det var hun.
"Gene Tierney was certainly good-looking." "Yes, she was." (*Lit.* Yes, she was that.)

Nei, 'no' indicates disagreement with a preceding statement not containing a negative:

– Gene Tierney var slem. – Nei, det var hun ikke.
"Gene Tierney was mean." "No, she wasn't."

Nei, 'no' indicates agreement with preceding statement containing negative:

– Historien om Gene Tierney er ikke bare trist. – Nei, den er ikke det.
"The story of Gene Tierney is not all sad." "No, it isn't."

Jo, 'yes' indicates disagreement with a preceding statement containing a negative:

– Gene Tierney var ikke snill. – Jo, det var hun, men hun var plaget.
"Gene Tierney was not kind." "Yes, she was, but she was troubled."

(c) When used after a statement without a negative, **jo** signals agreement, but with more reserve, less enthusiasm, than **ja** does:

– Napoleon var genial. – Jo, han var vel det.
"Napoleon was brilliant." "Yes, I suppose he was." (*Lit.* Yes, he was well that.)

(d) **Ja, jo, nei** may also be used sentence-initially even when the following expresses neither agreement nor disagreement:

– Hvorfor gikk David Cameron av? – Nei, det var fordi han tapte Brexit-avstemningen.
"Why did David Cameron resign?" "Because he lost the Brexit-vote."
(*Lit.*: No, because . . .)

– Hvorfor gikk David Cameron av? – Jo, det var fordi han tapte Brexit-avstemningen.
"Why did David Cameron resign?" "Because he lost the Brexit-vote."
(*Lit.* yes, because . . .)

(To answer this question with **ja** would be less likely.) In these examples, **nei** is slightly 'downtoning', but it does not really negate anything in an example like this; rather it is as if the speaker is modest and does not wish to over-emphasise the significance of his own words.

(e) **Nei** can also be used sentence-initially, at the beginning of a warning:

Nei, nå slutter du!   No, now you stop it!

(f) **Ja** and **nei** can also be used sentence-initially even when there is no obvious immediate context.

Ja, da drar vi, da.   Yes, we had better go.
                               (*Lit.* Yes, then we go, then.)

Nei, vi får vel dra.   No, we had better go.
(**Jo** here would be less likely.)

(g) **Ja** can also be used before a duplicating pronoun to signal that a topic is picked up from a previous statement:

Frankrike, ja, der er det jammen fint.
France, yes, that is a nice place.

(h) **Nei** can be used to express amazement or surprise:

Nei, har du vunnet på bingo nå igjen!
No, did you win at the bingo again!

Note 1 – Alongside **ja, jo** we also find the more 'hesitant' **Tja, Tjo.**

Note 2 – Others include **jaså, ja visst, jamen, neimen, jaha.**

8.3.1.1

Interjections may often be used to express feeling. Interjections expressing negative feeling (pain, displeasure, discomfort, negative surprise) include:

Au, 'ouch', the prototypical expression for physical pain.

> **Au, neslene brenner!**   Ouch, the nettles sting!
>
> **Huff, som det så ut på hybelen hans.**
> Ugh, you should see the state of his pad.
>
> **Isj**, Yuck, ugh; **Uff**, Oh; **Usj**, Ooh
>
> **Æsj, den osten smakte vondt.** Yuck, that cheese tasted foul!

While **au, usj** etc. typically convey the speaker's feelings, **fy** is often directed more towards someone else. **Fy** is the prototypical interjection to tell a dog that it has misbehaved, for example:

> **Fy deg, Fido!**   Naughty boy, Fido!

8.3.1.2

Interjections also express surprise; not necessarily negative:

> **Oi (sann)**, Oh; **Å**, Oh; **Ai**, Ouch; **Aha**, Aha; **Neimen**, My word;
> **Ops(sann)**, Oops!; **Jøss**, Jeeze

This last interjection may be felt unsuitable by some, due to its religious origin.

Da may be added to all monosyllabic words (except å) above: **auda, uffda, oida, jøssda.** The extended forms will mean roughly the same as the monosyllabic ones.

Interjections also express relief:

Gudskjelov!	Thank God!
Gudskjelov! Det gikk bra.	Thank God, it went well.

8.3.2 In conversation

Interjections can also serve a more pragmatic purpose in a conversation. They can signal:

(a) Hesitation:

Hm(m), Mm

(b) Agreement

Mm

(c) Disagreement, disparagement

Pøh

Pytt (sann)

Gjør det ikke vondt? Å pytt!	Doesn't it hurt? Naah!

8.4 Polite expressions

8.4.1 Greetings and farewells

8.4.1.1 Greetings

Hei, Hi there; **Hallo**, Hi; **Morn (God morn)**, Hello; **God dag**, Good morning/afternoon; **God kveld**, Good evening.

Hei and **Hallo** are perceived as more informal than the other greetings. **God dag, God kveld, Morn** are hardly used by the young.

When people meet and present themselves, it is not unusual – in addition to saying **Hei** and giving one's own first name (more seldom full name, except when the occasion is formal) – that one says **Hyggelig (å treffe deg)**, 'Nice (to meet you)'.

Hallo can also be used in a more confrontational sense:

Nei hallo, se og skjerp deg nå.   Hello! Get a grip on yourself now!

8.4.1.2 Words of farewell

Ha det/Ha det bra, Have a good day; **Morna (morn)**, Bye; bye bye;
Adjø, Goodbye; **Farvel**, Goodbye

Ha det is less formal than Morna and especially adjø, farvel. Adjø and
farvel are rather literary.

8.4.2 At mealtimes

Håper det smaker!	Hope you like it. (*Lit.* hope it tastes.)
Værsågod!	Please (go ahead, eat).

These two may be said by the host, but they are not normally said by any
of the guests. (There is no Norwegian expression corresponding to **Guten
Appetit!**)

Skål!	Cheers!
Takk for maten.	Thanks for the food/Thank you for the meal. Should be said by guests to the host or hostess directly after the meal.
Velbekomme.	You're welcome. Said by the host or hostess in response to Takk for maten.

8.4.3 Apologies

Unnskyld	Sorry/Pardon me
Beklager.	I do apologise.
Omforlatelse	Excuse me; Sorry
For all del	By all means/Don't mention it

8.4.4 Thanks

Takk	Thanks
Tusen takk	Many thanks

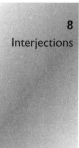

| **Takk så mye** | Thank you very much |
| **Takk for sist!** | Thank you for the last time! |

This last is a polite expression when meeting somebody again, especially if they have entertained you.

8.4.5 | Asking the interlocutor to repeat something

| **Hva?** | What? |

May be asked if you did not catch the words of your interlocutor.

| **Hva sa du?** | What did you say? |
| **Unnskyld?** | Excuse me? |

8.5 Onomatopoetic expressions and expletives

8.5.1 | Onomatopoetic words

8.5.1.1 | Animal sounds

Words that imitate the sounds of animals include:

Nøff, oink (pig); **Mø**, moo (cow); **Bæ**, baa (sheep); **Voff**, woof (dog); **Mjau**, miaouw (cat); **Kykeliky**, cock a doodle doo (cockerel)

8.5.1.2 | Other sounds

Words that imitate sudden sounds include

Bang, Bang; **Pang**, Bang; **Svisj**, Swoosh; **Dunk**, Thud

8.5.2 | Expletives

8.5.2.1 | Mild/literary expletives

Søren, Damn, darn; **Gid!**, Good grief, goodness gracious; **Pokker**, Hell!

8.5.2.2 | *Coarser swearwords*

The following swearwords are coarser; they are to be avoided.

Helvete!, Hell!; **Faen**, **Satan Damn**, Damn!

Note – English swearing may involve bodily functions ('Shit!', 'Fuck!'), while equally 'serious' swearing in Norwegian, at least until fairly recently, used to involve religious terms – **Faen i helvete**, 'The devil in hell' is still a forceful oath in Norwegian. Recently, some English and American 'taboo' words have been borrowed.

8.6 Other interjections

Vær så snill	Please

Note that **vær så snill** is much less used than its English translation.

God natt; Natta.	Night, night.
Prosit.	Bless you. (when someone sneezes)
Gratulerer.	Congratulations.
Gratulerer med dagen.	Many happy returns of the day.

Said on somebody's birthday or on some day of special significance to them, such as their wedding anniversary, Constitution Day . . .

Kondolerer.	Sorry for your loss./
	Please accept my condolences.

Said to someone who has been bereaved.

Hurra	Hooray!
Hurra for 17. mai!	Hooray for Constitution Day!
Hurra! Vi har vunnet!	Hooray! We've won!
Hysj	Shhh!
Heia Norge!	Come on, Norway!
Heia Viking!	Come on, Viking! (football team)
Bravo	Bravo!
Pst	Psst (to attract surreptitious attention)

Chapter 9

Conjunctions and subjunctions

9.1 Introduction

Conjunctions and subjunctions have a linking function. For main clauses (MC) and subordinate clauses (SC), see 10.4, 10.8; for the conjunction field 'f' which contains the link itself, see 10.7.3.6.

9.1.1 Classification

Traditional grammar uses an overarching term for the single word class of *conjunctions*, which includes both *coordinating conjunctions* (e.g. og, 'and'; men, 'but'; eller, 'or') and *subordinating conjunctions* (e.g. at, 'that'; om, 'if'; fordi, 'because'). However, *NRG* and several modern Norwegian grammars distinguish between the distinct word classes of *conjunctions* (coordinating, Nw. konjunksjon) and *subjunctions* (subordinating, Nw. subjunksjon), a practice we will follow in this book.

9.1.2 Coordination

Coordination involves linking together two clauses (either two main clauses or two subordinate clauses) or two clause elements of a similar grammatical type. The link itself is often a *conjunction* placed between the elements to be linked. See 9.1.4.1ff.

Subjects coordinated

Aksel og Anna liker jazz.   Aksel and Anna like jazz.

Objects coordinated

Selskapet vil utvikle kunnskap og kompetanse.
The company wishes to develop know-how and competence.

Verbs coordinated

De sitter og snakker.   They are sitting chatting.

Main clauses coordinated

Han tok bilen og jeg syklet.   He took the car and I cycled.

Subordinate clauses coordinated

De sa at de ville komme, *men* **at de ville komme for sent.**
They said that they would come, but that they would be late.

Note – The Norwegian term **konjunkt** is often applied to a phrase that is linked, and should not be confused with the English 'conjunct', which is a kind of adverb, with similarities to a conjunction, linking a clause or phrase with a previous part of the same sentence (see 6.2.5.3.) An English term sometimes used for **konjunkt** is 'conjoin'.

9
Conjunctions and subjunctions

9.1.3 | Subordination

Subordination is the incorporation of a subordinate clause (shown by round brackets in the examples below) into a main clause sentence (shown by < >). The link word used is often a *subjunction* (9.3) or *other subordinator* (9.4) which comes at the beginning of the subordinate clause. In the example below, the subjunction is **fordi**.

<Vi gikk inn i fjøset   **(fordi været var forferdelig)>.**
We went into the barn   because the weather was awful.
Main clause – Independent   *Subordinate clause – Dependent*

There is often a hierarchy of clauses, one within another like a Chinese box, by which clauses are subordinated. In the next example the subordinate clause marked [C – C] is subordinated to the subordinate clause (B – B), which in turn is subordinated to the main clause sentence <A – A>. See 10.8, 9.1.4f.

< Jag er glad (at ingen tapte noen penger [da de gikk konkurs]) >.
I am happy   that no one lost any money   when they went bankrupt.
<A   (B   [C   C] B) A>

9.1.4 | Position of conjunctions

9.1.4.1 | Conjunctions

Conjunctions are usually found between the two sentence elements, phrases or clauses to be coordinated. See 9.1.2 above and 10.4. The use of a conjunction does not usually affect the word order in the clause that follows.

Han hadde kanskje rett, men han burde ikke sagt det.
He may have been right but he shouldn't have said so.

Å være eller ikke være ...   To be or not to be ...

Occasionally, conjunctions occur at the beginning of a sentence. Certain conjunctions never start a sentence, however; these include explanative and conclusive conjunctions. See 9.2.5f.

Og dette er bare begynnelsen.   And this is just the beginning.

9.1.4.2 | Subjunctions

(a) Subjunctions introduce a subordinate clause and are found at the beginning of the subordinate clauses when the order is MC + SC:

Vi kjøper et nytt hus	***hvis* vi har råd til det.**
We will buy a new house	*if* we can afford it.
MC	*Sub.conj. SC*

Thus, when the order is SC + MC, they occur at the beginning of the sentence:

***Hvis* vi har råd til det,**	**kjøper vi et nytt hus.**
If we can afford it	we will buy a new house.
Sub.conj. SC	MC

(b) In the case of attributive clauses and certain consecutive clauses, the subordinate clause cannot precede the main clause, so a subjunction or other subordinator (9.1.5.3) cannot begin the sentence:

Læreren min,	***som* underviser i norsk,**	**er meget hyggelig.**
My teacher,	*who* teaches Norwegian,	is very nice.
	Other subordinator	
	Attributive clause	

Oljeresursene skal forvaltes *slik at*	**de kommer hele det norske samfunnet til gode.**	**9** Conjunctions and subjunctions
The oil resources will be managed *so that*	it benefits the whole of Norwegian society.	
Sub. conj.	*Consecutive clause*	

Jeg spurte	*om*	**de kunne veksle en hundrelapp.**
I asked	*whether*	they could change a hundred kroner note.
	Sub. conj.	*Indirect question*

9.1.5 | *Conjunctions, subjunctions, conjunctional adverbs and other subordinators*

9.1.5.1 | *Conjunctions and subjunctions*

Conjunctions normally consist of a single word (**og, eller, men, for, så** (cf.9.2), whereas subjunctions (9.3) may either be single words (**at**, 'that'; **da** (, 'as'; **ettersom**, 'because'; **fordi**, 'because'; **om**, 'whether/if'; **siden**, 'since'; **som**, 'as') or complex subjunctions comprising several words, often a combination of adverb or preposition + subjunction (**for at**, 'in order to'; **selv om**, 'although'; **slik at**, 'so that'; **som om**, 'as if'; **så at**, 'so that').

9.1.5.2 | *Conjunctional adverbs*

Clauses may also be linked by a conjunctional adverb (6.3.4.4) in a separate main clause. Compare:

Han dro hjem, *for* **det var sent.**
    Conjunction
He went home *because* it was late.

Cf.

Han dro hjem. Det var *nemlig* **sent.**
    Conjunctional adverb
He went home. It was late, *you see.*

The function is the same in both cases, but the conjunctional adverb may come first in the clause, causing inversion: finite verb – subject (FV–S). See 10.7.2. Subjunctions are found with subordinate clause word order: subject – clausal adverb – finite verb (S–FV). See 10.4.3.

Kasper klarte ikke lære å kjøre. *Likevel* **fikk han mye hjelp.**
                                      Conjunctional adverb FV   S
Kasper couldn't learn to drive. *Even so* he had a lot help.

Cf.

Kasper klarte å lære å kjøre, *selv om* **han ikke fikk mye hjelp.**
                              Subjunction S CA FV
Kasper could learn to drive *although* he did not have a lot of help.

9.1.5.3 Other subordinators

Other subordinators include interrogative and relative subjunctions/adverbs. These differ from conjunctions in that they introduce a subordinate clause and at the same time constitute a clause element within that clause:

Jeg spurte *hva* **hun ville.**
                  Subordinator = *object*
I asked *what* she wanted.

Jeg vet *hvor* **alle likene er begravd.**
                  Subordinator = *adverbial*
I know *where* all the bodies are buried.

Notice that an interrogative as subject must be followed by **som** (see 9.4.1.2 and 10.8.1.2(a)):

Jeg lurer på *hvem som* **gjorde det.**
                  Subordinator = *subject*
I wonder *who* did that.

9.1.5.4 Indicators of subordination

Not all subordinate clauses are introduced by a subjunction or other subordinator. Some have no introductory word, because the words **at** or **som** have been omitted (see (c) below). There are, however, various *indicators of subordination*. These are not necessarily a word class or sentence element, but may be a marker showing the clausal relationship. Such indicators include:

(a) An introductory word in the subordinate clause: for example, a subjunction, interrogative pronoun or adverb, or subjunction or adverb. See 9.3.1ff. and 9.4.1ff.

Han sier *at* han vil emigrere.
He says *that* he wants to emigrate.

Spør *hvorfor* han ønsker å emigrere.
Ask *why* he wants to emigrate.

Jeg vet *hvor* han ønsker å emigrere.
I know *where* he wants to emigrate.

(b) The position of the clausal adverbial immediately before the finite verb. See 10.3.6.3.

Han fortalte meg at han *aldri* ville se meg igjen.
He told me he never wanted to see me again.

(c) But note that, in the following examples, the subordinate clauses have no specific indicator of subordination:

Hunden som trodde (at) han var katt ... [at omitted: see 10.8.4.1]
The dog that believed he was a cat ...

Den gutten (som) Eva var forelsket i, bor i Tromsø. [som omitted: see 10.8.4.2]
The lad Eva was in love with lived in Tromsø.

9.2 Conjunctions

9.2.1 Introduction

There are very few conjunctions, but the conjunctional adverbs (9.1.5.2, 6.3.4.4) fulfil almost the same function. Conjunctions are classified according to their function into copulative, disjunctive, adversative, explanative and conclusive conjunctions.

Section	Term	Example
9.2.2	Copulative	**og, samt**, and; **pluss**, plus
9.2.3	Disjunctive	**eller**, or
9.2.4	Adversative	**men**, but **(ikke …) men**, (not…) but
9.2.5	Explanative	**for**, for
9.2.6	Conclusive	**så**, so

9.2.2 | *Copulative conjunctions*

Copulative means 'connecting'.

9.2.2.1 | *Og – 'and'*

Og ('and') is the most frequent word in Norwegian. In practice, /g/ is always omitted in pronunciation.

Og is used to link two (or more) main clauses, clause elements, words or phrases of the same kind.

> **Erik drakk øl og Eva drakk vin.**
> Erik drank beer and Eva drank wine.

> **Paret fikk femteplassen i tango, slowfox og quickstep.**
> The couple took fifth place in the tango, slow foxtrot and quickstep.

> **Bøkene hans er triste og morsomme.**
> His books are sad and funny.

As in English, one may sometimes coordinate elements that differ:

> **Hun er vakker og med barn.**   She is beautiful and pregnant.

Note – Sometimes, **å** is incorrectly used where the norm would have **og**:

> ***De sitter å snakker** instead of **De sitter og snakker**

9.2.2.2 | *Samt – 'as well as'*

Samt belongs to formal style and renders 'and', 'together/along with', 'as well as' but differs in usage from **og**. The most important difference is that **samt** cannot link clauses.

Vi skal invitere familie og venner samt naboer.
We will invite family and friends as well as neighbours.

$\boxed{9.2.2.3}$ *Double conjunctions (correlative conjunctions)*

(a) Både . . . og – 'both . . . and'

The coordination of two elements may be strengthened by the addition of the conjunctional adverb **både** to form **både . . . og**, a construction that emphasises that both elements have equal weight. Like **og** this can be used with clauses, clause elements or phrases.

Dette har vakt sterke reaksjoner blant både elever og lærere.
This has provoked strong reactions among both pupils and teachers.

Note – Unlike English 'both . . . and', **både . . . og** can coordinate more than two items:

Både Per, Pål og Espen . . .   Both Per, Pål and Espen . . .
[brothers in fairy-tales]

(b) Other double conjunctions include:

såvel . . . som, both . . . and [more formal than **både . . . og**];
dels . . . dels, partly . . . partly; **ikke bare . . . men også**, not only . . . but also

Det er ikke bare hva du sier, men også hvordan du sier det.
It is not only what you say but also how you say it.

$\boxed{9.2.2.4}$ ***Pluss** – 'plus'*

Originally used with numerals (**fem pluss fem er ti**, 'five plus five is ten'), Norwegian **pluss** is used increasingly as a conjunction with quantities.

Prisen er 1000 kroner pluss porto.
The price is 1000 kroner plus postage.

Note – In recent years, **pluss at** has also come to be used as a subjunction, ending a list:

Hun sier at han lyver, at han stjeler, at han slår, pluss at han løper etter andre.
She says that he lies, that he steals, that he is violent, and that he chases after other women.

9.2.3 | Disjunctive conjunctions

Disjunctive means 'alternative'. In addition to **eller** ('or') a number of double conjunctions consist of a conjunctional adverb + **eller**. These strengthen the element of choice.

9.2.3.1 | Eller – 'or'

Eller links all kinds of words, phrases or clauses.

> **Vil du ha te eller kaffe?**   Would you like tea or coffee?

9.2.3.2 | Enten ... eller – 'either ... or'

Enten ... eller ((og)så) usually causes inversion of the verb in both clauses.

> **Enten føler du for dem, eller så gjør du det ikke.**
> Either you feel for them or you don't.

9.2.3.3 | Verken ... eller – 'neither ... nor'

This expression implies negation ('neither . . . nor'), so no additional negative in the form of **ikke** is necessary (although this is not infrequently found). Note that **verken** (also spelled **hverken**) . . . **eller** may be extended to link more than two elements.

> **Hverken jeg eller min bror vet noe.**
> Neither my brother nor I know anything.

9.2.4 | Adversative conjunctions

Adversative means 'opposite' and expresses a contrast, restriction or correction. Note that opposition can also be expressed by the conjunctional adverbs **derimot**, 'on the other hand'; **dog**, 'yet'; **likevel**, 'yet'; **imidlertid**, 'however, nevertheless'; **enda**, 'yet'. See 6.2.5.3(a).

9.2.4.1 | Men – 'but'

Men ('but') links words, phrases or clauses.

> **De synes det er fint å være ute, men de liker ikke å gå langt.**
> They think it's good to be outdoors, but they do not like walking far.

Han er fra Bergen, men nokså stillferdig.
He is from Bergen, but still fairly quiet.

9.2.5 | *Explanative conjunctions*

Explanative means 'explaining'. The conjunctional adverbs **jo**, **nemlig** also express explanation. See 6.2.5.3(d).

9.2.5.1 | *For – 'for', 'as'*

For ('for', 'as') always links two main clauses:

Det var veldig spennende, for vi visste ikke hva vi skulle finne.
It was very exciting as we didn't know what we would find.

For is not used as much as the near-synonymous subjunction **fordi**.

9.2.6 | *Conclusive conjunctions*

Conclusive indicates 'conclusion, result'. Conclusion may also be expressed by means of conjunctional adverbs such as **altså**, 'therefore'; **derfor**, 'consequently'; **dermed** 'consequently'.

9.2.6.1 | *Så – 'so'*

Så ('so') links clauses and expresses a conclusion or result:

Vinden rev i teltet, så jeg regnet ikke med mye søvn.
The wind was pulling at the tent, so I wasn't counting on much sleep.

9.3 Subjunctions

9.3.1 | *Introduction*

9.3.1.1

(a) Subjunctions are more varied and more numerous than conjunctions. In addition to the simple general subordinators (**at**, **om**), they often comprise a compound (**ettersom**, 'because'; **fordi**, 'because'; **liksom**, 'as if') or a word group that, in many cases, is a combination of an adverb or preposition + **at** or **om** (**etter at**, 'since'; **uten at**, 'except that'; **for så vidt**, 'for that matter'; **selv om**, 'even if'; **som om**, 'as if'). In this way, they are able to express many subtle semantic distinctions.

(b) The general subordinators (9.3.2) may introduce subject and object clauses and clauses constituting the predicative complement, attribute or adverbial in the sentence. The infinitive marker (9.3.3) only occurs with infinitives. The semantically differentiated subordinators (9.3.4f) only introduce adverbial clauses, see 10.8.2.2.

(c) The infinitive marker **å**, 'to' (often omitted in grammars, or else given its own word class) is here classified as a subjunction (see 9.3.3).

| 9.3.1.2 | *Subjunctions* |

9.3.2	General subordinators
	Explicative
	• indirect speech **at** that
	• indirect question **om** whether
	See also **som** (9.4.1.2).
9.3.3	The infinitive marker **å**, to
9.3.4	Semantically differentiated subordinators
9.3.4.1 Temporal	**bare**, if only; **da**, as; **før**, before; **etter at**, after, since; **idet**, when, just as; **inntil**, until; **mens**, while; **når**, when; **siden**, since, as
9.3.4.2 Causal	**da**, as, since; **ettersom**, because; **fordi**, because; **idet**, as, since; **siden**, since, as
9.3.4.3 Conditional	**bare**, as long as, if only; **dersom**, in case, as long as; **hvis**, if; **ifall**, if, in case; **når**, when; **om**, if, whether; **så fremt**, if, provided (that)
9.3.4.4 Concessive	**enda**, although, even though; **selv om**, even though; **skjønt**, although, though

9.3.4.5	Final	**for at**, so that, in order that; **så**, so
9.3.4.6	Consecutive	**så**, so; **så ... at**, so ... that; **uten at**, unless
9.3.4.7	Comparative	**enn**, than; **jo ... jo**, the ... the...; **liksom**, as if; **som**, as; **som om**, as if

9.3.2 | General subordinators

The general subordinators **at**, 'that', and **om**, 'whether', merely indicate that the clause they introduce is a subordinate clause. They have only a very vague intrinsic meaning.

9.3.2.1 | At

(a) **At**, 'that' is as important among subjunctions as **og** is among conjunctions. As in English, this subjunction may often be omitted (10.8.4.1). **At** is used most often to introduce a statement in indirect speech, and follows a verb of saying or reporting:

De sa (at) de skulle undersøke saken.
They said (that) they would look into the matter.

Compare direct speech:

De sa: «Vi skal undersøke saken».

(b) **At** introduces subordinate clauses that have a nominal function. These clauses function in much the same way as a noun phrase, subject, object or prepositional object. When **at** introduces the sentence, it is obligatory.

At dette har skadet partiet, er udiskutabelt.
That this has damaged the party is undeniable.

Vi så (at) de var ulykkelige.
We saw that they were unhappy.

9.3.2.2 | Om

Om 'if, whether' corresponds to **at**, but is used to introduce indirect yes/no questions. See 10.8.1.2.(b). Unlike **at, om** may not be omitted. Note that **om** can also be used elliptically to respond to real or presumed questions. **Om** is also used as a conditional or concessive conjunction. See 9.3.4.3f.

Vi spurte *om* han ville være med på teater.
We asked whether he wanted to join us in the theatre.

Compare the direct question:

Vi spurte: «Vil du være med på teater?»

Note also the rather formal **hvorvidt**:

Det er ikke klart *hvorvidt* hun trekker seg.
It is not clear whether she is retiring.

9.3.3 | The infinitive marker å

For the use of the infinitive, see 5.3.1.

The infinitive marker **å**, 'to' is only used together with an infinitive form.

Han prøvde *å* bli valgt inn i nasjonalforsamlingen.
He tried to get elected to Parliament.

In some constructions **å** may be omitted (5.3.1.5):

Du behøver ikke (*å*) komme.   You don't need to come.

Perhaps because of the similarity in their pronunciation, **og**, 'and' is often incorrectly substituted for **å** (compare also 9.2.2.1, Note):

*Han prøver *og* bli et bedre menneske.
He is trying to be a better person.

9.3.4 | Semantically differentiated subordinators

Unlike **at** and **om**, most subjunctions indicate a specific semantic relationship between the main clause and subordinate clause, for example condition, cause or intention. They can, therefore, be categorised according to the meaning of the clause they introduce.

9.3.4.1 | Temporal subjunctions

Temporal means 'time-based'. See also 9.5.1.9.

Da vi kom hjem, var alt i orden.
When we got home everything was all right.

Man vet aldri når man kan ha bruk for det.
You never know when you might need it.

De rike blir enda rikere, mens de fattige blir hengende etter.
The rich are getting even richer while the poor lag behind.

9.3.4.2 | Causal subjunctions

Causal means 'expressing reason, cause'.

Siden det er så fint vær, går vi en tur.
As it's such fine weather, we will take a walk.

Fordi, ettersom and more rarely siden clauses may either precede or follow the main clause. Fordi is the most common causal conjunction.

Han gikk hjem, fordi hun uansett ikke ville snakke med ham.
He went home as, no matter what, she wouldn't speak to him.

Ettersom han var sent ute, måtte vi begynne uten ham.
As he was delayed, we had to begin without him.

Vi måtte begynne uten ham ettersom han var sent ute.
We will have had to begin without him as he was delayed.

9.3.4.3 | Conditional subjunctions

Conditional means 'expressing a condition'. See 10.8.5.2 for different kinds of conditional clause.

Hvis vi kommer til Oslo, skal vi besøke deg.
If we come to Oslo, we will visit you.

Hvor ville du reise, i fall du kunne velge?
Where you go if you could choose?

Om du ikke hadde kommet nå, vet jeg ikke hva jeg hadde gjort.
If you hadn't come now I don't know what I would have done.

| 9.3.4.4 | *Concessive subjunctions* |

Concessive means 'expressing a concession'. Such clauses express a contrast with the main clause. **Selv om** is the most frequent way of introducing such clauses.

Hun gir aldri opp *selv om* oppgaven virker håpløs.
She never gives up *even if* the problem seems hopeless.

Han hadde kjøpt seg nye, flotte, *enda* de andre var langtifra slitt.
He had bought new, smart ones, *even though* the others were scarcely worn.

Note – **Uaktet** and **skjønt**, 'despite, in spite of' are now rare. **Fordi om** is fairly frequent in the spoken language.

| 9.3.4.5 | *Final subjunctions* |

Final in this sense means 'expressing an intention or purpose'. These are sometimes difficult to distinguish from consecutive conjunctions.

For at vi skal bli bedre kjent...
In order for us to get better aquainted...

Du har jo bodd i Uppsala, så du må være flink i svensk.
You have lived in Uppsala, of course, so you must be fluent in Swedish.

| 9.3.4.6 | *Consecutive subjunctions* |

Consecutive means 'expressing a result or consequence'.

Kom, la oss stige ned og forvirre språket deres *så* den ene ikke forstår den andre!
Come, let's go down and confuse their language so they won't be able to understand each other. (Genesis 11: 7)

Så can also introduce a main clause (see also 9.2.6.1).

9.3.4.7	*Comparative subjunctions*

Comparative means 'expressing a comparison'. See also 2.5.

I **Det så ut *som om* lynet hadde slått ned.**
It looked *as if* lightning had struck.

2 **Det skal bli varmere *enn* det har vært.** (See also 2.5.10.3.)
It will be warmer *than* it has been.

3 ***Jo* mer vi trener, *desto/dess* flinkere blir vi.**
The more we train, *the* better we get.

These include the fairly formal **liksom**:

4 **Han smilte *liksom* han visste noe.**
He smiled *as if* he knew something.

Notice the fixed order of clauses in sentence 3 above; the subordinate clause introduced by **jo** + comparative must come first and the main clause with **desto** + comparative has inversion. There is no difference in meaning between expressions formulated with **jo . . . desto** and **jo . . . jo, dess . . . dess**.

***Jo* mer bonden produserer, *jo* mer støtte.**
The more the farmer produces, *the* greater the financial support.

9.4 *Other subordinators*

9.4.1	*Introduction*

Pronouns and adverbs used to introduce a subordinate clause are also subordinators.

9.4.1.1	Interrogative pronouns and adverbs	**hvem**, who; **hva**, what; **hvor**, where; **når**, when
9.4.1.2	Relative subjunctions and adverbs	**som**, who, which, that; **der**, where

9.4.1.1 | *Interrogative pronouns and adverbs*

(a) Interrogative pronouns (4.8) and interrogative adverbs (6.2.4.5) introduce **hv**-questions. See 10.7.4.2. When they are used to form subordinate clauses, i.e. indirect questions, no other subjunction is required before them as they also constitute a clause element.

Jeg vet ikke *hvor* han har gått.   I don't know *where* he has gone.

Compare direct question:

***Hvor* har han gått?**   *Where* has he gone?

(b) However, when an interrogative pronoun is the subject of a subordinate clause, **som** is introduced as a subject marker (4.8.1.1):

Jeg vet ikke *hvem som* kysser henne nå.   *Subject*
I don't know *who* is kissing her now.

Cf.

Jeg vet ikke *hvem* (som) hun kysser nå.   *Object*
I don't know *who* she is kissing now.

9.4.1.2 | *som*

See also 6.2.4.4 for relative adverbs.

Som is the most common of all subordinators, and introduces relative clauses.

When it correlates with the subject of the clause, **som** cannot be omitted:

Her er kvinnen *som* drømmer om Romeo.
Here is the woman that dreams of Romeo.

Contrast with the following example, in which **som** does not correlate with the subject:

Her er kvinnen (*som*) Romeo drømmer om.
Here is the woman that Romeo dreams of.

See also 9.4.1.1(b).

9.5 | Some problem conjunctions and subjunctions

9.5.1 | *Translation into Norwegian of some problem conjunctions and subjunctions*

Many English conjunctions and subjunctions have fairly direct equivalents in Norwegian, e.g. 'that' = **at** or **som**, 'if' = **om**, etc. However, the same word in English is often a conjunction or subjunction, preposition and adverb, with each part of speech possessing at least one equivalent in Norwegian. The conjunction or subjunction introduces a clause with a finite verb. While many Norwegian prepositions may govern an infinitive, they can do so only if there is no change of subject (from the main clause). If there is a change of subject, the sense can only be conveyed by means of a subjunction and a following clause.

Compare:

Vi må gjøre alt *for å* redde kjempepandaen. *Infinitive*
We must do everything *to* save the giant panda.

Vi må gjøre alt *for at* kjempepandaen skal reddes. *Subjunction*
We must do everything *so that* the giant panda is saved.

9.5.1.1 | *'After'*

(a) As a subjunction before a full clause (i.e. one with a finite verb), use **etter at**:

Security will have to be tightened *after* thieves have got into the premises.
Sikkerheten må skjerpes *etter at* tyver har tatt seg inn i lokalet.

(b) As a subjunction before a non-finite clause (10.10.2), use **etter å**:

To væpnede menn kom unna med 100 000 kroner *etter å* ha ranet en bank i Bergen.
Two armed men escaped with 100 000 kroner *after* having robbed a bank in Bergen.

(c) As a preposition, use **etter** (7.6.1).

After the robbery, the two robbers disappeared on foot.
Etter ranet forsvant de to ransmennene til fots.

(a) When 'as' = 'because', 'since', use **fordi**:

I had to walk *as* my car was at the garage.
Jeg måtte gå *fordi* bilen min var på verksted.

(b) When 'as' = 'just as', use **da, i det**:

As I was about to leave, it started to snow.
***Da* jeg skulle gå, begynte det å snø.**

(c) When 'as' = 'while', use **mens**:

She knits *as/while* she is watching TV.
Hun strikker *mens* hun ser på fjernsyn.

(d) When 'as' denotes 'in the capacity of', use **som** (cf. 9.5.1.3):

As a child she was promised in marriage to the count.
***Som* barn ble hun lovet bort til greven.**

9.5.1.3 'As . . . as'

When a comparison is made in a positive clause, use **like . . . som**. When a comparison is made in a negative clause, use either **ikke like . . . som** or **ikke så . . . som**.

You are *as* tall *as* your sister.	**Du er *like* lang *som* din søster.**
I'm not *as* rich *as* you think.	**Jeg er ikke *så* rik *som* du tror.**

9.5.1.4 'Before'

(a) As a subjunction use **før, innen**:

Before you go, have another beer.	**Før du drar, ta en øl til.**
We ate *before* we went home.	**Vi spiste *før* vi kom hjem.**
Before we take such a big step . . .	**Innen vi tar slikt et stort steg . . .**

This must be done *before* there is an accident.
Dette må bli gjort *før* det blir en ulykke.

(b) As an adverb = 'earlier', 'previously', use **før, tidligere:**

Have you been in Oslo *before?*   **Har du vært i Oslo *før/tidligere?***

(c) As a preposition of time use **før** (7.3.8), **innen:**

We will go home *before* Christmas. **Vi reiser hjem før jul.**

(d) As a preposition of place = 'in front of', use **foran:**

Two police cars drove *before* the president.
To politibiler kjørte *foran* presidenten.

9.5.1.5 *'Both . . . (and)'*

(a) As a conjunction use **både . . . og** (cf. 9.2.2.3 (a)):

The cells are equipped with *both* a shower *and* TV.
Cellene er utstyrt med *både* dusj *og* fjernsyn

(b) As an indefinite pronoun, where 'both' can be replaced by 'the two', use **begge** (4.9.1):

Both are possible.   **Begge er mulige.**
Both are good.   **Begge er gode.**

9.5.1.6 *'Either'*

(a) As a conjunction 'either . . . or' (meaning 'only one of A or B') after a positive, use **enten . . . eller:**

It has to be *either* today *or* tomorrow.
Det må bli *enten* i dag *eller* i morgen.

(b) As a conjunction 'either . . . or' (meaning 'both A and B') after a comparative, use **både . . . og:**

I'm younger than *either* Håkon *or* Frida.
Jeg er yngre enn *både* Håkon *og* Frida.

(c) As a conjunction 'either . . . or' (meaning 'both A and B') after a negative, use **verken . . . eller:**

He did not come *either* yesterday *or* today.
Han kom *verken* i går *eller* i dag.

(d) As an adverb, use **heller** (6.5.1.3(c)):

I'm not rich, but I'm not poor *either*.
Jeg er ikke rik, men *heller* ikke fattig.

(e) As an indefinite pronoun meaning 'both A and B', use **begge** (4.9.1):

a stream with houses on *either* side
en bekk med hus på *begge* sider

(f) As an indefinite pronoun after a negative meaning 'one of A or B', use **ingen** etc. (4.6.6):

I don't know *either* of them.
Jeg kjenner *ingen* av dem.

9.5.1.7 'Since'

(a) As a subjunction, when 'since' = 'because', 'as', use **fordi, ettersom, siden, da:**

Since you ask, I am sixty years old.
Ettersom du spør, er jeg seksti år gammel.

Since no one had any objections, the proposal was accepted.
Da ingen hadde noe å innvende, ble forslaget akseptert.

(b) As a preposition, when 'since' = 'after', use **siden, etter at:**

Since reading that I have not smoked a single cigarette.
Siden jeg leste det, har jeg ikke røkt en eneste sigarett.
Etter at jeg leste det, . . .

(c) As an adverb, when 'since' = 'since that time', use **siden (den gang)**:

> We haven't been there *since*.
> **Vi har ikke vært der *siden (den gang)*.**

| 9.5.1.8 | 'That' |

(a) As a subjunction, use **at**:

> I said (*that*) we were disappointed.   **Jeg sa (*at*) vi var skuffet.**

(b) As a relative pronoun, when 'that' = 'which', 'who(m)', use **som**. For the use of **som** and **at** in cleft sentences and existential sentences, see 10.3.2.4 and 10.7.3.4 respectively.

> He bought the house (*that*) we liked so much.
> **Han kjøpte huset (*som*) vi likte så godt.**

(c) For the use of 'that' as a demonstrative pronoun in Norwegian, see 4.3.2.

| 9.5.1.9 | 'When' |

(a) As a temporal subjunction, use **når** or **da** (9.3.4.1). Note that **når** can also be used as an interrogative adverb (6.2.2.1):

> Tell me *when* you're ready.   **Si fra *når* du er klar.**
> In 1975, *when* he was just ten ...   **I 1975, *da* han var bare ti år ...**

In a main clause reporting past events, **da** is used:

> **Da sprakk trollet.**   Then the troll exploded.

In a subclause reporting an isolated past event, **da** is used:

> **Da kongsdattera og Askeladden giftet seg, ble det turet vidt og bredt.**
> When the princess and Askeladden [figure in fairy tales] got married, there was a great celebration.

In a subclause reporting a repeated event in the past, however, **når** is used:

> **Når Stockholms-toget passerte, stod vi guttene alltid og så på.**
> When the Stockholm train went by, we lads always stood and watched.

(b) As a concessive subjunction, use **selv om, til og med, skjønt:**

He drives *even though* he might cycle.
Han kjører *selv om* han kunne sykle.

Even when she is really furious she does manage to stay calm.
***Til og med når* hun er virkelig rasende, klarer hun å holde seg rolig.**

Chapter 10

Sentence structure and word order

10.1   Introduction

10.1.1   *Word classes, clause elements and phrases*

10.1.1.1

In Chapters 1–9 of this book we largely examine word classes and the way some words inflect and are used. In the current chapter, we look at the syntax of Norwegian, that is how words are combined into longer phrases, utterances, clauses and sentences. By way of comparison, compare the main clause sentence below, analysed first by word classes and then by clause elements:

Hun	**har**	**alltid**	**undervist**	**studenter**	**ved**	**universitetet.**
She	has	always	taught	students	at	the university.
Pronoun	*Verb*	*Adverb*	*Verb*	*Noun*	*Preposition*	*Noun*
Subject	*Verb*	*Adverbial*	*Verb*	*Object*		*Adverbial*

10.1.1.2

The clause is one of the basic elements of sentence structure or syntax. It comprises clause elements as in the diagram below:

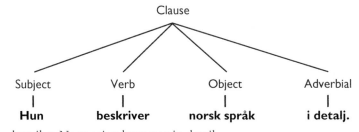

She describes Norwegian language in detail.

These clause elements consist of phrases. Phrases in turn comprise a head word alone or a head word and modifier. The structure of the clause can in this way be regarded as a hierarchy:

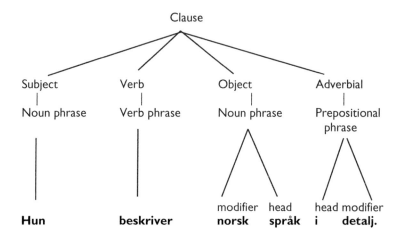

10.2 Phrases

10.2.1 Head words and modifiers

10.2.1.1

Phrases comprise a head word alone (H) or a head word with modifiers coming before or after the head:

Noun phrase	Verb phrase
tre *jenter* fra Tromsø	nesten måtte *gi* opp
H	H
three girls from Tromsø	almost had to give up

Adjective phrase	Adverb phrase
mye *eldre* enn henne	nesten *aldri*
H	H
much older than her	almost never

litt *innenfor* muren
   H

a little way inside the wall

Noun phrases may alternatively contain a pronoun as head (see also 10.2.2):

***hun* med det lyse håret**   she with the fair hair
H

10.2.1.2

The verb phrase in a narrow sense comprises the finite verb plus optionally a verb particle or reflexive pronoun: **klarnet opp**, 'cleared up'; **snu seg**, 'turn around'.

10.2.1.3

The infinitive phrase comprises an infinitive (and complements): **ikke å glemme passet**, 'not to forget the passport'.

10.2.1.4

The prepositional phrase consists of a preposition plus (optionally) a noun phrase:

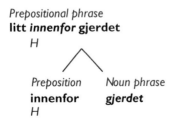

Prepositional phrase
litt *innenfor* gjerdet
    H

Preposition   *Noun phrase*
innenfor   **gjerdet**
H

10.2.2 Noun phrases

10.2.2.1 Determiners and attributes

The noun phrase (NP) consists either of a noun or pronoun alone (**boken**, 'the book'; **hun**, 'she') as head or an NP with optional determiners (**alle hans bøker om grammatikk**, 'all his books about grammar').

(a) Preposed determiner:
   The NP may have several preposed determiners, including:

   - An indefinite or definite article: *en* **ny bok**, 'a new book'; *den* **nye boken**, 'the new book'
   - One pronoun or several, used determinatively: *alle disse* **bøkene**, 'all these books'
   - A genitive expression: *Daniels* **nye bok**, 'Daniel's new book' (see also the '**sin** genitive' in 1.8.1.7)

(b) Preposed attribute:
   This consists of a single adjective phrase or several coordinated adjectives: *en liten norsk* **bedrift**, 'a small Norwegian firm'.

(c) The order of preposed determiners and attributes is usually as in the table below

| Determiners | | | | | | Adjective | Head |
Totality	Definite	Possession attribute	Quantity	Selection	Comparison	attribute	word
begge	**de**		**to**			**unge**	**søsknene**
samtlige		**Aksels**	**mange**			**nye**	**klær**
alle	**disse**	**mine**				**minste**	**brødre**
					slike	**gamle**	**biler**
	den			**siste**			**tiden**

Translations: both the two young siblings; all of Aksel's many new clothes; all of these my small brothers; such old cars, in recent times

(d) Postposed attributes:

   - Unlike English, Norwegian has a possessive that usually comes after the noun: **hytten** *min*, 'my cabin' (see 4.4.2)

- The '**sin**-genitive' (1.8.1.7) comprises a possessive that follows the noun: **Emma** *sin bil*, 'Emma's book'
- Adjective attribute: **en bok** *full av slurvefeil*, 'a book full of careless errors'
- A prepositional phrase: **forfatteren** *av boken*, 'the author of the book'
- An adverb: **huset** *der borte*, 'the house over there'
- An infinitive construction: **kunsten** *å skrive*, 'the art of writing'
- A subordinate clause: **huset** *som var til salgs*, 'the house that was for sale'
- Apposition: **Jo Nesbø**, *norsk forfatter og musiker*, er . . ., 'Jo Nesbø, Norwegian writer and musician, is. . .

| 10.2.2.2 | *Indefinite and definite noun phrase*

(a) Indefinite noun phrases introduce a new idea. Definite noun phrases refer back to a familiar idea:

Vi har to biler – *en liten og en stor bil*. *Den lille bilen* er gammel.
        Indefinite NP   ← Definite NP
We have two cars – a small and a large car. The small car is old.

(b) The indefinite noun phrase may consist either of a naked noun:

Har du øl?	Do you have any beer?
***Katter* liker ikke vann.**	Cats do not like water.

or one preceded by:

An indefinite article	***en* katt**, a cat
An adjective attribute	***alkoholfritt* øl**, non-alcoholic beer
A measurement attribute	***en liter* melk**, a litre of milk
A combination of these	***en kilo god* kaffe**, a kilo of good coffee

(c) The definite noun phrase consists of a proper noun or a common noun with an end article:

***Dahl* var forfatter.**	Dahl was a writer.
Fant du *ølet*?	Did you find the beer?

The noun in the definite NP may either occur alone: **katten**, the cat or it may be preceded by a definite attribute expressing:

totality	*alle* tilskuere, all the spectators
possession	*deres* kolleger, their colleagues
	USAs utenriksminister, the US Secretary of State
selection	*første* omgang, the first round
demonstrative	*dette* produktet, this product
determiner	*den* katten, that cat; *det* produktet, that product

or it may be followed by:

a possessive	kollegene *deres,* their colleagues
a prepositional phrase	fyren *i Washington,* the bloke in Washington
a relative clause	boka *som vi leste,* the book we read

A definite noun phrase may have a complement that agrees with it (see 2.1.1):

kattene er *hjemløse*   the cats are homeless

Generally speaking, only definite noun phrases are duplicated (see 10.7.3.5–6):

Bilen, *den* har automatgir.   The car, it has an automatic gear box.

BUT:

***Kaffe,* det er godt.**   Coffee, that's good.

10.2.2.3 Function

For clause elements see 10.3ff below. The functions of noun (and pronoun) phrases are:

(a) Subject:

***Den nye bilen* er grå.**   The new car is grey.

(b) Direct object:

Malin kjøpte *en terrengsykkel.*   Malin bought a mountainbike.

(c) Indirect object:

Barna gav *henne* en PC til jul.   The children gave her a computer for Christmas.

(d) Subject complement:

Han er *oversetter.*   He is a translator.

(e) Object complement:

De kalte kattungene   They called the kittens
Tom og Jerry.   Tom and Jerry.

(f) Part of a prepositional phrase

huset i *byen*   the house in town

10.2.3 | *Verb phrases*

10.2.3.1 | *A narrow view of the verb phrase*

A verb phrase consists either of a finite verb (FV, see 10.3.3.1) alone:

Barnet *skriker.*   The child is crying.

or of several verbs, including one finite and one or more non-finite (NFV, see 10.3.3.2) forms:

Barnet *hadde skreket* hele natten.   The child had cried all night.

Alle *kunne ha fått* det til samme pris.
Everyone would have been able to get it at the same price.

or a FV (+NFV) and a verb particle, i.e. an adverb or preposition (For compound verbs, see 5.7):

Vi *sender over* hans brev.   We are forwarding his letter.

or a FV (+NFV) and a reflexive pronoun (For reflexive verbs see 5.5.3):

Hun måtte *skynde seg.*   She had to rush.

10.2.3.2 | *A broader view of the verb phrase*

One view of the verb phrase includes elements governed by the main verb such as objects, complements and adverbials:

Finite verb	Particle	Indirect object Subject complement Potential subject	Direct object Object complement Particle	Free/Other adverbial
hengte	opp		et maleri	i hallen
satte	av		mjølkespannet	i vegkrysset
så		trett	ut	hele kvelden
utnevner	nok	Inger	til leder	neste år
hørte		sønnen	komme opp	om morgenen
kjørte	forbi		bussen	i høy fart

Translations: hung up a picture in the dining-room; set down the milk pail at the crossroads; looked tired all evening; will probably appoint Inger leader next year; heard the son get up in the morning; overtook the bus at high speed

10.2.4 Adjective phrases

10.2.4.1 Structure

The adjective phrase often consists of an adjective or participle (functioning as an adjective) as Head (H) either alone or with adverbial modifiers, primarily adverbs:

temmelig *nervøs*   rather nervous
        H

ti meter *høy*   ten metres tall
     H

forferdelig *urettferdig*   terribly unjust
       H

10.2.4.2 Function

Adjective phrases function as:

(a) Predicative complement:

De var *glade*.   They were happy.   subject comp.
Det gjorde henne *søvnig*.   It made her sleepy.   object comp.

(b) Preposed attribute in a noun phrase:

en *ikke spesielt vellykket* forfatter
a not particularly successful writer

det *i enhver henseende perfekte* hotellet
the in every respect perfect hotel

(c) Adverbially, as attributes/modifiers

– in an adjective phrase:

en *ekstremt* mislykket forfatter   an extremely unsuccessful author

– in a clause:

Han hopper *fint*.   He jumps well

10.2.5 Adverb phrases

10.2.5.1 Structure

The adverb phrase may consist of an adverb (H) either alone or with adverbial modifiers. These modifiers are preposed.

ganske *fort*   rather quickly
  H

nesten *aldri*   almost never
  H

Temporal and spatial adverbs can form postposed attributes:

på vei *ut*   on the way out
konkurransen *her hjemme*   the competition here at home

Prepositional phrases used adverbially as modifiers may be postposed:

ute *på landet*   out in the country
ut *fra sitt kontor*   out of his office

| 10.2.5.2 | *Function*

The adverb phrase functions mainly as:

(a) Clausal adverbial (see 10.3.6.1f.):

> **De har *aldri/ ikke/ jo/ kanskje/ ofte/ antakelig/ dessverre/ heldigvis* vunnet i lotteriet.**
> They have never/ not/ you know/ perhaps/ often/ presumably/ unfortunately/ luckily/ won the lottery.

Other adverbial (see 10.3.6.1):

> **Der bor Ivar.**   (*Lit.* There lives Ivar.) That is where Ivar lives.

(b) Modifier to a noun phrase:

> ***Ikke bare* politikerne, men *også* folket støtter presidenten.**
> Not only the politicians but also the people support the president.

(c) Modifier in an adjective or adverb phrase:

> **Hun virket *veldig* fornøyd.**
> She seemed very pleased.

> **Han kjørte *veldig* fort.**
> He drove very fast.

| 10.2.6 | **Prepositional phrases**

| 10.2.6.1 | *Structure*

Prepositional phrases comprise a preposition plus – often – a prepositional complement (7.1.3.1) which is governed by the preposition and may consist of a noun phrase, infinitive phrase or subclause:

> **Jenta *med den fantastiske stemmen* er min hustru.**
> The girl with the fantastic voice is my wife.

> **Vi funderer *på å skrive en bok.***
> We're thinking of writing a book.

> **Hun grubler *over hvordan hun skal lykkes.***
> She is pondering how she will succeed.

| 10.2.6.2 | *Function*

(a) Postposed attribute to a noun phrase:

toget *mot Lillehammer*
the train to Lillehammer

(b) Other adverbial (10.3.6.1):

Skuddet gikk *forbi den norske målvakten*.
The shot went past the Norwegian goalkeeper.

(c) Clausal adverbial (10.3.6.2):

***Uten tvil* er hopp vinterens beste norske gren.**
Ski jumping is without doubt Norway's best sport this winter.

(d) 'Prepositional object'

See 7.1.3.4.

De sto og ventet *på bussen*.
They stood waiting for the bus.

(e) Complement (10.3.5):

I år ble han utnevnt *til transportminister*.
This year he was appointed Minister of Transport.

10.3 Clause elements

The different clause elements (or 'building blocks') are each examined in the paragraphs that follow, whilst in 10.4 these are plotted in a scheme showing their relative order in the clause.

| 10.3.1 | *Subject*

In the Norwegian clause, the subject is compulsory except in imperative clauses (**Hjelp!**, 'Help!') and certain relative clauses where it may be omitted. Its form may vary.

| 10.3.1.1 | *Form*

The subject usually consists of:

(a) A noun phrase or pronoun:

Sofia er min søster.	Sofia is my sister.
Drosjen stanset utenfor.	The taxi stopped outside.
De kom ut av butikken.	They left the shop.

(b) A subordinate clause:

| **Om de liker meg, er tvilsomt.** | Whether they like me is doubtful. |

Note – An infinitive phrase can also form the subject, see 5.3.1.6.

| 10.3.1.2 | *Position*

The subject (S) is normally placed next to the finite verb (FV) in main clauses, and its position relative to the finite verb helps to indicate sentence type:

| **Jan spiste eplet.** | S – FV = Statement | Jan ate the apple. |
| **Spiste Jan eplet?** | FV – S = Yes/no question | Did Jan eat the apple? |

But notice that, when a non-subject (X) begins the clause, Norwegian usually has inverted statements, unlike English:

| **Hver dag spiser Jan et eple.** | Every day Jan eats an apple. |
| X   FV   S | |

In some imperative clauses, an implicit or explicit second person subject comes after the verb:

| **Gå (du) først!** | (You) go first! |

| 10.3.2 | **Constructions using the formal subject**

A formal subject is typically the pronoun **det**, 'it' that does not refer back to a word in the preceding text. We differentiate between four types in 10.3.2.1ff.

| 10.3.2.1 | *Type A*

In some sentences, **det** (= 'it') as subject has little real meaning and by means of its position is used to indicate sentence type, i.e. statement or question. It is sometimes called a 'place-holder subject':

Det regner/snør/hagler.	It is raining/snowing/hailing.
Det blir mørkt snart.	It will be dark soon.
Det ringte i telefonen.	The phone rang.
Er det ikke for varmt herinne?	Isn't it too hot in here?

This is particularly the case with verbs indicating meteorological phenomena (**regne**), but also applies to sensory verbs that could alternatively take a personal subject (**ringe**).

| 10.3.2.2 | *Type B*

When the subject is postponed (moved to the right in the sentence), an anticipatory **det** (= 'there') is inserted, which is known as the *formal subject* (FS, Nw. **formelt subjekt**). The postponed subject is then known as the *potential subject* (PS, Nw. **potensielt subjekt**). Type B is used to anticipate an indefinite noun phrase, i.e. a new idea, which rarely comes at the front of the sentence:

Det stod *en politimann* i forstuen.
FS   PS
There was a police officer standing in the hall.

Compare the following alternative, which is less likely, particularly in the spoken language:

***En politimann* stod i forstuen.**
S

This construction with **det** is called an *existential sentence* (10.7.3.4, Nw. **presenteringssetning**), because in English it is found only with forms of the verb 'to be'. In Norwegian, its use is more frequent, and it may be found, as above, with other intransitive verbs.

In Type C, the formal subject **det** (= 'it') anticipates an infinitive phrase or subordinate clause as potential subject:

> **Det blir interessant å følge klubben.**
> FS   PS
> It will be interesting to follow the club.

> **Det er uvisst *om noe er stjålet.***
> FS   PS
> It is uncertain whether anything has been stolen.

Alternatively, the infinitive phrase or the subclause may come at the front of the sentence:

> **Å følge klubben blir interessant.**
> S
> **Om noe er stjålet, er uvisst.**

10.3.2.4 Type D

Type D is in English called the *cleft sentence* (Nw. **utbrytning**). Here the construction **Det er/var X som. . .**, 'It was X that/who. . .' places emphasis on a particular element, and the remainder of the original clause is relegated to a subordinate clause (relative clause). The original sentence is, therefore, cleft in two:

> **Base clause**
> **Oskar sendte Sara blomster forrige uke.**
>   X
> Oskar sent Sara flowers last week.

> **Cleft sentence**
> **Det var 'blomster som Oskar sendte Sara forrige uke.**
> FS   X
> It was flowers that Oskar sent Sara last week.

Theoretically, almost any clause element may be emphasized in this way:

Det var Oskar som...
Det var forrige uke som...
Det var Sara som...

| 10.3.3 | **Finite and non-finite verbs**

| 10.3.3.1 | *Finite forms*

The finite verb shows tense, voice or mood (cf. 5.1.1f), and its forms include:

(a) Present tense: **kjører** **Politiet kjører fort.**
The police drive fast.

(b) Past tense: **kjørte** **De kjørte fort.**
They drove fast.

(c) Imperative: **kjør** **Kjør!**
Drive!

(d) Present (and, rarely, past) passive: **kjøres (kjørtes)** **Bilen kjøres av Erik.**
The car is (was) being
driven by Erik.

(e) Subjunctive (rare): **leve!** **Leve kongen!**
Long live the King!

Note 1 – When there are several coordinated finite verbs, the subject is as a rule placed either immediately before or after the first verb:

Erik ligger og sover. Erik is asleep.
$S - FV_1 \quad FV_2$

Nå ligger Erik og sover. Erik is asleep now.
$FV_1 - S \quad FV_2$

Note 2 – If there are both finite and non-finite verbs in a clause, the finite verb is usually an auxiliary and comes first:

Erik skal sove nå. Erik will sleep now.
$FV \quad NFV$

| 10.3.3.2 | *Non-finite forms* |

See also 5.2.1.1(e) – (h).

Non-finite forms include:

(a) Infinitive – without å: kjøre   **Han skal *kjøre*.**
                                           He will drive.

        – with å: å kjøre   **Hun liker *å kjøre*.**
                                           She likes to drive.

(b) Past participle (supine):   kjørt   **Han har *kjørt* hit.**
                                           He has driven here.

(c) Infinitive passive: kjøres   **Bilen må *kjøres*.**
                                           The car must be driven.

Note 1 – Several infinitives may occur together:

Han sa han ikke kunne *begynne å tenke på å skrive* boken.
He said that he could not begin to think about writing the book.

Note 2 – After a modal auxiliary both an infinitive and supine may be found:

De burde *ha tenkt* på det.   They should have thought of that.

Note 3 – The present participle in Norwegian is most often regarded as an adjective or adjectival noun, seldom as a non-finite verb form (5.2.1.1 (g), 5.3.13.)

| 10.3.4 | **Direct and indirect objects** |

| 10.3.4.1 | *Form of objects* |

(a) The direct object may be:

- A noun phrase (including pronouns):

    De spiste *lunsj*.   They ate lunch.
    Jeg møtte *ham*.   I met him.

- An infinitive phrase:

  Koret begynte *å synge*.   The choir began to sing.

- A phrase in direct speech:

  «*Helvete,*» ropte hun.   "Hell," she cried.

- A subordinate clause:

  Jeg vet *at han er korrupt*.   I know he's corrupt.

(b) Indirect objects are typically noun phrases or prepositional phrases:

Hermine gav *Harry* en dult.   Hermione gave Harry a nudge.
Harry gav blomster *til Gulla*.   Harry gave flowers to Ginny.

| 10.3.4.2 | *Direct and indirect objects* |

(a) Direct objects are found with transitive verbs (5.5.1.1):

De har bygget *huset* selv.   They have built the house themselves.

(b) Both direct objects (DO) and indirect objects (IO) are found with ditransitive verbs. The DO is usually an inanimate object affected by the action, whilst the IO is an animate being that is the recipient of the action:

De sendte *oldemor en gave*.   They sent great grandma a present.
          IO   DO

(c) The order of direct and indirect objects is in most cases the same as in English although, when both objects are pronouns, the order in Norwegian is always IO – DO:

Gi *meg det*!   Give me it/Give it me!
  IO   DO

(d) If the indirect object is a prepositional phrase, the direct object precedes it:

Han lånte *boken til en venn*.   He lent the book to a friend.
          DO   IO

Position of objects

When stressed, the object usually comes directly after the non-finite verb or verb particle:

Jeg har brent (opp) *brevene*.   I've burnt the letters.

(If there is only a finite verb, the object comes after that.)

The object may, however, begin the clause:

Brevene har jeg brent.   *Lit.* The letters I've burnt. I've burnt the letters.

Object clauses usually come at the end of the clause:

Karl spurte *hvem som hadde brent brevene*.
Karl asked who had burned the letters.

10.3.5 Complements

The *predicative complement* (Nw. **predikativ**) is found with a *copular* verb (Nw. **kopulaverb**), one that has little real content and which either describes a state, e.g. **være**, 'be'; **hete**, 'be called'; **se . . . ut**, 'look'; **virke**, 'seem', or which results in a change: **bli**, 'become'; **nominere . . . til**, 'nominate'. It occupies the same position as the object.

10.3.5.1 Phrases as complements

Complements may be:

(a) A noun phrase: **Bilen er *et vrak*.**
                        The car is a wreck.
                        Det er *henne*.
                        It is her.

(b) An adjective phrase: **Hun er *intelligent*.**
                            She is intelligent.

(c) A subordinate clause: **Dette er *hva det handler om*.**
                            This is what it is about.

(d) A prepositional phrase: **De valgte henne *til* leder.**
They elected her leader.

(e) An infinitive construction: **Poenget *er å leve livet.***
The point is to live your life.

| **10.3.5.2** | *Form* |

Predicative complements are of three kinds.

(a) Subject complement:

Hun er *professor.* She is a professor.
Vann blir *altfor dyrt.* Water is becoming too expensive.

(b) Object complement:

Dette gjorde ham *rasende.* This made him furious.
Paret kalte gutten *Shirley.* The couple called the lad Shirley.

(c) Free complement (Nw. **fritt predikativ**), which, unlike subject complements and object complements, can easily be dropped:

Trett og sliten kom hun sent hjem.
Exhausted she came home late.

Som ung var Martin utadvendt.
As a young man, Martin was extrovert.

| **10.3.6** | **Adverbials** |

| **10.3.6.1** | *Two types of adverbial* |

See also 6.2.1.3, 10.2.5.2.

Adverbials are of two types: *Clausal adverbials* (CA) and *Other adverbials* (OA):

Han har *visstnok ikke* syklet *på mange år.*
       CA   *OA*
He has *allegedly not* been on a bike *for many years.*

(a) Clausal adverbials, often adverbs, modify the sense of the clause as a whole:

Han sykler *aldri/ofte/sjelden* til arbeidet.
He never/often/rarely cycles to work.

(b) Other adverbials, often prepositional phrases or subordinate clauses, denote concepts such as manner, place and time, answering the questions how? where? when? why?:

Vi reiser ikke *til Norge om vinteren*.
                where?   *when?*
We don't go to Norway in winter.

Fordi Gene var så pen, undervurderte folk henne.
Because Gene was so beautiful, people underestimated her.
why?

|10.3.6.2| *Clausal adverbials*

The main types of clausal adverbial are:

(a) Modal adverbs:

    Det er *dessverre* for sent.
    It is unfortunately too late.

(b) Conjunctional adverbs:

    Du kommer *altså* på søndag.
    You will come then on Sunday.

(c) Prepositional phrases:

    Det er *tross alt* januar.
    It is after all January.

(d) Negations:

    Jeg gambler *ikke*.
    I don't gamble.

|10.3.6.3| *Position of adverbials*

(a) Clausal adverbials come *after* the finite verb (or the subject in inverted word order) in the main clause (unless they come in the 'F' position), and usually *before* the finite verb in the subordinate clause:

Main clause

Vi hadde *ikke* kjørt for fort. We had not driven too fast.
   FV   *CA*

Subordinate clause

Vi forklarte at vi *ikke* hadde kjørt for fort.
              CA FV
We explained that we had not driven too fast.

Note – One may also sometimes find the same word order in a subordinate
clause as in a main clause (**Vi forklarte at vi hadde ikke kjørt for fort**, see 10.8.5),
but this is less common in writing, and it has a special nuance of meaning.

(b) Other adverbials usually either come at the end or at the beginning of
the sentence:

Vi hadde ikke kjørt for fort *denne gangen*.
We had not driven too fast this time.

Denne gangen hadde vi ikke kjørt for fort.
This time we had not driven too fast.

10.4   The order of clause elements

The account of Norwegian word order in this book is based largely on a
positional scheme originally developed by Paul Diderichsen for Danish, a
syntactically similar language, though there are some minor differences.
Diderichsen's scheme has the great advantage of mapping the entire clause
(in principle the sentence), thus indicating the relative positions of all the
clause elements simultaneously. Diderichsen uses the following nomencla-
ture for the seven positions in the clause and the three fields:

Main clause

Front field | Mid field | End field

F(undament) – **v**(erbal) – **n**(ominal) – **a**(dverbial) – **V**(erbal) – **N**(ominal) – **A**(dverbial)

Subordinate clause

Front field | Mid field | End field

k(onjunksjon) – **n**(ominal) – **a**(dverbial) – **v**(erbal) – **V**(erbal) – **N**(ominal) – **A**(dverbial)

In what follows, 'k' has been replaced by 'f' (Norwegian **forbinderfelt**) in the
subordinate clause, to accord with Norwegian practice. In the diagram below,
the positions are shown for comparison with the terminology used above in
10.1–10.3. But see 10.6.3 for major exceptions regarding clausal adverbials.

Scheme A Main clause (MC)

Front field	Mid field			End field		
Front	Finite verb	Subject	Clausal adverbial	Non-finite verb	Object/ Complement/ Potential subject	Other adverbial
F	v	n	a	V	N	A
I dag	**hadde**	**de**	**ikke**	**laget**	**mat**	**da vi kom.**
Today	(they	had)	not	cooked	a meal	when we arrived.

Scheme B Subordinate clause (SC)

Front	Mid field			End field		
Sub-junction	Subject	Clausal adverbial	Finite verb	Non-finite verb	Object/ Complement	Other adverbial
f	n	a	v	V	N	A
...da	**jeg**	**ikke**	**hadde**	**sett**	**filmen**	**tidligere.**
...as	I	had	not	seen	the film	before.

10.4.1 Main clause and subordinate clause

10.4.1.1 Clause and sentence

A *clause* is part of a sentence that usually has a subject and finite verb (with the exception of most imperative constructions (5.4.4, 10.3.1, 10.3.3.1). A *sentence* comprises either a main clause alone or several coordinated main clauses, and may have one or more subordinate clauses.

De besøker oss, og det gleder jeg meg til.   *One sentence*
MC   MC
They're coming on a visit and I'm looking forward to it.

De besøker oss. Jeg gleder meg til det.   *Two sentences*

10

Sentence
structure and
word order

MC   MC

They're coming on a visit. I'm looking forward to it.

| 10.4.1.2 |

(a) While a main clause (MC) can occur on its own, a subordinate clause (SC) usually occurs together with a main clause, forming a clause element within it:

At de besøker oss, gleder meg.
SC=Subject   *FV*
That they're visiting us pleases me.

Jeg vet ikke *om de besøker oss.*
         SC=direct object
I don't know if they are visiting us.

Vi har mye å snakke om *når de besøker oss.*
                    SC=other adverbial (time)
We have a great deal to talk about when they visit us.

(b) Some subordinate clauses may occur without a main clause in exclamations or wish clauses, often where something is understood:

(Tenk) *at jeg kunne ta så feil*!   That I could be so wrong!

| 10.4.1.3 |

When there are several subordinate clauses, one may form part of another, forming a hierarchy (see 9.1.3):

. . . idet han sa   1

  at det ikke ville bli aktuelt   2

    fordi vi ikke hadde råd. . .   3

when he said/ that it would not be of interest/ as we could not afford it

10.4.2 | Scheme A – Order of clause elements in the main clause

Front	Finite verb	Subject	Clausal adverbial	Non-finite verb	Object/ Complement/ Potential subject	Other adverbial
F	v	n	a	V	N	A
1 Mia	kjøpte	–	–	–	en bærbar PC	i går.
2 Mia	kjøpte	–	ikke	–	en stasjonær PC	i går.
3 Hun	har	–	også	kjøpt	en skanner	i år.
4 I går	kjøpte	Mia	–	–	en PC.	
5 Hun	kjøper	–	alltid	–	dataprodukter	på Internett.
6 PCen	kjøpte	hun	–	–	–	i går.
7 I dag	laster	hun	–	ned	programvare	fra Internett.
8 Nå	kjøper	hun	ofte		utstyr	på avbetaling.
9 I går	kunne	hun	ikke	koble	PC-en sin	til Internett.
10 Mia	var	–	–	–	skuffet	i går.
11 Skuffet	har	hun	jo ofte	vært	–	tidligere.
12 Til våren skal		hun	faktisk	skrive	en ny bok.	
13 I dag	skal	hun	–	male	kjøkkenet	ferdig.
14 Male	kan	hun	i alle fall.			
15 Aksel	er	–	–	–	lærer.	
16 Det	har	han	–	vært	–	i mange år.
17 Det	sitter	–	–	–	to katter	på bilen.
18 De	må	–	–	ha vært	uheldige	denne gang.
19 –	Burde	du	ikke	barbere	deg	hver dag?
20 –	Har	du	ikke	villet lese	brevet	før?
21 Jeg	gav	–	–	–	henne blomster	på fødselsdagen.
22 Når	kommer	de	–	–	–	hjem fra skolen?
23 –	Legg	–	–	–	brevene	på skrivebordet!

Translations: 1 Mia bought a laptop yesterday, 2 Mia did not buy a desktop yesterday, 3 She has also bought a scanner this year, 4 Yesterday Mia bought a computer, 5 She always buys computer products on the internet, 6 The computer, she bought (that) yesterday, 7 Today she is download-ing programmes from the internet, 8 Now she often buys equipment on hire purchase, 9 Yester-day she could not connect her computer to the internet, 10 Mia was disappointed yesterday, 11 She has often been disappointed previously, you know, 12 In the spring she is actually going to write a new book, 13 Today she is going to finish painting the kitchen, 14 She can paint any way, 15 Aksel is a teacher, 16 That he has been for many years, 17 There are two cats sitting on the car, 18 They must have been unlucky this time, 19 Shouldn't you shave every day?, 20 Didn't you want to read the letter before?, 21 I gave her flowers on her birthday, 22 When do they come home from school?, 23 Put the letters on the desk!

10.4.2.1 Positions in Scheme A

(a) In the 'F' position we find various elements: noun phrases as subject or object, adverbials, and occasionally complements and non-finite verbs (1, 18, 21, 22). This is where the subject is usually placed when the main clause has unmarked (i.e. unemphatic) word order. The 'F' position rarely contains more than one element.

(b) In the 'v' position there are only finite verbs (1–23). In a normal, unabbreviated clause this is the only position that must be filled.

(c) The 'n' position contains a noun phrase or pronoun. If the subject of the clause is not in the 'F' position, then it will be placed here (so-called inverted word order) (4, 6–9, 11–14, 16, 19, 20, 22).

(d) The 'a' position contains negations and other clausal adverbials (2, 3, 5, 8–9, 12, 14, 19–20). There may be more than one (11).

(e) In the 'V' position are non-finite verbs (3, 9, 11–13, 16, 18–20) but also particles (7).

(f) In the 'N' position are noun phrases as objects (1–5, 7–9, 12, 13, 20, 21, 23) and complements (10, 15, 18). The potential subject is in this position when there is a formal subject (17). With ditransitive verbs, there is both a direct and an indirect object in this position (21).

(g) In the 'A' position come one or more other adverbials, often denoting time or place (1–3, 5–11, 16–23).

(h) There may also be extra positions before the 'F' position and after the 'A' position (see 10.7.3.5).

(i) There may also be a conjunction 'f' position before the extra position or 'F' position (10.7.3.6).

10.4.2.3 Summary of main clause order

(a) Main clause sentences are either statements, questions or commands.

(b) In statements, position 'F' is always filled, either by the subject or in principle by any non-verbal clause element (examples 1, 2 below).

(c) Questions are of two types: Yes/no questions in which 'F' is unfilled (3) and Hv-questions in which 'F' is always filled (4).

(d) In commands, position 'F' is unfilled and this usually also applies to 'n' (5)

Front field		Mid field				End field		
	F	**v**	**n**	**a**		**V**	**N**	**A**
Sentence type								
Statement	**Han**	**leser**	–	–	–	**norsk**	**i år.**	1
	I år	**leser**	**han**	–	–	**norsk.**		2
Yes/no question	**–**	**Leser**	**han**	–	–	**norsk**	**i år?**	3
Hv-question	**Hvorfor**	**leser**	**han**	–	–	**norsk?**		4
Command	**–**	**Les**	–	–	–	**norsk!**		5

Translations: 1 He reads Norwegian this year, 2 This year he reads Norwegian, 3 Is he reading Norwegian this year? 4 Why is he reading Norwegian?, 5 Read Norwegian!

10.4.3 Scheme B – Order of clause elements in the subordinate clause

	Sub-junc-tion	Subject	Clausal adverbial	Finite verb	Non-finite verb	Object/Comp lement	Other adverbial
Matrix	f	n	a	v	V	N	A
1 **Han spurte**	**om**	**hun**	**ikke**	**hadde**	**sett**	**filmen**	**før.**
2 **Jeg sa**	**at**	**jeg**	**alltid**	**skulle**	**støtte**	**dem.**	
3 **Hun lurte på**	**om**	**det**	**ikke**	**fantes**	–	**mat**	**hjemme.**
4 **Hanna visste**	**(at)**	**de**	**aldri**	**ville**	**hjelpe**	**henne.**	
5 **Dette er**							
en sang	**(som)**	**du**	**nok**				
			aldri	**har**	**hørt**	–	**før.**
6	**Hvis**	**du**	**bare**	**visste!**			

Translation: 1 He asked whether she hadn't seen the film before, 2 I said that I would always support them, 3 She wondered whether there wasn't any food in the house, 4 Hanna knew (that) they would never help her, 5 This is a song (that) you probably haven't heard before, 6 If you only knew!

10.4.3.1 Positions in Scheme B

(a) Notice that the *matrix* is that part of the sentence remaining when the subordinate clause is removed.

(b) In Scheme B, there is no 'F' position in the sense of a position which can house any element, but instead there is an 'f' position (Nw. **forbinderfelt**) containing a subordinator or **hv**-word.

(c) The subject position ('n') is always occupied in Scheme B.

(d) The subordinator **at** may sometimes be omitted (4), as may the subordinator **som** when it is not the subject of the clause (5), see 10.5.1, 10.8.2.3(b), 9.1.5.4 (c), 9.4.1.2.

(e) For independent clauses (6) with subordinate clause word order, see 10.8.7.

(f) An extra position may be inserted after the 'A' position, see 10.7.3.5.

(g) Where there are two subordinate clauses linked by a conjunction, this conjunction precedes the subordinator in the 'f' position.

10.5 Differences between main clause and subordinate clause positions

There are two major differences.

10.5.1 Subject and verb

While the main clause begins with any clause element in the 'F' position, the subordinate clause almost always begins with the subjunction (position 'f') and subject ('n'). Occasionally, however, (see 10.4.3.1) the subordinators **at** and **som** are omitted in the subordinate clause. So, while main clause order may be either S – FV ('straight') or FV – S ('inverted'), subordinate clause order is usually S – FV (straight).

10.5.2 The clausal adverbial

In the main clause, the clausal adverbial ('a') comes immediately *after* the FV ('v'). In the subordinate clause, the clausal adverbial (a) comes immediately *before* the finite verb (v), although there are exceptions (see 10.6.3.1).

10.6 Order within positions

In many sentences, there is more than one element in the 'a', 'V', 'N' and 'A' positions. This section discusses the relative order of elements within these positions.

417

10.6.1 Order of non-finite verbs and verb particles

With separable compound verbs, the verb particle occupies the 'V' position. When the separable verb is in the non-finite form, both verb and particle occupy this position.

F	v	n	a	V	N	A
De	**skal**	–	–	*betale tilbake*	**pengene.**	
De	**skal**	–	–	*tilbakebetale*	**pengene.**	

They are going to pay back the money.

For compound verbs, see 5.7.

10.6.2 Order of objects, complements and potential subjects (in 'N')

Potential subject	Subject complement	Indirect object	Direct object	Object complement

10.6.2.1 Order of objects

See also 10.3.4.2.

The order of objects is usually the same as in English: the indirect object (IO) precedes the direct object (DO) unless the indirect object is a prepositional phrase:

Jeg sendte *henne blomster.*   I sent her flowers.
           IO   DO

This is also true when the objects are pronouns (see also 10.3.4.2):

Jeg sendte *henne dem.*   I sent her them.
           IO   DO

BUT:

Jeg sendte _blomster til henne._   I sent flowers to her.
            _DO_   _IO (prep.phrase)_

When the DO is a subordinate clause, it is usually preceded by the IO, as in English:

Mor fortalte _meg at hun skulle gifte seg på nytt._
            _IO_   _DO=Subordinate clause_
Mum told me that she was going to get married again.

|10.6.2.2| _The direct object usually precedes the object complement (OC)_

I dag valgte partiet _ham til leder._
                 _DO_ _OC_
Today the party elected him leader.

|10.6.2.3| _The subject complement (SC) usually precedes its "objects"_

Hun er _verd en hederlig lønn._
               _SC_
She is a worth a decent salary.

Note – There are exceptions in some set phrases:

Han er alltid _situasjonen voksen._
             _DO_   _SC_
He is always equal to the situation.

|10.6.2.4| _Unstressed object pronouns and reflexive pronouns_

Unlike stressed objects, which go in the 'N' position, unstressed object pronouns (including reflexive pronouns) go in the 'n' position:

F |	v	n	a |	V	N	A

Stressed object

| **Jeg** | **så** | – | **ikke** | – | *Ivar* | **på møtet.** |

I didn't see Ivar at the meeting.

Unstressed object and reflexive pronouns

| **Jeg** | **så** | *ham* | **ikke** | – | – | **på møtet.** |

I didn't see him at the meeting.

Unstressed subject and reflexive pronouns

| **Da** | **lærte** | *han seg* | **aldri** | – | **språket.** |

Then he never learned the language.

Note – An exception is the clause with a complex verb (i.e. both finite and non-finite verbs):

Han har aldri lært seg språket.   He has never learnt the language.

10.6.3 Order of clausal adverbials

10.6.3.1 Positions 'a¹' and 'a²'

Clauses with an unstressed subject have the order seen in 10.4.2f., namely:

Scheme A   Main Clause: F | –v–n–a – | V–N–A

Scheme B   Subordinate clause: f | –n–a–v – | V–N–A

In these clauses, the clausal adverbial adopts the position marked in the table below as a². Note, therefore, that in normal (unmarked) use in Scheme A, the clausal adverbial frequently comes *after* the finite verb and in Scheme B, it frequently comes *before* the finite verb, i.e. in a¹.

But, with a stressed subject (marked ' below), the adverbial may come *either before or after* the finite verb, and some versions of the schemes in Norwegian grammar books consequently have the order where the clausal adverbial goes in a¹:

Scheme A   *Main Clause:*

F		v	a¹	n	a²		V	N	A

Normal use

I dag **har**   **hun**   **ikke fått**   **noe mat.**
Today she hasn't had any food.

Stressed subject

I dag **har** **ikke** **'katten**   –   **fått**   **noe mat.**
Today the cat hasn't had any food.

            Har **ikke** **'regjeringen** –   **diskutert dette**   **før?**
            Hasn't the government discussed this before?

Scheme B   *Subordinate clause:*

f		a¹	n	a²	v		V	N	A

Normal use

Da   –   **hun**   **ikke vil,**   –   –   –   **går vi ikke.**
As she doesn't want to, we won't go.

Stressed subject

Da **ikke** **'Eva**   –   **vil,**   –   –   –   **går vi ikke.**
As Eva doesn't want to, we won't go.

| 10.6.3.2 | *Order within position 'a'*

The order of clausal adverbials is usually:

1 Modal, 2 Context, 3 Empathy, 4 Epistemic, 5 Focus, 6 Negation

1 Modal: short modal adverbs (6.2.4.3), used to reinforce or moderate the
   content of the clause, e.g. **jo**, 'you know'; **nok**, 'I suppose'; **vel**, 'certainly'

2 Context, used to link the clause to a previous clause or to the context
   as a whole, e.g. **nemlig**, 'namely'; **altså**, 'therefore'; **derfor**, 'therefore';
   dessuten, 'moreover'

3 Empathy, used to express the speaker's attitude toward the content of the
   clause, e.g. **heldigvis**, 'luckily'; **dessverre**, 'unfortunately'; **forhåpentlig**,
   'hopefully'

4   Epistemic, used to indicate the truth value of the content in the clause, e.g. **faktisk**, 'actually'; **kanskje**, 'perhaps'; **sikkert**, 'certainly'; **trolig**, 'presumably'; **visstnok**, 'in all probability'

5   Focus, used to emphasize, focus on, parts of the clause, e.g. **bare**, 'simply'; **også**, 'also'

6   Negation: **ikke**, 'not'; **aldri**, 'never'

If several of these are used in the same clause, the order may be as above:

　　　 1 2　　 4　　 6
De har jo derfor faktisk aldri vunnet.
They have, you know, therefore never actually won.

　　　 1　 2　 3　　　 6
Vi får vel altså tross alt ikke gi opp.
We must probably therefore despite everything not give up.

10.6.4 Order of other adverbials and the passive agent

See also 10.6.3.3.

10.6.4.1 Order of other adverbials: manner, place, time, condition

(a) The relative order of other adverbials is quite flexible, and it is only possible to give two rules of thumb:

- Adverbials of *manner* usually precede those of *place* and *time:* manner – place – time (MPT).
- Long adverbials usually follow the MPT group.

(b) The order is often (but see 10.6.3.3):

1   Adverbial expressions of *manner*: **fort**, quickly; **dårlig**, badly; **sent**, late; **umiddelbart**, immediately
2   Adverbial expressions of *place*: **her**, here; **ute**, outside; **utenfor huset**, outside the house; **i Bergen**, in Bergen
3   Adverbial expressions of *time*: **i går**, yesterday; **neste uke**, next week; **før juleferien**, before the Christmas holidays
4   Longer adverbial expressions such as *cause, condition*, etc.: **av den grunn**, for that reason

　　　　 1　　 2　　 3　　 4
Han kom sent hjem i går fordi det var trafikkork.
He got home late yesterday because there was a traffic jam.

| 10.6.4.2 | *Position of the passive agent* |

The passive agent usually comes immediately before the Other adverbial expressions in position 'A'.

Vi ble ringt opp *av Olav* på hotellet sist lørdag.
      Agent *OA-Place* *OA-Time*
We were rung up by Olav at the hotel last Saturday.

10.7   Main clause transformations

Optional movements within the Norwegian main clause are often made for stylistic reasons.

| 10.7.1 | *The base clause* |

In order to discuss movements within the clause, we will assume a Norwegian base clause, that is one that is stylistically unmarked, for example:

1	2	3	4	5	6	7
F	| v	n	a |	V	N	A
Hun	**vil**	**–**	**ikke**	**spille**	**fotball**	**denne sesongen.**

She won't be playing football this season.

This base clause begins with the subject and therefore has straight (subject – finite verb) word order, with all the other positions filled except for 'n'. The subject is, therefore, the *theme* of the sentence, see 10.9.1.1.

Variations on this order are explored in the paragraphs that follow, where other sentence elements may become the theme. In 10.7.3.3–10.7.3.5 these changes involve a radical redisposition of elements.

| 10.7.2 | *Topicalisation* |

| 10.7.2.1 |

In topicalisation (or fronting, Nw. **framflytting, topikalisering**)), one of the clause elements usually located in positions 2 to 7 is placed in this first, 'F', position, and the subject in the 'n' position. The most common topicalisation is of adverbial expressions of time or place.

1		2	3	4	5	6	7
F	|	v	n	a |	V	N	A

Base clause

| **Hun** | | **vil** | – | **ikke** | **spille** | **fotball** | **i år.** |

She won't be playing football this year.

1 A to F

| **I år** | | **vil** | **hun** | **ikke** | **spille** | **fotball.** | |

2 N (Object) to F

| **Fotball** | | **vil** | **hun** | **ikke** | **spille** | – | **i år.** |

3 N (direct speech, object) to F

| «**Kronidiot!**» | | **sa** | **han.** | | | | |

"Bloody idiot", he said.

4 a (clausal adverbial) to F

| **Ikke** | | **tenker** | **hun** | – | **spille** | **fotball** | **i år.** |

5a V (non-finite verb and possible object, complement or adverbial) to F

| **'Lese** | | **gjør*** | **han** | – | – | | **stadig.** |

He reads constantly.

5b **'Spille**

| **fotball** | | **vil** | **hun** | **ikke** | **(gjøre)*** | – | **i år.** |

6 v (finite verb) to F (rare, mostly in spoken language)

| **'Forsvinner** | | **gjør*** | **de** | | | | **støtt** |

They are always disappearing.

---

* In these cases, the finite verb or non-finite verb may be replaced in 'v' and 'V' by a place-holder verb or pro-verb, usually a form of **gjøre**. The function of this verb is simply to indicate sentence type by means of the resulting word order, but it also gives the topicalised verb contrastive stress (marked ').

| **10.7.2.2** | *Why topicalise?*

See also 10.9.1.1f for theme and focus. Numbers below refer to examples in 10.7.2.1 above.

(a) Background information

For example, see 1 in 10.7.2.1 above: **I år vil hun ikke spille fotball.**

Adverbial 'A' – the element topicalised provides background information (often establishing time or place, see 10.7.2.4) to the new information that is to come in the clause. It is not emphasised.

(b) Linking information

De reiste til Roma. _Der_ besøkte de Vatikanet.

<————>

They travelled to Rome. There they visited the Vatican.

The adverbial (The word **der** in the second sentence) may serve to link the clause with a previous clause.

(c) Added emphasis

For examples see 2 in 10.7.2.1 above: **Fotball vil hun ikke spille i år (, men tennis vil hun spille)** and also 3–6. The elements topicalised are given added emphasis. The weight of the additional emphasis corresponds to the relative infrequency with which that element appears in 'F'. In cases 4–6 these topicalisations are not found in English. See also Emphatic topic 10.9.3.2.

| 10.7.2.3 | _One element is topicalised_

Note that (with the exception of example 5b in 10.7.2.1) only one clause element usually occupies the 'F' position (10.4.2.1 (a). For instance, only one adverbial is normally topicalised, which is different from English:

De spilte en match _i Bergen i august_.
                             OA-place OA-time
They played a match in Bergen in August.
cf.

I august spilte de en match _i Bergen_.
OA-time   _OA-place_

I Bergen spilte de en match i _august_.
OA-place   _OA-time_

| 10.7.2.4 | _Adverbial clause in position 'F'_

A subordinate clause otherwise found in the 'A' position may commonly be found in the 'F' position, where it provides background information, as in this temporal clause:

Når vi kom hjem, spiste vi alltid   middag.
_F_   _v_   _n a_   _– N_
When we got home we always ate dinner.

The weight principle and altering emphasis in the sentence

An unstressed element referring to a familiar idea (i.e. a short element) tends to be located to the left of the sentence, while a stressed element introducing a new idea (i.e. a longer element) tends to be located to the right. So, the natural balance of the sentence in spoken and informal written Norwegian is one of 'end weight' as in this example:

Han ble verdensmester i poker *i år*   *da han vant 8 millioner dollar.*
F   v   n   *OA-time OA-time (subordinate clause)*
He became world champion at poker this year when he won 8 million dollars.

The implications of the weight principle (Nw. **vektprinsippet**) are that:

(a) Elements losing stress move leftwards, though not necessarily all the way to 'F', e.g. the unstressed object pronoun which moves to 'n'.

Compare:

Jeg så ikke 'Eva i går.   I didn't see Eva yesterday.
Jeg så *henne* ikke i går.   I didn't see her yesterday.
          ←————

(b) In some cases, such as **ikke**, this requires the use of the 'a¹' and 'a²' positions; see 10.6.3.1. In this case, **ikke** goes in 'a¹':

I dag har *ikke* Erik fått avisen.
          ←————

Today Erik has not got his newspaper.

(c) Some stressed subjects introducing a new idea are postponed (moved rightwards) and are replaced (↑) by a formal subject (FS). When such 'potential subjects' (PS) comprise infinitive phrases or subordinate clauses, they move to the extra position. See 10.3.2.2f.

↑**Det ligger *en bok* på golvet.**   *Potential subject is a noun phrase*
FS   PS

————→

There's a book lying on the floor.

↑**Det er hyggelig *at dere kan følge med.*** *Potential subject is a*
subordinate clause

FS   PS
————————→

It's great that you can come along.

(d) Clauses and clause elements that are not formed in accordance with the
weight principle are sometimes found in formal written Norwegian and
have varying degrees of 'left weight'.

Han har *denne uken* gått av som pave. *Other adverbial in position 'a'*

←————————————————————

He has this week resigned as Pope.

At han skal bruke tid på å skrive upassende tweeter med hyster-
***iske utfall mot kvinnelige journalister,* har vakt forundring i vide**
kretser.

That he should spend time on writing inappropriate tweets with hysterical
outbursts against female journalists has caused surprise in many circles.

Long subordinate clause in position 'F'

Various implications of the weight principle are explored in 10.7.3.1–10.7.3.6
below.

10.7.3.1 | *Free and bound adverbials*

See also 10.6.4.

Other adverbials (10.3.6.1) are sometimes classified as either 'free' or
'bound'. Free adverbials are those whose position or content is not determined by a governing verb. They can adopt various positions in the clause.
Time adverbials are generally free:

1 **Hun har mottatt prisen *i dag.*** She has received the prize today.
2 ***I dag* har hun mottatt prisen.**
3 **Hun har *i dag* mottatt prisen.**

When the free adverbial is located in position 'a', as in example 3, this is usually an indication of formal written style.

Bound adverbials form a complement to the verb and are usually found in position 'A'. Place adverbials are bound more often than time adverbials:

Akkurat nå befinner de seg *i Sydvest-Frankrike*.
At this moment, they are in south-west France.

For adverbial subordinate clauses see 10.7.2.4, 10.8.2.2, 10.10.2.1.

$\boxed{10.7.3.2}$ *Negative elements*

(a) The adverb **ikke** usually has a fixed location in the mid field in position 'a', and may on occasion also attract other clause elements to this position when these include a negative. These include objects comprising or containing **ingen, ingenting**, etc., which are found *not* as one might assume in 'N' in the end field, but in 'a' in the mid field:

Jeg hadde ingenting gjort.   I had done nothing.
F   v   (n)   a   V

This also occurs in subordinate clauses:

(Vi ble overrasket) fordi de ingen penger ville ha.
                      f   n   a   v
(We were surprised) because they did not want any money.

This order is, however, stylistically marked, and usually it indicates an old-fashioned or literary style.

(b) In unmarked sentences **ingen(ting)**, etc. is replaced by **ikke noen**, etc., (see 4.6.3.1, 4.6.6.3) with **ikke** in position 'a' and the object in 'N':

Jeg hadde   ikke gjort noe.   I hadn't done anything.   MC
F   v   (n) a   V   N   (A)

(Vi ble overrasket) fordi de ikke ville ha noen penger. SC
                 f   *n*   *a*   *v*   *V*   *N*   *(A)*
(We were surprised) because they did not want any money.

| 10.7.3.3 | *Passive transformation*

(a) For passive verb forms and usage, see 5.6.1. The transformation from active to passive is a method for moving 'light' information leftwards and 'heavy' information rightwards in the sentence (10.9.1). There are two main reasons for using the passive:

   (i) The object in the base (active) sentence is unstressed, and some other element needs to be emphasised, and/or:

  (ii) The subject in the base sentence is unknown or unimportant ('agentless passive', examples 1–3 below).

(b) In the examples of passive transformations below, italics indicate stressed words:

Active		*Passive*
1 **Noen stjeler *biler*.**	→	**Biler *stjeles*.**
Someone steals cars.		Cars are stolen.
2 **De valgte *ham*.**	→	**Han *ble valgt*.**
They elected him.		He was elected.
3 **Man har invitert oss.**	→	**Vi har blitt invitert.**
They have invited us.		We have been invited.
4 ***Henrik* slo ham.**	→	**Han ble slått av Henrik.**
Henrik hit him.		He was hit by Henrik.

In examples 1–3 an expression containing an unimportant subject becomes an agentless passive expression with emphasis on the verb. In example 4 the subject in the base is important, and for emphasis, it is moved rightwards according to the weight principle. See 10.7.3.

(c) If the object of the base sentence in 5 below (**henne**) is not to receive emphasis, but this is instead to be placed on some other element, then passive transformation moves this object leftwards to become a natural (unstressed) topic. Now the verb (**sparket**) is emphasised, or alternatively the agent (**av sjefen**) if it is present.

5 **Sjefen sparket *henne* i går.**   The boss sacked her yesterday.
    S   O

5a **Hun ble *sparket*.**   She was sacked.
     S   (*No agent*)

5b **Hun ble sparket *av sjefen* i går.**   She was sacked by the boss
                                 yesterday.
     S   Agent

(d) Of the two methods available for radically altering emphasis in the sentence, topicalisation (10.7.2, 10.9.3) is possible only for the main clause, while passive transformation is possible for both main and subordinate clause:

6a **Sjefen sparket *henne*.**   The boss sacked her.

    ***Henne* sparket sjefen.**
    Topicalisation

6b **Hun ble sparket *av sjefen*.**   She was sacked by the boss.
    Passive MC

    Ryktet sier at hun ble sparket av sjefen.
               Passive SC
    Rumour has it that she was sacked by the boss.

| 10.7.3.4 | *Existential sentences and the place holder*

See 10.3.2.1f. for types.

(a) It is usual to postpone a subject containing heavy, new information. This postponed subject is then known as the *potential subject*. An extra subject, the *formal* or 'place-holder' subject, usually **det** (10.3.2.1ff) replaces it in the 'F' position.

In English, this construction is largely only found with the verb 'to be', hence the term 'existential sentence', but in Norwegian its use extends beyond verbs of existence or non-existence to what might be called 'presentative' verbs, i.e. any intransitive verb (cf. the Norwegian term **presenteringskonstruksjon**).

TYPE B (Potential subject = Noun phrase)

Det sitter en katt i stolen.　　There's a cat sitting in the chair.
FS　　　　　PS

cf.

En katt sitter i stolen.　　A cat is sitting in the chair.
S

TYPE C (Potential subject = Infinitive phrase)

Det er vanskelig å slanke seg.　It is hard to slim.
FS　　　　　　　　PS

cf.

Å slanke seg er vanskelig.　　Slimming is hard.
S

TYPE D (Potential subject = Subordinate clause)

Det var hyggelig at du kunne komme.
FS　　　　　　　PS
It was nice that you could come.
cf.
At du kunne komme, var hyggelig.
S

(b) Position of the formal and potential subject in the main clause:

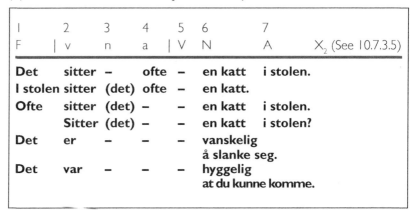

1	2	3	4	5	6		7	
F	| v	n	a	| V	N		A	X₂ (See 10.7.3.5)
Det	**sitter**	–	**ofte**	–	**en katt**		**i stolen.**	
I stolen	**sitter**	**(det)**	**ofte**	–	**en katt.**			
Ofte	**sitter**	**(det)**	–	–	**en katt**		**i stolen.**	
	Sitter	**(det)**	–	–	**en katt**		**i stolen?**	
Det	**er**	–	–	–	**vanskelig**			
					å slanke seg.			
Det	**var**	–	–	–	**hyggelig**			
					at du kunne komme.			

Translations: There's often a cat sitting in the chair; In the chair there's often a cat sitting; Often there's a cat sitting in the chair; Is there often a cat sitting in the chair?; It's hard to slim; It was nice that you could come.

10.7.3.5 Extra positions

Extra positions (X₁, X₂) are occasionally added at the beginning and end of the schema to accommodate clauses as potential subject, object clauses or free elements outside the clause.

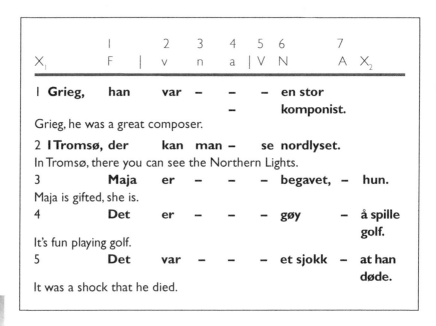

X₁	1 F	2 | v	3 n	4 a	5 | V	6 N	7 A	X₂
1 Grieg,	**han**	**var**	–	–	–	**en stor**		
						komponist.		

Grieg, he was a great composer.

2 I Tromsø, der		**kan**	**man**	–		**se nordlyset.**		

In Tromsø, there you can see the Northern Lights.

3	**Maja**	**er**	–	–	–	**begavet,**	–	**hun.**

Maja is gifted, she is.

4	**Det**	**er**	–	–	–	**gøy**	–	**å spille golf.**

It's fun playing golf.

5	**Det**	**var**	–	–	–	**et sjokk**	–	**at han døde.**

It was a shock that he died.

|10.7.3.6| *Position 'f' in main clauses*

A position 'f' – which one might call a 'conjunction field' (Nw. **forbinder-felt**) – is added before position 'F' in the main clause in order to accommodate conjunctions:

...men	**Leon,**	**han er lat, han.**	but Leon, he's lazy, he is.
f	X,	F v	

|10.7.4| *Questions*

This section deals with direct questions. For indirect questions, see 10.8.1.2. There are several different constructions.

|10.7.4.1| *Yes/no questions*

These questions are so called because they anticipate either affirmation or denial (see also 10.4.2.3). They have inversion of the finite verb and subject, and the 'F' position is usually empty.

1 F	2 v	3 n	4 a	5 V	6 N	7 A
	Reiser	**du**	–	–	–	**i morgen?**
	Solgte	**du**	**ikke**	–	**bilen?**	
	Har	**du**	**aldri**	**lest**	**Bibelen?**	
	Kan	**jeg**	–	**få se**	**fotoet?**	
I morgen,	**reiser**	**du**	–	–	–	**da?**

Translations: Are you going away tomorrow?; Didn't you sell the car?; Have you never read the Bible?; Can I see the photo?; Tomorrow, are you going away then?

| 10.7.4.2 | *Hv-questions*

The topic in this kind of question is an interrogative adverb or pronoun, most of which begin with **hv–** : **hvem**, 'who'; **hva**, 'what'; **hvor**, 'where'; **hvilken**, 'which', etc. (see 4.8) (but notice **når**, 'when') located in the 'F' position.

	1	2	3	4	5	6	7
	F	| v	n	a	| V	N	A
1	Hva	kan	du	–	se	–	der oppe?
2	Hvem	er	han?				
3	Hvor	reiser	vi	–	–	–	i sommer?
4	Når	kommer	hun	–	–	–	hjem i kveld?
5	Hvordan	kunne	de	–	gjøre	det?	

Translations: 1 What can you see up there? 2 Who is he? 3 Where are we going this summer? 4 When is she coming home tonight? 5 How could they do that?

The **hv**-question requests information about a specific clause element: in example 1 an object, 2 a subject complement, 3 an adverbial of place, 4 an adverbial of time, 5 an adverbial of manner.

| 10.7.4.3 | *Questions in statement form*

Some questions are found in statement form ('declarative' questions), when question intonation is used or a tag or tag clause is added:

Du reiser altså i morgen?	You are leaving tomorrow, then?
Du reiser ofte, gjør du ikke?	You travel often, don't you?
Det er ikke dårlig, hva?	That's not bad, eh?
Du kommer fra USA, ikke sant?	You come from the USA, don't you?
Du reiser mye, eller?	You travel a lot, don't you?

The last variant with **eller** as a tag is colloquial and mainly found in speech.

10.8 Subordinate clauses

10.8.1 Form

10.8.1.1 Conjunctional clauses

These clauses are introduced by a subordinator such as **at**, 'that'; **ettersom**, 'as'; **fordi**, 'because'; **hvis**, 'if, whether'; **når**, 'when'; **om**, 'if', etc (see 9.3.1):

Sigrid sa *at politikk er uforenlig med moral.*
Sigrid said that politics is irreconcilable with morality.

Hvis man fortsatt er sulten, **kan man bestille mer mat.**
If you are still hungry, you can order some more food.

10.8.1.2 Indirect question clauses

See also 10.7.4 for direct questions.

These clauses are introduced by:

(a) An **hv**-word:

Han visste ikke *hva han skulle tro.*
He didn't know what he was supposed to believe.

When the **hv**-word is the subject of the subordinate clause, the subject marker **som** must be added (cf. 10.8.4.2):

Han ville vite *hva som skjedde.*
He wanted to know what was happening.

(b) om (hvorvidt)

Jeg vet ikke *om (hvorvidt) vi kan fortsette.*
I don't know whether we can go on.

10.8.1.3 Relative clauses

These clauses usually occur as a postposed attribute to or are in apposition to a noun phrase, and are introduced by a subjunction or a relative adverb:

Den gutten *som kom med avisen,* **heter Jan.**
The lad who came with the paper is called Jan.

Den lille byen *hvor vi bor,* har tre kirker.
The small village where we live has three churches.

10.8.2 Function

Subordinate clauses can be classified according to their function, that is
according to the clause element they represent in the larger sentence.

10.8.2.1 Subject and object clauses

See also 10.3.1, 10.3.4.

(a) at-clauses

At du vegret, var meget klokt.	*Subject*
That you refused was very sensible.	

Jeg håper *at han vinner.*	*Object*
I am hoping that he will win.	

(b) Indirect question clauses

Det er uvisst *hvem som blir sjef.*	*Potential subject*
It is not known who will be the boss.	

Vi spurte henne *hva hun hadde tenkt å gjøre.*	*Object*
We asked her what she was considering doing.	

10.8.2.2 Adverbial clauses

These include:

(a) Temporal clauses (indicating time)

Vi får fortsette å høste *mens været er godt.*
We will have to go on harvesting while the weather holds.

Når jeg kommer hjem, bruker jeg å ta en kopp kaffe.
When I get home, I usually have a cup of coffee.

(b) Conditional clauses (indicating condition)

Hvis jeg vant i lotteriet, ville jeg kjøpe en vingård.
If I won the lottery, I would buy a vineyard.

Jeg har med melk, *i fall du glemte å kjøpe*.
I've brought milk in case you forgot to buy any.

(c) Comparative clauses (indicating comparison)

Det gikk lettere *enn vi hadde fryktet*.
It was easier than we had feared.

(d) Consecutive clauses (indicating consequence)

En mann skubbet borti ham, *slik at glasset gikk i gulvet*.
A man bumped into him so that the glass fell to the floor.

(e) Causal clauses (indicating cause)

Jeg spiller fotball *fordi det er kult*.
I play football because it's fun.

(f) Final clauses (indicating intention)

Det er bare små endringer som skal til *for at vi skal vinne*.
Only minor changes are necessary in order that we will win.

(g) Concessive clauses (indicating concession)

Hun kan ikke knytte skolissene sine, *enda hun er åtte år*.
She can't tie her own shoelaces even though she is eight years old.

| 10.8.2.3 | *Attributive clauses*

(a) Relative clauses with **som**

There are two types: restrictive and non-restrictive:

1) In a restrictive relative clause, the relative pronoun defines or modifies its antecedent in such a way that the relative clause cannot be omitted without drastically changing the meaning of the sentence:

De bileierne som allerede har betalt årsavgift, må ikke betale mer.
Those car-owners who have already paid road tax do not have to pay anything more.

2) In the non-restrictive relative clause, the relative clause provides extra information about the antecedent that may be omitted without changing the basic meaning of the sentence:

Bileierne, som for øvrig allerede betaler en årsavgift, må betale denne avgiften.

The car-owners, who incidentally already pay road tax, have to pay this charge.

(b) Relative clauses without **som**

When the relative clause relates to the subject, **som** is necessary, but in other cases it is often omitted (see 9.1.5.3f, 9.4.1.1(b), 10.8.4.2):

Compare:

Her er den boken som handler om språk.
Here is the book that is about language.
(den boken is the subject of handler om)

Har du sett den boken (som) jeg kjøpte i dag?
Have you seen the book I bought today?
(den boken is the object of kjøpte)

10.8.3 *Position of the subordinate clause in the sentence*

See also: 10.3.1.2, 10.3.4.1(a), 10.3.5.1(c), 10.4.1.2f., 10.7.2.4, 10.7.3.4).

10.8.3.1 *Subject and object clauses*

These usually occupy the 'F' or 'X_2' position.

1		2	3	4	5	6	7	
F		v	n	a	V	N	A	X_2
1 *At du er frisk,* gleder			–	–		–	**oss.**	
2 **Jeg**		**liker**	–	**ikke**	–		–	–	*at du lyver.*

1 *At du er frisk,* gleder – – – **oss.**

We are happy that you are better.

2 **Jeg** **liker** – **ikke** – – – *at du lyver.*

I don't like you telling lies.

| 10.8.3.2 | *Adverbial clauses*

(a) These clauses (temporal, conditional, causal, comparative, concessive, final) usually occupy the 'F' or 'A' position (cf. 10.8.2.2).

I		2	3	4	5	6		7	
F			v	n	a		V	N	A	X₂

Når Ida kommer, drar vi – – – **på hytta.**

When Ida arrives, we will go to the cabin.

Vi   **drar** – – – – **på hytta**
                                      når Ida kommer.

We'll go to the cabin when Ida arrives.

Hvis du oppfører

deg ordentlig,   **skal**   **du** –   **få en iskrem.**

If you behave, you can have an ice cream.

Du   **skal** – –   **få en iskrem**   **hvis du oppfører deg**
                                                ordentlig.

You can have an ice cream if you behave.

Note – It is also possible in formal written language to locate the adverbial clause in 'a'. See 10.7.3.1.

Some adverbial clauses (consecutive) usually only occupy the 'A' position:

I	2	3	4	5	6		7	
F		v	n	a		V	N	A	X₂

Han ble – – – **bankier** *så han skulle bli rik.*

He became a banker so he could get rich.

| 10.8.3.3 | *Attributive clauses*

Attributive clauses that are associated with the subject or object occupy the same position as these, i.e. 'F', 'n' or 'N':

I	2	3		4	5	6	7
F	|	v	n	a	|V	N	A X$_2$

Subject

Boken
jeg leser for tiden, **er**   –   –   –   **veldig interessant**

The book I am reading at present is very interesting.

Subject

I går   **kom** *min søster,*
              som er sykepleier.

Yesterday my sister, who is a nurse, arrived.

Object

De   **ville** –   – **se** *stedet*
                   der Ivar Aasen er født.

They wanted to see the place where Ivar Aasen was born.

10.8.4 **Subordinate clause with no indicator of subordination**

10.8.4.1 *Omission of* **at**

As in English, **at**, 'that' is often omitted after verbs of saying, thinking or perceiving:

De sa (at) de skulle komme   They said they were coming
neste uke.   next week.

Han synes (at) det er hyggelig.   He thinks it's nice.

10.8.4.2 *Omission of* **som**

(a) As in English, the subordinator **som**, 'that, which', is often omitted when it does not refer to the subject in the subclause:

Filmen (som) vi så, var kjedelig.   *Object*
The film we saw was boring.

Vi fant den skjorta (som) han lette etter. *Object*
We found the shirt he was looking for.

(b) When referring to an entire clause, **som** is often omitted (except when correlating with the subject), but the word **noe**, 'something' is then inserted:

Hun skriver krim, noe (som) publikum liker.
She writes detective stories, something the public like.

10.8.5 *Subordinate clauses with main clause order*

Subordinate clauses usually have no topic and possess subject-verb order. The order is usually subject – clausal adverbial – finite verb:

De sa at de ikke kunne komme.   They said they couldn't come.

But some subordinate clauses follow Scheme A (10.4.2). These are detailed in 10.8.5.1f below.

10.8.5.1 *at-clauses in indirect speech*

Main clause word order is found in some **at**-clauses after a verb of saying:

(a) Inversion after a non-subject following the subjunction **at**:

De sa at når de kom hjem, *skulle de* **spise middag.**
They said that when they got home they would eat dinner.

(b) The clausal adverbial follows the finite verb in the **at**-clause. This happens when the **at**-clause is reported speech and only when the matrix sentence is a positive statement.

De sa at de *kunne ikke* **komme.**   (cf. **'Vi kan ikke komme.'**)
cf. 10.8.5.

10.8.5.2 *Conditional clauses with no subordinator*

See also conditional subjunctions, 9.3.4.3.

Conditional clauses usually begin with a subordinator:

***Hvis pengene strekker til,* kan vi bygge et svømmebasseng.**
If there is enough money, we can build a swimming pool.

cf. **Vi kan bygge et svømmebasseng** *hvis* **pengene strekker til.**

Dersom du kommer, **får du middag med vin.**
If you come, you can have dinner with wine.

(a) Yes/no question word order (see 10.7.4.1):

This kind of conditional clause, which has no subordinator, but instead inverted word order and an unfilled 'F' position, usually comes at the beginning of the sentence. This type of conditional is much more frequent in Norwegian:

Hadde jeg nok penger, skulle jeg bygge et svømmebasseng.
If I had enough money, I would build a swimming pool.

Leser du bruksanvisningen nøye, vil det være lettere å sette det sammen.
If you read the instructions carefully, it will be easier to assemble it.

This construction exists in English elevated and formal style after 'had', 'were', 'should':

Were we to do so, we would be breaking the law.

'Had we but world enough and time,
This coyness, Lady, were no crime...' (Andrew Marvell)

(b) It is, however, always possible to use a subordinator such as **hvis** and normal Scheme B word order instead:

Cf.
Hvis jeg hadde nok penger,...
Hvis du leser bruksanvisningen nøye,...

10.8.7 *Main clauses with subordinate clause order*

Most main clauses follow Scheme A (10.4.2), but a few main clause sentences have Scheme B word order (10.4.3). These include three cases detailed below in 10.8.7.1ff.

10.8.7.1 *Clauses expressing a wish or exclamation*

Om de bare hadde visst!
If they just had known!

At han aldri ville hjelpe oss!
That he was never prepared to help us!

This construction is usually associated with emotional intensity.

10.8.7.2 *Clauses beginning with* **kanskje** *or* **kan hende**

Kanskje, 'perhaps' and **kan hende**, 'may be' are the remnants of verb phrases historically followed by **at: det kan skje at** and **det kan hende at.** Therefore, the sentences below may follow schema B:

Kanskje det ikke blir frost i kveld.
Perhaps there won't be frost tonight.

Kan hende vi ikke makter dette.
It may be that we won't manage this.

(Schema A is, however, also possible.)

10.8.7.3 *Echo questions*

These are a type of direct question that repeats part or all of what someone has just asked.

Question: «**Er du allerede ferdig?**» "Are you ready already?"

Echo question: «**Om jeg allerede er ferdig?**» "Am I ready already?"

10.9 Emphasis

10.9.1 *Factors determining word order*

In Norwegian, three factors determine the order of the words in the clause: the information structure, the syntactic function and the weight.

10.9.1.1 *Information structure*

The information structure of the sentence is such that it is divided into two parts, 'given' information and 'new' information. The given information is called the *theme* and the new information the *focus* (Nw. **tema** and **rema** respectively). The first element after any conjunction is the theme, while the rest is focus:

Theme	Focus
Jeg	**liker å leve i Frankrike**
I	like living in France.
Der	**kan jeg koble av.**
There	I can relax.
Det	**er bra for helsen min.**
That	is good for my health.
Derfor	**må jeg dra dit hver sommer.**
That's why	I have to go there every summer.

10.9.1.2 Syntactic function

As can be seen from the short text above, the element that forms the theme is governed by the context. The order within the focus is primarily governed by the syntactic function of the clausal elements involved (subject, object, etc.), compare:

I går slo Man U Chelsea.   Yesterday Man U beat Chelsea.
I går slo Chelsea Man U.   Yesterday Chelsea beat Man U.

10.9.1.3 Weight

Because the focus involves new information or new ideas, it is often longer and 'heavier' than the theme, so *end-weight* is natural in the sentence. See the weight principle, 10.7.3. The end of the sentence also forms a natural stress position, so we can also talk of *end-focus*.

cf.
Hun kjøpte *en ny platetopp*.   She bought a new hob.

Hun kjøpte *en ny elektrisk induksjonstopp med booster og bro-funksjon, som var ganske dyr.*
She bought a new electric induction hob with a booster and bridge function, which was rather expensive.

10.9.2 Contrastive stress in spoken language

In the spoken language, it is possible to use voice stress to emphasise any element without altering the word order:

'Neutral base' sentence:

Frida solgte hytta si i fjor sommer.
Frida sold her cottage last summer.

Stress on:

Subject   **'Frida solgte hytta si i fjor sommer.** (i.e. not Sara or. . .)

Verb   **Frida 'solgte hytta si i fjor sommer.** (i.e. did not give it away)

Object   **Frida solgte 'hytta si i fjor sommer.** (i.e. not her flat)

Adverbial **Frida solgte hytta si 'i fjor sommer.** (i.e. not this summer)

This is, of course, not possible in written Norwegian, and various strategies can be adopted in writing in order to provide an unequivocal marking of elements, such as fronting (10.9.3), raising (10.9.4), duplication (10.9.5) or the cleft sentence (10.3.2.4).

10.9.3 Fronting

As we have seen above, the front position 'F' usually, but not always, contains given information (10.9.1). It is in this context practical to think of topics (elements in 'F') as being of two kinds.

10.9.3.1 Natural topics

(a) The subject is the element most commonly found in 'F', and usually comprises a definite noun phrase, name or pronoun:

Læreren/Eva/Hun kom inn i forelesningssalen.
The teacher/Eva/She came into the lecture room.

This is regarded as an unmarked or base clause (10.7.1).

(b) When adverbials of time or place come in 'F', they often provide a
background or jumping-off point for the content of the sentence:

I neste uke **reiser jeg til Tyskland.** *Next week* I'm going to Germany.
I Berlin **skal jeg treffe Tobi.** *In Berlin,* I'm meeting Tobi.

(c) 'New' elements may occupy 'F' if they have a logical relation to what
has gone before:

Bilen kan ikke godkjennes. *Et frontlys* **er ødelagt.**
The car cannot pass its test. One headlight is broken.

It is clear that the headlight belongs to the car.

10.9.3.2 *Emphatic topics*

See also 10.7.2.1ff.

The 'F' position is, less frequently, used to add extra emphasis (marked ')
to an element already 'heavy' in information. Emphatic topics may include
the object, a verb phrase, infinitive phrase or negation. This kind of topicalisation is rare in English, but is considerably more frequent in Norwegian.

'*Vin* drikker hun, men *øl* kan hun ikke fordra.
She drinks wine, but beer she cannot stand.

'*Lære noe* gjør jeg hver dag. I learn something every day.
'*Jage etter jenter* gjør han stadig. He's always running after girls.
'*Aldri* har jeg sett maken. I have never seen the like.

10.9.4 *Raising*

10.9.4.1

Raising (often resulting in what Norwegians call **setningsknute**) is the term
used when an element in a subordinate clause is fronted in the matrix, thus
'raising' it to a higher level:

Jeg synes ikke	(at) *den filmen* var så vellykket.	**10** Sentence structure and word order

Matrix   *subject in the subordinate clause*

I don't think   that film was so successful.

cf.

Den filmen synes jeg ikke var så vellykket.

Topic in the main clause

That film I don't think was so successful.

10.9.4.2

Frequent kinds of raising are:

(a) Where an element is raised from a relative clause

Vi hadde en katt som het *Smilla*.   We had a cat called Smilla.

cf.

Smilla hadde vi en katt som het.

(raised subject complement in subclause)

(b) Where the verb in the matrix is a reporting verb, e.g. **si**, 'say'; **mene**, 'think'; **høre**, 'hear':

Jeg vil ikke si at de er *dyre*.   I wouldn't say they are

cf.   expensive.

Dyre *vil jeg ikke si (at) de er*.

(raised subject complement in subclause)

Jeg tror ikke at Shakespeare skrev *det dramaet*.

I don't believe Shakespeare wrote that drama.

cf.

Det dramaet tror jeg ikke (at) Shakespeare skrev.

(raised object in subclause)

Jeg regner med at vi har arbeidet ferdig *i neste uke*.

I expect we will have the work completed next week.

cf.

***I neste uke* regner jeg med at vi har arbeidet ferdig.**
(raised adverbial in subclause)

10.9.5 Duplication

See also extra positions, 10.7.3.5.

10.9.5.1 Duplication at the front

The theme in the 'F' position can be moved leftwards to the 'X₁' position and at the same time be represented in 'F' by a 'pro-word'. This is often a personal (subject or object) pronoun or an adverb like **så, da** or **der**:

Amundsen, han kom først til polen.	*Subject*
Amundsen, he arrived at the pole first.	*duplicated*
Sigrid Undset, henne gav de Nobelprisen i 1928.	*Object duplicated*
Sigrid Undset, they gave her the Nobel Prize in 1928.	
Forsiktig med penger, det var han ikke.	*Complement*
	duplicated
Careful with money he was not.	
***I Paris*, der vil jeg tilbringe påsken.**	*Adverbial*
	duplicated
In Paris, that's where I want to spend Easter.	
***I fjor*, så/da var vi i Sverige.**	*Adverbial*
	duplicated
Last year, then we were in Sweden.	

Although duplication is more characteristic of the spoken language, it does occur in written texts, especially when the element in 'X₁' is an adverbial clause:

Hvis det som skjedde onsdag, er opplegget for videre aksjoner, så mener vi det er å gå over streken.
If what happened on Wednesday is standard foretaste of future actions, then we think that this is going too far.

10.9.5.2 Duplication at the end

In the 'X₂' position one finds elements that are also represented inside the clause. The element in the extra position duplicates the sense of the one inside the clause, usually a pronoun, pro-word or adverb.

(a) The element inside the clause is often:

(i)   The subject

Maja er ikke frisk, *hun*.
Maja is not well (, she [isn't]).

(ii) A noun phrase that is not the subject

De arbeidsløse er det synd på, *de*.
The unemployed are to be pitied (they [are]).

(iii) An adverbial expression of time or place

På universitetet var det fint, *der*.
At the university (there) it was great.

(iv) An adverbial expression of degree, in practice most often så

Det var så spennende, *så*.
It was so exciting(, it was).

10.10 Ellipsis

10.10.1 Clauses with no subject or no finite verb

A clause usually contains both a subject and a finite verb. But there are some exceptions to this pattern.

10.10.1.1 Commands

See also 5.4.4.

These are usually found with the imperative form of the verb and have an implicit subject in the second person:

Spis (du) smørbrødet ditt nå!   Eat up your sandwich now!

Note 1 – The subject is occasionally explicit and then follows the finite verb:

Kjør du! You drive!

Note 2 – The negative can precede or follow the finite verb.

Ikke gjør dette hjemme! Don't do this at home!
Tro ikke at kjærlighet varer. Don't think that love lasts.
(H. Wildenvey)

| 10.10.1.2 | *Verb deletion and subject deletion*

(a) In coordinated phrases and clauses (9.1.2) linked by **og**, 'and'; **men**, 'but' or **eller**, 'or', either the subject or the finite verb can be omitted if it is identical in both cases:

Han kom fram til oss og (han) skrek. *Subject deleted*

He came up to us and (he) shouted.

Aksel spiser oksekjøtt og Emma (spiser) fisk. *Finite verb deleted*

Aksel is eating beef and Emma (is eating) fish.

(b) When the verb and object, complement or adverbial are identical, both elements can be omitted:

Han skal ta seg en kaffepause nå og hun *Finite verb and*
(skal ta seg en kaffepause) om en time. *object deleted*
He'll take a coffee break now and she ('ll take a coffee break) in an hour.

(c) In relative clauses, the subject may (as in English) be left out if it is identical with the main clause correlate of **som**:

Her er jenta som vant kampen.
Here is the girl that won the match.

Her er bilen jenta vant.
Here is the car the girl won.

10.10.2 | Non-finite clauses

In the example following, a preposition is followed by a finite subordinate clause:

Vi fikk beskjed om *at vi måtte betale 1000 kroner.*
We were told that we had to pay 1000 kroner.

But, in this case the finite verb (and here the subject) may be omitted if the subject is the same in both clauses. Then, an infinitive with å replaces them:

Vi fikk beskjed om *å betale 1000 kroner.*
We were told to pay 1000 kroner.

Clauses lacking a finite verb are of several different kinds, see 10.10.2.1ff.

10.10.2.1 | Ellipted adverbial clause

(a) Replacement of a finite verb with an infinitive may occur after a preposition in a number of adverbial clauses, for example:

Han var flere ganger alene med keeper *uten å score.*
He was alone with the goalkeeper several times without scoring.

Vi tar betalt *for å bringe* varene hjem til folk.
We charge for home delivery.

(b) This also occurs in some comparative clauses, for example:

Det er bedre *enn å slenge* rundt uten arbeide.
It is better than hanging about without any work.

Det er fortsatt tryggere å fly *enn å kjøre* bil.
It is still safer to fly than to drive.

10.10.2.2 | Object and infinitive constructions

(a) These constructions are found after verbs of perception such as **be**, 'ask'; **høre**, 'hear'; **kjenne**, 'feel'; **late**, 'allow'; **se**, 'see'. There is usually no infinitive marker å.

The noun phrase preceding the infinitive has a double function, both as object of the verb in the matrix and as the logical or implied subject of the infinitive:

Jeg så *ham* falle.   cf.   **Jeg så at han falt.**
I saw him fall.   I saw that he fell.

Other examples:

Redningmannskapene hørte *henne* rope på hjelp.
The rescue teams heard her cry for help.
cf.
Redningmannskapene hørte *at hun* ropte på hjelp.

Jeg bad *dem* bli til middag.   I asked them to stay for dinner.
Hun lot *meg* snakke videre.   She allowed me to go on talking.

(b) In the case of the verbs **forby**, 'forbid' and **tillate**, 'allow', the infinitive has the infinitive marker **å**:

Klubben tillater publikum å se på treningene.
The club allows the public to watch the training sessions.

| 10.10.2.3 | *Subject and infinitive constructions*

We may regard this as a development of the object + infinitive construction above (in an active sentence) in which the 'object' then becomes the subject of a passive verb. Compare the following:

I Vi ber om at *skoleelever* holder seg hjemme.   *Subordinate clause*
        subject
We are asking that schoolchildren stay at home.

2 Vi ber skoleelever holde seg hjemme.   *Object + infinitive*
        object
We are asking schoolchildren to stay at home.

3 *Skoleeelever* bes holde seg hjemme.   *Subject + infinitive*
    subject
Schoolchildren are being asked to stay at home.

| 10.10.2.4 | *Word order in non-finite clauses*

(a) Position within subordinate clauses and elliptical constructions

Matrix |	f |	n	a	v |	V	N	A
1a De ble							
løslatt	**etter**	–	–	–	**å ha legitimert seg.**		
1b	**Etter**						
	at	**de**	–	**hadde**	**legitimert seg,**	**(ble de**	
						løslatt.)	
1c	**Etter**	–	–	–	**å ha**		
					legitimert seg	**(ble de**	
						løslatt).	
2a Vi så	**at**	**han**	–	**reiste**	–	–	**bort.**
2b Vi så	–	–	–	–	**ham**		
					reise bort.		

Translations: 1a They were released after having identified themselves, 1b, c After having identified themselves, they were released, 2a We saw that he went away, 2b We saw him go away.

(b) Position of the non-finite clause in the sentence

F	|	v	n	a|	V	N	A X$_2$
1a De		**ble**	–	–	–	**løslatt**	**etter å ha**
							legitimert seg.
1b Etter å ha							
legitimert seg		**ble**	**de**	–	–	**løslatt.**	
2 Vi		**så**	–	–	–	**ham**	
						reise bort.	

Translations: 1a They were released after having identified themselves, 1b After having identified
themselves, they were released, 2 We saw him go away.

Chapter 11

Word formation

11.1 Introduction

11.1.1 Words, old and new

11.1.1.1

Word-formation deals with 'complex words', e.g. **saueull** 'sheep's wool'; **brukbar** 'useful'. Simplex words, such as **gutt**, 'boy'; **på**, 'on' and **hvit**, 'white' are outside the purview of word-formation. Inflection, such as we find in **gutter**, 'boys' and **hvite**, 'white', plural, is also outside the purview of word formation.

11.1.1.2

We may distinguish between existing words and new words. Existing Norwegian words include, for example, **tre**, 'tree'; **båt**, 'boat'; **synge**, 'sing' and **leve**, 'live'. These examples may be recognisable to the English reader, and they are of Indo-European origin, common to English and Norwegian. However, other Norwegian words are not recognisable in the same way, e.g. **språk**, 'language'; **snakke**, 'speak', and **slange**, 'snake'. These do not go back to Indo-European; they are borrowings from (Low) German. A large proportion of the Norwegian vocabulary consists of borrowings from (Low) German. This has to do with Norwegian history; the Hanseatic League was very important throughout Scandinavia for several hundred years. English has a larger share of loans from French than does Norwegian, and this has to do with English history (the Norman Conquest), so many English words seem alien to a Norwegian, such as 'adore', 'admire', 'adroit'. While German (Low or High) stands out as the most important source of loanwords ever in Norwegian, there are also loans from other languages. Compare e.g. **gutt**, 'boy', perhaps from Dutch; **sjenert**, 'shy', from French; **drosje**, 'taxi' from Russian, and **alkohol**, 'alcohol' from Arabic. In recent years, English has been *the* donor language (see also 11.4.8.2ff.), witness fairly recent words such as **sjekke**, 'check', from English 'check', **kjip** (colloq.), 'unpleasant', 'mean', from English 'cheap' and **seive**, 'save data on a computer'.

Note – Often, English loanwords acquire a more 'specialised' or slightly different meaning in Norwegian. For example, while Norwegians can **seive** on their computer, they will still **spare**, 'save in a bank'; while, colloquially, people can be called **kjip**, 'mean', 'unpleasant', things cannot be called **kjip** to indicate that they are of low price. Since Norwegian already had the useful and familiar word **spare**, for instance, there would have been little point in replacing it to denote the familiar action of saving money in the bank. Saving data on the computer, however, may have been perceived as a new thing – and a new term may have seemed useful.

11.1.2 | *Compounding and derivation*

11.1.2.1

There are two main ways of forming words in Norwegian, viz. *compounding* and *derivation*. These are the two main branches of word formation, i.e. the processes by which new words are formed – and by which existing complex words are motivated. Simplified, compounding involves creating a (new) word by 'putting two words together', while in derivation one word is combined with an *affix*, an element that is less than a word, a non-word element.

An example of compounding is **kenguru|genser**, 'kangaroo sweater', formed by putting together the two words **kenguru** and **sweater**. An example of derivation is **spise|lig**, 'edible', formed by combining the word **spise**, 'eat' (more technically, the verb stem **spis–**, cf. below) and the non-word **–lig**.

Note 1 – In this chapter, we use | to indicate the juncture between parts of words. This is, of course, not part of Norwegian orthography.

Note 2 – It is not always easy to distinguish derivation from compounding.

11.1.2.2

It may be debated whether it is really words that are being combined to produce new words. Many linguists would argue that the first element in

Norwegian **spise|lig**, 'edible, palatable', for instance, is not the verb, but the verb stem, that part of the verb that is common to all its inflectional forms. Compare the adjective **spis|bar**, 'edible', which clearly contains this stem and not the entire infinitive (as in *__spise|bar__). In this book, we shall often say that two words are put together, but the reader should bear in mind that it might be two stems.

11.1.2.3

Like English, Norwegian contains much compounding. In English, compounds are often written as two words, e.g. 'arms race', 'drugs dealer', but the rules are not always clear, cf. 'taxpayer', 'blackboard', or even the hyphenated 'well-being' and 'on-site'. The rule in Norwegian is quite clear; compounds should be written as one word: **våpen|kapp|løp**, 'arms race'; **narkotika|handler**, 'drug dealer'; **skatte|betaler**, 'taxpayer'.

Compounding may be an even more productive aspect of Norwegian word-formation than is derivation; at least, many learners find compounding more striking. Compounding is dealt with in 11.2, derivation in 11.3. Section 11.4 deals with some lesser used ways of forming new words, and with loans.

11.1.3 | *Productive and non-productive patterns*

11.1.3.1

The fact that there are regular patterns in word-formation is helpful both when speakers wish to coin new words and when they try to infer the meaning of existing words. The example **kenguru|genser**, 'kangaroo sweater' above may not have been heard by a native before, while the example **spise|lig**, 'edible', certainly has. In both cases, however, there may be similar words elsewhere in the vocabulary, e.g. **Donald|slips**, 'Donald tie'; **elske|lig**, 'loveable', respectively, and by means of these, we may understand both **kenguru|skjorte** and **spise|lig**, if they are new to us.

11.1.3.2

Some words have been coined by means of a pattern no longer in use. For example, many agent noun formations referring specifically to females are obsolete today. Cf. Nouns, 1.3.4.2f., and 11.3.1.3 below. The wife of an oberst, 'colonel' is no longer called an oberst|inne, 'colonel's wife', and the younger generation will prefer lærer, 'teacher' to lærer|inne, 'female school-teacher', irrespective of 'real-life gender'. However, witness the still current venn|inne, 'female friend', cf. venn, 'friend'; elsker|inne, 'female lover', cf. elsker, 'lover'. If somebody were to encounter the word landsmann|inne and already knows the word landsmann, 'compatriot', they are – by means of the similarity with elskerinne, venninne – able to guess the meaning of landsmanninne.

11.1.3.3

A pattern such as that of adding –inne to a noun is no longer in use to coin new words. We call such patterns *unproductive*. By contrast, patterns that are used to coin new words are referred to as *productive*. An example is derivation by means of –bar; this suffix may be added to transitive verbs (or rather stems, cf. 11.1.2.2), in order to coin new words: digg|bar, 'enjoyable' cf. digge, 'enjoy'; bær|bar, 'portable; laptop computer', cf. bære, 'carry'; spis|bar, 'edible', cf. spise, 'eat'. The distinction between productive and unproductive is not always straightforward.

11.1.4 *Lexicalisation*

Both compounds and derivations may be *lexicalised*, for example when the meaning of a word is not transparent from the elements brought together to compose it. Thus, the compound grønn|saker, 'vegetables' consists of the parts grønn, 'green' and saker, 'things', but many green things do not qualify as grønnsaker. The derivation barns|lig contains the noun barn 'child' and the suffix –lig, but it is not self-evident that the adjective should mean 'childish' rather than 'child-like'. The term lexicalised is also used about cases where the 'parts' are not recognisable from elsewhere, such as the derivative deilig, 'lovely; delicious' or the compound pult|ost, 'sour milk cheese flavoured with caraway seeds'. Deilig resembles other derivations in –lig, such as venn|lig from venn, hus|lig from hus – but there is no noun *dei. Pultost clearly resembles other compounds with ost 'cheese' as their second part, such as brun|ost, 'brown cheese', gul|ost, 'yellow cheese', but there is no relevant related noun pult. In practice, the difference between lexicalised and transparent (analysable) can be very tricky. See also 11.2.1.3 below.

11.2 Compounding

11.2.1 Introduction

11.2.1.1 A common technique

(a) There are many examples in Norwegian where, simplified, one word is formed from two or more words. Compare **skole|jente**, 'school girl' and **blå|gul** *lit.* 'blue-yellow', i.e. 'Swedish', which may be said to be formed from **skole**, 'school' and **jente**, 'girl' and **blå**, 'blue', **gul**, 'yellow' respectively. Words from many word-classes may be combined to create compounds; **skolejente** is related to two nouns, **blågul** to two adjectives. Cf. further 11.2.2.1–14 below. A common pattern of compounding is that of noun + noun, as in **skolejente** (cf. 11.2.2.1). This pattern is productive (11.1.3.1), witness the relatively new formations **tennis|albue**, 'tennis elbow' and **tuja|krangel**, 'thuja quarrel; quarrel over a Thuja tree'. The combination of two adjectives, as in **blågul**, is not equally common. (This difference may partly reflect the fact that nouns are by far the most numerous word-class.)

(b) Also in English, compounding (especially of noun + noun) is a very common method of word-formation. Notice, however, that Norwegian compounds are written as one word (11.1.2.3), cf. **krim|serie**, **taxi|sjåfør** vs. English 'crime series (on TV)', 'taxi driver'. So, from an Anglophone perspective, some Norwegian compounds look long; **sammen|set|nings|konferanse|middags|deltaker**, 'compound conference dinner participant' is a constructed example.

(c) Compounds may be formed from or related to more than two parts. These parts may in turn consist of parts, as illustrated by **sammensetningskonferansemiddagsdeltaker**, cf. **sammensetning**, 'compound', **konferanse**, 'conference', **middag**, 'dinner' and **deltaker**, 'participant'. Normally, we can divide larger compounds into two at first. Thus, **stor|vilt|jakt**, 'big game hunt/ing' is related to the two nouns **stor|vilt**, 'big game' and **jakt**, 'hunt'; **stor|vilt** is in turn related to the adjective **stor**, 'big' and the noun **vilt**, 'game'. **elefant|kirke|gård**, 'elephant churchyard' relates to **elefant**, 'elephant' and **kirkegård**, 'churchyard'; **kirke|gård** is in turn related to both **kirke**, 'church' and **gård**, 'yard'.

11.2.1.2 Determinative compounds – and those that are not

(a) Compounds (in particular noun + noun) are often 'determinative', in Norwegian as in English; the last 'element' of the compound is often central to both its meaning and its grammatical properties – word-class and inflection class. The first element will tell us what kind of subgroup of the second element is meant. For example, **skolejente**, 'school girl' is a kind of girl and not a kind of school. Furthermore, **skolejente** is not any kind of girl, but a girl with a relation to school. **helse|studio**, 'health studio' is a kind of **studio**, and not a kind of **helse**, 'health'; it is a **studio** that relates to **helse**, 'health'. A **musikk|studio**, 'music studio' is also a kind of **studio**, one that relates to **musikk**, 'music'. Similarly, **helsestudio** is a neuter gender noun like **studio**, but unlike **helse** (which is of feminine [common] gender). **Geografi|bok**, 'geography text book' is a kind of **bok**, not a kind of **geografi**, and its plural will be **geografibøker**, i.e. **geografibok** inflects in the same way as **bok**, 'book' (**bøker**) and not as **geografi**.

(b) However, many compounds are not so clearly determinative – or even clearly not determinative. For example, **blå|gul**, 'blue-yellow' is not a kind of yellow; it will normally mean 'blue *and* yellow' or 'Swedish' (because of the colours of the Swedish flag).

| 11.2.1.3 | *Meaning of compounds: lexicalisation* |

(a) The meaning of a compound is normally related to that of its elements. As many compounds are determinative (11.2.1.2), the meaning of **kjemi|time**, 'chemistry lesson' is no surprise, given the meaning of **kjemi**, 'chemistry' and **time**, 'hour, school lesson'. Similarly, the meaning of **synge|dame**, 'female singer' may seem to follow logically from that of **synge**, 'sing' and **dame**, 'lady', 'woman'. However, compounds are words; the meaning of (simplex) words is something we have to learn, and the meaning of compounds does not necessarily follow automatically, either. While there is nothing derogatory about the words **synge** and **dame**, the compound **syngedame** is perceived as being derogatory. The compound **kenguru|genser**, 'kangaroo sweater' would probably in isolation be understood as a sweater decorated with small kangaroo figures, but it could be a sweater designed for or used by a kangaroo, the way that **herre|skjorte**, 'gentleman's shirt' means a shirt designed for or used by men – or it could mean a sweater used when handling kangaroos, the way that **ski|genser** can mean a sweater used when skiing.

(b) While many compounds have an element of predictability in their meaning, many also have an element of unpredictability. **blå|bær**, 'blueberry' clearly relates to **blå**, 'blue' and **bær**, 'berry', but **blåbær** does not mean any blue berry, such as crowberry or boysenberry, but only blueberry/bilberry. (Compare English.) Often, the term 'lexicalised' (see 11.1.4, 11.2.1.3) is used to refer to compounds whose meaning is less predictable, such as **blåbær**. In practice, the difference between lexicalised and non-lexicalised compounds can be tricky.

11.2.1.4 Word knowledge and world knowledge

(a) In order to guess the meaning of a compound, speakers have to come up with a reasonable interpretation, involving not only their knowledge of grammar, but also their knowledge of the world. Consider e.g. **heste|kjerre**; given that **hest** means 'horse' and **kjerre** means 'cart', speakers may guess that a **hestekjerre** is a cart pulled by horses, cf. English 'horse-cart'. From a grammatical perspective, the compound **fiske|båt** looks very similar to **hestekjerre** (noun + link –e–, cf. 11.2.3, + noun). Given that **fisk** means 'fish' and **båt** means 'boat', one possible interpretation might have been 'boat pulled by fish' but, given our knowledge of fish, this is less likely; it means 'fishing-boat'.

(b) In a number of cases, the reason why a compound exists at all has to do with societal factors (as is the case for other words). Thus, **vill|svin**, 'wild boar' tells us that we have to do with the kind of pigs that are wild – in contrast to normal domestic pigs. It is presumably no accident that there is no noun *vill|ulv, 'wild wolf' or *vill|elg, 'wild elk' – the norm for wolves and elk is to be wild. The fairly recent compound **vil|laks**, 'wild salmon' was coined when it became common to breed salmon commercially. Only then was the word **villaks** perceived as being useful.

(c) If the first part of a compound is related to a noun, the second part to a transitive verb, then the relation between the second and the first part of the compound may resemble that between a transitive verb and its object. Examples include **fugle|fanger**, 'bird-catcher'; **bok|føring**, 'book keeping' which may be compared to **fanger fugler**, 'catches birds' and **fører bøker**, 'keeps books' respectively. If the second part of the compound is related to an intransitive verb, the relation between the second and the first part may resemble that between an intransitive verb and its subject. Examples include **gutte|bryting**, 'boys wrestling' and **par|dans**, 'partner dance', cf. **gutter bryter**, 'boys wrestle' and **par danser**, 'couples dance' respectively. However, these are tendencies only.

11.2.2 Different combinations

We shall now look at a number of different types of compounds.

Noun + noun

skole|gutt, schoolboy	cf. **skole**, school and **gutt**, boy
jakt|hund, hunting dog	cf. **jakt**, hunt and **hund**, dog
nakke|skade, neck injury	cf. **nakke**, neck and **skade**, injury
bil|eier, car owner	cf. **bil**, car and **eier**, owner
skog|s|vei, forest road	cf. **skog**, forest and **vei**, road
geit|e|bonde, goat farmer	cf. **geit**, goat and **bonde**, farmer

This is a very frequent and productive pattern. Noun + noun compounds often contain a linking element, a 'link', such as the –s– in **skogsvei** or the –e– in **geitebonde**. Cf 11.2.3 below. Proper nouns may serve as first 'element'; the compound may either be well established or a 'temporary compound' formed for the occasion:

Bergen\|s\|banen 'the railway line to Bergen' cf. **Bergen** and **bane** 'railway line'
Midsomer-seer 'person who watches Midsomer Murders' (TV programme) cf. **Midsomer** and **seer**, 'viewer'

In writing, temporary ('on the spot') formations (such as **Midsomer-seer**) more often contain a hyphen. If they become more common, the hyphen is less used (see 12.3.4.2).

Often, the elements of a noun + noun compound may themselves be compounds, cf. 11.2.1.1(c). On the meaning of noun + noun compounds, cf. 11.2.1.

Adjective + noun

grå\|spurv, house sparrow (*lit.* grey sparrow)
cf. **grå**, grey and **spurv**, sparrow

halv\|liter, half a litre
cf. **halv**, half and **liter**, litre

gammal\|ost, *lit.* old cheese, Norwegian cheese
cf. **gammal/gammel**, old and **ost**, cheese

| 11.2.2.3 | *Verb + noun* |

sitte|stilling, sitting posture   cf. **sitte**, sit and **stilling**, posture
danse|skole, dance school   cf. **danse**, dance and **skole**, school
leke|plass, playground   cf. **leke**, play and **plass**, place
lene|stol, reclining chair   cf. **lene**, lean, recline and **stol**, chair

This pattern is fairly common. The second element can denote a location for the activity denoted by the first element, or a way of carrying out the activity denoted by the first element, for instance.

| 11.2.2.4 | *Adverb + noun* |

nå|tid, present   cf. **nå**, now and **tid**, time
ute|time, school lesson outdoors   cf. **ute**, out and **time**, hour, lesson
hjemme|sitter, *lit.* home sitter,   cf. **hjemme**, at home and
i.e. non-voter   **sitter**, sitter

It can be difficult to distinguish adverbs from prepositions (cf. 6.1.2.2, 7.2.1).

| 11.2.2.5 | *Pronoun + noun* |

selv|respekt, self-esteem   cf. **selv**, self and **respekt**, respect
hun|kjønn, feminine   cf. **hun**, she and **kjønn**, sex, gender

This pattern is not found in very many words.

| 11.2.2.6 | *Noun + verb* |

skam|slå, beat up   cf. **skam**, shame and **slå**, beat
ovn|s|bake, bake in the oven   cf. **ovn**, oven and **bake**, bake
grunn|gi, substantiate, give reason for   cf. **grunn**, reason, ground and **gi,** give

This pattern is found in a number of words, also new ones. Often, the noun in these compounds plays a role comparable to the object of the verb (**grunngi**) cf. 11.2.1.4(c).

| 11.2.2.7 | Adverb + verb |

sammen|fatte, summarise   cf. **sammen**, together and **fatte**, formulate
ute|stenge, exclude, shut out   cf. **ute**, out and **stenge**, close
fram|gang, progress   cf. **fram**, forwards and **gang**, going

| 11.2.2.8 | Adjective + Adjective |

grå|grønn, grey green   cf. **grå**, grey and **grønn**, green
små|sjuk, a bit under the weather   cf. **små**, little and **sjuk,** ill
halv|gal, half-crazy   cf. **halv**, half and **gal**, crazy

Under this heading, we may also include compounds that have a participle as a second element, since participles in many ways resemble adjectives cf. 5.2.1.1(f),(g):

ny|klippet, newly cut   cf. **ny**, new and **klippe**, cut
syk|e|meldt, reported in sick   cf. **syk**, ill and **melde**, report
tynt|flytende, thin, liquid   cf. **tynn**, thin and **flyte**, flow,
                                          cf. also **flyte tynt**
hardt|slående, hitting forcefully; striking   cf. **hard**, hard and **slå**, hit

In such cases, there can be a 'link', cf. 11.2.3 below, as in syk**e**meldt. If the adjective is followed by a present participle, as in tyn**t**flytende, the adjective is usually in the neuter.

| 11.2.2.9 | Verb + Verb |

fryse|tørre, freeze dry   cf. **fryse**, freeze and **tørre**, dry
trøste|spise, eat as   cf. **trøste**, comfort, console and **spise**, eat
consolation

This type is less frequent.

| 11.2.2.10 | Adjective + verb |

svart|male, paint a gloomy picture   cf. **svart**, black and **male**, paint
fri|gjøre, liberate   cf. **fri**, free and **gjøre**, make
fin|pusse, polish, perfect   cf. **fin**, fine and **pusse**, brush, polish

| 11.2.2.11 | Noun + adjective |

mat|glad, fond of food   cf. **mat**, food and **glad**, fond of
gryte|klar, ready to cook   cf. **gryte**, casserole and **klar**, ready
kull|svart, pitch black   cf. **kull**, coal and **svart**, black
tanke|full, pensive, thoughtful   cf. **tanke**, thought and **full**, full

This pattern is found with a rather large number of adjectives, old and new.

| 11.2.2.12 | Preposition + adjective |

over|ivrig, excessively eager   cf. **over**, over and **ivrig**, eager
bak|full, hung-over   cf. **bak**, back and **full**, drunk

| 11.2.2.13 | Verb + adjective |

snakke|salig, chatty   cf. **snakke**, chat and **salig**, happy
danse|glad, fond of dancing   cf. **danse**, dance and **glad**, fond of

| 11.2.2.14 | Preposition + verb |

under|bygge, substantiate   cf. **under**, under and **bygge**, build
ned|legge, kill, close down   cf. **ned**, down and **legge**, lay
av|gjøre, decide   cf. **av**, off and **gjøre**, do

This type is quite frequent. There are basically two different kinds of preposition + verb combinations, referred to as inseparable vs. separable verbs (or 'faste og løse sammensetninger'), cf. 5.7. Compare the following examples:

Du må underbygge påstandene dine. vs. ***Du må bygge under dine påstander.**
You must substantiate your claims.

***Du må innkoke kraften.** vs. **Du må koke inn kraften.**
You must reduce the broth.

underbygge is a so-called inseparable compound; the preposition cannot be separated from the verb. By contrast, **koke inn** will typically not behave as one word. (See 5.7.)

| 11.2.2.15 | *Preposition + noun*

inn|tog, entry   cf. **inn**, in and **tog**, act of marching
ut|gang, exit   cf. **ut**, out and **gang**, progress

This is a fairly common pattern. It is not always easy to distinguish this from adverb + noun.

| 11.2.2.16 | *Preposition + preposition*

Norwegian has a number of examples where a compounded preposition relates to two simplex ones:

innenfor, within   cf. **innen**, inside of and **for**, for
bakfra, from behind   cf. **bak**, behind and **fra**, from
innved, close to   cf. **inn**, in and **ved**, by, near

It is not always easy to deduce the meaning of the compound from the simplexes (cf. **innenfor**), but in a number of cases, one can (cf. **bakfra**).

See also 7.4.1.

| 11.2.2.17 | *Complexes inside compounds*

So far, we have looked at compounds that consist of two simplexes. However, nothing prevents either element from being complex (cf. 11.2.1.1 (c)):

kjøkken|inngang, kitchen entrance cf. **kjøkken**, kitchen and
inn|gang, entrance
(last element is a compound)

danseskole|lærer, dancing school teacher cf. **danse|skole**, dancing
school and **lærer**, teacher
(first element is a compound, second element a derivative of the
verb **lære**)

barnetime|hørespill, children's hour radio play cf. **barne|time**, children's hour (radio programme until 2010) and **høre|spill**, radio play
(both elements are compounds)

skytter|lag, marksmen's team
(first element is a derivative of the verb **skyte**)

nyhets|s|tjeneste, news service (first and second elements are both derivatives from **ny|het** and the verb **tjene**)

<h2>11.2.2.18   *Others*</h2>

In addition to the types outlined above, there are many words that look like compounds, but deviate from the patterns outlined so far. For example, there are words that look like noun + noun compounds, but do not relate to two independent words, e.g. **bom|ull**, 'cotton'. **bomull** is not usually considered a kind of **ull**, 'wool', and it does not relate to a noun **bom**, either. Compounds like these are clearly lexicalised (see also 11.1.4).

<h2>11.2.3   *Links*</h2>

<h3>11.2.3.1</h3>

Many compounds relate to two words; cf. **båt|hus**, 'boat house' and **hus|båt**, 'house boat', both relating to **båt** and **hus**. However, many other compound nouns not only contain the two words (or stems, 11.1.2.2) the compound is related to, but also an additional element smaller than a word. Compare **bruk|s|hund**, 'working dog' **geit|e|bonde**, 'goat farmer'. Apart from the two words **bruk**, 'use' and **hund**, 'dog', **brukshund** contains an –s–; apart from the nouns **geit**, 'goat' and **bonde**, 'farmer', the noun **geitebonde** also contains an additional –e–.

<h3>11.2.3.2</h3>

We shall call such elements as –s–, –e– 'links'. As noted, many compounds do not contain a link; cf. **bord|bein**, 'table leg' (compare **bord**, 'table' and **bein**, 'leg'), **regn|vær**, 'rainy weather' (compare **regn**, 'rain' and **vær**, 'weather'). If a compound contains a link, then –s– is by far the most frequent one. Compare **skip|s|hund**, 'ship's dog', which is related to **skip** and **hund**; **gard|s|gutt**, 'farm boy', which is related to **gard** and **gutt**. However, there are also some compounds where the link is –e–. Compare **gutt|e|lag**, 'boys team', related to **gutt**, 'boy' and **lag**, 'team'; **hund|e|elsker**, 'dog lover', related to **hund**, 'dog' and **elsker**, 'lover'.

11.2.3.3

In some few cases, a compound contains a rare link, such as in **rose|n|knopp**, 'rosebud', where an –n– is found. Compare also **berlin|er|bolle** lit. 'Berlin bun' vs. **Berlin** and **bolle** 'bun', where the link –er– is historically a loan from German; cf. the more 'normal' **Berlin-avtalen**, 'the Berlin treaty'. (The first element can even, very rarely, occur in a form otherwise unknown – cf. **vass|hjul**, 'water wheel' vs. **vann** and **hjul**.)

11.2.3.4

The link –s– occurs mainly after nouns forming the first element of compounds. It is rare after other word classes (though found after some adjectives). It can be difficult to know which compounds take links and which do not. Here are some rules of thumb:

1) Links are unusual outside noun + noun compounds.
2) Links are rare if the first element ends in a vowel, even more so if that vowel is stressed, and after **n–, sj–, s–, st–, t–, er–**.
3) It is more likely that a compound – especially a new one – does not contain a link.
4) If we know that the compound does contain a link, it is more likely that it contains –s– rather than –e– (not to mention the other candidates); –s– is by far the most common link.
5) If a particular first element selects a particular link in one compound, it probably does so in all. Let us suppose that we have encountered the compound **bruk|s|hund**, 'working dog' before, and that we are now uncertain whether there should be a link when we combine **bruk** 'use' with **måte**, 'way, approach'. Given that **bruk** takes the link –s– in **brukshund**, **bruk|s|måte** (not *brukmåte) is the more likely alternative – and is indeed correct.
6) Similarly, if we know the compound **geit|e|bonde** 'goat farmer', then we know that **geit**, 'goat' takes an –e–. We may then guess that **geit**

will probably also take an –e– when combined with **fjøs** 'byre'or **flokk**, 'herd', 'flock' – compare **geit|e|fjøs, geit|e|flokk**. Conversely, if we know that a certain first element does not select a particular link in a particular compound, it probably never does. For example, if we know that **hus**, 'house' is not followed by a link in **hus|eier**, 'house-owner', we may guess that there will be no link in **hus|båt**, 'house boat' or **hus|leie**, 'rent', either.

Note – No rule of thumb is infallible. For example, **geit|ost**, 'brown cheese made from goat whey' does not contain an –e–, even though we find **geite–** in other compounds. The links have also become less productive than they were (cf. 3) above; so, in a number of examples, an old compound contains an –s–, a new one does not, even if the two share the same first element.

11.2.3.5 | First element is a compound

(a) So far, we have mainly considered compounds consisting of two simplex 'words'. The linking element indicates the internal structure of the compounds; it shows where the 'dividing line' goes. The preferences for linking elements can be different if the first element of the compound is itself a compound. Given the noun **vei|trafikk**, 'road traffic', we can guess that other compounds with **vei–** will also contain no link – cf. **vei|prosjekt**, 'road project'; **vei|arbeider**, 'road worker'. However, if the first element of the compound is itself a compound, then a link is somewhat more likely, cf. **spor|vei**, 'tramway', without link (cf **spor**, 'track'; **vei**, 'road') vs. **sporvei|s|trafikk**, 'tramway traffic' with a link. Similarly, compare **mål|mann**, 'goalkeeper' vs. **tomål|s|seier**, 'win by two goals'; **språk|forsker**, 'language scholar' vs. **andrespråk|s|forsker**, 'second language scholar', **vin|flaske**, 'wine bottle' vs. **rødvin|s|flaske**, 'red wine bottle'.

(b) Again, the link indicates the structure; it helps us see where the first element ends. **En andrespråk|s|forsker** is a scholar working on second language, not a second scholar working on language; compare **andre|styrmann**, 'second mate on a ship', where there is no link; the elements are **andre** and **styrmann**.

If a stem normally takes a link in compounds, and this stem is compounded with another stem to make up a first element, then it is somewhat less likely that the latter should take a link, cf. **gutt|e||lag**, 'boys' team' (cf. **gutt**, 'boy'; **lag** 'team') with link vs. **smågutt||lag**, 'small boys' team' (cf. **små**, 'small', plural) without; **bjørn|e||jakt**, 'bear hunt' vs. **isbjørn||jakt**, 'polar bear hunt'. This tendency probably applies mainly to older compounds, but again, the link helps us see the internal structure.

11.3 Derivation

Simplified, in derivation one word (or its stem, cf. 11.1.2(b)) is combined with an affix, an element that is less than a word, a non-word element. Derivation may thus be contrasted with compounding, which involves 'putting two words together' (11.2). Here are some examples of derivation:

Derived word	'Word'	Affix 'less than a word'
spiselig, adj edible	**spise**, vb eat	**–lig** (suffix)
bærbar, adj portable	**bære**, vb carry	**–bar** (suffix)
unormal, adj abnormal	**normal**, adj normal	**u–** (prefix)
beholde, vb keep	**holde**, vb hold	**be–** (prefix)

We may classify derivational patterns according to whether the new words are formed by means of suffixes (11.3.1), prefixes (11.3.2) or fall into a different category (11.3.3). In suffixation, the affix is found at the end, as in spise*lig*, 'edible', where the suffix –lig is found at the end, compare spise, 'eat' and –lig. In prefixation, the affix is found at the beginning, as in *u*normal, 'abnormal', where the prefix u– is found initially before the word normal. Suffixation is the most common kind of derivation in Norwegian, as in English. There are many prefixes and many suffixes. We can only mention a few.

11.3.1 Suffixes

11.3.1.1 General remarks

(a) Change of word class

Suffixes are elements smaller than words that follow their stem (11.1.2.2). Suffixes are contrasted with prefixes (dealt with in 11.3.2), affixes that precede their stem.

Suffixes can – but need not – change the word class of the preceding element. When, for example, the suffix –lig is added to the verb spise, 'eat', the resulting word is an adjective spiselig, 'edible', so there has been a change of word-class. When the suffix –bar is added to the verb **digge** 'enjoy' (of English origin, cf. 11.1.1.2), the result is an adjective **diggbar**, 'enjoyable' (colloq.), again with a change of word-class. Such word-class change is not found with prefixes. For example, when the prefix **u–** is added to the noun **dyr**, 'animal', the resulting **udyr**, 'beast' belongs to the same word-class as **dyr**; when **u–** is added to the adjective **glad**, 'happy', the resulting **uglad**, 'unhappy' belongs to the same word-class as **glad**. However, word-class change is not found with all suffixes, either. For example, the noun **fløytist**, 'flautist' is related to the noun **fløyte**, 'flute'; the addition of a suffix **–ist** has not entailed any change of word-class.

(b) Several suffixes, one function (example: nouns denoting people)

Several suffixes may have related functions. Thus, a number of suffixes create nouns denoting people, e.g. **–er** as in **amerikaner**, 'American' **skytter** 'marksman'; **–ing** as in **dumming**, 'fool'; **hedmarking**, 'person from Hedmark'; **–ist** as in **harpist**, 'harpist'. It is not always easy to say exactly what the difference is between the suffixes, although there often is one (for example a noun in **–ing** will never denote agents, but nouns in **–er** can).

(c) One suffix, several functions (example: **–er**)

While several suffixes may seem to serve one purpose, there are also suffixes that have several meanings (sometimes related, sometimes not). For instance, the suffix **–er** does not only create nouns denoting people, such as **skytter**, 'marksman'; **hopper**, 'long-jumper', but also nouns denoting instruments, such as **bryter**, 'power switch'; **åpner**, 'opener'. There is a connection between these two uses. Such nouns as **skytter**, **hopper** are examples of the 'nomen agentis'; they focus on people as doing something – and instruments are the means by which actions are carried out. A power switch is the thing that carries out the action of switching electricity off, just as a jumper is a person that jumps.

| 11.3.1.2 | *Suffixes used to form adjectives*

(a) **–aktig**
This suffix can be added to nouns and adjectives and the result is an adjective:

skolemester, schoolmaster   **skolemesteraktig**, schoolmasterish
skurk, crook   **skurkaktig**, crooked

liv, life	**livaktig**, vivid
grønn, green	**grønnaktig**, greenish

The suffix –**aktig** may be compared to English '–ish' or '–like'. For example, **Peter er skolemesteraktig**, 'Peter is schoolmasterish' will normally imply that Peter is in fact not a schoolmaster, but that he resembles one in some way. While –**aktig** is found with a large number of existing words, it is not as productive as it used to be.

(b) –**bar**

This suffix is found with adjectives; typically –**bar** has been combined with transitive verbs (or rather stems cf. 11.1.2.2). The meaning is typically 'that can be verbed':

bære, carry	**bærbar**, portable
tenke, think	**tenkbar**, imaginable

To some extent, –**bar** has replaced –**lig** in this function; i.e., –**bar** is productive (cf. 11.1.3 above).

(c) –**en**

This suffix is not very productive any more, and its meaning is not very clear, but it is found in a large number of adjectives that are related to nouns and verbs:

ull, wool	**ullen**, pertaining to wool; woolly; unclear
lyst, lust, pleasure	**lysten**, willing; lusty
gå, go	**gåen**, exhausted
slite, work hard, toil	**sliten**, worn-out

Many words created with the suffix –**en** are lexicalised (cf. 11.1.4, 11.2.1.3). The adjective **holden**, 'wealthy' derives from the verb **holde**, 'hold', historically, but this relation will go unnoticed by most speakers. A number of formations do not relate to any simplex word, e.g. **lumpen**, 'mean'; **doven**, 'lazy'.

(d) –**ende**

This suffix is used to form present participles. Compare **leende**, 'laughing' vs. **le**, 'laugh'; **dansende**, 'dancing' vs. **danse**, 'dance'. The Norwegian participle in –**ende** is seldom verbal, unlike its English counterpart in –**ing**, and more seldom used. Often, a word in –**ende** functions as an adjective, cf. **en svært spennende bok**, 'a very exciting book' (see also 5.2.1 and 5.3.13). Participles may have an unexpected meaning. Given **spenne**, 'tighten', the meaning of **spennende** is not expected, and given **slå**, 'hit', it is not expected that **slående** will most often mean 'striking' (hardly ever 'hitting'). The suffix –**ende** is sometimes found in nouns denoting people: **reisende**, 'traveller'; **troende**, 'believer'. Some words in –**ende** are unrelated to any verb, cf. **bekende (mørkt)**, 'pitch (dark)', related to the noun **bek**, 'pitch'.

(e) –et/–a/–d/–t
On such adjectives as **nyforelsket**, 'newly in love'; **storkjefta**, 'boastful'; **firbeint**, 'four-legged'; **rødøyd**, 'red-eyed', cf. 11.4.3.2 below.

(f) –ete
This suffix is added to verbs and nouns. The result is an adjective.

From nouns:

støv, dust	**støvete**, dusty
dust, jerk, fool	**dustete**, stupid
soss, posh person, snob	**sossete**, snobbish

From verbs:

krangle, quarrel	**kranglete**, quarrelsome, difficult
grine, cry, weep	**grinete**, grumpy
bråke, make too much noise	**bråkete**, noisy

When an adjective in –ete is related to a verb, it will typically characterise somebody (or something) as having a propensity for doing what the verb denotes. Thus, saying **Jo er bråkete** means that Jo (man's name) is likely to **bråke** 'cause trouble', saying **Jo er kranglete** means he is likely to **krangle**, 'quarrel', etc. Yet, **Jo er grinete** does not mean that he is likely to **grine**, 'weep', but that he is grumpy – the meaning of derivations is not completely predictable, some derivations can be lexicalised (11.2.1.3). De-nominal adjectives in –ete typically characterise somebody or something as having qualities associated with the typical referent of the noun. Given that **dust**, 'fool' means what it does, we may guess that the derived adjective **dustete** will not be a word of praise (and it means 'stupid'). The suffix –ete is productive; it is found in fairly new formations, such as (colloq.) **nerdete**, 'nerdy', cf. **nerd**, 'nerd', **bløffete** (colloq.), 'that tends to bluff', cf. **bløffe** (colloq.), 'bluff' (vb).

(g) –før
This suffix is not very productive (and not found with very many words), but it is found with some verbs, in which case the adjective means 'able to + verb', 'good at + verb':

talefør, eloquent; rhetorically good	cf. **tale**, speak
skrivefør, able to write; skilled at writing	cf. **skrive**, write

(h) –ig

This suffix is not very productive these days, but it is found with a large number of words. Adjectives in –ig are usually related to nouns (noun stems). Not all adjectives in –ig are related to a noun (e.g. there is no noun corresponding to the adjective **riktig**, 'correct').

nytte, use, help	**nyttig**, useful
lyst, lust; cheer	**lystig**, cheerful
hånd, hand	**hendig**, handy, useful

(j) –lig

This suffix is added to verbs, adjectives and nouns. The result is an adjective. The suffix –lig is not very productive (11.1.3) these days. However, it is found with a large number of older words. In a number of cases, the meaning may be paraphrased as ' –like, –ly'.

Added to nouns

kvinne, woman	**kvinnelig**, female, feminine
venn, friend	**vennlig**, friendly

Added to verbs

elske, love	**elskelig**, charming, adorable
leve, live	**levelig**, tolerable

Added to adjectives

kjær, dear	**kjærlig**, warm, caring
grønn, green	**grønnlig**, greenish

Not all adjectives ending in –lig relate to another word. Thus, related to **liflig**, 'good', 'sweet', there is no **lif** (see also 11.1.4). In the case of some adjectives in –lig, we find linking elements, 'links' (cf. 11.2.3). Thus, the adjective **barnslig**, 'childish, immature' is related to **barn** 'child' and –lig, but the word also contains a link –s– ; **fredelig**, 'peaceful' is related to **fred**, 'peace' and to –lig, but the link –e– has also been inserted.

(k) –messig

This suffix is used to form adjectives, usually related to a noun:

rettmessig, correct, lawful   cf. **rett**, right, law
kjempemessig, great, excellent   cf. **kjempe**, giant
emnemessig, topic-wise   cf. **emne**, topic

Some adjectives in –**messig** are old formations, some rather new. The latter typically have a meaning comparable to English ' –wise' cf. **emnemessig** above.

(l) –som

This suffix is not very productive these days. Adjectives ending in –**som** are usually formed from verbs, and they are often used of 'people that are likely to + verb':

strevsom, taxing; hard-working   cf. **streve**, work hard
pratsom, talkative, chatty   cf. **prate**, chat
tenksom, pensive   cf. **tenke**, think

(m) –sk/ –isk

We shall treat these two as one suffix forming adjectives, typically from nouns, but also from verbs:

bedragersk, fraudulent   **bedrager**, fraud, impostor
synsk, visionary   **syn**, vision
skotsk, Scottish   **Skotte,** Scotsman, Scot
glemsk, forgetful   **glemme**, forget
dyrisk, bestial   **dyr**, animal

The corresponding noun is not always clear. There is, for instance, no obvious corresponding noun for the adjective **grisk**,'greedy'.

11.3.1.3 Suffixes used to form nouns

(a) –as

This suffix is not found in many words. It is stylistically marked; nouns in –**as** are at best colloquial, and they usually denote negative properties.

tjukkas, 'fatty'; thick mat
smukkas, (ironically) (too) good – looking man

(b) –dom

This suffix is not very productive, but is found in some nouns related to adjectives, nouns (and the odd verb):

kristendom, Christianity	cf. **kristen**, Christian
ungdom, youth, youngster	cf. **ung**, young
spådom, prophecy	cf. **spå**, prophesy, foretell

(c) –else

This suffix is not very productive these days, but it is found in a large number of older words. The stem is usually a verb or an adjective. –else is less productive with adjectives. After an adjective stem, the –else noun will often mean 'the act of making + adjective', after a verb stem 'the process or product of verbing'.

forsnakkelse, slip of the tongue	cf. **forsnakke seg**, say something unintended
ergrelse, irritation	cf. **ergre**, irritate
tykkelse, thickness, density	cf. **tykk**, thick
forargelse, irritation; uproar	cf. **forarget**, incensed

(d) –er

This suffix may be added to a verb, and the result will be a masculine (common gender) noun denoting a person doing the activity denoted by the verb (cf. English):

fiske, fish	**fisker**, fisher
synge, sing	**sanger**, singer
flå, skin	**flåer**, skinner; extortionist

Many nouns ending in –er and denoting persons are related to nouns (see also 11.3.1.1(b)):

lutheraner, Lutheran	cf. the proper noun **Luther**
løgner, liar	cf. the noun **løgn**, lie, fib

Not – Vowel change accompanies the suffix –er in some cases. The noun **sanger**, 'singer' is related to the verb **synge**, 'sing' by both suffixation and vowel change, the noun **morder**, 'murderer' to the verb **myrde**, 'murder'. See also 11.3.3

Some nouns ending in –er denote animals (including birds and insects):

støver, hound	cf. **støv**, dust
øyenstikker, *lit.* 'eye-stabber', dragon fly	cf. **øye,** eye and **stikke**, tab

There are also nouns ending in –er that denote instruments associated with an action:

skriver, printer (also, historically: clerk)
gressklipper, lawn mower
skrutrekker, screwdriver

There are also formations in –er that resemble agent nouns, but that do not correspond to any verb. Corresponding to **kelner**, 'waiter'; **skomaker**, 'shoemaker', there is no verb **kelne; *(sko)make*, for example.

Note – There are also nouns ending in –er that correspond to numerals, cf. Numerals 3.2.1.1.

–er can also be added to a place-name, and the result will be an inhabitant name, a masculine (common gender) noun denoting a person from that place:

en sveitser, a Swiss	cf. **Sveits**, Switzerland
en ålesunder, a person from Ålesund	cf. **Ålesund** (town)
en drammenser, person from Drammen	cf. **Drammen** (town)

(In **drammenser** we also find a link –s–, cf. 11.2.3.)

Some nouns in –er are related to phrases or to complex words. See 11.4.3.

(e) –iker

This suffix may be considered a variant of –er. It is only found in nouns denoting humans: **alkoholiker**, 'alcoholic' cf. **alkohol**, 'alcohol', **alkohol-isme**, 'alcoholism'; **psykotiker**, 'psychotic', cf. **psykose**, 'psychosis'.

(f) –eri

This suffix is not very productive these days, but it is found in a number of neuters. They can denote a product of the process denoted by the corresponding verb, not infrequently with derogative connotations:

lureri, trick, cheating	cf. **lure**, to dupe, cheat
smøreri, bad painting: 'daub'	cf. **smøre**, spread butter/oil on

There are not always negative connotations, however:

brenneri, distillery	cf. the verb **brenne**, burn, distil
maleri, painting (work of art)	cf. the verb **male**, paint

Nouns in –**eri** need not relate to a verb; they can be related to another noun:

tjuveri, theft	cf. **tjuv**, thief
falskneri, fraud	cf. **falskner**, fraudster

Neuter nouns in –**eri** can denote a place where some activity is carried out:

bakeri, bakery	cf. **bake**, bake
slakteri, slaughter-house	cf. **slakte**, butcher (vb)
trykkeri, printing-house	cf. **trykke**, print

There need not always be a corresponding verb or noun: **meieri**, 'dairy', does not relate to the verb **meie**, 'cut down', or the noun **meie**, 'runner on a sled'.

(g) –**het**

The result of adding –**het** to an adjective will be a feminine (common gender) noun denoting the corresponding quality:

dum, stupid	**dumhet**, stupidity
vennlig, friendly	**vennlighet**, friendliness
kjærlig, caring, warm	**kjærlighet**, love

This suffix is productive (11.1.3); compare the fairly recent **tøffhet**, 'toughness'; **kulhet**, 'coolness' related to the adjectives **tøff**, 'tough'; **kul**, 'cool' respectively.

(h) –**ing** (–**ling**, –**ning**)

This is a highly productive suffix, found also in a large number of older words. It is found with verbs, adjectives and nouns.

–**ing** can be added to verbs. In that case, the 'result' is a noun denoting an activity associated with the verb. That noun may be of feminine (common) gender.

danse, dance	cf. **dansing**, dancing
somle, delay	**somling**, delay

This use of –ing is also found with (relatively) new words, e.g. **sponsing**, 'sponsoring'; **kødding**, 'taking the mickey'.

However, –ing is also found in nouns denoting persons. In that case, the noun is of masculine (common) gender. If related to adjectives, it denotes people having the (often negative) quality denoted by the adjective. For example:

dum, stupid	**dumming**, stupid person
lur, smart	**luring**, smart-aleck

The adjective is usually monosyllabic. This use of –ing is also found with (relatively) new words, e.g. **tøffing**, 'toughie', cf. **tøff**, 'tough'.

–ing can also be added to a place-name, and the result will be a masculine (common gender) noun denoting a person from that place (see also 11.3.1.1(b)); thus, the noun **hedmarking** means 'a person from Hedmark' 'Inhabitant names' are also formed in other ways, cf. –er, and the names are numerous (perhaps because Norway is a country where local identity has been perceived as important).

The suffix –ning is often seen as a variant of –ing.

bygning, building (house)	cf. **bygge**, build
belysning, light	cf. **belyse**, light up

It is not easy to give clear rules for the distribution of –ning and –ing, but after l–, r–, nd–, stressed vowels, consonant clusters and the stem –er, –ing is the norm, compare **stjeling**, 'act of stealing'; **fyring**, 'act of heating'; **binding**, 'act of binding; something that holds in place'; **klåing**, 'groping'; **plystring**, 'whistling'; **sementering**, 'act of cementing'; formed from **stjele**, **fyre**, **binde**, **klå**, **plystre**, **sementere** respectively. After d–, –ning is more common: **ladning**, 'load' (noun), cf. **lade**, 'load' (verb).

In some cases, e.g. **forsking/forskning**, 'research'; **bøying/bøyning**, 'inflection', there is almost free variation. Some writers prefer **bøying, forsking**, others **bøyning, forskning**.

In some few cases, there is a clear difference in meaning between –ing and –ning, such as **bygging**, '(act of) building' (process) vs. **bygning**, 'a building that has been finished' (product); **dekking**, 'the act of covering', as in **tildekking**, 'covering over' vs. **dekning**, 'cover'; **holding**, 'the act of holding' vs. **holdning**, 'attitude'. In such cases, the formation with –ning is often lexicalised (11.1.4). Most formations in –ing denote both process and product; cf. **stevning**, 'issuing a writ' (process) or 'a formal letter summoning someone to court' (product).

A few nouns end in –ling:

lærling, apprentice	cf. **lære,** learn, teach
tjømling, person from Tjøme	cf. **Tjøme**, (place-name)
sjukling, (derog.) person in poor health	cf. **sjuk**, ill

–ling is restricted to nouns denoting humans, always of masculine (common) gender.

In some cases, words in –ing relate not to simple stems, but perhaps rather to phrases (cf. 11.4.3). For example, **nykomling**, 'newcomer' does not relate to *komling; there is no such word. A **nykomling** is somebody who is **ny** and who carries out the action of **komme**, 'come'.

Derivations can take part in compounding, and because –ing is used so much in derivation, we find many compounds containing –ing: **skiskyting**, 'biathlon' is related to **ski**, 'ski' and to **skyting**, 'shooting'; **potetopptaking**, 'potato harvesting' is related to **potet**, 'potato' and **opptaking** *lit.* 'picking up'.

Note – Some few nouns in –ing are historically direct loans, e.g. **camping**, **doping**, **pudding**, all from English.

(j) –is
This suffix is not found in many words, but it is sometimes used to coin new ones. It is stylistically marked; nouns ending in –is are informal.

tyggis, chewing-gum	cf. **tygge**, chew
grovis, bawdy joke	cf. **grov**, crude

(k) –sel
This suffix is not very productive today, but it is found with some adjectival and verbal stems:

redsel, fear	cf. **redd**, afraid
gjemsel, hide and seek	cf, **gjemme**, hide

(l) –skap
This suffix is not very productive these days, but it is found in many words. The result of adding –skap to an adjective will be a masculine (common gender) noun denoting the corresponding quality, in the abstract:

dum, stupid	**dumskap**, stupidity
lat, lazy	**latskap**, laziness

Nouns in –skap that are formed from adjectives often denote a quality, so their meaning may be rather abstract. –skap can, however, also be added to nouns, and will then typically denote a state or property:

vennskap, friendship   cf. **venn**, friend
statsborgerskap, citizenship   cf. **statsborger**, citizen
farskap, paternity   cf. **far**, father

(m) –sjon

This suffix is found in loans, more specifically of masculine/common gender. Here are some examples:

nasjon, nation; **visjon**, vision; **refusjon**, rejection (of e.g. manuscripts); refund (of money)

(n) Suffixes reserved for female agent nouns, such as –inne, –esse, –ske are largely obsolete these days, as a result of language debates and conscious policy. Cf. 1.3.4.2f., and 11.1.3.2. Some remain, such as:

danserinne, female dancer, cf. **danser**; **elskerinne** female lover, cf. **elsker**; **fyrstinne**, princess, cf. **fyrste**; **grevinne**, countess, cf. **greve**; **hertuginne**, duchess, cf. **hertug**; **lærerinne**, female teacher; **løvinne**, female lion, cf. **løve**, lion; **skuespillerinne**, actress, cf. **skuespiller**; **venninne**, friend, cf. **venn**; **prinsesse**, princess, cf. **prins**; **pleierske**, nurse, cf. **pleier**

| 11.3.1.4 | *Suffixes used to create verbs*

Verb-creating suffixes are rare, but we find a few.

(a) –er(e)

This suffix is typically found in Latinate verbs:

produsere, produce; **revidere**, revise; **protestere**, protest, object

However, some exceptions exist, e.g. **grublisere** (humorous) 'ponder', cf. **gruble**, 'ponder'; **halvere**, 'divide into halves', cf. **halv**. Neither **gruble** nor **halv** have anything to do with Latin.

−iser(e) and −ifiser(e) can be seen as variants of this suffix:

balkanisere, 'make like the Balkans'   cf. **Balkan**

mummifisere, 'mummify'   cf. **mumie**, 'mummy'

(b) −n(e)

This suffix is not very productive these days, but it can be found with an inchoative meaning (becoming) in a few old words:

gulne, become yellow   cf. **gul**, yellow

blekne, become pale   cf. **blek/bleik**, pale

(c) −s

As a derivational verb-creating suffix, −s is not very productive these days, but it is found in a few new verbs and some old ones, having e.g. a reciprocal meaning (mutuality) or reflexive meaning (acting upon oneself). See 5.6.3.

mailes, send e-mails to each other   cf. **maile**, send an e-mail

møtes, meet (each other)   cf. **møte**, meet (someone)

Note − When indicating the passive, −s functions as an inflectional suffix. See 5.6.2.

11.3.2 | Prefixes

11.3.2.1 | Introduction

This brief survey can only deal with some of the many prefixes to be found. Since prefixes, unlike suffixes, cannot 'change word-class' (11.3.1.1(a)), we simply list them alphabetically.

(a) **an−**

angå, concern   cf. **gå**, go

anta, presume   cf. **ta**, take

ansette, hire   cf. **sette**, place

ansettelse   act of hiring

This prefix is not very productive anymore. It is often difficult to tell what the meaning will be. Verbs in **an−** are often transitive.

(b) **be−**

Usually, verbs beginning in **be−** are transitive and related to other verbs, while nouns beginning in **be−** are related to verbs in **be−**.

beskrive, describe	**skrive** write
beskrivelse, description	
bevise, prove	**vise**, show
begå, commit (a crime)	**gå**, go
beholde, keep	**holde**, hold
beholdning, holding	

(c) er–

This prefix is hardly productive today; it is found in some verbs (mostly of German origin) and in related nouns:

erkjenne, realise	**kjenne**, know
erfare, experience (vb)	**fare**, travel
erfaring, experience (noun)	

The semantic relation can be unclear, cf. **erfare** and **fare**; and there need not be any related word at all. Related to **erstatte**, 'replace; compensate', there is no *statte. Verbs in er– are usually transitive.

(d) for–

This prefix is found in a number of words, often related to verbs, not so often nouns and adjectives. Verbs in **for–** are usually transitive.

fortelle, tell	cf. **telle**, count
forlede, lead astray	cf. **lede**, lead
forsølve, silver-plate	cf. **sølv**, silver
forklare, explain	cf. **klar**, clear
forklaring, explanation	

(e) fore–

This prefix is found in a number of words, usually related to verbs (or nominal derivations of verbs). Verbs in fore– are usually transitive.

forelese, lecture	cf. **lese**, read
forelesning, lecture	
forestille, pretend to be	cf. **stille**, set, put
forestilling, show	
foregripe, anticipate	cf. **gripe**, take, grasp

(f) mis– 'mis–, dis–'

This prefix is found in a number of words related to verbs and nouns and adds the sense of 'badly, wrongly':

mishandle, mistreat, abuse	cf. **handle**, act
misfarge, stain	cf. **farge**, colour
mistenke, suspect	cf. **tenke**, think
mistanke suspicion	cf. **tanke**, thought

Verbs in **mis–** are usually transitive.

(g) **u–** 'un, not'

This is perhaps the most common prefix. When **u–** is added to an adjective, the result will be a somehow negative adjective. Compare **glad**, 'happy'; **uglad**, 'unhappy'; **vennlig**, 'friendly'; **uvennlig**, 'unfriendly'. The meaning of **u–** is negative, but it is more specialised than that. Consider **ufin;** the 'base' adjective **fin**, 'fine' can mean 'good; well-behaved':

Den boka var fin.	That book was fine/good.
Det var fin oppførsel.	That was decent/fine behaviour.

However, **ufin** 'coarse' can only be used about vulgar or unpleasant behaviour and people, and not about bad books, for example. **u–** can also be added to noun stems, as in **uvenn**, 'enemy'; compare **venn**, 'friend'; **ufisk**, 'bad, inedible fish', cf. **fisk**, 'fish'; **uskikk**, 'bad habit', cf. **skikk**, 'habit'; **ugress**, 'weed' cf. **gress**, 'grass'. Some nouns formed with **u–** are less easily analysable: cf. **vær**, 'weather' with **uvær**, 'storm'; **dyr**, 'animal', with **udyr**, 'beast'.

(h) **van–** 'not, badly'

This prefix is not very productive these days. It combines with both verbs, nouns and adjectives, and its meaning is usually negative, denoting 'badly', or 'lacking'.

vanstell, neglect	cf. **stell**, care, order
vanfør, invalid (old word)	cf. **før**, able-bodied
vanvidd, madness	cf. **vidd**, wit
vanskjøtte, neglect, mismanage	cf. **skjøtte**, take care of

11.3.3 | Other techniques: Conversion and vowel change

Derivation need not always be a matter of suffixation (11.3.1) or prefixation (11.3.2), compare:

Verb stem	Noun stem
slå, 'hit'	**slå**, 'old-fashioned door-handle'
skriv, 'write'	**skriv** (noun), 'official letter'

The verb stems **slå, skriv** may be taken as basic; they are 'converted' to noun stems. Simplified, conversion is when a word usually associated with one word-class is used as if it belonged to another word-class. In English, there is much conversion, cf. e.g. 'to have a go', in which 'go', normally a verb, is used as a noun. Conversion may be rarer in Norwegian, but it is fairly common also in Norwegian for a verb stem and a noun stem to be related without any affixation:

Verb stem	Noun stem
øks, 'use an axe, chop'	**øks**, 'axe'
bil, 'travel by car'	**bil** 'car'
kyss, 'kiss'	**kyss**, 'kiss'
kast, 'throw'	**kast**, 'throw'

It may vary whether the noun or the verb is basic; the important point is that they are related. As **bil** illustrates, this is a productive kind of word-formation.

There are cases in which derivation shows in vowel change:

Verb stem	Noun stem
syng, 'sing'	**sang**, 'song'
myrd, 'murder'	**mord**, 'murder'

The verb stems **syng–** and **myrd–** respectively relate to the nouns; vowel change has taken place. This word-formation technique is not very productive.

More often, vowel change occurs in combination with affixes. Compare:

Verb	Noun
fange, 'catch'	**fengsel**, 'prison'
Vestlandet, 'West Norway'	**vestlending**, 'person from West Norway'

In these cases, we find vowel change ($a \rightarrow e$) in combination with the suffixes –**sel** (11.3.1.3. (h)) and –**ing** (11.3.1.3(k)).

11.4 Other patterns

Not all word-formation can be described as neatly as in the preceding sections; word-formation is not always a matter of glueing bits together. In this section, we survey a number of word-formation patterns that are better described in other ways. See also 11.3.3.

11.4.1 Affixoids

In colloquial language in particular, one may find so-called affixoids, elements that come close to affix status. Examples include **kjempe–**, **drit–**, **døds–**; **mega–** and many others. The case of **kjempe–** is illustrative. In isolation, **kjempe** means 'giant'. It is easy to recognise that meaning in the compounded adjectives **kjempestor**, 'very big'; **kjempesterk**, 'very strong'; giants are supposedly big and strong. However, the meaning relation is more unclear in e.g. **kjempesøt**, 'very cute' and **kjempeliten**, 'very small'. Giants are not supposed to be cute or small; **kjempe–** has developed into an intensifying element meaning 'very'. Similarly, in isolation, **død** means 'death', **syk** means 'ill', and the meaning of **dødssyk**, 'mortally/terminally ill' will come as no surprise. However, in a word like **dødskjedelig**, 'deadly boring', **døds–** cannot be taken equally literally, nor in such colloquial formations as **dødskul**, 'very cool'; **dødssexy**, 'very sexy'.

While the prefixoids **drit–** and **døds–** may be perceived as improper, **kjempe–** is very well established.

In addition to the prefixoids, we find a number of 'suffixoids', such as **–bevisst**, 'conscious', **–vennlig**, 'friendly', **–fri**, 'free', **–løs**, 'loose'. Thus, while **menneskevennlig**, 'friendly (towards humans)' is usually seen as a compound of **menneske**, 'human' and **vennlig**, 'friendly', the word **prisvennlig**, related to **pris**, 'price', means 'cheap'.

11.4.2 Words that are not easily segmented

Some words have features in common both in terms of meaning and form, and yet they do not really consist of stems and affixes. This is evident for some verbs ending in **–le** and **–re**, e.g. **fomle**, 'fumble'; **fikle**, 'fumble'; **kakle**, 'cackle'; **somle**, 'delay'; **romle**, 'rumble'; **vrimle**, 'swarm'; **gomle**, 'chew repeatedly'; **stotre**, 'stutter'; **sitre** 'shiver'; **plapre**, 'blabber'; **knitre**, 'crackle'. These verbs have an element of iterativity, i.e. repetition (or intensification). For example, to make one brief noise does not qualify as **kakle**; to utter one empty word does not qualify as **plapre**; to shake briefly just once not as **sitre**. However, if we isolate a derivational suffix **–l**, **–r** in these verbs, we are left with elements that never occur elsewhere. Many of these verbs are also onomatopoetic (cf. 11.4.7).

11.4.3 | *Words formed from phrases*

11.4.3.1

While Norwegian words normally may be said to consist of stems and affixes, sometimes they relate to phrases. For example, the noun **tre|master**, 'three-masted sailing ship', is most straightforwardly related to the phrase **tre master**, 'three masts'. Similarly, a **sam|boer**, 'life partner' is not a particular kind of **boer**, since the noun **boer** is used only of South Africans of Dutch descent. Rather, **samboere** are people who live together –**bor sammen**. Also, **vel|gjører**, 'benefactor', cf. **vel**, 'well' and **gjøre**, is not a compound involving a noun as second element; there is no noun *****gjører**. Rather, a **vel|gjører** is somebody who **gjør vel**.

11.4.3.2

There are also adjectives that appear to be derived from a phrase, cf.:

storkjefta, mpolite	cf. **stor kjeft,** big mouth
femårig, five years long	cf. **fem år,** five years
rødøyd, red-eyed	cf. **røde øyne**, red eyes
langbeint, long-legged	cf. **lange bein**, long legs

(There are no adjectives *****kjefta**, *****årig**, *****øyd**, *****beint**.)

The most common of such formations are those ending in **–et/–a**, which are alternatives here. For some few colloquial formations, **–a** is more frequent than **–et**, but **–et** is much more frequent in writing. Even in writing, **storkjefta** is more frequent than **storkjeftet**, whereas **storsinnet**, 'magnanimous' is more frequent than **storsinna** (which is rare in writing).

The two other suffixes here, **–d** and **–t** have no alternatives, and they are less frequent, especially **–d**. The distribution of **–a, –et, –t** and **–d** here resembles that of the verbal suffixes for the past participle of the verb (cf. 5.3.12).

The formations above typically characterise properties, often associated with inalienable (permanent) possession (such as having long legs, a big mouth).

11.4.5 | Abbreviations

11.4.5.1

Some few words have originated by means of abbreviation. Thus, **SV** comes from **Sosialistisk Venstreparti**, 'Socialist Left Party'; **OSSE** from **Organisasjonen for sikkerhet og samarbeid in Europa**, 'The Organisation for Safety and Security in Europe'. This kind of word-formation presupposes a written language; most other types of word-formation do not. If we go back a thousand years in Norwegian language history, there will still be compounds and derivations, but there will not be any words formed on the basis of abbreviation. Normally, abbreviations stand out. They tend to be written with capital letters, cf. above; compare also **NRK**, 'The Norwegian Broadcasting Company' (**Norsk Rikskringkasting**); **FN**, 'The United Nations' (**De forente nasjoner**); **SSB** 'The Norwegian Central Statistics Bureau' (**Statistisk sentralbyrå**). These are read as a sequence of letters and are sometimes called 'initialisms'. So is the now frequent **sms**, but unlike the previous examples, this noun is common (not proper) and inflectable (compare **Hun sendte ham sms-er dagen lang**, 'She sent him text messages all day long').

11.4.5.2

A few abbreviations have made it all the way to common nouns. Examples include **moms**, 'VAT' (originally **merverdiomsetningsavgift**); **tv**, often written **teve** (**televisjon**), 'television'; **wc**, 'wc'; **bh**, 'bra' (**brystholder** *lit.* 'bosom holder'). These can be inflected like other common nouns; compare **momsen**, 'the VAT'; **tv-er**, 'televisions'. Abbreviations like **moms** or **NATO**, pronounced as if they were a word, are sometimes called 'acronyms'.

11.4.5.3

Another set of words that have presumably originated in journalese or in colloquial language are sometimes called 'short forms' or 'clippings'. Examples include **krim**, 'crime'; **pop**, 'pop'; **porno** 'porn'; **narko**, 'narcotics, drugs'. They have their origin in the longer **kriminal(roman/serie)**, **populær(musikk)**, **pornografi**, **narkotika**. Where the longer form still exists, it may have a more formal or slightly dated feel, but not necessarily in all contexts. Thus, few Norwegians will talk of **kriminalserie**, only of **krimserie**, 'crime series' (as TV entertainment), yet still **kriminalpoliti**, 'criminal police' is preferred. The longer form **fotografi**, 'photo' is formal compared to **foto**, but not dated; the longer form **automobil** is by contrast dated compared to **bil**, 'car'.

11.4.6 Reduplication

This is a form of word-formation in which there is partial or complete identity between two parts. This is found in some very few compounds with a strengthening effect, e.g. **finfin**, 'very fine'; **mannemann**, '*lit*. man-man; macho man'; **tipptippoldefar** 'great-great-great-grand-father'. There are some more examples to be found in child-directed language, such as **vovvov**, 'bow-wow; dog'; **bittebitteliten**,'teeny-weeny'.

11.4.7 Onomatepoetics

These are words that imitate sounds, such as **nøff**, (sound made by a pig), 'oink'; **breke** (verb for sound made by a sheep), 'bleat'; **kykeliky**, 'cock-adoodledo'. While one might think that pigs, sheep and cocks sound the same all over the world, Norwegian onomatepoetics are not identical to the English ones, as the examples illustrate, neither for the sounds emitted by these animals, nor for a number of other words imitating sounds, such as **klask**, 'smack'; **pang**, 'bang'.

11.4.8 Foreign influences on the vocabulary

11.4.8.1

Historically, Norwegian has (like any other language) always received words, in particular nouns, from other languages. For instance, the word **språk**, 'language' is historically of German origin, **møbel**, 'piece of furniture' comes from French; the word **akevitt**, 'aquavit' from Latin; the word **alkohol** from Arabic, and the word **nydelig**, 'lovely' from Danish.

From a historical perspective, Danish and German (Low and High) stand out, in that loans from these languages are very numerous, and even affixes have been borrowed, e.g. –het (11.3.1.3(g)). Unlike words, affixes are seldom borrowed; when they are, such borrowings indicate intense contact.

It is often uncertain how long a loan remains a loan, and whether speakers know. Such words as **tsunami** or **rendez-vous** are clear loans, since they contain unusual letters (**rendez-vous**) or unusual combinations (**tsunami**). At the other extreme, no 'average' Norwegian has any idea that **jern**, 'iron' is historically a loan from Irish or **språk**, 'language' from German. These words are perceived as Norwegian, just as speakers of English perceive the word 'bag' to be English, although it was borrowed from Scandinavian some thousand years ago (and then borrowed back again into Norwegian after 1945).

11.4.8.2 | English influence

Today, English stands out as the central language for borrowing (11.1.1.2), to an extent that has worried many Norwegians. This may in part be because English loanwords catch the eye (or the ear).

11.4.8.3 | English affixes

Some English affixes are borrowed, testifying to the depth of English influence – but also to the vitality of Norwegian, in that the affixes are not merely 'taken over'. A case in point is the English plural suffix '–s'. It has been borrowed into Norwegian in a number of nouns that often occur in the plural in English. Examples include **caps** (also spelled **kæps**), **pins**, **pyjamas**; compare English 'cap', 'pin', 'pyjama'. In Norwegian, the English plural '–s' has become part of the noun stem itself; compare e.g. **kæpsen** 'the cap'. In some words, the ' –s' was, for a time, a proper plural ending, compare the archaic plural forms **fotos, gangsters**. As these words have become less 'alien', they have got a more regular Norwegian inflection: **et foto – flere foto, en gangster – flere gangstere**. See 1.4.7.1 (b)–(e).

A more recent example of a borrowed affix is the derivational ' –ish', used by some younger people at least: **Skal vi møtes sånn to-ish?**, 'Should we meet at two-ish?' How stable this will be remains to be seen.

11.4.8.4 | Pseudo-loans

Although most Norwegians now have a considerable knowledge of English, and English enjoys high prestige in Norway, Norwegian has some very English-sounding neologisms that in fact do not exist in the supposed donor language. Examples include **rocka**, 'that is reminiscent of rock, fine, unconventional, rough'; **snacksy**, 'appetising, appealing'; **grillparty**, 'barbecue'. In Norwegian, but not in English, one can be **fit for fight**, and Norwegians use **after ski** where the English would use the French 'après ski'.

| 11.4.8.5 | *Neo-classical influences*

Like many other European languages, including English, Norwegian contains considerable 'classical' or 'Neo-classical' word formation. Thus, there are suffixes of Latinate origin that may create agent nouns, notably –ant, –ist, –ør:

(a) –ist

> **korist**, choir singer, cf. **kor**, choir; **Donaldist**, eager reader of (specialist in) Donald Duck, cf. **Donald**; **fløytist**, flute player, cf. **fløyte**; **jurist**, law scholar, cf. **jus** law, jurisprudence

(b) –ant

> **trafikant**, road user, cf. **trafikk**, traffic; **praktikant**, trainee, cf. **praktisere**, practice

(c) –ør

> **kontrollør**, controller, cf. **kontrollere**, control; **inspektør**, inspector, cf. **inspisere**, inspect, check

The suffixes –ant and –ør occur after loan stems. For the other word classes, there are also other Latinate suffixes, such as the adjective-forming suffixes –al as in **nasjonal** 'national' and –ibel as in **irreversibel**, 'irreversible'. As these suffixes are rather similar to English, we do not go into detail.

Chapter 12

Orthography

12.1 Symbols and sounds

12.1.1 *Letters of the alphabet*

12.1.1.1

(a) There are twenty-nine letters in the Norwegian alphabet:

A B C D E F G H I J K L M N O P Q R S T U V W X Y Z Æ Ø Å

The order of the three vowels at the end of the Norwegian alphabet, . . . Æ Ø Å, is the same as in Danish, but unlike Swedish . . . Å Ä Ö.

(b) The Norwegian Å, å, is a separate letter, not an accent or diacritic on **A**. The letter Å, å was introduced to Norway in 1917 to replace the earlier **AA, aa**. The letter Ø, ø similarly, is not a diacritic but a separate character.

12.1.1.2 *Q, W, X, Z*

In modern Norwegian Q, W, X and Z only occur in the proper names for people such as **Willy, Winther, Wergeland, Xavier, Zachariassen,** and countries such as **Qatar, Wales, Zimbabwe**. In common nouns, they show that a word has been borrowed from another language, as in **quiche, wok, xylofon, zucchini**.

The word **wc** is pronounced as if written **vc**, and in web addresses **www** is pronounced as if spelt **v v v**. There are very few loanwords in Norwegian with a **w**, for example: **weekend, whisky, windsurfing**.

12.1.1.3 **C, K**

The letter c in loanwords is usually pronounced as s: **centiliter; cisterne,** 'water tank'; **cirka.** In a very few loanwords c has the same pronunciation as k: **camping, cocktail, container, cup, cognac.**

Some personal names in which C is pronounced as K vary between the use of these two letters in spelling: **Carl/Karl, Christoffer/Kristoffer, Caspersen/ Kaspersen.**

12.1.2 **Diacritics**

In addition to the standard Norwegian alphabet given in 12.1.1.1, the following characters can be found in Norwegian spelling dictionaries or are frequent when spelling foreign names:

á à ã ä ç é è ê ë í ï ñ ó ò ô ö ú ü

The following occur in the *Språkrådet* list of foreign place-names:

ă â ã ā ć č đ ð ę ğ î ł ń ň ŋ ő ř ś š ş ţ ŧ þ ù ý ź ž f

12.1.2.1 **Acute accent**

A relatively few loanwords in Norwegian have an acute accent, including:

allé, avenue; **diaré**, diarrhoea; **entré**, entrance; **idé**, idea; **kafé**, café; **komité**, committee; **kupé**, compartment; **moské**, mosque; **supé**, evening meal; **trofé**, trophy

Here the –e is stressed, unlike such native words as, say, **hule**, 'cave', and this means that, in the definite and plural form, nouns like **allé**, 'avenue' take –en, –er:

alléen, the avenue BUT **hulen**, the cave; **alléer**, avenues BUT **huler** caves

Note that the accent can be dropped in the definite singular and the plural forms (**alleen, alleer** are also possible).

12.1.2.2 **Grave and circumflex accents**

(a) A grave accent is found on the preposition à in phrases loaned from French and pronounced as short a.

tre billetter à 50 kroner	three tickets at 50 kroner each
vis-à-vis, à jour, à la carte; déjà vu	

Neither of these accents is common in modern Norwegian.

(b) The circumflex is less common and optional in loanwords and phrases such as: **châteauvin,** 'chateau wine'; **crème fraîche; tête-à-tête,** and such loanwords are usually found without diacritics, cf. also **ampere, entrecote.**

Note the rare Norwegian exceptions **fôr,** 1. 'fodder', 2. 'lining'; **òg,** 'also, too'.

12.1.2.3 | Indigenous accents

(a) In certain loanwords, especially in names and titles from European languages, indigenous accents such as diaeresis are retained.

Aïda, aloë, Boëtius, Citroën, Faëton, Golda Meïr, Noël, Zaïre

In such cases each vowel is pronounced separately, unlike, for example, Norwegian **hai,** 'shark'; **kai,** 'quay', which have diphthongs.

Others include:

Coruña, señor, São Paulo, João, Antonín Dvořák

(b) The letters **ä ö ü** are found in Swedish and German names:

Östertälje, Köln, Lübeck

12.1.2.4 | Internet and e-mail addresses

In internet and e-mail addresses the Norwegian letters **æ, ø, å** are usually written **a, o, a,** though some people prefer to write **ae, oe, aa.**

12.2 Spelling

12.2.1 | Miscellaneous spelling rules

12.2.1.1 | Double and single consonants

(a) Norwegian words as a general rule have a double consonant after a short stressed vowel in both closed and open syllables (i.e. those with a following consonant and those without):

bygg – bygget	building site, the building site
hette – hetter	hood [noun, singular and plural]

hopp – hoppe   jump [noun], jump [verb]
trygg – trygge   secure [adjective, singular and plural]

If the vowel is long and stressed, there will, on the contrary, be a single consonant:

byge, shower; **hete**, be called; **håpe**, hope [verb]; **håp**, hope [noun]

Exceptions:

(i) In inflected forms, there is a single consonant before a new consonant:

tynn – tynt, thin [common, neuter]; **sommer – somrer**, summer, summers; **spenne – spente**, tighten, tightened

But this does not occur before the link –s in compounds because it is not an inflexional ending: **rett|s|bok**, court record

(ii) In derivatives ending in –**ning**, –**ne**, –**sk** there is a single consonant in the stem:

bygning, building (cf. **bygge,** build); **kvikne,** revive (cf. **kvikk,** lively); **glemsk,** forgetful (cf. **glemme,** forget)

(iii) **v** is never doubled: **støvel,** boot

(iv) Many monosyllabic words, especially function words of high frequency are written with a single consonant even when the vowel is short:

an, ad, at, den, et, for, han, hen, hos, hun, hvis, kan, man, men, nok, skal, til, vel, vil

In compounds three similar consonants can be juxtaposed if a hyphen is inserted:

fjell-land or **fjelland**, mountain country

(b) The letter **m** is not doubled at the end of a word, even if the vowel is short:

dam, pool; **dom**, sentence; **krim**, detective story

But **m** is doubled between vowels:

> **dammen**, the pool; **barndommen**, the childhood; **krimmen**, the detective story

(c) Loanwords have often been adopted to Norwegian orthographic principles with a double consonant:

> **buss**, bus; **hipp**, hip; **klubb**, club; **penn**, pen; **snobb**, snob

However, some more recent (often English) loans retain their spelling with a single consonant:

> chip, fan, pickup

Alternative forms exist for some recent loans:

> **bag** or **bagg**; **hit** or **hitt**; **lab** or **lab**; **jet** or **jett**; **pop** or **popp**

Derivatives formed from such loans double the consonant, however:

> **shop** (noun) [noun] but **shoppe**, 'to shop' and **shopping**.

(d) Some loanwords retain a single consonant after a short stressed vowel:

> **apostrof**, apostrophe; **graffiti**

12.2.2 | Some general points on spelling and pronunciation

Norwegian is, when compared to English, a fairly phonemic language (one phoneme or sound is represented by one grapheme or written letter), but there are exceptions. While this is no place for a comprehensive account of Norwegian pronunciation, a brief summary follows of the major departures from phonemic pronunciation. Note that graphemes (written letters) are indicated by < >, phonemes (sounds) by / /.

12.2.2.1 | g, k, sk, etc

(a) Before the vowels /i/ and /y/ and diphthongs /ei/ and /øy/, the graphemes <k> and <sk> are all pronounced /ç/ and /ʃ/ respectively: **kikke, kineser, kyle; skift, sky, skøyte**

Loanwords are generally exceptions. Note /k/ in: **kickboksing, kilt, kimono, kyrie**

(b) Before other vowels the same phonemes /ç/ and /ʃ/ are represented by the graphemes <kj> and <tj>, <skj> and <sj> respectively: **kjede, kjole; tjern, tjære; skje, skjorte; sjø, sjelden**

(c) Before the vowels /i/ and /y/ and diphthongs /ei/ and /øy/ the grapheme <g> is usually pronounced /j/: **gift, gyllen, geit**

Loanwords are generally exceptions (**general, ginseng**), and there are some other exceptions too (**gidde, gøy, Geir** (man's name)).

(d) Before other vowels the same phoneme /j/, often represented by <j> **Jan, jøde**, is sometimes represented by the grapheme <gj>: **gjøre, gjeld, gjødsel**

Note 1 – Other graphemes that in some loanwords may represent /ʃ/, are <sch>, <sh>, <ch>, <rs>, <g>, <j>: **schæfer, sherry, charter, børs, gelé, jour.**

Note that <rs> can also represent /ʃ/ in words of native origin, e.g. **kors, verst.**

Note 2 – <tj> is pronounced as 'soft' <t>, namely /ç/, before all vowels: **tjeld, tjene, tjue, tjære**

| 12.2.2.2 | *Silent consonants at the beginnings of words* |

/j/	silent <d> in <dj>:	**djup**
/j/	silent <h> in <hj>:	**hjelp, hjort, hjul**
/j/	silent <l> in <lj>:	**ljome, ljuge**
/j/	silent <g> in <gj>:	**gjerne, gjøre**
/v/	silent <h> in <hv>:	**hva, hvem, hvile**

| 12.2.2.3 | *Silent consonants at the ends of words* |

silent <d> after a stressed long vowel: glad, god, hud

But there are exceptions, such as **Gud**

silent <d> in <ld>:	**kveld, kald, sild**
silent <d> in<nd>:	**hund, hånd, ond**
silent <d> in<rd>:	**fjord, gård, hard**
silent <g> in the suffix <ig>:	**heldig, lykkelig, viktig**
and in the conjunction **og**	
silent <v> sometimes in <lv>:	**selv, sølv, tolv, halv**

But there are many examples where <v> is not silent: **gulv, kalv, elv, Sølve** [man's name]

silent <t> in the definite article neuter **–et** and in the pronoun **det**:

bordet, gulvet, huset

But <t> is pronounced /t/ before a genitive **–s**, as in: **husets, dets**

| 12.2.2.4 | *Vowels*

(a) The vowel phonemes in Norwegian are long and short /i/ /y/ /u/ /o/ /e/ /ø/ /å/ /æ/ /a/.

They are written <i> <y> <u> <o> <e> <ø> <å> <æ> <a>:

bil, ikke, fly, sykkel, gul, gutt, stor, most, pen, penge, kjøpe, grønn, blå, gått, kopp, ære, herre, bra, takk

Length is indicated by a double consonant or consonant group following the short vowel, e.g. there is a long vowel in **ta, tak**, but a short vowel in **takk, tank** respectively. See also 12.2.1.1.

Note – The vowels <o> /o/, <u> /u/, <å> /å/ are represented in the International Phonetic Alphabet by [u], [ʉ], and [o] in e.g. **stor, blå**, but, as these may cause confusion, the standard Norwegian notation is used here.

Long /å/ is usually written <å>: **lås**

But in some words before **v, g** it is written <o>: **lov, sove, svoger, tog**

Short /å/ is written <å> when it is a shortened form of /å/: **blått** (from **blå**), **gått** (from **gå**) but otherwise it is written <o>: **topp, sogn, dommer**

(b) The phoneme /æ/ occurs in East Norwegian speech before /r/ and retroflex consonants in, for example: **vær, populær; hvert, jern**

The diphthongs are:	/æi/ written<ei>:	grei
	/æu/ written <au>:	sau
	/øi/ written <øy>:	høy
And less frequent:	/ai/ written <ai>:	mai
	/åi/ written <oi>:	koie

12.3 Upper-case and lower-case letters

12.3.1 *Upper-case or lower-case letters?*

Only an outline of this subject can be given here. More detailed information can be found in, for example, Finn-Erik Vinje, *Skriveregler*. (See Bibliography.) The general rule, in Norwegian, as in English, is that an upper-case capital initial letter is used in proper nouns:

Aftenposten [newspaper], **Harald V, Munchmuseet, Roald Amundsen, Skagerrak, Stortinget,** the (Norwegian) Parliament

A lower-case initial letter is used in common nouns and all other word classes.

museet, the museum; **hytter**, cabins; **kong**, king; **dansk**, Danish

But see 12.3.1.2.

12.3.1.1 *Major similarities between Norwegian and English*

Norwegian and English use upper-case letters in the same way in the following instances:

(a) to start a sentence.

Vi kommer.   We are coming.

Note, however, that names like **de Saussure, von Falkenhayn** or **bin Laden**
retain their lower-case letter even when they comprise the first word in a
sentence. On the other hand, abbreviations that normally have an initial
lower-case letter take a capital at the beginning of a sentence: **E-posten kom
ikke fram**, 'The email did not arrive'.

(b) to introduce direct speech. See 13.1.6.2.

> **De spurte: «Hva gjør du?»**   They asked: 'What are you doing?'

(c) to show respect when addressing or referring to deities, royalty, etc.:

> **Allah, Buddha, Den hellige ånd**, the Holy Spirit; **Frelseren**, the Saviour;
> **Gud**, God; **Herren**, the Lord

> **Lenge leve Hans Majestet Kongen!** Long live His Majesty the King!

Other titles and epithets are normally rendered with lower-case letters:

> **dronning Maud**, Queen Maud; **herr og fru Thoresen**, Mr and
> Mrs Thoresen; **pave Benedikt XVI**, Pope Benedict XVI; **statsminister
> Gerhardsen**, Prime Minister Gerhardsen

| 12.3.1.2 | *Major differences: Norwegian lower-case – English upper-case*

There are six main areas where Norwegian uses a lower-case initial letter
while English has an upper-case initial letter:

(a) days of the week, months, festivals and national holidays

> **tirsdag**, Tuesday; **juli**, July; **sankthans**, Midsummer

(b) nouns and adjectives denoting nationality or derived from placenames.

> **en bergenser**, a resident of Bergen; **en brite**, a Brit; **europeisk**,
> European; **en islending**, an Icelander

(c) nouns and adjectives denoting religious or political persuasion

> **en jøde**, a Jew; **en kristen**, a Christian; **kristendommen**, Christianity;
> **islam**, Islam; **katolsk**, Catholic (adjective); **kommunistisk**, Communist
> (adjective); **en sosialist**, a Socialist

(d) people's titles. But see 12.3.1.1(c).

> **herr Jensen**, Mr. Jensen; **fru Johansen**, Mrs. Johansen; **frøken Smilla**, Miss Smilla; **professor Lie**, Professor Lie; **kong Olav Tryggvason**, King Olav Tryggvason; **president Kekkonen**, President Kekkonen

Note – Academic qualifications traditionally have small letters: **bachelor, dr.philos., cand.med.**, cf. English 'BA', 'PhD'.

12.3.2 | Upper-case letters in proper nouns – the basic rule

A Norwegian proper noun is written with an upper-case initial letter. Norwegian recognises five main categories of proper nouns, described in 12.3.2.1–5 below.

12.3.2.1 | Names of people, animals, boats, buildings, etc

This applies to both first names and family names.

> **Kirsten Flagstad** [Norwegian opera singer]; **Bamse** [cartoon bear]; **Fram** [Nansen's ship]; **Akershus** [fortress in Oslo]

12.3.2.2 | Place-names

This category includes not only geographical place-names but also public buildings and street names written as one word.

> **Tromsø, Geirangerfjorden, Nordkapp**, North Cape; **Telemark, Østersjøen**, the Baltic; **Skippergata, Håkonshallen, Stortorvet**

12.3.2.3 | Names of firms, institutions, organisations, etc

The names of many institutions, organisations and commercial companies are written with an upper-case initial letter.

> **Hæren**, the Army; **Posten**, the Post Office; **Senterpartiet**, the Centre Party; **Språkrådet**, the Language Council; **Stortinget**, the Norwegian Parliament

Exceptions:

> **politiet**, the Police; **tollen**, the Customs

In many instances, nouns used eponymously to describe a company's products are treated as common nouns and therefore have an initial lower-case letter:

Jeg kjøpte en ny volvo.   I bought a new Volvo

12.3.2.4 | Heavenly bodies, etc

While **jorda**, 'the Earth', **sola**, 'the sun' and **månen**, 'the moon' are usually written with a lower-case initial letter in Norwegian, the names of most other heavenly bodies are written with an upper-case initial letter.

Jupiter; **Uranus**; **Mars**; **Melkeveien**, the Milky Way

12.3.2.5 | Titles of books, plays, films and other works of art

Bibelen, the Bible; **Sult**, Hunger; **Vildanden**, the Wild Duck; **Skrik**, the Scream

12.3.3 | Upper-case letters in proper nouns of two or more words

It is only possible to provide rules of thumb.

12.3.3.1 | The basic rule

The basic rule in Norwegian is that only the first word of a proper noun expression of two or more words takes an initial upper-case letter. But see 12.3.3.3f. for exceptions.

Den røde armé, The Red Army; **Drammen kommune**, the Municipality of Drammen; **En flyktning krysser sitt spor**, A Fugitive Crosses His Tracks (title of a novel)

This means that, as the first word in the expression, it is often the article alone that takes the initial upper-case letter.

De forente nasjoner, The United Nations; **Et dukkehjem**, A Doll's House (drama title)

Proper noun within the expression

If a word in a proper noun expression is itself a proper noun (12.3.2.1), it too is capitalised.

> **Lille Eyolf**, *Little Eyolf* (drama title); **Republikken Sør-Afrika**, the Republic of South Africa; **Tarjei Vesaas** (first name and family name)

Note also the usage with a hyphen:

> **Nazi-Tyskland**, Nazi Germany; **Sør-Atlanteren**, the South Atlantic; **Vest-Berlin**, West Berlin

| 12.3.3.3 | *Names of firms, institutions, organisations, etc*

When the names of firms, etc. comprise more than one word, only the first word is usually capitalised:

> **Statens pensjonsfond**, the Government Pensions Fund of Norway; **Statistisk sentralbyrå**, Statistics Norway

But when the first word is itself a name, the second word is often given an initial capital in order to avoid any confusion as to the status of the phrase as a name:

> **Norges Statsbaner**, Norwegian State Railways; **Tromsø Private Sykehus**, Tromsø Private Hospital

| 12.3.3.4 | *Fixed epithets without the definite article*

Many fixed epithets have upper-case initial letters in all elements, unless they consist of a name (+ **den**) + adjective:

> **Eirik Blodøks**, Erik Bloodaxe; **Mikke Mus**, Mickey Mouse; **Pippi Langstrømpe**, Pippi Longstocking

but:

> **Olav den hellige**, Saint Olav; **Peter den store**, Peter the Great

12.3.4 | The use of upper-case letters in compound proper nouns

A proper noun may be incorporated into a compound noun (11.2) in one of two different ways. In both instances, the compound itself usually begins with an upper-case letter, as shown below.

12.3.4.1 | As the first element of a compound, usually without a hyphen

In the examples below the upper-case letters indicate an awareness of the origin and significance of the proper noun for an understanding of the compound. Compare 12.3.2.2.

Golfkrigen, the Gulf War; **Osebergskipet**, the Oseberg (Viking) ship

But note either **Oslo-folk** or **oslofolk**, 'people from Oslo'. As in this case, when the compound has become familiar, there is a tendency to use a lower case initial letter. Compare also: **nobelpris**, 'Nobel Prize', **wienerbrød**, 'Danish pastry'.

12.3.4.2 | Where the proper noun comprises several words, with a hyphen

New York-korrespondent, New York correspondent; Nordahl **Grieg-monumentet**, the Nordal Grieg Monument

12.3.5 | The use of upper-case letters in abbreviations

12.3.5.1 | Initialisms that are proper nouns

See also 11.4.5.

Initialisms that are abbreviations of proper nouns are written in upper case letters, regardless of their conventional unabbreviated form.

GT (Det gamle testamente), The Old Testament; **NRK (Norsk rikskringkasting)**, the Norwegian Broadcasting Corporation

Acronyms (initialisms pronounced as words) may occur either as all capital letters or with an initial capital:

Nato/NATO, Stami/STAMI (Statens arbeidsmiljøinstitutt), the National Institute of Occupational Health

| 12.3.5.2 | *Initialisms that are not proper nouns*

These largely comprise three groups.

(a) Either with small or capital letters:

dvd/DVD; edb/EDB, electronic data processing; **html/HTML; pc/PC; tv/TV**

(b) With capital letters in some initialisms for common nouns:

AS (Aksjeselskap), Company; **BNP (bruttonasjonalprodukt)**, Gross Domestic Product; **GPS, SMS**

(c) With small letters for some initialisms no longer regarded as abbreviations as such:

behå (< **BH, brystholder**), bra(ssiere); **hiv, laser, radar**

12.4 Miscellaneous

| 12.4.1 | *Hyphenation*

Most word processing programs on computers have a hyphenation feature, but occasionally it is necessary to hyphenate manually. The following basic rules for word division may prove helpful on occasions when dividing a word becomes unavoidable. Two methods are used:

(a) The single consonant rule (often used for simple words):

Words starting a new line begin with a consonant: **ek-sem-pel, bile-ne, ep-ler, pæ-rer, bol-ler**

(b) The morphological rule (often used for compounds and derivatives):

A division is made between the morphological elements in a word: **an-melde, bil-ene, eks-emp-el, kunn-skap**

Note 1 – Exceptions: The digraphs <dh>, <gh>, <gj>, <kj>, <sc>, <s>, <ch>, <sh, <sj>, <sk> are not hyphenated where they represent a single phoneme: **af-ghaner, re-gjering**.

Note 2 – It is possible to use both rules in the same text.

12.4.1.1 | *No hyphenation*

Generally speaking, the following should not be hyphenated:

(a) Monosyllabic words: **benk, byks, fangst**
(b) Abbreviations, dates, numbers: **21.4.2017; 1944; 17. mai**

12.4.1.2 | *Hyphenation of simple words*

These comprise at most two syllables and are usually hyphenated using the single consonant rule: **fren-de, ka-nin, skul-le**.

12.4.1.3 | *Hyphenation of compounds and derivatives*

When hyphenating compounds (made up from several single words, see 11.2) and derivatives (a single word plus an affix, see 11.3), the morphological rule is usually applied:

pike-skole, girls school; **før-skole**, preschool; **god-het**, goodness

When there is an –s link between elements, this –s stays with the first element, cf. 11.2.3:

parkerings-plass, car park

Note – Triple consonants are hyphenated after the second consonant:

ball-lek, ball game

12.4.2 | **Words or figures?**

In Norwegian, cardinal numbers are written either as words or figures. If numbers are not too long or are approximate, they are written as words in running text. Consistency of use within a text or a paragraph is called for. Note that numbers are not used to begin a sentence.

12.4.2.1 Words

Words are, therefore, generally used to express the figures 1–12 and for round numbers.

Erik er åtte år. Han har tre brødre.
Erik is eight. He has three brothers.

De ventet i fire–fem timer.
They waited for four to five hours.

12.4.2.2 Figures

See also Chapter 3. Figures are used:

(a) For large numbers. With the exception of telephone numbers (where usage varies, see 3.2.6), large numbers are usually written as groups of three counted from the end. Round numbers over a million are sometimes written as a combination of figures and words.

143 000 innbyggere, 143,000 inhabitants
2   700 000 [to millioner syv hundretusen] or 2,7 millioner

(b) In mobile telephone numbers:

Mob. +47 123 45 678

(c) But notice the landline number:

Tel. +47 55 31 60 67

(d) With units of measurement stated in abbreviated form:

20 kg; 300 m²; 211 cm; 50 km; 20°C

(e) In dates and times. See 3.5f.

1939; 10. desember; 11.15

(f) Prices:

Billetten koster 120 pund.   The ticket costs £120.

12.4.3 *One word or two in fixed expressions?*

See also 11.2.

There are some rules of thumb for ascertaining whether word pairs are written as a compound or as two separate words:

(a) When the stress (marked ') comes on the second word, they are written as two words:

Ingrid kom i 'går.   Ingrid arrived yesterday.

(b) When the words each have a distinct stress, they are written as two words:

Torkel rodde 'ut 'på sjøen.   Torkel rowed out into the lake.

(c) When the stress comes on the first word, they are written as one word:

Det var mange båter 'utpå fjorden.
There were a lot of boats out on the fiord.

(d) One way of ascertaining whether we are dealing with a compound or a phrase is to try to insert a word between the two 'elements':

i dag   two words because **i hele dag** is possible.
igjennom   one word because nothing can be inserted.

12.4.3.1 *Prepositions in two-word phrases*

A general rule is that two-word phrases beginning with the prepositions **av, for, i, med, om, over, på** and **til** are written as two words:

etter hvert, gradually; **for øvrig**, for that matter; **i kveld**, this evening; **med mindre**, unless; **på nytt**, anew; **til lands**, in this country

But if two prepositions are merged, they generally form a compound:

iblant, sometimes; **ifra**, from; **imellom**, between; **imot**, against (see also 7.4.2.)

12.4.3.2 *Semantic differences*

Occasionally there may be a difference in meaning between two or more words written separately and compounded:

cf. **Presidenten er overalt.**	The President is everywhere.
Presidenten står over alt.	The President is supreme.
cf. **Alt for Norge.**	Everything for Norway.
Jakken er altfor stor.	The jacket is far too big.

12.4.3.2 *Stylistic differences*

(a) In many instances, the difference between two or more words written separately and compounded is merely a matter of style and practice. For example, the following may be either:

for di/fordi, because; **for resten/forresten**, besides; **så fremt/såfremt**, provided that; **så pass/såpass**, this much; **visst nok/visstnok**, in all probability

(b) For separable and inseparable verbs, see 5.7.2f.

Chapter 13

Punctuation

13.1 Introduction

In many instances English and Norwegian practice are similar as regards punctuation. This section is a résumé of the most important points of use and includes the main differences between English and Norwegian punctuation.

13.1.1 *Punctuation marks*

The names of the principal punctuation marks in Norwegian are:

.	**punktum**
,	**komma**
:	**kolon**
-	**bindestrek**
–	**tankestrek (lang strek), replikkstrek**
()	**parentes, bueparentes**
[]	**hakeparentes**
;	**semikolon**
' . . . ' " . . . " « . . . »	**anførselstegn, hermetegn, sitattegn, gåseøyne, vinkeltegn**
?	**spørsmålstegn (spørretegn)**
'	**apostrof**
!	**utropstegn**
@	**krøllalfa** [used only in e-mail addresses]

13.1.2 | The comma

The system for using commas in Norwegian has been called a 'grammatically-based pause comma', as the comma separates sections of speech demarcated by clear signals such as pauses or changes in tempo. Use is in fact based on the clause (see 10.1.1). What follows outlines only major uses. For a full version of comma rules, see e.g. Finn-Erik Vinje, *Skriveregler*.

13.1.2.1

Between main clauses in the same sentence linked with the conjunctions **og**, 'and'; **eller**, 'or'; for 'because' or **men**, 'but', see also 9.2:

Ranerne hadde hansker, og politiet har ikke funnet finger-avtrykk.
The thieves wore gloves, and the police have found no fingerprints.

Maten er sikkert rik på kalorier, men neppe særlig lekker.
The food is certainly full of calories, but hardly tasty.

Exception – A comma is better left out, however, when the subject is the same in both clauses and is, therefore, omitted in the second clause.

Landene vil beholde sine egne atomvåpen og dermed beholde egen maktstilling i verden.
The countries want to keep their nuclear weapons and thereby keep their position of power in the world.

13.1.2.2

Between two coordinated subordinate clauses:

Politiet spurte hvor jeg bodde, og når jeg hadde kommet til Norge.
The police asked where I lived and when I had arrived in Norway.

After a subordinate clause that comes before the main verb:

Da vi kom, hadde de allerede spist.
When we got there, they had already eaten.

After an inserted restrictive subordinate clause:

Bilen som vi kjørte, var en Mercedes.
The car we drove was a Mercedes.

Usually before and always after an inserted restrictive relative clause (see 10.8.2.3):

Ingrid, som er lege, så på benet hans.
Ingrid, who is a doctor, took a look at his leg.

See 9.2.2.3, 6.2.5.3(e), 9.3.4.7.

With dels. . ., dels; jo. . ., desto/jo. . ., jo:

TV-programmet er dels på norsk, dels på amerikansk engelsk.
The TV programme is partly in Norwegian, partly in American English.

Jo mer hun trente, desto flinkere ble hun.
The more she trained, the better she got.

In order to separate interjections (8.1.1), tags (10.7.4.3), forms of address, etc. from the main body of the sentence.

Tobias, kan du komme hit?   Tobias, can you come here?
Hei, hvordan går det med deg?   Hi, how are things with you?

13.1.2.8

Note the following occasions when the use of the comma in English is *not* reflected in Norwegian.

(a) Around adverbs like 'however', 'too', 'though':

This, however, is uncertain. **Dette er imidlertid usikkert.**

(b) In letters after introductory phrases (13.1.5) and closing phrases:

Dear Mr Smith, **Kjære herr Smith!**
(or **Kjære herr Smith**
without anything)

Yours sincerely, **Vennlig hilsen**

(c) After an introductory prepositional phrase:

From your point of view, this may seem fine.
Fra ditt ståsted virker dette kanskje bra.

13.1.2.9

Note the difference in Norwegian and English usage of the comma in certain numerical or mathematical expressions.

(a) Norwegian has a decimal comma, English a decimal point. See also 3.2.7.2.

4,75 [fire komma syttifem] 4.75

499,90 499.90 [= 499 kroner 90 øre]

(b) Norwegian has a space (or sometimes a full stop) where English has a comma to mark thousands.

2 000 3,000

1 234 567 1,234,567

13.1.3 *The full stop*

The full stop is used at the end of a sentence (statement):

Tiden går. Time flies.

Otherwise it is chiefly found in the following instances:

| 13.1.3.1 | *In abbreviations*

(a) Generally speaking, words that are abbreviated in written Norwegian but not in the spoken language take a full stop (but see Note 1 below):

Written	*Spoken*	*English*
adr.	**adresse**	address
aug.	**august**	August
ca.	**cirka**	approx.
et.	**etasje**	floor
ev.	**eventuelt**	possibly
kl.	**klokka**	o'clock
maks.	**maksimum**	maximum
mva.	**merverdiavgift (moms)**	VAT
nr.	**nummer**	No.
pst.	**prosent**	per cent
s.	**side**	p. (page)
tlf.	**telefon**	tel.

(b) Abbreviations of more than one word are of two types:

1) Those with a full stop between the words:

bl.a.	**blant annet**	inter alia
f.eks.	**for eksempel**	e.g.
f.Kr.	**før Kristi fødsel**	BC
m.a.o.	**med andre ord**	in other words
m.m.	**med mer**	etc.

Note that there is no space after the first full stop.

2) Those with only one full stop after the last word:

dvs.	**det vil si**	i.e.
etc.	**et cetera**	etc.
istf.	**i stedet for**	instead of
mfl.	**med flere**	etc.
moh.	**meter over havet**	metres above sea level
osv.	**og så videre**	etc.

dvs.	**det vil si**	i.e.
pga.	**på grunn av**	because of

(c) Ordinal numbers:

**1. – første; Olav 5. – Olav den femte;
17. mai – den syttende mai; 9.11.2018**

(d) As punctuation in time expressions:

kl. 15.00 (or kl. 1500)

Note 1 – Some abbreviations have no full stop, including:

Weights and measures: **mm, cm, mg, kg, t, ml, l, min, sek** (**sekund,** second), **ts** (**teskje,** teaspoon)

Currencies:	**kr, nkr, NOK, EUR**
Chemical elements:	**Au, He**
Books of the Bible:	**1. Mos** (**Første Mosebok,** Genesis)
	Rom (**Romerbrevet,** Romans)

Note 2 – As a general rule there is no full stop in words that are abbreviated in both the written and spoken language, including initialisms (see 11.4.5):

FN, NRK, SAS, NATO/Nato, TV/tv, WC/wc

13.1.4 | *The colon*

The colon is used chiefly as follows in 13.1.4.1–13.1.4.3 below.

13.1.4.1 | *Quotations and direct speech*

Before quotations, dialogue in a play or thoughts in direct speech coming after a reporting phrase. The word after the colon usually has an initial capital letter, especially if what follows the colon is a complete sentence.

Hamlet: «Å være eller ikke være: Det er spørsmålet.»
Hamlet: To be or not to be, that is the question.

Note that there is no colon after **at**.

| 13.1.4.2 | *Lists* |

Before lists, examples, explanations and summaries.

Det var flere forskjellige typer blomster: roser, tulipaner og påskeliljer.
There were several different kinds of flowers: roses, tulips and daffodils.

| 13.1.4.3 | *Numerical expressions and abbreviations* |

In some numerical expressions and a handful of abbreviations.

et kart i målestokk 1:25 000   a map with a scale of 1:25,000
20:4   20 divided by 4
20:30   20.30 hours

[increasingly used on digital clocks in preference to a full stop]

| 13.1.5 | **The exclamation mark** |

| 13.1.5.1 |

The exclamation mark is used after exclamations, greetings, commands and imperative verb forms (5.4.4). Traditionally, it has also been used after introductory phrases in letters, but this usage is becoming less common.

Stopp tyven!   Stop thief!
Au!   Ouch!
Leve kongen!   Long live the King!
Kom hit!   Come here!
Kjære Jenny!   Dear Jenny,

[Increasingly omitted]

The exclamation mark is retained before saying verbs:

Ops! sa mor.   Oops! said mum.

| 13.1.5.2 |

If the exclamation, greeting, command, etc. is followed by a clause (except in the case of a clause reporting direct speech), it is usually best to omit it at the end of the sentence.

Forsvinn, ellers får du bank. Scram, or else you'll get a thick ear.

13.1.6 | *Direct speech and quotations*

13.1.6.1 | *Direct speech, dramatic dialogue*

Norwegian has several ways of showing dialogue, including double inverted commas and the guillemet (see 13.1.6.2(b) below). It also uses the dash (see 13.1.10). Neither the guillemet nor the dash are found in English to indicate dialogue.

– Hjelp, ropte hun.   – Jeg drukner.
"Help!" she cried. "I'm drowning."

Note – The dash here only indicates where the quotation begins, not where it ends.

13.1.6.2 | *Quotations*

(a) Norwegian often has double inverted commas of one of two types:

„sitat" or "sitat"

The first form used to be common in handwritten texts. The second is now common in texts produced on a computer. Note that the form of the inverted commas (". . .") differs from that in English (". . .").

(b) Norwegian also uses guillemets around direct speech.

«sitat»

This form is common in books and newspapers.

«Husk, det å leve er en kunst», skrev Ibsen.
"Remember, living is an art", wrote Ibsen.

Guillemets are also used with names of boats, pieces of music, ballets, paintings, buildings and book titles, although in textbooks it is common instead to use italic script.

Note – In Swedish the guillemets point right » », in Danish inwards » «.

13.1.8 The apostrophe

13.1.8.1 Omission

The apostrophe is used (sparingly!) to show that certain letters have been omitted in less common elisions.

'n Ola	him, Ola
slakter'n	the butcher

13.1.8.2 With genitives

Unlike in English, apostrophes are not normally found after genitives (**mors bil**, 'mother's car'), but there are two exceptions:

(a) The apostrophe is found before the genitive –s in special cases including initialisms in lower case written without a full stop, letters of the alphabet, certain abbreviations and words not usually found as nouns:

min pc's tastebord	the keyboard of my PC
Olsen & Co's forlag	Olsen & Co's publishing firm

(b) Norwegian has an apostrophe instead of the genitive –s in words ending in –s, –x or –z. See 1.8.1.2.

Vesaas' romaner	Vesaas's novels

13.1.8.3 French words

Apostrophes are found in some French words and phrases:

Côte d'Azur; D'Artagnan; Jeanne d'Arc, Joan of Arc

13.1.9 | The hyphen

In addition to indicating a word break at the end of a line of text, in Norwegian the hyphen is used chiefly as shown in paragraphs 13.1.9.1–13.1.9.5.

13.1.9.1 | Compound names

In certain compound names.

Mette-Marit; Mona Larsen-Asp; Oslo-Filharmonien

13.1.9.2 | ikke–

As in English, in compounds formed with **ikke-**:

ikke-røyker	non-smoker
ikke-vold	non-violence

13.1.9.3 | Compounds

As in English, to replace **og** 'and' in certain compounds.

svart-hvitt	black and white
svensk-norske forbindelser	Swedish-Norwegian relations

13.1.9.4 | Avoiding repetition

To avoid repetition of the second (and very occasionally the first) element of a compound in expressions.

søn- og helligdager	Sundays and holidays
hev- og senkbar	height-adjustable
	[*lit.* possible to raise and lower]

13.1.9.5 | In compounds with an acronym

In compounds where one of the elements is an acronym, initialism or number:

EU-motstander, an EU opponent; **pc-en**, the pc; **Oves 70-årsdag**, Ove's 70th birthday; **A4-format**, A4 size; **2000-tallet**, the 21st century

Note, however, that there is no hyphen if the number is written out:

etthundreårsdagen, the centenary

13.1.10 *The dash*

The short dash or n-dash (double the length of the hyphen) is used chiefly as shown in paragraphs 13.1.10.1–13.1.10.3.

13.1.10.1 *Pause*

To indicate a pause before an unexpected conclusion to a statement.

I kofferten fant man – en halv million kroner.
In the suitcase, they found – half a million kroner.

13.1.10.2 *Parenthetical comment*

To mark a parenthetical comment, exclamation, etc.

Johansen kom – takk og pris – i dette øyeblikk med kaffen.
Johansen came – thank goodness – at that moment with the coffee.

13.1.10.3 *Period*

To indicate period, extent, distance when used without a blank space on either side between figures, place-names, dates, etc.

Strekningen Oslo–Narvik er 1400 kilometer.
The distance between Oslo and Narvik is 1,400 kilometres.

Åpningstid kl. 8–12. Stengt 1.–31. juli.
Opening hours 8–12. Closed 1–31 July.

13.2 Addresses

13.2.1 *Letters within Norway*

Note that, if used, the addressee's title is written out in full (**Herr**, **Fru**, etc.) unless very long. However, titles are often dropped nowadays in favour of first name and surname alone. The house number always follows the street name. The street name is best written out in full. If the addressee lives in a block of flats, the floor number + **et.** (= **etasje**) should be added after a comma following the street address. Notice that otherwise there is no punctuation.

House or flat:

Johan Hansen	[Name of recipient]
Langgata 35A	[Street address: street name + house number]
0566 OSLO	[postcode + city/town.]

With a post box:

Anna Dahl	[Name of recipient]
Postboks 10	[Post box number]
1371 Asker	[postcode + city/town.]

13.2.2 Letters to Norway from abroad

On letters from abroad to an address in Norway the nationality marker NO- should precede the postcode, and be separated from it with a hyphen.

Stine Hansen	[Name of recipient]
c/o Per Olsen	[Name on the letter box if different from above]
Leilighet 425	[Number of flat, room, dorm etc]
Storgata 6	[Street address: street name + house number]
NO-7321 Trondheim	[**NO**-prefix, postcode + city/town.]
NORWAY	

13.2.3 E-mail addresses

E-mail addresses follow the international pattern. Note that Norwegian **ø, æ, å** are often replaced by **o, a** and **a** respectively. See 12.1.1.1(b).

mathilde.nygard@transnorsk.no

13.3 Dates and times

13.3.1 Dates in running text

In running text, the most common Norwegian convention is (**den**) + date in figures followed by full stop + month written out + year in figures. See also 3.5.2.1.

Ibsen døde (den) 26. mai 1906.   Ibsen died on May 26, 1906.

13.3.2 | Dates in figures only

There are various conventions for giving the date in figures only (see also 3.5.2.1(e)). The official form for giving dates shown by the Language Council of Norway, *Språkrådet*, is in the order day – month – year:

1.4.2018   01.04.2018   1.4.18   01.04.18

Norwegian Standard NS 4129 for 'office documents and forms' specifies the order: year – month – day, i.e. **2018–04–01**, whilst the US norm has the day before the month: 2018–01–04. (cf. '9–11' = 11 September 2001). When abbreviated, dates have no apostrophe, unlike English:

08   '08 i.e. 2008

13.3.3 | Times

Clock times may be written as follows:

kl. 13   kl. 1300   kl. 13.00   kl. 13:00
kl. 9.05   kl. 0905   kl. 09.05   kl. 09:05

If there are three figures, the full stop is obligatory.

Appendix I

Linguistic terms

This list comprises only those terms that are not explained in the text or that may not be familiar to students of Norwegian. In some cases, these are not directly transferable to English grammar.

abstract nouns   refer to unobservable notions, e.g. **kjærlighet**, 'love'; **lykke**, 'happiness'.

adjective phrase   consists of an adjective or a participle with optional words which modify or limit its meaning, e.g. **Han er** *(ganske) trett*, 'He is (rather) tired'.

adverb phrase   consists of an adverb with optional words which modify or limit its meaning, e.g. **Han kjørte** *(meget) fort*, 'He drove (very) fast'.

adverbial   (see **clausal adverbial, other adverbials**)

affix   is a prefix added to the beginning or a suffix added to the end of a word, e.g. *u*forkortet, 'unabridged'; svak*het*, 'weakness'.

agent   is the person or thing carrying out the action (in a passive construction), e.g. **Huset er eid** *av hennes eksmann*, 'The house is owned by her former husband'.

agreement   is a way of showing that two grammatical units have a particular feature in common, e.g. plural: **bøk*ene* mine**, 'my books'; neuter: **område*t* er stor*t***, 'the area is big'.

anaphoric   reference means that a word in a text refers back to a previous word or words, e.g. *Erik* **er solbrent.** *Han* **har vært ute i sola for lenge**, 'Erik is sunburned. He (i.e. Erik) has been out in the sun too long.' (Compare **cataphoric**.)

apposition	is where two noun phrases describe the same phenomenon, e.g. *Anna, min søster,* er professor', 'Anna, my sister, is a professor.'
attributive	is used to describe adjectives that precede the noun and modify it, e.g. et *vakkert* hus, 'a beautiful house'.
cataphoric	reference means that a word in a text refers to another word or words occurring later in the text, e.g. **Da** *han* **døde, var** *Elvis* **kun 42 år gammel,** 'When he died, Elvis was only 42 years old.' (Compare **anaphoric.**)
clausal adverbial	denotes an adverb modifying the sense of the clause as a whole, e.g. **Han er** *ikke* **dum,** 'He's not stupid'; **Jeg kommer** *aldri* **til å forstå det,** 'I'll never understand it'.
clause	usually comprises a **noun phrase** and a **verb phrase** (**subject** and **predicate**), e.g. **Han skriver en bok,** 'He's writing a book'.
collective nouns	are nouns denoting a group, e.g. **søsken,** 'brothers and sisters'; **kveg,** 'cattle'.
common nouns	are all nouns that are not **proper nouns,** e.g. **en katt,** 'a cat'; **to filmer,** 'two films'; **farger,** 'colours'.
complements	1) express a meaning that adds to (or complements) that of the subject or object. They can be either an **adjective phrase** or a **noun phrase,** e.g. **Emil og Emma er** *unge.* **De er** *skolekamerater,* 'Elin and Emil are young. They are school friends.' In this sense, cf. **predicative complements.** 2) are 'additions' to a head word. In Å **bake kake er gøy,** 'Baking cakes is fun', **kake** is a complement of Å **bake.**
complex verb	is one that has two or more parts: **Jeg** *har spist* **froskelår,** 'I have eaten frogs' legs.'
compound verb	is a verb consisting of a **stem** and a prefixed **particle,** which may be inseparable from the stem, e.g. **av** in *av*folke, 'depopulate', or separable: cf. *opp*finne and **finne** *opp,* 'invent'.
congruence	(= **agreement**)
conjugation	(or verb class) denotes the way a verb is inflected, its pattern of endings, and also a group of verbs

with the same endings, e.g. weak past tenses in: Conj. I –et; Conj. II –te, –de, Conj. III –dde.

copular
verbs (or copulas) link the noun or adjective **complement** to the subject, e.g. **Emma** *er* **fysioterapeut**, 'Emma is a physiotherapist'; **Gabriel** *ble* **fornøyd**, 'Gabriel was satisfied'.

copulative
means 'linking', (see **copular**).

correlative
is the word or phrase that a pronoun replaces or refers to. For example, **Jakob kjøpte** *en ny sykkel*. **Den var dyr**, 'Jakob bought a new bike. It was expensive.'

count nouns
are nouns that describe an individual countable entity and therefore usually possess a plural form, e.g. **by, byer**, 'town, towns'; **mann, menn**, 'man, men'. (Cf. non-count noun.)

declension
denotes the different ways of **inflecting** the noun in the plural, e.g. **stol*er***, 'chairs'; **uk*er***, 'weeks'; **spill*ere***, 'players'; **egg**, 'eggs'. It is also used to describe adjective inflection in constructions such as the indefinite declension of the adjective, e.g. **et stort hus**, 'a big house', or the definite declension of the adjective, e.g. **det store huset**, 'the big house'.

definite
(see **indefinite**)

derivative/derivation
refers to a word derived from a **stem**, usually by the addition of an **affix**, e.g. *ang*å, 'concern', *fore*gå, 'happen' and **en gå*ende***, 'a pedestrian' are all derivatives of the verb **gå**, 'go'.

direct object
refers to a person or thing directly affected by the action of a (transitive) verb, e.g. **Kai sparket** *ballen/sin søster*, 'Kai kicked the ball/his sister'.

duplication
involves the repetition of a subject, object or adverbial, usually in a pronoun or adverb form, e.g. *Frida* **er flink,** *hun*, 'Frida is clever, she is.'

durative verb
(or verb of duration) denotes a continued action (e.g. **sove**, 'sleep'), a constant change (e.g. **vokse**, 'grow') or an intermittent action (e.g. **dryppe**, 'drip').

ellipsis
involves the omission of a word or word group in the sentence, e.g. **Jeg ville røyke, men jeg fikk ikke** (*røyke*), 'I wanted to smoke but I was not allowed to (smoke)'.

end focus	is the principle that new, unfamiliar information comes at the end of the sentence, e.g. **Da reiste han** *til San Francisco*, 'Then he went to San Francisco.'
end weight	is the principle that long, heavy expressions come at the end of the sentence, e.g. **Han reiste deretter** *i en gammel lastebil uten lys*, 'He then travelled in an old truck without lights.'
figurative sense	is a sense other than the literal, e.g. **Det koster skjorta!**, 'It costs an arm and a leg [*lit.* 'the shirt'].'
finite verb	is a verb whose form shows tense, mood or voice (active/passive) (cf. **non-finite verb**).
first element	in a compound often modifies the **second (subsequent or final) element**, e.g. *tre*|hus, 'wooden house' and *stein*|hus, 'stone house' are both types of house.
focus	is new information imparted in an utterance (i.e. its message), e.g. **Hanna** *kommer til å gifte seg i morgen*, 'Hanna is going to get married tomorrow.'
formal subject	(FS) is **det** in cases when the **potential subject** (PS) is postponed, e.g. *Det* (FS) **står** *en trafikkbetjent* (PS) **der borte**, 'There's a traffic warden standing over there', or there is no real subject, as in **Det snør**, 'It's snowing'.
fronting	is moving an element to the beginning of the sentence. Compare **Vi elsker gravlaks**, 'We love cured salmon' and *Gravlaks* **elsker vi**, 'Cured salmon we love.'
gender	means classes of nouns, reflected in the behaviour of associated words. This can be due to sex, as is often the case for pronouns (**fyren – han,** 'the boy – he'; **jenta – hun,** 'the girl – she'), or it can be due to other factors, as is often the case for the articles/determiners (**en rus,** 'a high, an intoxication'; **ei lus,** 'a louse'; **et hus,** 'a house').
grammatical subject	(= **formal subject**)
head word	is the word that determines the syntactic type of the phrase: e.g. in **en stor hvit hund**, 'a large white dog', the word **hund** is head, determining that this is a noun phrase.
homonym	is a word that is identical in pronunciation or spelling to another word, cf. **et egg**, 'an egg', and **en egg**, 'a blade'.

hv-question	is a question introduced by an **interrogative** pronoun or adverb (so named because many of these words begin with the letters **hv** in Norwegian, e.g. **hva, hvem, hvor, hvorfor, hvordan,** etc).
idiom(atic)	indicates a usage that is not readily explicable from grammar.
imperative	is the **mood** of the verb expressing command or warning or direction, e.g. **Kom!**, 'Come on!'; **Se opp!**, 'Look out!'.
impersonal	constructions do not involve a person, but are usually formed with the impersonal pronoun **det**, e.g. **Det snør**, 'It's snowing.'
implied subject	is actually an object in a main clause which functions similarly to a subject in a non-finite clause, e.g. **Vi bad _henne_ å ringe oss**, 'We asked her to ring us'.
indeclinable	describes a word that does not inflect, e.g. the adjectives **bra**, 'good'; **gratis**, 'free'; **ekte**, 'genuine'. Unlike other adjectives these take no endings for neuter or plural.
indefinite	noun phrases typically refer to a new entity, e.g. _**En tyv**_ **ble arrestert i dag**, 'A thief was arrested today.' In contrast, **definite** refers to a previously mentioned (or familiar) entity, e.g. _**Tyven**_ **hadde stjålet en bil**, 'The thief had stolen a car.'
indirect object	is usually a person or animal benefiting from an action, e.g. **Jeg ga _henne_ boka**, 'I gave her the book.'
infinitive phrase	is a phrase consisting of an infinitive accompanied by optional words which modify it, e.g. **å spille ishockey**, 'to play ice hockey.'
inflect	means to change the form of 'one and the same word'. This is often done by adding different endings, cf. **drikke**, 'drink' vs. **drikker**, but it can also be done by vowel change, cf. **drikke** vs. **drakk**, or by a combination of the two, cf. **drikke** vs. **drukket**.
inflexible (= indeclinable)	
inflexion	(see **inflect**)
interrogative	means having to do with question, e.g. an interrogative pronoun asks a question, e.g. _**Hvem**_ **var**

det?, 'Who was that?'; *Hva* **brakte deg hit?**, 'What brought you here?'

inverted
: word order denotes verb – subject order, e.g. *I dag* **drar vi**, 'Today we leave.'

matrix
: is that part of a main clause sentence remaining when the subordinate clause is removed, e.g. *Eva lovet* **at hun skulle skrive til oss**, 'Eva promised that she would write to us.'

modal verbs
: express possibility, intention or obligation, e.g. **jeg kan**, 'I can'; **han vil**, 'he wants to'; **du må**, 'you must'.

mood
: is the quality of a verb that conveys the speaker's attitude. The indicative mood conveys factual statements or poses questions; the imperative mood makes a request or command, and the subjunctive mood expresses a wish, doubt, or something contrary to fact.

mutated vowel
: is one that changes in different forms of the word, e.g. o → ø in **bok – bøker**, 'book – books'; **stor – større**, 'big – bigger'.

nomen agentis
: A noun derived from an action verb, e.g. **en leser**, 'a reader', from lese 'to read'.

nominal
: means noun or acting as a noun, e.g. *Svømming* **er morsomt**, 'Swimming is fun'; *Å svømme er* **morsomt**.

non-count nouns
: are nouns, often denoting a substance or an abstract, that do not usually take a plural, e.g. **mel**, 'flour'; **bensin**, 'petrol'; **luft**, 'air'; **avsky**, 'loathing'; **glede**, 'joy'. Cf. count noun.

non-finite verb
: forms are those forms not showing tense or mood, namely the infinitive, supine and participles.

noun phrase
: is a noun (see **head word**) or pronoun often accompanied by one or more words before or after the noun which modify it, e.g. **en fantastisk** *roman* **som jeg leste**, 'a wonderful novel that I read'.

number
: is a collective term for singular and plural, e.g. **en gutt**, 'a boy' (sg.) – **to gutter**, 'two boys' (pl.).

object
: (see **direct object, indirect object**)

other adverbials
: (or content adverbials or sentence adverbials) are usually an adverb, noun phrase or subordinate clause

denoting manner, place, time or condition, e.g. **Han reiser** *med tog* (manner) *til Bergen* (place) *i morgen* (time) *hvis han har tid* (condition), 'He will travel by train to Bergen tomorrow if he has time.'

part of speech	means word class, e.g. noun, adjective, conjunction, etc.
particle	is a stressed adverb or preposition appearing together with a verb to form a single unit of meaning, a particle verb, e.g. *ut* in **se ut**, 'look'; *opp* in **gi opp**, 'give up'.
partitive	indicates that a part is implied, e.g. *en del av* **pengene**, 'some of the money'; *en flaske* **vin**, 'a bottle of wine'; *et kilo* **poteter**, 'a kilo of potatoes'.
pejorative	means deprecating as in e.g. **fjols**, 'idiot'.
postposed (or post-positioned)	means coming after something. Cf. **preposed**. In **oss kvinner imellom**, 'between us women', the word **imellom**, normally a preposition, is postposed.
potential subject	is the postponed subject, e.g. **Det er gøy** *å løse kryssord*, 'It's fun to solve crosswords' (see **formal subject**).
predicate	forms the only compulsory part of the clause other than the **subject**. The predicate is the verb plus any object, complement or adverbial: **Han** *løper (ti kilometer hver dag)*, 'He runs (ten kilometres every day).'
predicative complement	is a word or word group (often a **noun phrase** or **adjective phrase**) which complements, i.e. fills out, the subject, e.g. **Hun er** *hans trener* **og hun sier at han er** *bedre enn noensinne*, 'She is his trainer and she says that he is on top form.'
preposed (or pre-positioned)	means coming in front of something. In **før daggry**, 'before dawn', **før,** 'before' is preposed; it is a preposition.
prepositional phrase	consists of a preposition plus a prepositional complement (usually a **noun phrase** or **infinitive phrase**), e.g. **jenta** *med det lange håret*, 'the girl with the long hair'; **De dro** *uten å si adjø*, 'They left without saying goodbye.'
productive	implies that a method of word formation (or inflection) is still being used to produce new words, e.g. the suffix **–vennlig** in **barnevennlig**, 'child-friendly'

proper nouns	are names of specific people, places, books, etc., e.g. **Aksel, Pedersen; Åndalsnes; Det nye testamente**, 'the New Testament'.
raising	is the practice of moving an element from a subordinate clause to (the front of) the main clause (see **fronting**), e.g. *Det* sa Sofia at vi ikke skulle gjøre, 'Sofia said that we should not do that.' (← **Sofia sa at vi ikke skulle gjøre** *det*.)
reciprocal	or **reciprocating** indicates a mutual activity either by the use of a pronoun – **De avskyr** *hverandre*, 'They detest one another' – or a form of the verb – **De møttes i Oslo**, 'They met in Oslo.'
reflexive	pronouns refer to the subject in the same clause. They have a distinctive form in the 3rd person, e.g. **Han har solet** *seg*, 'He has been sunning himself.' Reflexive verb constructions incorporate a reflexive pronoun: **Vi har** *lært oss* **fransk**, 'We have learned French.'
second (subsequent or final) element	in a compound determines the word class of the compound, cf. **fri**, 'free' (adjective: **first element**) with fri|*het*, 'freedom' (noun) and fri|*gi*, 'liberate' (verb).
semantic	has to do with the meaning of words.
simple verb	is one that only consists of one word, e.g. *Hjelp!*, 'Help!'; (jeg) *kjører*, '(I) drive'; (han) *gikk*, '(he) went'. Compare **complex verb**.
stem	is the part of the word common to all of its forms and onto which the inflexional endings are added. For the verb **danse**, the stem is **dans–**, compare infinitive *dans/e*, present *dans/er*, past *dans/et* or *dans/a*, supine *dans/et* or *dans/a*, imperative **dans!**
subject	is a **nominal** sentence element which together with the **predicate** forms a clause.
syllable	consists of (typically) a vowel plus one or more consonants, e.g. å, da, båt, bånd, in–du–stri–ar–bei–de–re.
tag question	in English consists of verb + subject (+ negative) at the end of a statement to invite a response from the listener, e.g. 'He likes salmon, *doesn't he?*' In Norwegian **hva?** or **ikke sant?** usually suffices, e.g. **Han liker laks**, *ikke sant?*, 'He likes salmon, doesn't he?'

terminative verbs	denote an action or process implying a state of change or leading to a change or cessation, e.g. **sovne**, 'fall asleep'; **låse**, 'lock'.
topic	is the position at the beginning of all main clause **statements** and **hv-questions**. It is often occupied by the subject, e.g. *Vi/Studentene* **liker hennes forelesninger**, 'We/The students like her lectures.' Words other than the subject, especially **adverbial** expressions of time or place, may however occupy the topic position, e.g. *I morgen* **skal jeg spille golf**, 'Tomorrow I shall play golf.'
verb phrase	consists of a **finite verb** alone or several finite and non finite verbs in a chain, e.g., **Han** *reiser*, 'He is travelling'; **Han** *sitter* og *leser*, 'He is (sitting) reading'; **Han** *må kunne løpe*, 'He must be able to run.'
voice	indicates whether the subject of a verb acts (active voice, e.g. **Man skjærer potetene i små biter**, 'You cut the potatoes into small pieces') or is acted upon (passive voice, e.g. **Potetene skjæres i små biter** 'The potatoes are cut into small pieces').
voiced	describes a consonant produced with vibration of the larynx, e.g. **b, d, g, v, m, n, r, l**.
voiceless	describes a consonant produced without vibrating the larynx, e.g. **p, t, k, f**.

Appendix 2

English-Norwegian and Norwegian-English linguistic terms

Different grammars use different terms, so this list is meant as an aid only.

accusative	**akkusativ, objektsform**
active	**aktiv**
adjective	**adjektiv**
adverb	**adverb**
adverbial	**adverbial**
affix	**affiks**
agent	**agens**
agreement	**kongruens (samsvarsbøying)**
apposition	**apposisjon**
article	**artikkel (determinativ)**
aspect	**aspekt**
attributive	**attributiv**
auxiliary verb	**hjelpeverb**
cardinal number	**grunntall**
case	**kasus**
clausal adverbial	**setningsadverbial**
clause	**setning**
clause element	**setningsledd**
cleft sentence	**utbrytning**
command	**ordre, bydesetning, imperativsetning**
common gender	**felleskjønn, utrum**
common noun	**fellesnavn, appellativ**
comparative	**komparativ**
comparison	**komparasjon, gradbøying**
complement	**utfylling, predikativ**
complex preposition	**sammensatt preposisjon**
compound	**sammensatt ord, sammensetning**
concessional clause	**innrømmelsessetning**
conditional clause	**vilkårssetning, betingelsessetning**

Appendix 2

English-
Norwegian
and
Norwegian-
English
linguistic
terms

conjunction	konjunksjon, bindeord
conjunction field (f position)	forbinderfelt
consonant	konsonant
coordinating conjunction	sideordnende konjunksjon
count noun	tellelig substantiv
copular verb	kopulaverb
declarative sentence	deklarativsetning, fortellende helsetning
degree	grad
deictic	deiktisk
definite article	bestemt artikkel
demonstrative pronoun	demonstrativt pronomen, påpekende pronomen, pekeord
derivation	avledning
determiner	determinativ, bestemmerord
diphthong	diftong, tvelyd
direct object	direkte objekt
direct speech	direkte tale
ellipsis	ellipse
echo-question	ekkospørsmål
exclamation	utrop
existential sentence	presenteringssetning
extra position	ekstraposisjon
feminine	femininum, hunkjønn
finite clause	finitt setning
finite verb	finitt verb
focus	rema
formal subject	formelt subjekt
free complement	fritt predikativ
fronting	framflytting
future	futurum
gender	grammatisk kjønn
genitive	genitiv, eieform
headword	kjerne, hode
imperative	imperativ, bydeform
indefinite article	ubestemt artikkel/determinativ
indefinite pronoun	ubestemt pronomen
indirect object	indirekte objekt, hensynsledd
indirect question	avhengig spørresetning
indirect speech	indirekte tale
infinitive	infinitiv

Appendix 2
English-
Norwegian
and
Norwegian-
English
linguistic
terms

infinitive marker	infinitivsmerke
inflexion	bøyning, bøying
inflexion class	bøyingsklasse
interjection	interjeksjon, utropsord
interrogative pronoun	spørrepronomen
intransitive verb	intransitivt verb
inversion	inversjon, omvendt ordstilling
main clause	helsetning
masculine	maskulinum, hankjønn
matrix clause	hovedsetning, oversetning minus leddsetning
modal auxiliary	modalt hjelpeverb
mood	modus, utsagnsmåte
modifier	adledd, beskriverledd, tillegg, utfylling
nominative	nominativ, subjektsform
neuter	nøytrum
non-finite clause	småsetning
non-finite verb	infinitt verb
non-count noun	utellelig substantiv, massesubstantiv
noun	substantiv
noun phrase	nomenfrase, substantivfrase
number	numerus, tall
object	objekt
optative	optativ
ordinal number	ordenstall
orthography	ortografi, rettskrivning
paradigm	paradigme
participle	partisipp
passive	passiv
past participle	perfektum partisipp
past perfect	(pluskvamperfektum), preteritum perfektum
past tense	preteritum, fortid
personal pronoun	personlig pronomen
phrase	frase
plural	flertall
pluperfect	preteritum perfektum (pluskvamperfektum)
possessive	possessiv, eiendomspronomen
predicative complement	predikativ
prefix	prefiks, forstavelse

Appendix 2
English-
Norwegian
and
Norwegian-
English
linguistic
terms

preposition	preposisjon
present participle	presens partisipp
present perfect	perfektum, presens perfektum
present tense	presens, nåtid
pro form	proform
pronoun	pronomen
proper noun	egennavn, proprium
punctuation	tegnsetting
quantifier	kvantor
question	spørsmål
raising	løfting
real subject	egentlig subjekt, potentielt subjekt
reciprocal pronoun	resiprokt pronomen
reflexive pronoun	refleksivt pronomen
relative clause	relativsetning
relative pronoun	relativpronomen
rheme	rema
sentence	helsetning, periode
s-genitive	s-genitiv
singular	entall
statement	utsagn
stem	stamme
subject	subjekt
subjunctive	konjunktiv, optativ
subordinate clause	leddsetning (bisetning)
subordinating conjunction	underordnende konjunksjon, subjunksjon
suffix	suffiks
superlative	superlativ
syntax	syntaks
tag-question	halespørsmål, tilhengerspørsmål
tense	tempus, tid
theme	tema
topicalisation	framflytting, topikalisering
unstressed pronoun	trykklett pronomen
verb particle	verbpartikkel
voice	diatese
vowel	vokal (selvlyd)
weight principle	vektprinsipp
word class	ordklasse
word formation	orddanning, ordlaging

word order	leddstilling, ordstilling	**Appendix 2** English- Norwegian and Norwegian- English linguistic terms
yes/no question	ja/nei-spørsmål	

adjektiv	adjective
adledd	modifier
adverb	adverb
adverbial	adverbial
affiks	affix
agens	agent
akkusativ	accusative
aktiv	active
appellativ	common noun
apposisjon	apposition
artikkel	article (determiner)
aspekt	aspect
attributiv	attributive
avhengig spørresetning	indirect question
avledning	derivation
beskriverledd	modifier
bestemmerord	determiner
bestemt artikkel	definite article
betingelsessetning	conditional clause
bindeord	conjunction
bøying	inflexion
bøyingsklasse	inflexion class
bydeform	imperative
bydesetning	command
deklarativsetning	declarative sentence
determinativ	determiner, article
diatese	voice
diftong	diphthong
direkte objekt	direct object
direkte tale	direct speech
egennavn	proper noun
egentlig subjekt	real subject
eieform	genitive
eiendomspronomen	possessive
ekkospørsmål	echo-question
ekstraposisjon	extra position
ellipse	ellipsis
entall	singular

Appendix 2
English-
Norwegian
and
Norwegian-
English
linguistic
terms

fellesnavn	common noun
felleskjønn	common gender
femininum	feminine
finitt setning	finite clause
finitt verb	finite verb
flertall	plural
forbinderfelt	conjunction field (f position)
formelt subjekt	formal subject
forstavelse	prefix
fortellende helsetning	declarative sentence
fortid	past tense
framflytting	fronting, topicalisation
frase	phrase
fritt predikativ	free complement
futurum	future
genitiv	genitive
grad	degree
gradbøying	comparison
grammatisk kjønn	gender
grunntall	cardinal number
halespørsmål	tag-question
hankjønn	masculine
helsetning	main clause
hensynsledd	indirect object
hjelpeverb	auxiliary verbs
hode	headword
hunkjønn	feminine
ikke-finitt leddsetning	non-finite clause
imperativ	imperative
imperativsetning	command
indirekte tale	indirect speech
indirekte objekt	indirect object
infinitiv	infinitive
infinitivsmerke	infinitive marker
infinitt verb	non-finite verb
interjeksjon	interjection
intransitivt verb	intransitive verb
inversjon	inversion
ja/nei-spørsmål	yes/no question
kasus	case

kjerne	headword	**Appendix 2** English- Norwegian and Norwegian- English linguistic terms
kjønn	gender	
kommando	command	
komparasjon	comparison	
komparativ	comparative	
kongruens	agreement	
konjunksjon	conjunction	
konjunktiv	subjunctive	
konsonant	consonant	
kopulaverb	copular verb	
kvantor	quantifier	
leddsetning	subordinate clause	
leddstilling	word order	
maskulinum	masculine	
massesubstantiv	non-count noun	
modalt hjelpeverb	modal auxiliary	
modus	mood	
nåtid	present tense	
nomenfrase	noun phrase	
nominativ	nominative	
numerus, tall	number	
nøytrum	neuter	
objekt	object	
objektsform	accusative	
omvendt ordstilling	inversion	
optativ	optative, subjunctive	
orddanning	word formation	
ordenstall	ordinal number	
ordklasse	word class	
ordlaging	word formation	
ordstilling	word order	
ortografi	orthography	
påpekende pronomen	demonstrative pronoun	
paradigme	paradigm	
partisipp	participle	
passiv	passive	
pekeord	demonstrative pronoun	
perfektum partisipp	past participle	
perfektum	present perfect	
periode	sentence	
personlig pronomen	personal pronoun	

Appendix 2
English-
Norwegian
and
Norwegian-
English
linguistic
terms

pluskvamperfektum	past perfect
pluskvamperfektum	pluperfect
possessiv	possessive
potensielt subjekt	real subject
predikativ	(predicative) complement
prefiks	prefix
preposisjon	preposition
presens	present tense
presens partisipp	present participle
presens perfektum	perfect tense
presenteringssetning	existential sentence
preteritum	past tense
preteritum perfektum	past perfect, pluperfect
proform	pro form
pronomen	pronoun
proprium	proper noun
refleksivt pronomen	reflexive pronoun
relativpronomen	relative pronoun
relativsetning	relative clause
rema	focus, rheme
resiprokt pronomen	reciprocal pronoun
rettskrivning	orthography
sammensatt ord	compound
sammensatt preposisjon	complex preposition
selvlyd	vowel
setning	clause
setningsadverbial	clausal adverbial
setningsknute	result of raising
setningsledd	clause element
s-genitiv	s-genitive
sideordnende konjunksjon	coordinating conjunction
småsetning	non-finite clause
spørrepronomen	interrogative pronoun
spørsmål	question
stamme	stem
subjekt	subject
subjektsform	nominative
subjektsløfting	subject raising
subjunksjon	subordinating conjunction
substantiv	noun
substantivfrase	noun phrase

suffiks	suffix
superlativ	superlative
syntaks	syntax
tegnsetting	punctuation
tellelig substantiv	count noun
tema	theme
tempus	tense
tid	tense
tilhengerspørsmål	tag-question
tillegg	modifier
topikalisering	topicalisation
trykklett pronomen	unstressed pronoun
tvelyd	diphthong
uavhengig setning	sentence
ubestemt artikkel	indefinite article
ubestemt pronomen	indefinite pronoun
underordnende konjunksjon	subordinating conjunction
utbrytning	cleft sentence
utellelig substantiv	non-count noun
utfylling	complement, modifier
utrop	exclamation
utropsord	interjection
utrum	common gender
utsagn	statement
utsagnsmåte	mood
vektprinsipp	weight principle
verbpartikkel	verb particle
vilkårssetning	conditional clause
vokal	vowel

Appendix 2
English-
Norwegian
and
Norwegian-
English
linguistic
terms

Bibliography

Norwegian Grammar

Hans-Olav Enger & Kristian Emil Kristoffersen, *Innføring i norsk grammatikk. Morfologi og syntaks*, 2000, Oslo: Cappelen akademisk forlag.

Jan Terje Faarlund, Svein Lie & Kjell Ivar Vannebo, *Norsk referansegrammatikk*, 1997, Oslo: Universitetsforlaget.

Anne Golden, Kirsti MacDonald & Else Ryen, *Norsk som fremmedspråk Grammatikk*, 4th ed., 2014, Oslo: Universitetsforlaget.

Jon Erik Hagen, *Norsk grammatikk for andrespråkslærere*, 1998, Oslo: Universitetsforlaget.

Peter Hallaråker, *Norwegian nynorsk: an introduction for foreign students*, 1983, Bergen: Universitetsforlaget.

Harald Morten Iversen, Hildegunn Otnes & Marit Skarbø Solem, *Grammatikken i bruk*, 3rd ed., 2011, Oslo: Cappelen Damm akademisk.

Bjørn Kvifte & Verena Gude-Husken, *Praktische Grammatik der norwegischen Sprache*, 3rd ed., 2005, Wilhelmsfeld: Egert.

Svein Lie, *Innføring i norsk syntaks*, 5th ed., 2003, Oslo: Universitetsforlaget.

Svein Lie, *Norsk morfologi*, 2nd ed, 2011, Oslo: Ling.

Tom Lundskær-Nielsen, Michael Barnes & Annika Lindskog, *An Introduction to Scandinavian Phonetics*, 2005, Copenhagen: Alfabeta.

Kirsti MacDonald, *Spørsmål om grammatikk. Når norsk er andrespråk*, 1997, Oslo: Cappelen.

Kirsti MacDonald & Marianne MacDonald, *Exploring Norwegian Grammar*, 2013, Oslo: Cappelen Damm.

Olav Næs, *Norsk grammatikk. Elementære strukturer og syntaks*, 4th ed., 1979, Oslo: Fabritius.

Åse Berit & Rolf Strandskogen, *Norwegian. An Essential Grammar*, London & New York, 2nd ed., 1989, Abingdon: Routledge.

Finn-Erik Vinje, *Moderne norsk. En veiledning i skriftlig framstilling – morfologiske og syntaktiske vanskeligheter,* 5th ed., 2002, Bergen: Fagbokforlag.

Finn-Erik Vinje, *Norsk grammatikk – det språklige byggverket*, 2005, Oslo: Kunnskapsforlaget.

Finn-Erik Vinje, *Skriveregler*, 9th ed., 2011, Oslo: Aschehoug.

Other Nordic grammars

Erik Hansen & Lars Heltoft. *Grammatik over det Danske Sprog*, 2011, Copenhagen: Det Danske Sprog-og Litteratur Selskab.

Philip Holmes & Ian Hinchliffe, *Swedish. A Comprehensive Grammar*, 3rd ed., 2013, Abingdon: Routledge.

Tom Lundskær-Nielsen & Philip Holmes, *Danish. A Comprehensive Grammar*, 2nd ed., 2010, Abingdon: Routledge.

Ulf Teleman, Staffan Hellberg & Erik Andersson, *Svenska Akademiens Grammatik*, 1999, Stockholm: Svenska Akademien.

Websites

Språkrådet online:
  http://sprakrad.no/nb-NO/Sprakhjelp/Skriveregler_og_grammatikk/

Online dictionaries

Bokmålsordboka/Nynorskordboka: http://ordbok.uib.no

Online corpus material

Oslo-korpuset: http://www.tekstlab.uio.no/norsk/korpus/bokmaal/netscape/treord/oktntb.shtml

Avis-korpuset: http://avis.uib.no/sok/sok-i-hele-korpuset

Special studies

John Ole Askedal, 'Norwegian' in Peter O. Müller et al (eds): *Word-Formation – An International Handbook of the Languages of Europe*, 2016, Berlin / Boston: De Gruyter.

Eli Anne Eiesland, *The Semantics of Norwegian Noun-Noun Compounds.* 2015, Ph.D. thesis, University of Oslo.

Sigurd Waldemar Mong-Nybo, *I forhold til preposisjoner*, 2016, MA thesis, University of Oslo. https://www.duo.uio.no/handle/10852/53991

Eivor Finset Spilling, Gradbøying i norsk, 2012, MA thesis, University of Oslo. https://www.duo.uio.no/handle/10852/35125

Maria Theresa Robles Westervoll, 2015, *Dødsinteressant eller sykt unyttig?* MA thesis, University of Oslo. https://www.duo.uio.no/handle/10852/49988

Index

English words are in *italics*, Norwegian words are in **bold**. Words are listed in Norwegian alphabetical order, namely **a ... z, æ, ø, å**. Reference is to paragraph; *n* indicates Note.

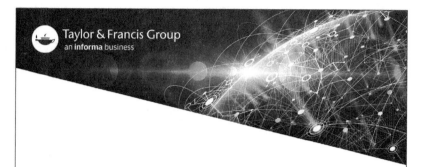